W9-ATH-153

WHAT'S WITHIN?

PHILOSOPHY OF MIND SERIES
Series Editor
Owen Flanagan, Duke University

SELF EXPRESSIONS
Mind, Morals, and the Meaning of Life
Owen Flanagan

THE CONSCIOUS MIND
In Search of a Fundamental Theory
David J. Chalmers

DECONSTRUCTING THE MIND
Stephen P. Stich

THE HUMAN ANIMAL
Personal Identity Without Psychology
Eric Olson

MINDS AND BODIES
Philosophers and Their Ideas
Colin McGinn

WHAT'S WITHIN?
Nativism Reconsidered
Fiona Cowie

WHAT'S WITHIN?

Nativism Reconsidered

Fiona Cowie

New York   Oxford

Oxford University Press

1999

Oxford University Press

Oxford   New York
Athens   Auckland   Bangkok   Bogotá   Buenos Aires   Calcutta
Cape Town   Chennai   Dar es Salaam   Delhi   Florence   Hong Kong   Istanbul
Karachi   Kuala Lumpur   Madrid   Melbourne   Mexico City   Mumbai
Nairobi   Paris   São Paulo   Singapore   Taipei   Tokyo   Toronto   Warsaw

and associated companies in
Berlin   Ibadan

Library of Congress Cataloging-in-Publication Data
Cowie, Fiona, 1963–
What's within? : nativism reconsidered / Fiona Cowie.
p.   cm. — (Philosophy of mind series)
Includes bibliographical references.
ISBN 0-19-512384-0
1. Nativism (Psychology)   2. Innate ideas (Philosophy)
3. Language acquisition.   4. Chomsky, Noam.   I. Title.   II. Series.
BF341.C68   1999
149'.7—dc21   98–5364

1 2 3 4 5 6 7 8 9

Printed in the United States of America
on acid-free paper.

I thought that nature was enough
Till Human nature came
And that the other did absorb
As Parallax a Flame—
Emily Dickinson

To Stephen P. Stich,
with gratitude

Preface

By the end of World War II, a new paradigm for the scientific understanding of human development had emerged. For a variety of reasons—methodological, metaphysical, political, even empirical!—the idea that human nature is the preeminent force at work in shaping the character of a person and the contours of her life had given way to a resolute empiricism. For the first time since the Enlightenment of the eighteenth century, experience, and not our innate endowment, was universally accorded the primary role in the making of ourselves and our society. By the time of the war in Vietnam, however, the newly resurrected empiricist orthodoxy was being challenged by a vigorous resurgence of nativism. Far from playing a minor role in the making of a person, human nature was again taken to be the chief factor at work in determining the nature of people and the milieux in which they live.

Today, "Nativism Rules, OK." In both the popular and academic presses, books and articles claiming to have found a 'substantial genetic basis for,' or 'instinct for,' or even 'the gene for' a variety of traits and behaviors have proliferated. Features as diverse as scholastic performance, sexual orientation, violence, "[a]ltruism, compassion, empathy, love, conscience, the sense of justice," poverty, alcoholism and other substance abuse, susceptibility to diseases, sexual mores, the desire to rape women, the attainment of concepts, language use, even attitudes toward divorce and religion—features that were formerly held to be substantially under environmental control—are now routinely claimed to be largely, if not wholly, innate.[1]

---

1. The quotation is from Wright (1994:12). See Herrnstein and Murray (1994), esp. 317–68) for the innateness of IQ and poverty; Hamer and Copeland (1994) and LeVay (1993) for the innateness of sexual orientation; Nobel et al. (1991), Bruner et al. (1993), and Wright (1995) for the innateness of violence; Williams and Nesse (1991) for the innateness of disease susceptibility; Thornhill and Thornhill (1992) for the genetic basis of men's alleged compulsion to rape; Nesse (1994) for nativist perspectives on substance

But what is nativism? What does it mean to say that some trait is innate? What kinds of evidence should support such a claim? What implications should be drawn from it? This book aims to present a partial answer to the first three of these questions, and in so doing, to sound a note of caution regarding the fourth.

Nativism about the mind will be my focus. In part I, I examine the history of the controversy over innate ideas and, in the light of that examination, develop an account of what nativism about the mental is. On the view I urge, the doctrine is not univocal; there are two quite distinct positions that proponents of 'innate ideas' have espoused. First, nativists have defended the view that (some of) our inborn faculties of mind are task- or domain-specific. Whereas empiricists assert that learning in all domains is underpinned by the same, very general learning strategies, nativists hold that in some domains, learning must be subserved by special-purpose mechanisms. This psychological hypothesis about the nature of our inborn learning mechanisms is not, however, the only view nativists have upheld. An ostensible commitment to innate ideas has also signified their sanctioning of a second and much more radical view, namely, that our acquisition of a mental life will forever resist explanation. Whereas empiricists take it for granted that the furnishing of a mind is a natural process, amenable at least in principle to rigorous, scientific explanation, nativists hold that the processes responsible for our attainment of ideas and beliefs are, and are likely to remain, deeply mysterious.

There is thus a deep tension within the nativist camp. On the one hand, nativists offer accounts of the mechanisms responsible for acquisition. On the other, they deny that such accounts can be given. I argue that this duality stems naturally from the two quite different kinds of argument that have been used to support nativists' claims, and that it accounts, once recognized, for the air of unclarity and confusion surrounding the nativist position. This dual nature—and corresponding unclarity—is apparent also, as I then go on to show in parts II and III, in modern-day nativist thought.

In part II, I argue that the radical concept nativism once proclaimed by Jerry Fodor is of a piece with the explanatory pessimism evinced by his historical predecessors. His claim that almost all our concepts are innate is not an attempt to explain how concepts are attained. Rather, I suggest, its purpose is to underscore the difficulty—even the impossibility—of providing a properly psychological account of the acquisition process. Recently, Fodor has tried to moderate his nativism, urging that rather than being brutely inexplicable, our acquisition of concepts is to be seen as a necessary concomitant of the 'fact' that most things in the world owe their existence to our being able to think about them. I argue that this 'Constitution Hypothesis' is nothing more nor less than an attempt to make metaphysical necessity

abuse; Fodor (1975, 1981b) for the innateness of concepts; Chomsky (1988) and Pinker (1994) for the innateness of language; and E. O. Wilson (1975) and Wright (1994) for the innateness of just about everything.

play the role played by God in the systems of earlier nativists: since natural science cannot explain how our minds are furnished, God—or in Fodor's case, metaphysical necessity—is the only thing left to appeal to in our explanatory endeavors. As against the mystery-mongering of Fodor and his predecessors, I urge that such appeals to a deus ex machina—whether cloaked in the garb of metaphysical necessity or not—are unwarranted. Acquiring a concept requires that one somehow or another develop the ability to distinguish what falls under it. While sometimes, perhaps, we may be born with the requisite recognitional capacities, in most cases they must be learned. I conclude that there is, therefore, a real prospect of developing a properly scientific (that is, psychological) understanding of how we acquire concepts. The notion that concept acquisition must remain forever beyond our ken is a mistake.

Part III discusses the fate of the nativist's faculties hypothesis, as exemplified in the views of Noam Chomsky. On this view, language learning is subserved by a dedicated 'Language Faculty,' a biologically-specified 'mental organ' that is distinct from any general-purpose capacity for learning we might possess. Chomsky goes further than asserting that a faculty for language learning exists. He also famously propounds a theory about the nature of the postulated language faculty. On his view, the language faculty incorporates (in some straightforward way) the principles of Universal Grammar.

In discussing Chomsky's position, I seek to establish two claims. First, I argue, there is no reason to accept the Chomskyan view in toto. Chomsky's nativism consists of a number of largely independent theses, which have (as I argue in chapters 8, 9, and 10) very different levels of evidential support. I urge that empiricist approaches to learning possess resources that have hitherto not been properly appreciated, and demonstrate how the apparent plausibility of the Chomskyan position derives from the nativist's helping himself to a variety of more or less implausible assumptions about language learners and their experience.

Nonetheless, I argue in chapter 11, there is reason to accept a nativist (if not altogether Chomskyan) view of language learning. This brings me to the second main aim of my discussion of linguistic nativism, which is to emphasize that *we really do not know* how language—or anything else, indeed—is learned. Our ignorance about the human mind and the processes by which it acquires knowledge is profound. So although the evidence now available tends to suggest that nativism might be right in the domain of language, the case to be made in favor of nativism, and against its empiricist alternatives, is nowhere near overwhelming enough to justify the almost religious conviction with which nativism about language has been defended over the last thirty or so years. I urge the need to develop empiricist learning theories—if not for language, then for the myriad other spheres in which learning unproblematically takes place in the absence of a special faculty—and argue that the truth or falsity of a nativist approach to a given area cannot be settled in advance of the development of a successful learning theory for that domain.

There are thus no short answers to the questions, "What is nativism about the mind?" and "Should we believe it?" Depending on what arguments the nativist uses to support his thesis as to what is within us, that thesis could be one of two very different things: an empirical psychological theory about learning mechanisms, on the one hand, or an expression of metatheoretical gloom on the other. If I am right in my assessments of these two positions, then nativist doctrines are far from indefeasible even in the psychological domain—the domain where the hypothesis of innateness has received its most articulate, intelligent, and sustained defense. How much more cautious, then, should we be about nativisms in other areas, particularly in areas where there is, apparently, much more at issue? The truth of Fodorean or Chomskyan nativism, while of course of great intellectual interest, is of little social consequence: the lives of the vast majority of people will be entirely unaffected by the outcomes of these debates, whatever those outcomes may be. The same, however, cannot be said of the resurgence of nativism in other spheres. Where what is at issue is the innateness or not of our intelligence, or our morals, or our sexuality, the stakes are arguably much higher.

Nativism's potential for effecting profound changes in our views about ourselves and our society is already becoming apparent. The nativist's shifting of explanatory emphasis from the environment to the genes—or from the knowable and manipulable to the imponderable and immutable—seemingly supports the more general shift in sociopolitical attitudes that is occurring as the twentieth century lurches to a close. The growing obsession here and abroad with racial, national, and sexual differences; the widely perceived failure of social welfare programs to cure society's ills; the newly fashionable backlash against attempts to enforce ideals of equality and civil rights; the calls for a reinstatement of 'traditional morals' and 'family values'; the nostalgia for a time when everyone had a place and knew that place and stayed in it—these kinds of views find a fertile seeding ground in the New Nativism. Conservative politicians, moralists, and jurists apparently find overwhelming the inference from 'innate' to 'right' and 'inevitable.'[2] If the poverty and violence of our inner cities are coded in the genotypes of their inhabitants, then government program aimed at ameliorating these conditions are pointless.[3] If poor scholastic performance among minority children is a consequence of their substandard genes, then forget about Head

2. See Wright (1994:13): "I believe some—some—of the conservative norms that prevailed in Victorian England reflect, if obliquely, a surer grasp of human nature than has prevailed in the social sciences for most of this century; and that some of the resurgent moral conservatism of the past decade, especially in the realm of sex, rests on an implicit rediscovery of truths about human nature that have long been denied."

3. See Jeffrey (1994): "Social variables used by sociologists . . . are only weakly associated with the violent career offender. This indicates that possibly the career offender is different in kind. . . . These individuals may differ in terms of genetic and neurological factors." (1994:167) Jeffrey advocates medical intervention (administration of neuroactive drugs to 'at risk' populations) as a crime-preventive measure.

Start and other educational reforms.[4] If the kind of serial monogamy practices in our society destroys some men's biological 'right' to reproduce, then we should tighten the divorce laws.[5] If women are by nature less aggressive than men, and if aggression is a factor in achieving social status and economic success, then sexual inequality and the 'glass ceiling' are here to stay. And so on. Of course, these inferences are highly questionable. 'Innate' does not in general imply 'impervious to environmental adjustment.'[6] And to suppose that something is right just because it is innate is to commit the fallacy of deriving 'ought' from 'is.' But although the fact that there is no short argument—and perhaps no argument at all—from nativism to political, moral, or economic prescriptions is sometimes acknowledged by the New Nativism's proponents,[7] the inference from some state of affairs' being natural to its being right is being made all the time, with potentially devastating consequences.[8]

All the more reason, then, to be very clear about what nativism is, and on what considerations its claims to credibility lie. If we as a society cannot help but draw social and political conclusions from claims about innateness—perhaps our tendency to do so is inborn!—we can at least take care to investigate the validity of those claims themselves. This book is intended to be a small step toward doing exactly that.

4. Herrnstein and Murray (1994:389–416).
5. See Wright (1994:101): "When some men dominate more than twenty-five years' worth of fertility, some man, somewhere, must do with less. . . . It is not crazy to think that there are homeless alcoholics and rapists who, had they come of age in a pre-1960s social climate, amid more equally distributed female resources, would have early on found a wife and adopted a lower-risk, less destructive lifestyle. . . . if polygyny would indeed have pernicious effects on society's less fortunate men . . . then it isn't enough to just oppose legalized polygyny. . . . We have to worry about the de facto polygyny that already exists. We have to ask . . . whether [monogamy] can be restored."
6. This point is argued eloquently by Alper and Beckwith (1993).
7. See Wright (1994:13): "If modern Darwinism indeed has some morally conservative emanations, does that mean it has politically conservative emanations? This is a tricky . . . question . . . the question of innate human goodness casts a political shadow that can't be so casually disregarded."
8. See Kevles (1985) and Gould (1981) for historical accounts of what ensued last time such inferences were accepted uncritically. See Lewontin, Rose, and Kamin (1984); Billings, Beckwith, and Alper (1992); and Block (1995) for cautionary scientific and philosophical responses to some of these claims.

Acknowledgments

My most immediate and pressing debt is to Steve Stich. Without his eleventh-hour intervention, this book would never have been published. Thank you, Steve, for your efforts, advice, and help.

As great, though different in kind, is my debt to my philosophical colleagues at Caltech: Jim Woodward, Alan Hájek, and David Hilbert (now of University of Illinois at Chicago). Your encouragement and support over the last few years are much appreciated: many thanks.

This book was 'innate, in a way,' in my Ph.D. dissertation. I'd like again to acknowledge the aid provided by my thesis advisers, Gil Harman and Scott Soames, and the faculty, students, and staff at Princeton University between 1988 and 1992, in my production of that prototype of the present work.

Diana Barkan, Michael Devitt, Dave Hilbert, Bill Lycan, Andrew Milne, Kim Sterelny, Steve Stich, and Jim Woodward read versions of the present manuscript and improved it enormously by giving me detailed comments thereon. In addition, Diana, Dave, and Jim, displaying heroic supererogation, have read much of it more than once, and Jim thought up the excellent title. For your generous help and insights, I thank you all.

Others have read bigger or smaller chunks of this material over the last few years, some anonymously in their capacity as journal referees. To those I know about—Frank Arntzenius, Bill Demopoulos, Peter Godfrey-Smith, Alan Hájek, Ned Hall, Paul Hoffman, Dan Kevles, Marc Lange, Oscar Mandel, David Papineau, Stephen Pinker, Chris Ryan, Tad Schmaltz, Margaret Wilson, and the late David Stove—thank you. To those I don't know about (and who said helpful things): thank you also.

I'd like also to acknowledge the various audiences who have endured—and in some cases thoroughly taken to pieces—talks based on this material.

Barbara Estrada and Doreen Domb have helped with the technical details of manuscript production; Alan Turring in Graphic Arts at Caltech did the illustrations. And hearty thanks go also to Robert Miller and Lisa Stallings at Oxford University Press, New York, for the astonishing efficiency with which they dealt with this book's production.

Finally, my heartfelt thanks go to my dear husband, Steve Novak, who couldn't give a damn what I say about nativism—and, miraculously, loves me anyway.

Contents

THE HISTORICAL DEBATE

1

What Nativism Is Not

1.1 What Is Nativism? Preliminary Spleen

The doctrine of innate ideas really is as old as philosophy itself. The claim that the character of our mental furniture is to a large extent internally rather than environmentally determined found its first substantive defense in the works of Plato, was resurrected by rationalist philosophers in the seventeenth and eighteenth centuries, and has been defended most recently by two of the twentieth century's foremost mentalists, Noam Chomsky and Jerry Fodor. Fodor has argued that the vast majority of our concepts are innate. Chomsky's view, less radical than Fodor's but radical enough, is that much of our knowledge of natural languages is inborn.

But what are innate ideas? What is one committed to when one is committed to them? What do Plato, Descartes, Leibniz, Fodor, Chomsky, and a host of lesser-known philosophers and psychologists have in common such that they are all nativists? Unfortunately, and as numerous commentators have lamented, a general understanding of nativism is hard to come by.[1] Nativists' claims do not wear their content on their sleeves; and although their thesis is one of philosophy's most venerable, the historical record is surprisingly unhelpful to one seeking to elucidate what, in fact, that thesis is.

Suppose that, as a first approximation, one were to say that nativism about the mind is the view that (some of) what is in our minds is innate, born with us, part of our biological endowment as members of the species *Homo sapiens*. Saying this adds precious little to our understanding of nativist doctrine. Yet saying even this much is enough to raise a host of interpretive difficulties.

---

1. See, e.g., Adams (1975:71); Scott (1987, 1988); Hacking (1975:57). Such complaints are not merely a recent phenomenon—see Locke's *Essay*, Bk.1 (Locke 1975).

Problems arise in the first instance because there are several different kinds of cognitive equipment the innateness of which may be at issue. In general, 'what is in our minds' receives a threefold classification into ideas (or concepts), beliefs (and other propositional attitudes), and faculties or capacities (such as our ability to reason or to learn a language). The innateness of all these kinds of equipment has, over the years, been defended. But, because different writers have focused on different aspects of the mental, there is considerable variation in the views expressed by those within the nativist camp. Consider, for example, the extent to which a contemporary nativist, like Noam Chomsky, would agree with the claims and motivations of nativists in the first part of seventeenth century. At that time, many were dismayed to see the influence of traditional Christianity being eroded by the rise of modern scientific materialism. Hoping to buttress Christian dogma and values against spreading skepticism, the so-called Cambridge Platonists sought to defend their favored moral and religious precepts by establishing their innateness.[2] They argued that such 'congenite truths' as 'There is a God,' 'Promises are to be kept,' and 'The obscene parts and actions are not to be exposed to publick view' (!) are immune to question on the grounds that they are written "euen [even] in thine owne bosom, written by the finger of God, in such plaine Characters, and so legible, that though thou knowest not a letter in any other booke, yet thou maist read this."[3]

Chomsky has not, to my knowledge, considered whether we have any innate opinions as to the probity of indecent exposure. But it is surely not essential to his being a nativist about language that he should accept the claims of his nativist forebears as to the innateness of moral and religious beliefs. So although Chomsky and his Cambridge cohorts share the view that *something* mental is innate, they may disagree as to *what* is innate. We therefore need a characterization of nativism that is both 'deep' and yet general enough to accommodate substantial doctrinal differences like these: an account that links nativism too closely to the innateness of some particular psychological trait is ipso facto inadequate.

A more important source of confusion derives from the fact that parties to the debate over nativism typically rely on metaphors to elucidate their positions. In explaining what it is for some mental item to be innate, nativists—where they do not invoke near synonyms like 'natural' or 'inborn'—make airy reference to veins in marble, hereditary diseases, imprints in wax, writings on the soul, and *prêt à porter* coats; which their empiricist opponents just as breezily counter with talk of blank slates, plain pages, empty storehouses, and made-to-measure suits. If taken as serious attempts to ex-

---

2. Patrides (1970) contains a selection of writings of the Cambridge Platonists. See Yolton (1956:30–48) for a more general survey of nativist writings prior to the publication of Locke's *Essay*.

3. The examples of innate precepts, from Sir Matthew Hale's *The Primitive Origination of Mankind* (1677), are due to Yolton (1956:34). The passage is from Richard Carpenter's *The Conscionable Christian* (1623), quoted in Yolton (1956:31).

plain what nativism is, these metaphors generate a plethora of interpretive puzzles. Even the small sample of analogies just mentioned suggests at least two quite different ways to understand what it means to say that something is innate. Descartes's comparison of innate ideas with inherited illnesses, and Leibniz's likening them to veins in a slab of marble, support a dispositional reading.[4] Just as the symptoms of hereditary gout are not present at birth, and just as the statue of Hercules is only implicit in the layout of the faults in the stone, innate ideas are not literally *there* in the mind of the neonate. Rather, their emergence is conditional upon the occurrence of certain other events or processes, in much the same way as uncovering the statue in the marble requires the sculptor's skillful chiseling or the manifestation of the disease requires that the unfortunate individual reach (say) middle age. To liken innate mental items to the statue implicit in the marble, or to the disease coded into the genes, then, is to suggest that those items are initially present in the mind only implicitly or potentially or partially, requiring something extra—experience, perhaps, or maturation—to emerge fully.

By contrast, the Cambridge Platonists' talk of principles' being written or imprinted or engraven in the soul, and the modern nativist's analogy between the mind's stock of innate concepts and a store's stock of suits, are most naturally read as implying that beliefs and ideas are present in the mind at birth in some quite straightforward and non-dispositional sense.[5] So, in addition to the three variants of the doctrine mentioned above—as concerning, that is, concepts or beliefs or capacities—we now get an orthogonal division of nativism into its dispositional and non-dispositional versions. The doctrine of innate ideas, which at first appeared to be a univocal position, has degenerated into a motley disjunction. And the fragmentation does not stop here: further analysis of the nativist's 'explanations' just makes things worse. Stich, for instance, canvasses several ways to understand Descartes's analogy between innate ideas and hereditary diseases, each of which has some intuitive appeal and none of which is wholly satisfying.[6] Samet (unpublished manuscript) does the same, at rather greater length, for Leibniz's statue of Hercules metaphor. But these attempts at elucidation do little to further our understanding of what nativism is. Instead, they serve to underscore how entirely unhelpful the nativist's metaphors are, and to demonstrate how hard it is to interpret them in such a way that different nativists come out saying—even roughly—the same thing.

---

4. See Leibniz's Preface to his *New Essays* (1981:52) and Descartes's "Comments on a Certain Broadsheet" (CSM I:303–4; AT VIIIB:358). (I shall give references both to the standard twelve volume edition of Descartes's works, edited by Adams and Tannery (AT) and to the two-volume edition edited by Cottingham, Stoothoff, and Murdoch (CSM). All quotations are as translated by CSM, unless otherwise indicated.)

5. The contemporary analogy between innate ideas and off-the-rack suits is due to Piattelli-Palmarini (1986, 1989).

6. See Stich, Introduction to Stich (1975).

The threat of a massive proliferation of different nativisms suggests that it may be a mistake to regard the nativist's metaphors as anything more than colorful *façons de parler*. They do, after all, often seem to be intended more rhetorically than explanatorily.[7] If so, it is a mistake to rely too much upon them. Further, to insist on a literal reading of the nativist's words is in many cases to violate a central imperative of interpretation—namely, that one shouldn't be too quick to ascribe stupid views to smart people. Particularly problematic in this regard is the attribution of a commitment to 'naive' or non-dispositional nativism to those who favor the 'writings on the soul' and *'prêt à porter'* conceits. This view, according to which concepts or beliefs are, as it were, 'fully present' in the mind at birth, has for so long been known to be susceptible to so many and such obvious objections, that charity alone might prevent our attributing it to anyone, his or her taste in similes notwithstanding.[8]

1.2 The Oblique Approach

Such considerations as these suggest that nativists' explicit attempts to explain their position are unreliable as guides to an understanding of what nativism is. Too great a focus on the nativists' analogical glosses leads inexorably to trouble of one sort or another. Insofar as one is concerned to answer the question, "What is nativism?," then, a more subtle approach is in order.

Unfortunately, however, our path to enlightenment is little clearer once we break free of the metaphorical undergrowth. The most obvious alternative method of finding out what nativists believe would be to figure out what problem they think nativism is a solution to and why they think nativism solves that problem, inferring thence what nativism must be in order that it solve that problem for that reason. But employment of this 'method of triangulation' is stymied by a further confusing feature of the nativism controversy, namely, that it is extremely unclear just what question nativism is designed to answer. Or rather, it is clear that there are two different

7. The passage from Carpenter quoted above, for example, was taken from a sermon. It is therefore perhaps inappropriate to read his talk of what is 'written in our souls' by the 'finger of God' as the outline of any kind of theory, it being intended rather as an exhortation to religious faith.

8. The classic articulation of nondispositional nativism's embarrassments appears in Book I of Locke's *Essay* (Locke 1975)—see §1.5.2 below. The charitable principle just mentioned is sometimes used as a basis for criticizing Locke, the charge being that no one could really have been stupid enough to subscribe to the views he criticizes in the *Essay*. Yolton (1956:30–44), however, gives scores of passages in which seventeenth-century nativists certainly wrote as if they held the naive theory Locke lampoons. The operative idea behind Yolton's defense of Locke is that—charity notwithstanding—we ought to suppose that nativists both understand and mean what they say.

questions to which nativists have taken themselves to be responding; what is unclear is why one should think that their responses to those questions deserve the name 'nativism.' In the rest of this chapter, I look at the two problems to which nativism has, historically, been proposed as a solution. The first is that of providing a foundation for a rationalist epistemology. I argue, in §1.4, that nativism has (or should have) at best a subsidiary role to play in that enterprise. For, to the extent that the rationalist succeeds in his project, the real epistemological work is being done by God. The second problem to which nativists have traditionally seen themselves as responding is that of providing an answer to the psychological question, "Where does what is in our minds come from?" In §1.5, I argue that insofar as the nativist has a plausible answer to this 'genetic' question, that answer is indistinguishable from the empiricist's.

1.3 Two Problems

Especially during the heyday of nativist theorizing in the seventeenth century, questions about how beliefs are acquired were frequently mixed up with questions as to their justification. Nativism seems to have been regarded not only as answering the psychological question, "How did what is in our minds come to be there?" but also, in virtue of its alleged contribution to an explanation of why beliefs that are arrived at a priori are justified, as forming the keystone of a rationalist epistemology.

Leibniz, for example, in the Preface to his *New Essays*, outlines two questions on which he is particularly concerned to take issue with Locke. First, he writes, "There is the question whether the soul in itself is completely blank like a writing tablet on which nothing has as yet been written . . . whether everything which is inscribed there comes solely from the senses and experience. . . ." (1981:48). This is a psychological question about the causal history of our beliefs and concepts; and Leibniz's position on this issue is, of course, that the *tabula* is far from *rasa*: "The soul inherently contains the sources of various notions and doctrines, which external objects merely rouse up on suitable occasions" (1981:48).

Having outlined his response to this question, Leibniz immediately turns to "another question, namely, whether all truths depend on experience, that is on induction and instances, or if some of them have some other foundation" (1981:49). This is an epistemological question concerning the sources of justification for our beliefs. Taking necessary truths as his example, Leibniz argues that they could not get their warrant from sense experience. For, he says, the senses can give us only "instances, that is particular or singular truths" (1981:49), and "however many instances confirm a general truth they do not suffice to establish its universal necessity" (1981:49). Where, then, does the 'extra' warrant required by necessary truths come from? The nativist hypothesis again saves the day: "It appears that necessary truths . . .

must have principles whose proof does not depend on instances nor, consequently, on the testimony of the senses . . . proof of them can only come from inner principles, which are described as innate" (1981:50).

Thus, Leibniz holds that the innateness of certain 'inner principles' answers two quite different questions. The first is the psychological question, "Why do we have certain beliefs (and concepts) despite an apparent absence of the kinds of sense experiences that could give rise to them?" The second is an epistemological question, "What justifies beliefs (such as our beliefs about necessities) that, apparently, could not get their warrant from sense experience?" As we will see, Leibniz is not alone in asking an innateness hypothesis to perform both these tasks. In §§1.4 and 1.5, I shall argue that it performs neither of them.

1.4 Nativism and Epistemology: Foundations for Rationalism

Let us look first at nativism's role in epistemology. So closely have nativism and rationalism been associated that the *Encyclopedia of Philosophy* actually identifies a commitment to innate ideas with a commitment to the possibility of obtaining substantive knowledge of the world a priori: "The theory of innate ideas, in any of its philosophically significant forms, claims that all morally right judgment or all science, or both, rest upon or consist in a knowledge *a priori* either of (a) universal principles governing reality or (b) objects transcending sensory experience" (Nelson 1967:166). Not only does this formulation make the connection between rationalism and innatism rather too intimate, it also seems to ignore nativism's other role as a psychological theory of belief and concept acquisition (see §1.5). The fact nonetheless remains that for many years a priori knowledge and an innateness hypothesis were regarded as a package deal.

But to try to characterize nativism in terms of its role in a rationalist epistemology is immediately to run up against a serious problem. The problem is that while a nativist hypothesis is, at least prima facie, a reasonable sort of response to the psychological question, "Where do beliefs arrived at a priori come from?" it is not a reasonable sort of answer to the epistemological question, "What *justifies* those a priori beliefs?" Why should the mere fact of my belief's being innate, or of its following from certain innate 'principles,' serve to justify it? A belief I acquired as a result of being brainwashed or drugged or hit on the head would not be justified. Why should beliefs I acquire as a result of being built the way I am be any better off?

They would be better off if a belief's innateness somehow guaranteed its truth; or if a principle's innateness somehow guaranteed its reasonableness. But it does not—or not by itself, at any rate. It is possible, after all, that our heads at birth should be stuffed full of all kinds of rubbish: false beliefs, faulty inferential strategies, misleading ideas, or what-have-you. It's therefore possible that (say) the belief that a triangle's angles sum to 180°

is rigorously derived, using our innate faculty of Reason, from innately spec-ified axioms—and yet false, because the innate axioms, or Reason itself, or both, are unreliable. Since innateness per se brings with it neither truth nor reasonableness, it will not, pace Leibniz, explain why our a priori beliefs are justified.

Of course, if there were some additional reason to suppose that what is innate is somehow epistemologically privileged, then the nativist would be on surer ground. Suppose, for example, there were reason to think that innate beliefs and so on were implanted in our minds by a benevolent God, concerned to give us a head start in our attempts to negotiate the sublunary wilderness. Then that would be reason to think that those beliefs are true; that our innate inferential strategies are truth-preserving; and that any innate concepts we possess are such as to carve the world at its joints. Or suppose, in a more contemporary vein, that a case could be made for the claim that natural selection would favor organisms whose innate beliefs were true over those with false beliefs. Then that would equally be grist to the nativist's mill.[9] Or suppose, to take a third possibility, that there were some episte-mological 'principle of conservatism' to the effect that if we believe that p and have no reason to think that not-p, then we are justified in continuing in that belief. Then, innate beliefs, being built in and believed by default, so to speak, would be justified unless positive grounds for rejecting them were discovered.[10]

But whatever extra machinery one chooses to wheel in here, the fact remains that an innateness hypothesis is at best only a part of the episte-mological edifice: the real foundation for a rationalist epistemology is pro-vided by God or Mother Nature or our 'principle of conservatism' or whoever or whatever it is that stands guarantor that our a priori beliefs—be they innate or not—track reality. So we have the situation alluded to above: an innateness hypothesis will not solve the epistemological problem; and what will solve that problem does not deserve to be called an 'innateness hypothesis.'

1.4.1 Doin' the Nativist Shuffle

I think that nativists themselves have always recognized, albeit very reluc-tantly, the shortcomings of nativism in its role as epistemological foundation stone. This recognition, and nativists' uneasiness with it, show up time and again in their tendency to shuffle their feet whenever the moment comes for

9. Carruthers (1992) makes exactly this case in response to exactly this problem. I myself have doubts about this strategy. It is, after all, a commonplace of evolutionary theory that natural selection will often favor organisms with a tendency to err: a creature that forms the belief 'Predator nearby!' whenever anything moves in its vicinity will be wrong more often than not, but it may well live longer than another that, valuing truth over prudence, sticks around to determine what really caused that moving shadow.

10. This last suggestion was made by Scott Soames.

them to take a stand as to the exact role that nativism is playing in their epistemology. On the one hand (or foot), they write as if nativism by itself were an epistemological doctrine; as if, that is to say, to propose an innateness hypothesis were in itself to answer all our questions about the justification of beliefs arrived at a priori. But on the other, there is evidence too that they also believe that nativism is only a psychological theory about the origins of our ideas and that, as I have argued, to advance an innateness hypothesis is at most only a part of explaining how the a priori is to be justified.

Henry More, to take one example, is a shuffle virtuoso. He begins his *Antidote Against Atheism* (1653) with a discussion of exactly the issues I have just raised. His central argument for the existence of God (§§3–8) is based on the claim that 'God necessarily exists' follows, with 'mathematical' certainty, from the "indelible Idea of a Being absolutely perfect in the Mind of Man," an idea that is "Natural [i.e., innate] and Essential to the Soul of Man" (§3). But More admits at the outset that such an argument can never be apodictic, not because of any doubts about the cogency of ontological arguments in general but because, as he eloquently puts it:

> it is possible that Mathematicall evidence [i.e., demonstrative proof] it self, may be but a constant undiscoverable delusion, which our nature is necessarily and perpetually obnoxious unto, and that either fatally or fortuitously there has been in the world time out of mind such a Being as we call Man, whose essential property is to be then most of all mistaken, when he conceives a thing most evidently true. (§2)

Yet, and despite having thus effectively undermined his own project, More carries on as if nothing at all had happened. His only response to the crushing objection that he himself has raised is the remark that "you may as soon un-soul the Soul, as divide her from perpetuall assent to those Mathematical truths, supposing no distemper or violence offered to her Facultyes" (§3). Cold comfort, in the light of the possibility raised in the previous quotation. Nonetheless, More feels able to summarize his argument and its conclusion as follows:

> For this Idea of God being no arbitrarious Figment . . . but the necessary and naturall Emanation of the mind of Man, if it signifies to us that the Notion and Nature of God implyes in it necessary existence as we have shown it does, unless we will wink against our own naturall light, we are without any further Scruple to acknowledge that God does exist. (§8)

Without any further scruple, indeed!

Similar uneasiness about the role of nativism in epistemology is apparent in Descartes's argument for the existence of God in the Fifth Meditation. As a preliminary to presenting his version of the ontological argument, Descartes attempts to explain both why it is that we seem to believe certain propositions in the absence of any relevant experience and why those propositions should compel our assent—why, that is, a priori knowledge is *knowledge*, not mere belief. As to the former question, Descartes's view is that such beliefs are got from reflection upon ideas possessed innately. And as to the question of why we should trust the beliefs so acquired—crucial to Descartes's subsequent demonstration that God exists—nativism seems to be supposed to do the trick there as well.

Although he has already argued that what the mind perceives 'clearly and distinctly' must be true (because guaranteed by God), Descartes seems not to rely here on the clarity and distinctness of a priori beliefs about God as the ground for our acceptance of them. Recognizing, perhaps, the imminent threat of the notorious 'Cartesian circle,' he implies instead that their justification resides in their innateness. After a long discussion of the etiology of mathematical beliefs, in which he describes how they arise out of reflection upon ideas that he 'finds within' himself and that do not come from experience, Descartes writes of those beliefs:[11]

> And even if I had not demonstrated this [that clear and distinct ideas, such as mathematical ideas, must be true], the nature of my mind is such that I cannot but assent to them, at least so long as I clearly perceive them . . . I always held that the most certain truths of all were the kind which I recognized clearly in connection with shapes, or numbers, or other items relating to . . . pure and abstract mathematics. (CSM I:45; AT VII:65)

But is Descartes here claiming merely that the innateness of his mathematical beliefs explains why, as a matter of psychological fact, he feels compelled to regard them as true? Or is he making the much stronger claim that the beliefs' innateness provides him with reason to accept them? Descartes waffles shamelessly between these alternatives.

On the one hand, his argument requires the stronger claim. There's no doubt whatsoever that Descartes takes himself to have shown not just that we all must, in virtue of our psychological makeup, believe that God exists, but also that that belief is true: God does exist. As he puts his conclusion: "from the fact that I cannot think of God except as existing, it follows that existence is inseparable from God, and hence that he really exists" (CSM I: 46; AT VII:67). But it doesn't follow that God exists because I can't help but think he does! Something more in the way of argument is required. Assuming, as I have done, that an appeal to the belief in God's clarity and distinctness is out of the question, an appeal to its *innateness* might look appetizing as an alternative explanation of its justification. After all, such an appeal had even at that time a venerable philosophical ancestry. And Descartes's constant references to innate ideas and the 'natural light' of Rea-

---

11. Two notes about terminology. First, as Greene (1985:1–22) has argued, an idea for Descartes is the primary vehicle of truth; hence his 'idea' is often closer to our 'belief' or 'proposition' rather than our 'concept.' I therefore use 'idea' and 'belief' interchangeably in what follows. Second, I regard as unimportant for present purposes the distinction between beliefs or ideas that are themselves innate, and those that are acquired solely via reflection on beliefs or ideas that are innate. For simplicity's sake, I call both 'innate.'

son in presenting this argument certainly give the impression that nativism was the explanation he had in mind.

On the other hand, however, Descartes is too good and too honest a philosopher to be entirely happy with this strategy. He never comes out and says in so many words that because his belief in God is innate, it is justified. Rather, he again makes use of his analogy between that belief and his mathematical beliefs. Pointing out that his beliefs about God and his beliefs about mathematics have the same causal history, both being a result of reflection upon innate ideas, he claims only that they should be accorded the *same* epistemological status: "I ought still to regard the existence of God as having *at least the same level of certainty* as I have hitherto attributed to the truths of mathematics" (CSM I:45; AT VII:65–6, emphasis added). But Descartes's careful avoidance here of any claims as to exactly how certain those truths are, makes clear that he has doubts about the cogency of his 'demonstration.' As he should. For we remember, even if Descartes chooses not to mention it, that the truths of mathematics cannot be known with certainty until the hypothesis of the Deceitful Demon has been ruled out. And we remember too that it is God himself who keeps the demon at bay. As Descartes apparently sensed, though he nowhere explicitly acknowledged, an appeal to innateness as a way of justifying a priori beliefs about God brings with it a new, but equally damaging, 'Cartesian circle.'

The real foundation of seventeenth-century rationalism, then, is God. But, given the broader theological ends that that epistemology was designed to serve, this was the last thing that theorists like More or Descartes could bring themselves openly to admit. By writing as if nativism were in itself an epistemological theory—as if, that is to say, the mere fact of an idea's being innate were enough to justify it—the rationalist tried (perhaps unconsciously) to mask the deity lurking at the bottom of his epistemology. But this is mere sleight of hand. Nativism is not an epistemological theory; and insofar as an appeal to a benevolent God constitutes such a theory, it cannot with any justice be called 'nativism.'

1.4.2 Taking a Stand

Oddly enough, it is Plato alone among nativists who offers a story about innate knowledge that has at least some hope of avoiding the kinds of difficulties I have been discussing. I say 'oddly enough,' because to the extent that Plato was concerned with the kinds of epistemological issues that exercised seventeenth-century rationalists—certainty, justification, the distinction between knowledge and mere belief, and so on—he seems not to have regarded his nativism per se as bearing essentially on those questions. Nonetheless, it is instructive to consider Plato's theory in the light of the present discussion, as it throws into particularly sharp relief the problems faced by a rationalist who attempts to base his epistemology on an innateness hypothesis.

Plato's doctrine of *anamnesis* is introduced in the *Phaedo* and the *Meno*. On this view, so-called learning is a matter of 'recollecting' knowledge that was in fact acquired before our birth, as our souls communed in incorporeal congress with the Forms. In the *Phaedo*, Plato's defense of the theory is part of his broader project of establishing the immortality of the soul. He argues that since some of the knowledge we possess could not have entered the soul through the bodily senses, it must have been acquired prenatally. This in turn implies that our souls can and do exist, in disembodied state, prior to our birth.[12]

In the *Meno*, the recollection theory is invoked to declaw a paradox that seemingly undermines the Socratic inquiry into what virtue is. Philosophical inquiry, Meno suggests (80d–e), is impossible. For if you don't know what you're inquiring after, you won't be able to recognize it when you find it; but if you do know what you're inquiring into, your inquiry is superfluous. Socrates responds by pointing out that if learning is recollection of what is within you, then there is a sense in which you do know what you seek before you begin. But since that knowledge is buried or forgotten, there is also a sense in which you do not know. So philosophical inquiry, and Socrates' own promotion of its practice, is not pointless after all (81c–e, 85c–86b).

The fact that *anamnesis* serves such divergent philosophical ends in the two dialogues has led to much scholarly controversy about the relation of the *Meno* and *Phaedo* theories.[13] In my view, however, the theories of the *Meno* and the *Phaedo*, and the arguments Plato marshals in their support, are essentially identical. In both dialogues, *anamnesis* is developed primarily as a solution to the psychological 'acquisition problem', "How does what is in our minds come to be there?" The doctrine's success in providing an account of concept and belief acquisition is then used to lend independent support to a view—namely, transmigration of souls—that, notwithstanding its usefulness in furthering Plato's 'deeper' philosophical ends, rather lacks something in the way of intuitive plausibility.[14]

Plato's argument for the recollection theory proceeds in two steps. First, he seeks to establish that much of what is in our minds must be innate. Employing, in effect, a version of the 'argument from the poverty of the stimulus,'[15] Plato argues that the information provided by sensory experience

---

12. The existence of the soul after death—a rather more compelling issue, given Socrates' predicament in the *Phaedo*—is established by separate arguments.

13. See in particular Scott (1987) and the literature discussed therein.

14. As evidence that Plato regarded the theories presented in the *Phaedo* and *Meno* as being identical, note that he has Cebes introduce the doctrine of *anamnesis* in the *Phaedo* by describing what is, in essence, the experiment performed in the *Meno*: ". . . when people are asked questions, if the question is put to them in the right way, they can give a perfectly correct answer, which they could not possibly do unless they had some knowledge and a proper grasp of the subject. And then if you confront people with a diagram or anything like that, the way they react is an unmistakable proof that the [recollection] theory is correct" (*Phaedo* 73a,b).

15. To be discussed more fully in §2.2.

is too meager to account for our acquisition of certain concepts or beliefs. In the *Phaedo* (74b–75e), he begins by noting that when we are presented with two sticks, we can tell that they are not exactly equal (in length, say): they "fall short" of Equality itself (74d).[16] The fact that we can make this judgment, he argues, shows that we must have had "knowledge of the Equal before that time when we first saw" (74e) the sticks and "realized that [they] strive to be like the Equal but are deficient" (74e–75a). But since *all* sensible objects, on Plato's view, necessarily fall short of perfect equality—since "all we perceive through [the senses] is striving to reach that which is Equal but falls short of it" (75b)—it follows that we couldn't have got our idea of equality from the senses. Hence, Plato concludes, "before we begin to see or hear or otherwise perceive, we must have possessed knowledge of the Equal itself" (75b): the idea of equality is innate.[17] In the *Meno*, Plato is concerned with our acquisition of certain kinds of beliefs, such as mathematical beliefs, for which experience is again insufficient. Although Meno's slave has never been taught anything about geometry, and although Socrates merely asks him questions (rather than supplying him with any explicit mathematical information), he is able to acquire true opinions about Pythagoras's Theorem. Since the boy's opinions did not come from without, Plato argues, they must have been in him from the start: they too are innate.

The second step of Plato's defense of *anamnesis* involves establishing that the psychological process that we naively call 'learning from experience' is in fact a process of recollection. Just as "the sight of Simmias often reminds one of Cebes" (*Phaedo* 73d), so experience of the world of sense reminds one of the things one had previously encountered in the realm of the Forms. Sense experience does not teach us anything new; rather, it serves to remind us of the things that we know already but have forgotten. Initially haphazard and therefore unreliable, the learner's recollections become (under the right kind of stimulus, such as a chat with Socrates) increasingly orderly and methodical. By paying attention to what he is recollecting, and by recollecting 'in order, as he should,' the learner converges on the truth. Finally, and insofar as he can confirm his 'memories' by arriving at the same point from a variety of different starting points, the learner attains a state of knowledge.

This brings us to the point about Plato that is of particular interest in the context of a discussion of the relation of nativism and rationalism in epistemology. Recall the thrust of my earlier arguments: a belief's innateness does not guarantee its truth, for our heads at birth could be full of trash; and insofar as our a priori beliefs can be justified, something other than their innateness is doing the epistemological work. What is interesting about Plato is that he, alone among nativists, is actually quite explicit on this point. He alone, that is to say, has a theory that shows how the psychological hy-

16. Quotations from the *Phaedo* are taken from the translation of Hackforth (1955); those from the *Meno* are from that of Grube (1981).

17. Bostock (1986:60–102) gives a similar reading of the *Phaedo* argument.

pothesis of innateness is connected to the epistemological question of justification.

Hinted at in the *Meno*, and more fully developed in the *Phaedrus* (247c–
252b), his view is that the concepts and beliefs that are recollected during
learning were acquired by the soul during its prenatal sojourn in a "place
beyond the heavens" where "true being dwells" (247c).[18] There, using "reason alone, the soul's pilot" (247c), the soul acquires "veritable knowledge
of being that veritably is" (247e). It being, according to Plato, a necessary
condition of a soul's entering a human body that it have in this manner
"journeyed with [its] god . . . gazing up to that which truly is" (249c), all
human souls can be guaranteed to have innate beliefs about the Forms. And
because our beliefs concerning the unchanging world of the Forms were
acquired by a soul unencumbered with bodily senses (and hence immune to
the errors that the senses bring with them), those beliefs are guaranteed to
be true. So as long as one takes care to recollect in the orderly manner that
Socrates recommends, one can be sure that the beliefs one acquires a priori
are true.[19]

The point is that regardless of what one might think about the wisdom—
not to say sanity—of basing one's epistemology on a doctrine of metem-
psychosis and the theory of Forms, Plato alone among rationalists explicitly recognizes that an innateness hypothesis will not by itself solve any epistemological problems. He recognized, that is to say, what I have been arguing throughout this section: that nativism is not an epistemological
doctrine.

It is, in the light of all this, an interesting question why nativism and
rationalism have been so closely associated throughout the history of philosophy. Perhaps this association is due to rationalist philosophers' having
given in to the (apparently overwhelming) temptation to conflate psychological compulsion with rational compulsion. Nativism, as I have already
remarked, might look plausible as an explanation of why it is that there are
things that we can't help but believe: just as our genes make sure that hearts
and blood and brains are, as it were, 'standard features' of the human machine, so they might ensure too that certain beliefs are non-optional. But it
is one thing to explain why I am compelled to believe that *p* in this sense;
and it's quite another to explain why I am compelled to believe that *p* in
the sense that interests the epistemologist. To think otherwise is to confuse

18. Quotations from the *Phaedrus* are taken from the translation of Hackforth (1955).
19. As Alan Hájek pointed out to me, this does not go all the way toward solving the
problem of justification. For although Plato argues for the reliability of innate beliefs, his
talk about orderly recollection does not guarantee the reliability of our access to them: as
we in the post–Freudian age recognize, it's possible that no matter how hard I try to
remember, I might fail to access knowledge that is in me. But Plato does at least go one
better than his nativist descendants, who explicitly recognized and responded to neither
problem.

the lack of doxastic choice that we might well have qua human beings, with whatever lack of choice we have qua rational beings.

1.5 Nativism and Psychology: The 'Genetic' Question

Dominic Scott remarks that, in thinking about nativism, there is "a fundamental choice to be made: are we to use one or another brand of innatism merely to tell us something about the origin of certain beliefs or about their justification?" (1988:136).[20] In §1.4, I argued that nativism per se has nothing to tell us about the justification of our beliefs. I left it open, however, that nativism may have something to say about their origins. Indeed, in arguing that it is only in conjunction with certain further assumptions (such as that God is good, or that souls can commune before birth with the Forms) that nativism can play a role in a rationalist epistemology, I tacitly assumed that nativism is indeed a psychological theory of belief and concept acquisition. In the present section, I shall argue that this assumption is, in fact, problematic. It is unobvious, to say the least, what the nativist is claiming about the origins of what is in our minds.

1.5.1 Internalism and Externalism: The Debate over
Nature versus Nurture

When it is not characterized as being identical with rationalism in epistemology, nativism is often equated with rationalism in psychology. Rationalism in psychology, in turn, is understood in terms of its opposition to empiricism, the two doctrines being viewed as constituting radically different answers to the 'genetic' question, "How did what is in our minds come to be there?" Nativism (or rationalism), on this conception, is the view that what is in our minds did not (in any very interesting sense) *come to be there* at all. Rather, it always was there; it was born with us; it is innate. Empiricism, by contrast, is the view that the contents of our minds are not (in any very interesting sense) born with us. Instead, they come 'from experience' or 'from the senses.'

Godfrey-Smith's recent discussion (1996) exemplifies this popular account of what nativism is, and reveals some of the difficulties inherent in it. Godfrey-Smith begins by making a general distinction between 'internalist' and 'externalist' explanations of an organism's traits: externalists explain "properties of organic systems in terms of properties of their environments" (1996:30), while internalists explain "one set of organic properties in terms of other internal or intrinsic properties of the organic system" (1996:30). He then proceeds to classify a wide variety of views and positions, including

---

20. See also Scott (1987:346–47; 1988:125–36).

those of nativists and empiricists, according to this schema.[21] On his view, empiricists such as Locke, Berkeley, and Hume are externalists: "The central empiricist claim . . . is the claim that the contents of thought are determined, directed or strongly constrained by the properties of experience. In strong forms, this is the claim that there is nothing in the mind that was not previously in sense" (1996:32). Leibniz and Chomsky, by contrast, are by this account internalists: they claim that "there is no way ideas which come into the mind from outside can be formed into beliefs and judgments without the operation of specific internal mechanisms. Inputs will not just coalesce into beliefs." (1996:39)

But while something like this understanding of nativism and empiricism is more or less the standard one, distilled as it is in popular references to the debate over "nature vs. nurture," it is clearly inadequate as it stands to capture what actual empiricists and nativists were up to. For, rhetoric aside, *both* empiricists *and* nativists are *both* internalists *and* externalists about the origins of what is in our minds. That is to say, each side accepts what is, on this account, the core of the other's position, for both sides agree that our minds are a product of a highly complex *interaction* of the experiential with the inborn. Admittedly, this meeting of minds is sometimes obscured by the rhetoric (not to say caricature and abuse) hurled from one side to the other. As I have mentioned (§1.1), this is a battle that is largely fought over, and with, metaphors: blank slates and empty warehouses clash with engraved souls and well-stocked department stores. But in this philosophical Balkans, as perhaps in the real thing, the rhetoric seems only to mask the absence of a substantive disagreement—at least so far as the appropriateness of internalist and externalist explanatory strategies in psychology is concerned. Force the warring parties to lay down their similes and negotiate the disputed territory in plain language, and there seems precious little that they disagree about. Nativists agree with the empiricists' 'externalist' insistence that very special sorts of interactions with the environment are necessary for the acquisition of a mental life. And empiricists agree with the nativists' 'internalist' claim that were it not for our possession of some rather special inborn equipment, we, like most of the natural world, would have no mental lives at all.

1.5.2 A Case Study: Locke and Leibniz

The interchange between Locke, arch empiricist, and Leibniz, paradigmatic rationalist, amply illustrates the pitfalls of understanding the innateness controversy in internalist versus externalist terms. In the first book of the *Es-*

---

21. In fact, Godfrey-Smith does not restrict his attention to theories about organisms: as well as finding an opposition between internalism and externalism in psychology and biology, he applies his taxonomy to epistemologies and philosophies of science according to the ways they explain the properties of a given (not necessarily organic) system in terms of intrasystemic, as opposed to extrasystemic factors (1996:30ff.)

say,[22] Locke takes issue with three claims commonly made by his nativist contemporaries. The first is that certain ideas (such as ideas of Being, Substance, God) are innate. The second is that we have innate knowledge of various, very general 'speculative principles' (such as the laws of identity and noncontradiction). The third is that there is innate knowledge of certain 'practical principles' (such as 'God is to be worshiped').

Locke distinguishes a strong and a weak version of the nativist's claim that such mental items are innate. The strong thesis asserts that since anything that is 'in the mind' must be 'imprinted' in the understanding, a proposition that is known (or an idea that is possessed) innately must be present in the mind at birth. But if this were true of (for example) logical principles, Locke argues, then "Infants, and all that have Souls must necessarily have them in their Understandings, know the Truth of them, and assent to it" (I.2.v). For it is, he reckons, "near a Contradiction, to say, that there are Truths imprinted on the soul which it perceives or understands not" (I.2.v). But, Locke points out, it is obvious that "Children, Ideots, Savages and the grosly Illiterate" (I.2.xxvii) are totally unaware of the logical principles at issue. Since the same goes for the allegedly innate ideas and practical principles—which, Locke maintains, are recognized, if at all, only as a result of experience—he concludes that the strong version of the claim that ideas or principles are innate is simply false.

Locke then goes on to consider the weaker claim that ideas and principles are dispositionally innate—innate, that is, only in the sense that people will recognize and assent to them at some determinate point in their intellectual development, such as when they 'come to the use of Reason' (I.2.vi). Taking his consideration of the case for the innateness of logical truths as illustrative of his general strategy, Locke argues (with characteristic overkill) that the claim that such truths are innate even in this weaker sense is self-defeating, false, and ultimately frivolous. If the claim is meant to be that we use reason to discover logical truths, then it is self-defeating: How, Locke asks (I.2.xi), can something that is the 'foundation and guide' to our reason require the use of reason for its discovery? If the claim is merely that our recognition of and assent to logical truths is coincidental with our coming to the use of reason, then, Locke argues, it is false: what in fact coincides with our coming to the use of reason is our discovery of lots of particular matters of fact, not general logical laws. The latter are formulated much later—if, of course, they are formulated at all: Locke's 'savages,' after all, may never explicitly recognize the laws of logic, despite behaving in other respects quite rationally (I.2.xii). Locke concludes that the weaker version of the nativist's claim that logical truths are known innately is frivolous, amounting to no more than the uninteresting observation, with which not even the most rampant empiricist will disagree, "That they are never known, nor taken notice of before the use of Reason, but may possibly be assented to sometime after, during

22. Locke (1975).

a Man's Life; but when, is uncertain . . ." (I.2.xiii). And since, as Locke goes on to point out, exactly the same is true of 'all other knowable truths,' logical principles "therefore have no Advantage, nor distinction from others, by this Note of being known when we come to the use of Reason; nor are they thereby proved to be innate, but quite the contrary" (I.2.xiii).

Locke's arguments highlight a recurring problem for nativists as they seek to make clear the content of their putatively 'internalist' claim that such and such ideas or beliefs are inborn, rather than being got from experience. If this claim is read as asserting that ideas are literally in the mind at birth— present in the mind, that is, in some straightforward and non-dispositional sense—then it is easy to dispute. For the concepts and principles that are alleged to be innate lack certain crucial features, such as being accessible to consciousness (Locke's favorite) or playing a role in reasoning, that pertain to the things whose presence 'in our minds' is uncontroversial. But if, on the other hand, nativists are read as asserting, as is prima facie more plausible, that concepts or beliefs are in our minds at birth only potentially, or dis- positionally, then they must find some mark that distinguishes what is innate from what is not. But such marks are, as a matter of fact, very hard to come by. Whatever features the nativist proposes as definitive of the innate—being assented to on first hearing, for example, or being recognized when we come to the use of Reason—can typically be shown to apply equally to almost everything that comes to be in our minds. And if it turns out that 'all know- able truths' or ideas are innate according to some analysis, then, the empir- icist can argue, by reductio ad absurdum, none are: the nativist hypothesis loses all its explanatory bite.[23]

If his critique of nativism underscores the nativist's dilemma, Locke's attempt to provide an alternative explanation of the origins of our ideas and beliefs highlights an equally curly difficulty faced by the empiricist. As he himself explicitly recognizes (Introduction to the *Essay*, §2), the empiricist's case against nativism rests not just on his arguments against that doctrine but also upon the cogency of his own account. The difficulty resides in developing an empiricist psychology that differs, not just verbally but also substantively, from that of the (sophisticated) nativist.

At least initially, the differences between nativism and Locke's empiricism appear stark. At the beginning of Book II of the *Essay*, for example, Locke states his position on the genetic question as follows:

> How comes [the mind] to be furnished? Whence comes it by that vast store, which the busy and boundless Fancy of Man has painted on it, with an almost endless variety? Whence has it all the materials of Reason and

---

23. It is striking that nativists tend not to be unduly bothered by the empiricist's at- tempted reductio. Indeed, they often write in ways that suggest they are more than happy to embrace it. In Chapter 3, I offer an interpretation of what nativists mean when they claim that all our ideas are innate.

Knowledge? To this I answer, in one word, From *Experience*. . . ." (Locke 1975: II.1.ii)

This is indeed an externalism to warm a Godfrey-Smithian heart! Yet as he further elucidates his psychology, Locke makes free appeal to various innate mental faculties, including in particular our 'natural powers' for forming ideas of sense and reflection, and our inborn capacity for performing various 'operations of Reason,' such as comparison, compounding, and abstraction, upon the ideas so formed. And as Leibniz argues, responding to Locke in his *New Essays*, this somewhat underhanded reliance on innate faculties lends a remarkably nativist or internalist flavor to Locke's theory. So much so, indeed, that Leibniz alleges that "fundamentally his [i.e., Locke's] view on this question is not different from my own or rather from the common [i.e., nativist] view . . ." (1981:53).

And such seems to be the case. The substantive differences between Leibniz and Locke, at least as regards the respective contributions of experience and our innate endowment to our acquisition of a mental life, are minimal. Leibniz, after all, explicitly endorses the Lockean contention that "the senses are necessary for all our actual knowledge" (1981:49). And, as he goes on to emphasize, Locke implicitly agrees with the Leibnizian contention that the senses are not by themselves sufficient to account for all our knowledge. For, as we have seen, Locke (1) postulates the existence of innate dispositions (or 'powers' or 'faculties') to form ideas of sense; (2) allows that there are ideas got not from experience of the world but from reflection upon the operations of our own minds; and (3) recognizes that we are innately able (thanks to the 'light of nature') to discern relations among our ideas (and hence to reason). In so postulating, allowing, and recognizing, Leibniz maintains (1981:51–53, 84), Locke is, although he does not acknowledge it, granting the nativist more or less everything that he could wish.

The same theme is struck repeatedly in the literature. Philosophers on each side continually accuse their opponents of differing from them only verbally in their accounts of the origins of our minds. Leibniz's charge against Locke was aired above. But Locke had said it first. Speaking of his nativist predecessors, he asserts that their claims about innate principles "amount to no more, but only to a very improper way of speaking; which whilst it pretends to assert the contrary, says nothing different from those, who deny innate Principles" (1975:I.2.v). Descartes too gets into the act. In his *Comments on a Certain Broadsheet*, for example, he expresses the following thought in response to the criticisms of the empiricist philosopher Regius:

> the author's disagreement with me seems to be merely verbal. When he says that the mind has no need of ideas, or notions, or axioms which are innate, while admitting that the mind has the power of thinking (presumably natural or innate), he is plainly saying the same thing as I, though verbally denying it. (CSM I:303; AT VIIIB:357)

It augurs ill for the attempt to understand nativism and empiricism in terms of their internalist/externalist takes on the genetic question when even the participants in the debate recognize that once the opposing positions are deprived of their rhetorical varnish, each collapses into the other!

1.5.3 Softening the Distinction

Nativists and empiricists, then, agree that both experience and our innate endowment play critical roles in our mental development. This much convergence is, of course, all to the good: that the human mind is a product of an interaction between our genes and our experience of the world is hard to deny. However, once the agreement of our protagonists as to this truism is acknowledged, it is impossible to view them as being internalists and externalists in the senses outlined above. Enshrined though this erroneous picture may be in the popular imagination, nativists do not hold that what is in our minds is innate, rather than coming from experience; and empiricists do not hold that what is in our minds comes from experience alone. The present taxonomy will need some refining if it is to shed real light on the innateness debate.

Godfrey-Smith himself is quite aware of the crudeness of his initial characterizations of internalism and externalism: "When I say that externalists place great weight on external factors and neglect internal factors, this does not imply that they deny that internal factors exist and are necessary in producing the behavior of the system we are interested in" (1996:51)—and the same, mutatis mutandis, presumably goes for internalists too. But if "everyone agrees that, in almost all real systems, there will be *some* role played by both internal and external" (1996:51), and if "the amount of emphasis placed on the two types of factors can vary continuously" (1996:53), then the difference between internalist and externalist explanatory strategies apparently becomes one of degree. On what I take to be a more careful statement of his view, Godfrey-Smith's externalists no longer "explain properties of organic systems in terms of properties of their environments" *simpliciter*; instead, they explain properties of organic systems *more* in terms of environmental properties than in terms of organismic ones. Internalists no longer "explain one set of organic properties in terms of other internal or intrinsic properties of the organic system" period; instead, they *place more emphasis on* internal or intrinsic properties than on environmental factors in their explanations.

Applying this revised taxonomy to the debate over innate ideas, as Godfrey-Smith urges, leads us to view nativists and empiricists as disagreeing about which factors—innate or environmental—play more of a role, or a more important role, in the genesis of our ideas. Nativists, on this interpretation, think that innate factors play a more important role in the acquisition process, while empiricists accord explanatory primacy to experience. In my view, however, even this more nuanced characterization, while certainly seductive, is ultimately unhelpful. First, as I shall argue in chapter 3, there are deeper things at issue between nativist and empiricist than the question of what sort of global explanatory strategy to use in understanding the mind. Nativists and empiricists disagree not just about how to explain the various phenomena of acquisition, but also about whether giving such an explanation is possible at all. Viewing their conflict in terms solely of an internalist–externalist opposition, even of the present 'softer' sort, obscures these vital concerns. A second reason to beware the Godfrey-Smithian reading is that as it stands, it does little to discourage the worry, expressed by Locke, Leibniz, and others, that the debate over innate ideas is at bottom just a verbal one. For while I do not deny that there can be substantive disagreements as to whether an internalist or an externalist explanatory strategy is appropriate in a particular case (see §1.5.4), many apparent such conflicts are simply artifacts of differing explanatory emphases. Viewing nativist and empiricist as quarreling merely over how 'important' the various factors in belief and concept acquisition are can incline us to see their dispute as insubstantial too.

To see how easily pseudo conflicts between internalist and externalist explanations can arise, consider the following sketches of how normal facial features develop in a human fetus. According to Gus, a geneticist, genetic factors are more important in ensuring that a fetus comes to have (say) two normally shaped eyes fairly close together on the front of its head; according to Harry, an epidemiologist, environmental factors (such as the absence of a high concentration of alcohol in the maternal bloodstream) are what ensure that normal development takes place. While one can certainly classify the former explanation as "internalist" and the latter as "externalist," it makes no sense to view them as being in any way in conflict. For Gus and Harry are addressing two subtly different aspects of fetal development. The 'internalist,' Gus, is explaining why a fetus normally comes to have eyes on the front (rather than the sides or top or back, say) of its head. The 'externalist,' Harry, is explaining how a fetus comes to have normal-sized eyes close to the center of its face rather than the larger, elongated eyes toward the side of its face that are characteristic of fetal alcohol syndrome. Both explanations are perfectly good ones, and it would be absurd to see them pitted one against the other as an instance of internalist–externalist strife.

I take the moral here to be a general one. The appropriateness of giving an internalist as opposed to an externalist explanation of a particular trait often depends purely on what one's interest in that trait happens to be or on what (to use a bit of philosophy of science jargon) the implied 'contrast class' for the explanandum is. Different explanatory strategies will suit different explanatory aims, and to argue about which strategy is the 'right' one to use in explaining a given trait is often just plain silly.

Viewing nativists and empiricists as quarreling simply about the 'right' way to explain how a normal mind develops can make them look silly too. On the present interpretation, what makes you a nativist is that you stress the psychological contribution made by our innate endowment and dismiss as comparatively unimportant the offerings of experience. What makes you an empiricist, by contrast, is that you stress the role of experience, attaching the epithet 'not very important' to the innate contribution. And the problem is that you and I could be nativists and empiricists in *this* sense, and yet disagree about nothing of substance whatsoever. I, perhaps, am interested in how we can acquire beliefs at all (rocks, after all, cannot), so I emphasize the importance, say, of having a brain. You, on the other hand, are interested in why we have *these* beliefs rather than *those*, so you stress that we have these, not those, experiences. Our respective appeals to the innate and the experiential are perfectly appropriate to answering the questions we are asking, our views about the mind are not in conflict, and the great innateness controversy that we might take ourselves to be involved in is, at best, an artifact of our different explanatory emphases and, at worst, merely verbal.

1.5.4 Where the Meaty Issues Lie

In arguing that the internalist–externalist interpretation of the innateness issue is undesirable because it inclines us to dismiss the whole debate as verbal, I've been talking as if internalists and externalists disagree about which factor plays "more" of a role, period, in mental development. But perhaps this is unfair to the intuition that lies behind Godfrey-Smith's distinction. For, as I mentioned above, there are contexts in which questions about the relative importance of various components in a causal story can be sensibly asked and substantively answered.[24] Suppose, for example, that Chloe and Minnie are both interested in why the facial features characteristic of fetal alcohol syndrome (rather than normal features) develop in a certain class of cases. Chloe, a molecular biologist, attributes the development of those features to a defective gene, FAS1. Minnie, an epidemiologist, attributes it to alcohol consumption during pregnancy. In this instance, Chloe and Minnie are genuinely disagreeing. Moreover, their disagreement obviously concerns the propriety of an internalist as opposed to an externalist explanation for the trait in question. So if the nativist–empiricist controversy could be shown to be more like Chloe and Minnie's, and less like Gus and Harry's, then it might after all be appropriate to view it in internalist–externalist terms.

Before we can assess this possibility, we need to inquire why the Chloe–Minnie dispute seems so much more "meaty" than that between Gus and Harry. Note first that Chloe and Minnie, unlike Gus and Harry, are in complete agreement as to what explanandum they're addressing. They are both asking the question, "Why do these features, rather than normal features, develop in some infants?" This is what prevents their 'talking past' each other in the way that Gus and Harry did in the previous example.

---

24. Both Peter Godfrey-Smith and Kim Sterelny stressed this point in their comments on an earlier draft of this section.

Second, Chloe and Minnie's quarrel is not about which sorts of factors are *in general* more important in fetal development, or even in fetal facial development. Instead, it is a narrow and very well-defined one, concerning the roles played by two specific factors, the hypothesized gene FAS1 and maternal drinking, in the development of the features characterisic of a particular disorder. Finally, and relatedly, the dispute between Chloe and Minnie is susceptible of definitive, empirical resolution. Gus and Harry, by contrast, could have argued and experimented until the world ends, with neither ever being convinced that his theory was wrong and the other's, right.

These contrasts suggest that disputes between internalists and externalists are substantive when they concern the *particular* ways that *particular* causal elements contribute to *particular* causal processes. While it's hard, as we've seen, to find a genuine opposition between internalism and externalism construed as global views about the relative importance of intrinsic and extrinsic causal factors, conflicts between internalist and externalist explanations of specific phenomena can quite easily arise. Thus, although it will not do to equate nativism and empiricism with internalism and externalism construed as comprehensive theoretical orientations across explanatory domains, it might be possible to view nativists and empiricists as quarreling over the merits of specific explanations.

But there is in fact no evidence that nativists and empiricists were working against the kind of background—of agreement as to the question being asked, the space of candidate answers to that question, and the ways the question could be resolved—that allows such quarrels to arise. It's far from obvious that Locke and Leibniz, for instance, had the same questions in mind as they pushed their respective views; or that they shared a conception of the space of possible answers to those questions; or that their theories were well enough articulated for it to be clear, to them or anyone else, where the conflict between them lay and how it could (even in principle) be resolved. The substantive issues between nativists and empiricists (assuming that such there be) arise at a level different from those at which internalism and externalism can meaningfully clash.

In sum, if internalists (the defenders of "nature") are supposed to hold that external factors play no important role in the development of a mind, then no nativist was ever an internalist. (And similarly, mutatis mutandis, for empiricists and externalism.) For nativists and empiricists have always agreed that minds are products of an extraordinarily complex set of interactions between nature and nurture. And while it might seem natural to think of internalism and externalism instead as being different views as to the relative weights to be accorded intrinsic and extrinsic factors, respectively, it's hard to see how this taxonomy applies to the nativism–empiricism debate. There was and is a lot more to the nativism controversy than the question of "when one factor plays 'more' of a role than the other" (Godfrey-Smith 1996:51) in our psychological development.

1.6 What Nativism Is Not: More Spleen

Should we then conclude that nativism—or empiricism, for that matter—is nothing at all? Should we conclude that, apart from its sociological importance in illustrating our all-too-human tendency to get carried away with our own rhetoric, and our all-too-philosophical penchant for making the evident obscure, the great controversy over innate ideas is not worth the paper it's written on? Should we, perhaps, simply pack up and go home?

Appealing though this last suggestion might be, to quit now would be a mistake. For it is possible to characterize nativism in a way that is both fair and accurate: fair in that nativism ends up being a substantive thesis about the mind; accurate in that it not only makes sense of the historical debate but also sheds some light on contemporary discussions of the issue. In chapters 2 and 3, I try to give an account of what nativism is, such that these desiderata are satisfied. In order to do so, it will be necessary to confront a final confusing feature of the nativist doctrine, namely, that there are two quite distinct forms of argument used to support the nativist position. One is the celebrated 'poverty of the stimulus' argument; the other is what I call the 'impossibility argument.' Both seek to establish nativism by undermining alternatives to it—each, that is, points to difficulties faced by empiricist accounts of the mind, claims that they are insurmountable, and concludes, on this basis, that nativism must be true.

The argument from the poverty of the stimulus, to be discussed in chapter 2, asserts that what is 'in our minds' is (in some sense) too rich or too complex to have come (in ways so far suggested) 'from the outside.' The environment lacks those properties that it would need to have, were the contents of a human mind to be explicable in terms of our interaction with the external world. Impossibility arguments, by contrast, contend that certain mental items must be inborn, not because the environment is de facto too impoverished to give rise to them but because empiricist accounts of their acquisition are in some way incoherent or self-undermining (see chapter 3). The moral in each case is the same: if our minds are not furnished as a result of our interaction with the external world, at least some of what they contain must be inborn. There is, after all, nowhere else it could have come from.

Both these arguments appear to be purely negative. Their conclusions should, in the first instance, be simply that (such and such version of) empiricism is false. Yet the nativist draws the apparently stronger conclusion: nativism is true. And the difficulty, if one is concerned to come to some view about what nativism is, is to find something in the latter claim that goes beyond the former. The difficulty, in other words, is that the assertion of nativism often seems to be merely the denial of empiricism. And if that is so, then nativism is not a theory of the mind at all: it signifies merely our lack of such a theory. And if that is so, then the doctrine is philosophically uninteresting.

So the burden of chapters 2 and 3 is to find some substance for the nativism debate, and this book, to be about. I argue that there are in fact two substantive issues over which nativists and empiricists clash. One concerns the natural architecture of the mind: Has nature equipped us with general-purpose, or domain-specific, learning devices? The other concerns the scope of natural science: What are our prospects for domesticating the mind and locating it within our overall scientific worldview? With this background in place, I turn in parts II and III to a consideration and evaluation of the views of contemporary nativists.

2

What Nativism Is (I)

The Hypothesis of Special Faculties

One central claim of the previous chapter was that nativism is not an epistemological doctrine. The hypothesis that ideas or beliefs are innate does not by itself explain why what is believed a priori is justified. If it is anything at all, then, nativism is a psychological doctrine. But what psychological thesis does the nativist assert? In chapter 1, I examined the idea that nativism is an 'internalist' (as opposed to an 'externalist') response to the 'genetic' question, asserting that what is in our minds is a result of 'nature' rather than—or at least more than—'nurture.'

Although I ultimately rejected it, the internalist interpretation of the nativist position looked attractive for two reasons. First, it seemed to explain the association of nativism with rationalism in epistemology: nativism, while not an epistemological theory strictly speaking, is relevant to epistemology because it provides an account of the relation between an a priori belief and what justifies it. For Plato, a belief is justified if it is acquired as a result of our (so to speak) eyeballing the Forms. Since embodied souls like us, however, are incapable of the requisite kind of contact with Reality, Plato invokes the hypothesis that our beliefs are innate, acquired prior to our embodiment and birth, to show how they can have the kind of justification that he envisages. Similarly for the early modern rationalist. What justifies our a priori beliefs is, on his view, the fact that they are implanted in our minds by a benevolent God. God having better things to do than to spend his time splicing beliefs into psyches at the appropriate experiential moment, the rationalist supposes him instead to have adopted the strategy of incorporating them into the human *esse* at the start. The rationalist's innateness hypothesis, construed as a commitment to a strongly internalist approach toward the explanation of the mental, thus functions as an account of the psychological mechanism by which God's goodness expresses itself in our day-to-day epistemic lives.

The internalist construal of nativism was attractive, second, because it seemingly made sense of the other, nonepistemological aspects of the empiricist–rationalist controversy. In addition to their disagreements as to the status of the a priori, philosophers in the seventeenth and eighteenth centuries were exercised by the more narrowly psychological puzzles that are raised by the phenomena of belief and concept acquisition. A natural way to express one's puzzlement over acquisition phenomena is to ask, "Where does what is in our minds come from?" Once the issue has been formulated along these genetic lines, it becomes tempting to read the nativist as asserting that what is in our minds is inborn rather than coming from experience; and the empiricist as asserting the contrary. But, as I argued in §1.5, viewing the controversy as a debate over 'nature vs. nurture' is unhelpful. Rhetoric aside, both nativists and empiricists acknowledge that, insofar as it can be said to 'come from' anywhere, what is in our minds is a product of both internal and external factors; and as to the question of which factor is more important, disagreements over this issue seem, if not trifling consequences of different explanatory interests, then pitched at the wrong level to capture what is at issue in the innateness controversy.

That said, however, it is impossible to deny that the rationalist–empiricist imbroglio has *something* to do with belief and concept acquisition, and the way that experience and our innate endowment combine to bestow on us a mental life. In the next section, I outline the two issues over which, in my view, nativist and empiricist clash.

2.1 Empiricism and Nativism: An Overview of the Dispute

I mentioned at the end of the previous chapter that nativists' arguments for their position are negative ones. Nativists proceed, that is to say, by demonstrating the shortfalls of empiricist accounts of acquisition, concluding that empiricism is false, and embracing nativism in its stead. Their position, therefore, should be viewed as a reactive one: nativism essentially involves the denial of (some aspect of) empiricist psychology. As will become clear below, there are in my view two elements of empiricism to which nativists take exception. As a preliminary to elucidating them, we need a brief sketch of the empiricist's position.

The acquisition theory of the classical empiricist[1] asserts that experiences of very particular sorts are necessary to the acquisition of all concepts and all beliefs. As to concepts, the empiricist view is that they are either 'simple' or 'complex.' Simple concepts are those that are acquired directly from experiences of their objects. Complex concepts are those that are constructed by means of certain operations of Reason, such as compounding, compari-

1. E.g., Locke (1975); Hume (1977).

son, or abstraction, out of simple concepts. The empiricist embraces a similarly two-stage account of the acquisition of beliefs. Some beliefs are acquired directly as a result of sensory stimulation by the facts they are about. Others are acquired by a more complicated process that involves the application of certain other operations of Reason, such as deduction or induction, to beliefs already held.

Three points about the empiricist theory deserve emphasis. First, it is worth reiterating that this kind of theory is based on the assumption that there is a substantial organismic contribution to the learning process. On the empiricist view, our minds are innately structured such that we can acquire 'primitive' ideas directly from sense experience.[2] And we are born with the ability to combine those ideas in divers ways to form complex ideas and beliefs.[3] Thus, as was noted in my earlier discussion of Locke (§1.5.2), there is a strongly 'internalist' air about the empiricist's belief that we possess an inborn ability to register, manipulate, and interpret sensory information. The standard "nature vs. nurture" gloss on the nativism–empiricism debate errs because it fails to see the importance of this fact.

A second distinguishing feature of empiricist accounts of acquisition is that they postulate learning strategies that are very *general*. Although theorists like Locke, Berkeley, and Hume may differ among themselves as to how, exactly, to characterize our combinatorial and ratiocinative faculties, they are in agreement that all acquisition phenomena are to be explained in fundamentally the same way. All concepts are either primitive or derived by combination or abstraction out of other concepts; all beliefs are either direct consequences of sensory stimulation or got from other beliefs through induction or deduction. The generality of this acquisition theory derives from the empiricist's conception of the processes responsible for belief and concept acquisition as purely formal. On this view, abstraction, for example, is a process that can be applied to any concept, no matter what its content. All deductive reasoning employs the same rules, rules that are indifferent to the exact subject matter of our reflections. Our methods of inductive reasoning, whatever they might be, are the same no matter what we are reasoning about. And so on.

2. It is an empirical matter, unimportant for present purposes, which items are acquired in this "brute causal" (Fodor 1981b:262) manner, though traditional examples include ideas of sense like RED and beliefs about the nature of one's own immediate experience, such as 'I am now sensing redly.' What is important is that there are, on the empiricist view, some things that we are able to learn from experience solely in virtue of the way the human 'sensorium' is built.

3. Classic examples of items acquired in this less direct manner include general concepts formed by abstraction, like MAN; compound concepts, like TALL MAN; and general beliefs formed by induction from instances, like 'All NBA players are tall men.' While they need not rule it out that these higher-order cognitive capacities—for abstraction, compounding, induction, and so on—are *modifiable* in the light of experience, empiricists must assume that they are at least to some extent inborn: experience cannot teach us how to learn from experience unless some learning strategies are already in place.

From this derives the first real point of disagreement between nativist and empiricist, for one central element of the controversy, as I shall show in this chapter, concerns the nature of the mind prior to any experience. While both sides agree that we must be born with an ability to register, interpret, and store information got from experience, they disagree about the character of that capacity. Whereas empiricists stress the generality of our innate learning mechanisms, nativists use arguments from the poverty of the stimulus to defend their view that since certain learning tasks require special kinds of skill, the mind must contain special-purpose, or task-specific, learning mechanisms in addition to those that empiricists allow. Thus, I argue, one major point of disagreement between nativists and empiricists concerns the 'task specificity' or 'domain specificity' of our innate faculties. Nativism, seen from this perspective, is the view that our inborn intellectual skills are domain-specific: each is peculiarly adapted to the performance of one of the various learning tasks with which we will, as we mature, be confronted.

But surely there must be more to nativism than this so to speak 'architectural' hypothesis if we are to account for all the fuss it has occasioned. I will argue that there is indeed a second, deeper, and—at least at first glance—more exciting point of disagreement between nativists and empiricists. While both sides agree that there is both a genetic and an experiential contribution to our mental development, they disagree in a very fundamental way as to our prospects for *understanding how* these two factors could combine to produce a human mind. This difference of opinion can be brought out by reflecting on a third noteworthy feature of empiricist acquisition models, emphasized in particular in Carruthers' very helpful (1992) discussion of the nativism–empiricism debate. Empiricists take it completely for granted that our acquisition of beliefs and ideas is, in fact, explicable. By providing their sketches of the causal–mechanical processes underpinning acquisition, they make clear their assumption that the phenomena of the mind are in principle open to our comprehension, even if in practice they prove very hard to understand. Nativists, I suggest, are much less optimistic. On their view, the interactive processes responsible for our acquisition of a mind are, and are likely to remain, an enigma.[4]

My view, then, is that nativism is a univocal doctrine only in the weak sense that it essentially involves the denial of empiricism. I urge that since there are two ways in which empiricism may be thought to be misguided, there are two quite distinct (indeed, probably inconsistent) strands in nativist theorizing. One strand emphasizes the falsity of the empiricist's view that

4. Although Carruthers notes, as do I, the naturalistic tenor of empiricists' theoretical sorties, his reading of the overall controversy is rather different from mine. He argues that the status of the a priori was the crucial point at issue between nativist and empiricist: nativists thought that substantive knowledge a priori was possible; empiricists denied this to be so. Carruthers thus sees nativists' nonnaturalism as deriving from their overarching commitment to a priori knowledge, whereas I see it as a critical, positive element in the nativist approach.

our inborn abilities to learn from experience are general-purpose ones, and postulates the existence of special faculties for the performance of certain sorts of learning tasks. Nativism in this sense will be discussed in the current chapter. I argue that in claiming that certain ideas or beliefs are innate, the nativist should be seen to be proposing a substantive alternative to the cognitive architecture envisaged by the empiricist. The other element in nativist thought stresses the naïveté of the empiricist's assumption that the processes of learning are explicable in straightforwardly natural-scientific terms. Viewed from this perspective, nativism is a metapsychological doctrine. As I shall argue in chapter 3, the nativist who asserts that everything in our mind is innate or inborn is emphasizing the deepness, darkness, and difficulty of the issues that the theorist interested in acquisition phenomena must confront.

2.2 The Argument from the Poverty of the Stimulus

Arguments from the poverty of the stimulus constitute one central means by which nativists have sought to undermine empiricism and thereby establish their own position. Such arguments seek to establish a 'gap' between what in the way of information about the world is provided by sensory experience and what we end up knowing. What is in our minds, nativists argue, is richer than what could be learned from experience. Hence, nativists conclude, what is in our minds must be innate.

There are seemingly two ways that the existence of a gap between experience and what is learned from it may be urged. One method involves emphasizing the sketchiness of the empiricist's acquisition theory. Although they assert that there are psychological mechanisms responsible for our acquisition of concepts and beliefs, empiricists offer few details as to how these mechanisms operate. Such reticence is, perhaps, appropriate in the case of 'primitive' concepts and beliefs. For the empiricist holds that since we acquire them just because that is what creatures like us *do* when their senses are stimulated, the full explanation of how these basic items are acquired is not properly the task of the psychologist.[5] In the case of complex concepts and higher-order beliefs, however, such burden-shifting is less permissible. For the processes allegedly responsible for our acquisition of these items are, as Fodor (1981b:273) puts it, 'rational–causal,' not 'brute-causal': they are subject to rational evaluation (in the case of beliefs) and (in the case of concepts) they seem less 'stimulus-driven' and more under the control of our background beliefs, desires, and interests. Hence the workings of processes like abstraction, induction, and deduction do seem to be the province of the psychologist. But while empiricists have, thanks to the logician, at least the

---

5. A modern-day empiricist would hold this to be, rather, the job of the physiologist or neuroscientist.

beginnings of a story about one rational–causal mechanism, namely, deductive reasoning, they have virtually nothing to say about abstraction or induction.[6] This is a serious problem, for these faculties are precisely the ones that according to empiricists are responsible for our ability to think thoughts that go beyond the particularities of experience. So empiricists' failure to explain the workings of these processes entails that there is a gap between our experience and what (at least according to their theory as it stands) we could learn from it.

This mode of attack, though pointing to the existence of an explanatory gap, differs in emphasis from true poverty of the stimulus arguments. It contends that empiricists provide no adequate recipe for turning the raw materials of experience into concepts and beliefs, rather than stressing, as do poverty of the stimulus arguments, that some of the ingredients are missing. And while claims to the effect that empiricists' explanatory pretensions outrun their explanatory capacities should, perhaps, give us pause, the immediate message of this argument is that empiricists should elaborate their theory; not that they are wrong.

Poverty of the stimulus arguments, by contrast, bear much more directly on the truth of the empiricist's acquisition theory. Rather than stressing the meagerness of the empiricist's account of processes like abstraction, they stress instead the meagerness of the experiential input to those processes. The proponent of this argument acknowledges that it may be premature to criticize empiricists on the grounds that their theory is underdeveloped: these are, after all, difficult questions. He acknowledges too that there is some initial plausibility to the empiricist's account. It doesn't, for instance, really seem all that unreasonable to think that there is some mental process, call it 'abstraction,' that enables us to formulate the general concept MAN, given enough experiences of particular men.[7] Nor does it stretch credulity overmuch to agree that there is some mechanism, call it 'induction,' that leads us to form the general belief 'All NBA stars are tall men' given enough exposure to individual NBA players.

The nativist's poverty of the stimulus argument grants, in short, that the empiricist can account for certain central cases of belief and concept acquisition. But, it maintains, empiricism, though likely true enough as far as it goes, simply does not go far enough: empiricists cannot make good their claim to explain the acquisition of all our cognitive equipment. There are items in our mental stock that cannot be accounted for on the empiricist model, no matter how generous we are in allowing empiricists their mechanisms of abstraction and induction, and so on. For there is nothing in experience from which they could be derived.

6. It should be noted that the empiricist's co-opting of formal logic to do duty as a theory of deductive reasoning is not without its critics—see, e.g., Harman (1986); Johnson-Laird (1983).

7. Terminological note: I use the uppercase when mentioning ideas.

2.2.1 Descartes

In the *Meditations*, Descartes obviously accepts that at least some ideas are straightforwardly acquired through sensory stimulation. In Meditation Three, he taxonomizes ideas according to their genesis: 'adventitious' ideas are "derived from things existing outside me"; 'fictitious' (or, as it's sometimes translated, 'factitious') ideas are "invented by me"; and 'innate' ideas "derive simply from my own nature" (CSM II:26; AT VII:38). Although he goes on to remark that his belief that "there exist things distinct from myself which transmit to me ideas or images of themselves throught the sense organs" is based on "blind impulse" rather than "reliable judgment" (CSM II:27; AT VII:39), Descartes's skepticism here derives not from any general worries about ideas' 'coming from outside' but, rather, from the fact that at this stage in the *Meditations* dialectic, he does not know whether there is anything 'outside' whence any ideas could come. In Meditation Six, this doubt is put to rest. For the fact that at least some ideas *are* 'transmitted' to us via the senses from material things there forms the core of Descartes's resurrection of the material world.[8] Asserting on introspective grounds that there is a mental 'faculty of sense perception' in which ideas of sense are formed, Descartes argues that since that faculty is passive (that is, incapable of initiating any change, including the production of ideas), there must be some active faculty, "either in me or in something else, which produced or brought about these ideas" (CSM II:55; AT VII:79). The producer of sensory ideas cannot be some further faculty in Descartes, however, for their appearance in his mind is entirely involuntary—even, at times, positively contrary to his will. So the ideas must come from outside himself: either from God or from material bodies. But since God is not a deceiver, and since Descartes has "a great propensity to believe that they are produced by corporeal things" (CSM II:55; AT VII:79–80), Descartes's sensory ideas must indeed be produced by external bodies. As he puts it: "I do not see how God could be understood to be anything but a deceiver if the ideas were transmitted from a source other than corporeal things" (CSM II:55; AT VII: 80). It follows, of course and as Descartes desired, that corporeal things exist. But it follows too that they can give rise to ideas: ideas can be learned from experience.

So the Descartes of the *Meditations* accepts the empiricist tenet that ideas can be 'transmitted' from material things via sense experience. He emphasizes, however, that the empiricist 'transmission' theory cannot be true root and branch. Offering a series of arguments from the poverty of the stimulus, Descartes argues that there are some ideas that cannot be acquired through experience of the material world.

---

8. See also Descartes's claim in the Fifth Replies that "I did not assert that the ideas of material things are derived from the mind . . . I explicitly showed that these ideas often come to us from bodies, and that it is this that enables us to prove the existence of bodies" (CSM II:253; AT VII:367).

That the idea of God is one of these is argued in the Third Meditation and in the *Comments on a Certain Broadsheet*. The latter discussion (CSM I:305; AT VIIIB:360) straightforwardly appeals to the impoverished nature of sense experience as a basis for holding GOD to be inborn. Descartes argues that "strictly speaking, sight in itself presents to us nothing but pictures, and hearing nothing but utterances and sounds" (CSM I:305; AT VIIIB:360). If we acquired GOD from the senses, therefore, all we could "ever understand about God is what he is called . . . or what corporeal form painters use to represent him" (CSM I:305; AT VIIIB:360). But our idea of God includes much more than this—more than the senses could supply. "So," Descartes concludes, "everything over and above these utterances and pictures which we think of as being signified by them is represented to us by means of ideas which come to us from no other source than our own faculty of thinking." (CSM I:305; AT VIIIB:360). The idea of God is innate.

The argument of Meditation Three, though leading to the same conclusion, is more complex. Having taxonomized ideas into innate, fictitious, and adventitious, Descartes articulates his (in)famous 'reality principle,' which states that "there must be at least as much reality in the efficient and total cause as in the effect of that cause" (CSM II:28; AT VII:40). He explains that where the etiology of our ideas is the issue, this principle is to be taken as implying that the cause of an idea "must contain at least as much formal reality as there is objective reality in the idea" (CSM II:28–29; AT VII:41). What this means in this context is that the cause of an idea must be at least as 'real' or 'perfect' in fact, as the resultant idea represents its object as being.[9] So, since our idea of God represents him as being supremely perfect, the cause of that idea must be supremely perfect also.

Descartes devotes most of his attention in this part of the Third Meditation to showing how the reality principle—which he regards as manifest by the natural light—provides grounds for thinking that the idea of God is not fictitious. Since he himself is a finite, mutable, dependent substance of limited intelligence and power, he could not have been the cause of an idea representing God as "infinite, eternal, immutable, independent, supremely intelligent, [and] supremely powerful" (CSM II:31; AT VII:45): the comparatively puny formal reality that he possesses is simply not up to the task of giving rise to such a rich objective reality as is contained in his idea of God. Hence GOD could not be fictitious, or 'invented' by Descartes.

If GOD is not fictitious, then it must (given Descartes's taxonomy) be either innate or adventitious. Descartes's case against the possibility that

---

9. CSM explain that "if an idea A represents some object X which is F, then F-ness will be contained 'formally' in X but 'objectively' in A" (CSM II:28, n. 1). It may be added further that the idea A has its own formal reality that "applies to the idea itself not as it represents something but as an entity in its own right" (Descartes, Fifth Replies—CSM II: 199; AT VII:286). Thus, the formal reality of a painting of the Notre Dame includes its being made of paint applied in a certain way to canvas; its objective reality includes beauty and majesty.

GOD 'comes from outside himself' is not made explicitly. Instead, he tacitly relies on another argument from the poverty of the stimulus to show that that idea does not come from the senses. The reality principle, as we have seen, implies that the cause of our idea of God must be altogether perfect. Descartes has argued in detail that a human mind is not perfect enough to have caused the idea. But our minds, on Descartes's view, are created in God's image. If *they* are incapable of causing GOD, how much less so is the material world, acting upon our bodies! Given the reality principle, the idea of God could not be caused by our experience, any more than it could be invented by us.

Thus, Descartes's reality principle supplies the arguments from the poverty of the stimulus that he needs to make his case that his idea of God is innate. Once it has been shown why that idea could not derive from the operations of our minds, it is obvious that, for precisely the same reasons, it could not derive from the senses either: the world lacks a property, namely, a supreme degree of perfection, that it would have to have were our idea of God derived from experience of it. God himself is the only possible source of Descartes's idea of him and, barring the possibility of revelation, the only conclusion is that that idea is innate: as a craftsman stamps his mark upon his work, so "God, in creating me [has] placed this idea in me . . ." (CSM II:35; AT VII:51).

In the Fifth Meditation and the Fifth Responses, Descartes offers further poverty of the stimulus arguments to establish the innateness of mathematical ideas. In the Fifth Meditation, he argues that although one might off-hand think that mathematical ideas such as TRIANGLE could have been learned from experience of triangular bodies, such a thought is "beside the point" (CSM II:45; AT VII:65), "[f]or I can think up countless other shapes which there can be no suspicion of my ever having encountered through the senses" (CSM II:45; AT VII:65). We have, that is to say, ideas—such as the idea of a chiliagon—that have no sensible instances and therefore could not be learned from experience. Mathematical ideas, Descartes concludes, are thus to be numbered amongst the "true ideas which are innate in me" (CSM II:47; AT VII:68).

This argument is invalid as it stands. The fact that I have had no experience of chiliagons (hence could not have acquired CHILIAGON from experience) does not establish that I did not acquire TRIANGLE from my experiences of triangles. What Descartes seems to be relying on here is a suppressed premise to the effect that these two ideas are acquired in the same way. If there were a single mode by which all our ideas of shapes are attained, then clearly a method that will not account for our acquisition of CHILIAGON could not be that by which TRIANGLE is obtained either. This premise is, in effect, what Gassendi attacks in the Fifth Objections to the *Meditations*. In his comments on the Third Meditation, Gassendi had argued that "all ideas seem to be adventitious—to proceed from things which exist outside the mind and come under one of the senses" (CSM II:195; AT VII: 279–80). Describing how the mind constructs new ideas from sensory ideas through its "faculty of putting these ideas together and separating them in various ways, of enlarging them and diminishing them and so on" (CSM II: 195; AT VII:280), Gassendi argues that even the idea of God is "compounded and augmented from the ideas of . . . finite things" (CSM II:200; AT VII:287), and hence is "partly derived . . . from the senses and partly . . . made up" (CSM II:212; AT VII:305). In his objections to the Fifth Meditation, Gassendi makes use of this apparatus in arguing, contra Descartes, that sense experience is sufficient for the acquisition of ideas of shapes: "You say that you have many ideas in you which never come into your mind via the senses. But of course it is easy for you to have these ideas, since you fashioned them from ideas which did come to you via the senses, and you formed them into various other ideas, in the ways explained above" (CSM II:223; AT VII:321–22). His claim, in other words, is that an idea like CHILIAGON could be got by composition or abstraction (he isn't clear which) from other ideas (such as, perhaps, STRAIGHT LINE and CLOSED FIGURE) that are supplied by experience.[10] On Gassendi's empiricist view, therefore, and contrary to what Descartes assumes in the argument just given, there is more than one way that mathematical ideas can be acquired. Some of them are got directly from experience, and then form the basis for the acquisition of others that we abstract and/or assemble from them.

Descartes responds to Gassendi's objection with yet another poverty of the stimulus argument, this one designed to show that not even the most basic of geometrical ideas could come from experience:

> although the world could undoubtedly contain figures such as those the geometers study, I nonetheless maintain that there are no such figures in our environment . . . no part of a line that was really straight could ever affect our senses, since when we examine through a magnifying glass those lines which appear most straight we find they are quite irregular and always form wavy curves. Hence, when in our childhood we first happened to see a triangular figure drawn on paper, it cannot have been this figure that showed us how we should conceive of the true triangle studied by geometers, since the true triangle is contained in the figure only in the way in which a statue of Mercury is contained in the rough block of wood. (CSM II:262; AT VII:382)

Experiences of straight lines or triangles, Descartes maintains, could not give rise to STRAIGHT LINE or TRIANGLE because they are not in fact experiences of straight lines or triangles at all! Since the world contains only rough approximations to mathematical objects, Gassendi's hope of deriving CHILIAGON by a process of abstraction from other mathematical ideas is vain. TRIANGLE and CHILIAGON are, as Descartes had tacitly assumed in his *Meditations* argument, in exactly the same boat. Neither can be got from experience; both of them are innate.

---

10. Or—again Gassendi is less than explicit—perhaps STRAIGHT LINE and CLOSED FIGURE are derived by abstraction from other ideas, like TRIANGLE, that are acquired directly from experience.

2.2.2 Leibniz

In the *New Essays*, Leibniz too employs arguments from the poverty of the stimulus against empiricism. As we will see below (§3.3), Leibniz's 'deep metaphysics'[11] entails that empiricist acquisition theories must be false, his own opinion being that "all the thoughts and actions of our soul come to it from its own depths and could not be given to it by the senses" (1981: 74). But because his aim in the *New Essays* was to write a popular work in the hopes of "[gaining] a more favorable reception for my thoughts" (1981: 44), he there downplays this aspect of his views, especially in Book I, where he responds to Locke's critique of innate ideas. Rather than embarking on the massive task of arguing that empiricism is wholly false, Leibniz there adopts the more modest aim of showing that empiricism is not wholly *true*:

> in the meantime I shall set aside the inquiry into that [i.e., why empiricism is wholly false] and ... conform to accepted ways of speaking ... since ... the outer senses can be said to be, in a certain sense, partial causes of our thoughts. I shall thus work within the common framework ... and I shall look into why, even within this framework, one should in my opinion say that there are ideas and principles which do not reach us through the senses, and which we find in ourselves. ...(1981:74)

Leibniz's weapon here is the poverty of the stimulus. Necessary truths, for example, are claimed (1981:79–80) to be innate on the grounds that "the senses are inadequate to show their necessity" (1981:80). Although empiricist accounts of belief fixation are true in some cases—"other truths come from experience or from observations of the senses" (1981:80)—necessary truths could not be gleaned from experience. For, Leibniz argues, "however often one experienced instances of a universal truth, one could never know inductively that it would always hold. ... The senses can hint at, justify and confirm these truths, but can never demonstrate their infallible and perpetual certainty" (1981:80).[12]

In each of these cases, and in Plato's case too (§1.3), the point is to show that there exists a gap between the information provided by experience about some domain—be it God, necessities, arithmetic, equality, whatever—and the ideas or beliefs we acquire concerning that domain. In every case the explanatory gap is alleged to arise not because we lack a worked-out recipe for making beliefs and so on out of experiences: the point is not that empiricist theories need elaboration. It is, rather, that although empiricism provides us with a recipe for making ideas from experience, we lack certain of the ingredients that that recipe calls for. Empiricist theories are, in at least some cases, just plain false.

---

11. The term is due to Jolley (1984).
12. See also his letter to Thomas Burnet of December 3, 1703 (Leibniz 1989:284–85).

2.3 A Trilemma

In stressing the existence of a gap, these arguments confront the empiricist with a trilemma. Empiricists must either acknowledge the falsity of their contention that all beliefs and concepts are derived ultimately from experience in the ways that they sketch; or they must deny that we do in fact possess the concepts or beliefs at issue; or they must somehow argue that our acquisition of those items can, contra the critic, be explained by an empiricist theory. The first of these options is obviously undesirable from the empiricist's point of view, being tantamount to abandoning empiricism. The second too looks unappetizing: denying outright that we have the kinds of concepts and beliefs alluded to by the nativist seems a somewhat drastic and counterintuitive step. Nonetheless, empiricists do sometimes pursue this strategy, maintaining that *precisely because* they could not be derived from experience, the problematic items should not be included in our mental inventory. Berkeley, for example, denies that we have any ideas or knowledge of mind-independent objects;[13] Hume denies that we have an idea of necessity;[14] Quine, to take a more contemporary figure, denies that we have knowledge of meanings.[15] More often, though, empiricists favor the third horn of the trilemma and attempt to show that the gap can be bridged. One bridging strategy they have favored involves getting experience and our minds to meet, as it were, in the middle. Rather than eliminating the problem beliefs and concepts outright, empiricists offer a revisionist account of their contents such that they are closer to the contents of experience. At the same time, they may defend a revisionist ontology such that the things in the world that we have concepts of, and beliefs about, are not so different in kind from the things we learn of in experience. Thus, for example, Hume can be seen as seeking to preserve both our intuition that we have beliefs about causation and the empiricist story about how those beliefs are acquired, by arguing that causation is nothing more than regular succession and contiguity, and that our beliefs about causes and effects *just are* beliefs about the spatiotem-

---

13. See, e.g., the *Principles of Human Knowledge*, §§9ff. "As for our senses, by them we have the knowledge only of our sensations, ideas or those things that are immediately perceived by sense, call them what you will: but they do not inform us that things exist without the mind" (§18). (Ayers 1975:82)

14. See the *Treatise*, I.III.xiv: ". . . the simple view of any two objects or actions, however related, can never give us any idea of power, or of a connexion between them" (Hume 1978:166). Note that Hume denies we have an idea of necessity only in case it is supposed to be a real relation holding among things in the world. He does not deny that we can conceive necessities understood in a less metaphysically objectionable way as relations holding among ideas: "Upon the whole, necessity is something, that exists in the mind, not in objects; nor is it possible for us ever to form the most distant idea of it, consider'd as a quality in bodies. Either we have no idea of necessity, or necessity is nothing but that determination of the thought to pass from causes to effects and from effects to causes, according to their experienc'd union" (*Treatise*, I.III.xiv [Hume 1978:166]).

15. Quine (1960). Quine, of course, also denies that there are any meanings, precisely because meanings are not the sorts of things of which we could acquire knowledge.

poral relations of events.[16] The phenomenalism of Berkeley is also an attempt to bridge the gap. On the phenomenalist view, our beliefs about so-called material objects *just are* beliefs about congeries of sensible qualities. And since there is nothing more to the world than experience can reveal to us, the information provided by experience is ample to provide us with knowledge of it.[17]

2.4 The Nativist Response to the Gap: Domain-Specific Faculties

The three strategies just mentioned—of eliminating problematic concepts, of enriching experience, and of revisionism in semantics and ontology—as a matter of fact exhaust the options that empiricists have explored in responding to poverty of the stimulus arguments. But there is another obvious way to react to the problem of the gap. The discrepancy between what we experience and what we know could be removed *by enriching the resources available to the learner,* that is, by offering an account that attributes to the learner inborn learning strategies that are in some sense richer or more powerful than those the empiricist postulates.

One way to increase the resources available to the learner would be to augment her intellectual powers across the board. One might claim, for instance, that the problematic beliefs or concepts *can* be acquired from experience, empiricist-style, because the learner's capacity for induction is in fact far more sophisticated than standard empiricist accounts allow. On this view, induction is an extemely high-powered faculty that enables learning to occur even where there is an apparent paucity of relevant experiences. But absent an account of how, exactly, this faculty for 'power induction' is supposed to differ from that for ordinary induction—absent an account, for instance, of how it could work as well to produce beliefs in situations where there are relevant sensory inputs as in situations, like those described by Plato, Descartes, and Leibniz, where there are no such inputs—an appeal to it is nothing more than the ad hoc invocation of a 'something-we-know-not-what' that explains how we learn the things we do. Its obscurity and blatant ad hockery aside, the 'power-induction' hypothesis has another flaw: it is not in fact licensed by the poverty of the stimulus argument that provoked it. Recall that this argument grants that the empiricist succeeds in explaining some acquisition phenomena. Its point is that explanatory difficulties arise only in certain cases, cases where the experiential input to learning is radically impoverished. That being so, parsimony might incline us to opt for a

16. He can be read as offering a similarly revisionist account of necessities and our beliefs about them.
17. Indeed, Berkeley is quite explicit that his phenomenalism is a response to the skeptical claim that experience is insufficient to give us knowledge of the world—see especially §§1–4 of the Introduction to the *Principles* (Ayers 1975:65–66).

second enrichment strategy whereby we increase the resources of the learner only as much as we need to to account for her acquisition of the items in question. Let the empiricist story suffice as regards concepts like RED or HOT, and propose a special mechanism for our acquisition of concepts like GOD or EQUAL. Let the empiricist story suffice for most beliefs and postulate a special faculty for those beliefs, like our mathematical or modal beliefs, that the empiricist cannot account for. But to take this kind of piecemeal approach to enriching the learner *just is* to postulate the existence of domain-specific faculties. It is to take the view that since some kinds of learning cannot be explained on the general empiricist model, we need to invoke special-purpose learning strategies to account for our performance of those tasks.

This, I contend, is what the nativist is gesturing toward when he claims, in light of his arguments from the poverty of the stimulus, that certain mental items must be innate. He does not mean that they arise in the total absence of experience, and he does not mean that experience plays a comparatively unimportant role in their acquisition.[18] Instead, he means to say something about learning mechanisms. On the nativist view, some concepts and beliefs are acquired by means of special-purpose, or task-specific, mental faculties.

2.4.1 Leibniz

There is some textual evidence that seventeenth- and eighteenth-century nativists had something like this 'faculties hypothesis' in mind when claiming that certain classes of ideas or beliefs are innate. Leibniz, for instance, seeks to explicate the sense in which he views ideas and beliefs as being innate by comparing the mind at birth to a piece of marble (1981:52). There are two ways the marble may be. It may be totally homogeneous, hence susceptible of being sculpted into a variety of different shapes. This Leibniz takes to be analogous to the empiricist view of the mind. Or it may be veined in such a way as to be more easily and naturally fashioned into a statue of Hercules than into something else (such as a bust of Caesar). The latter is the comparison Leibniz favors. Just as the veined marble is disposed, on being struck by the sculptor's tools, to fracture in ways appropriate to the shape of Hercules rather than some other shape, the mind at birth is disposed to take one 'shape,' rather than another, as a result of experience. As Leibniz puts it, "if there were veins in the block which marked out the shape of Hercules rather than other shapes, then that block would be more determined to that shape and Hercules would be innate in it, in a way" (1981:52).

Leibniz's nativism, as reflected in this analogy, accords in three crucial respects with the postulation of dedicated faculties. First, his metaphor, like the hypothesis of domain-specific learning, is clearly a response to arguments from the poverty of the stimulus. The idea behind them both is that the

---

18. That is, although it may be a *consequence* of his view that experience plays less of a role in acquisition than does the innate contribution, this is not the nativist's main point.

mind must somehow be structured in ways that allow some things to be learned despite limited amounts of experiential input. In likening the process of learning from experience to the process by which a sculptor fashions the marble into a finished statue, Leibniz makes the point that just as a sculptor who is able to exploit the veins in the marble will need fewer taps of the chisel when creating the finished work, so the learner who is able to exploit analogous 'veins' in her mind will need less input from experience when acquiring her mature complement of mental states. Second, both Leibniz's analogy and the hypothesis of domain specificity embody a particular conception of the sense in which the nativist's learning strategies are 'richer' than those of the empiricist. They are not richer in that they view the learner as being somehow endowed with extra, or more complex, or more powerful general strategies for turning experiences into beliefs or concepts (as if the sculptor possessed power tools in addition to his hammers and chisels). Rather, the nativist's domain-specific mechanisms are held to be richer in the sense that the content of the final state is partly specified in advance, or constrained by features of the learning device. And again, Leibniz's analogy reflects this view: facts about who the statue represents (its being a statue of Hercules rather than a bust of Caesar) are partly determined by the layout of the veins in the marble. And third, both Leibniz and the proponent of domain specificity emphasize that experiential input is still necessary to learning, more powerful learning mechanisms notwithstanding. Leibniz emphasizes that further "labour would be required to expose the veins and to polish them into clarity" (1981:52) in order fully to determine the form the statue takes. Similarly, the defender of special faculties holds that some features of the cognitive state ultimately attained by the learner are fixed by the vagaries of experience.

In sum, the picture of concept or belief acquisition implicit in Leibniz's analogy, and that supplied by a hypothesis of special faculties, share a number of crucial features. Both view experiential input as being necessary to learning; both view the content of the end product as being partly specified in advance by inbuilt features of the learning device; and both are naturally fitted to overcome the problems for empiricism that are revealed by poverty of the stimulus arguments. For these reasons, Leibniz's claim that some ideas or beliefs are innate in the sense that Hercules is innate in the slab of marble is fairly easily interpretable as the claim that they are acquired by a domain-specific device.

2.4.2 Descartes

There is some support for the 'special faculties' interpretation in the writings of Descartes too. It is clear that in calling some ideas innate, Descartes does not mean to make the kind of naive suggestion that Locke ridiculed in the *Essay*, namely, that some ideas are actually present in the mind from birth. Not only is this claim manifestly false, but Descartes explicitly rejects it. Hobbes had argued, in the Third Objections to the *Meditations*, that the fact that people sometimes sleep without thinking shows that "no idea is innate; for what is innate is always present" (CSM II:132; AT VII:187–88). In his response to Hobbes, Descartes repudiates the Hobbesian (and Lockean, for that matter) gloss of 'innate' as meaning 'always present to the mind': "when we say that an idea is innate in us, we do not mean that it is always there before us. This would mean that no idea was innate" (CSM II: 132; AT VII:189). He explains that by 'innate,' "[w]e simply mean that we have within ourselves the faculty of summoning up the idea" (CSM II:132; AT VII:189). And in the *Comments* (speaking of the innateness of GOD), he writes that "by 'innate ideas' I have never meant anything other than . . . that 'there is present in us a natural power which enables us to know God.' " (CSM I:309; AT VIIIB:366).

Yes, but what kind of 'faculty' or 'power'? Presumably Descartes does not intend to point to a 'power' that can operate in the absence of all experience. As Gassendi remarked in his objections to Descartes, and as Descartes himself must have been well aware, "if you had up till now been deprived of all your sensory functions, so that you had never either seen or touched . . . various surfaces or extremities of bodies, do you think you would have been able to acquire or form within yourself the idea of a triangle or other figure?" (CSM II:223; AT VII:321–22). Since a mental life cannot develop in an experiential void, Descartes cannot be taken to be denying the relevance of sense experience to our attainment of ideas. He is not asserting an extreme internalism. Perhaps, then, he is asserting the existence of a disposition to acquire ideas given appropriate experiences? Again, presumably not, for as we saw in the Locke–Leibniz exchange (§1.5.1), any empiricist can agree with this: that we have dispositions to acquire ideas given experience is hardly the point at issue.

I suggest that, like Leibniz, Descartes is disagreeing with his empiricist opponents about the *nature* of our dispositions to acquire ideas consequent upon experience. The empiricist sees the basis of that disposition as consisting in a few, very general learning strategies. Descartes, on the other hand, thinks that our dispositions to acquire ideas are more finely tuned than this. Since ideas of God and triangles are not got in the normal way from experience—and recall that in presenting his poverty of the stimulus arguments, Descartes does not deny that many ideas *are* straightforwardly acquired from experience (§2.2.1)—there could not be a single global faculty for concept acquisition. Since we patently have dispositions to acquire GOD and TRIANGLE, these dispositions must be grounded in some further, specialized faculties of mind.

This line of argument is borne out by Descartes's analogy, in the *Comments on a Certain Broadsheet*, between innate ideas and inherited illnesses. There are, he says,

> certain thoughts within me which came solely from the power of thinking within me; so I applied the term 'innate' to [these] ideas or notions. . . . This is the same sense as that in which we say that . . . certain diseases such as gout or stones are innate in [certain families]: it is not so much

that the babies of such families suffer from these diseases in their mother's womb; but simply that they are born with a certain 'faculty' or tendency to contract them. (CSM I:303–4: AT VIIIB:358)

The analogy implies, first, that on Descartes's view there are only *some* innate ideas: only "certain thoughts" are candidates for innateness, the rest being acquired from experience in the normal way. It intimates, second, that these ideas are of particular *kinds*, as is implied by the hypothesis of domain specificity: Descartes does not compare innate ideas with our tendency to contract diseases, period. Instead, he compares them with our tendency to contract diseases *of certain sorts*. But perhaps the most intriguing support for the present interpretation comes from Descartes's use of the word 'faculty' to describe the process by which innate illnesses are manifested. Just as there are particular genetic mechanisms, at least partially distinct from the usual disease-forming processes like infection by microorganisms, that are responsible for an individual's displaying the symptoms of inherited illnesses, so there are specialized mechanisms, distinct from the usual idea-forming operations, for the 'contraction' of certain ideas.

Further corroboration for the interpretation I am urging comes from the peculiarity of Descartes's initial *Meditations* argument for the innateness of mathematical ideas (discussed in §2.2.2). He claimed, recall, that the idea of a triangle must be innate not because experience of triangles is lacking but, rather, because he has ideas of other shapes for which experience *is* lacking. This inference, as I noted, is invalid unless we attribute to Descartes some view along the lines of that which I am now proposing. *If* his view were that there is a single mechanism responsible for the acquisition of all ideas of shapes, *then* it would follow that if CHILIAGON is not got from experience, neither is TRIANGLE. His argument for the innateness of mathematical ideas thus lends itself naturally to a faculties interpretation.

In implying that the acquisition of innate ideas is due to the operation of special faculties dedicated to the production of particular sorts of ideas, Descartes is apparently committed not only to the view that the mind possesses more inherent structure than is allowed by the empiricist; but also to the view that that structure is, as it were, directed toward certain ends. This is in keeping with the hypothesis of domain-specific learning: not only do we have kinds of learning mechanisms different from those allowed by the empiricist, but those mechanisms are responsible for the acquisition of particular sorts of ideas.

2.5 Architecture versus Development:
The Genetic Question Revisited

In this section, I want to elaborate on two features of the present interpretation. First, it explains what was attractive about the 'internalist' interpretation of nativism (discussed in §1.5). Because nativists insist that the mind must contain dedicated faculties (in addition to whatever general-purpose mechanisms the empiricist envisages), they will naturally be more inclined than empiricists to stress the role of internal factors in explaining acquisition. In order to understand how we learn, nativists cannot merely wave their hands in the direction of 'general-purpose learning mechanisms' like induction and deduction; they need also to recognize the existence, and figure out the characteristics, of the additional faculties that they postulate. Thus there is a sense in which the nativist is saying that internal factors *are* 'more important'—not more important than external factors in producing ideas, but more important in the sense of being more worthy of study and explication than empiricist accounts typically recognize.

A second feature of my view is that it involves the rejection of yet another interpretation of the nativism–empiricism controversy that has recently been aired. We saw in chapter 1 that nativism can't satisfactorily be equated with 'internalism' with respect to the psychological query, "Where does what is in our minds come from?" In the present chapter, I have argued that it's to be read as a hypothesis about the nature of the psychological mechanisms whereby what is in our minds comes to be there. However, one might try instead to read the nativism–empiricism controversy as being a debate at a slightly different explanatory level, concerning the relative plasticities of various developmental processes.[19] What is 'innate,' on this reading, would be what develops as a result of (neural or psychological) processes that are highly implastic, that is, relatively impervious to environmental manipulation. What is 'learned from experience,' by contrast, would be that which develops through processes that are more plastic, ones that are sensitive to a much broader range of environmental inputs. Ariew (1996) explains the degree of 'plasticity' possessed by a trait in terms of its degree of 'canalization.' On his view, the extent to which a trait counts as innate (for some genotype) is to be identified with the extent to which the developmental pathway for that trait is canalized, where a pathway is canalized to the extent that it is bound to produce its end state (i.e., to result in acquisition of the trait) regardless of environmental variation either initially or during development.

On this view, the innate and the learned represent points toward the ends of a continuum of traits, a continuum determined by the different degrees of autonomy possessed by the developmental processes responsible for them. Nativists in this sense (nativists*, as I'll call them) think that most of what is in our minds is the product of developmental processes that are highly canalized, that is, that are robust under changes in the environment. Empiricists* think that what is in our minds is produced by processes that are highly sensitive to environmental factors. Thus, the disagreement is not (as I have argued) about the sorts of *cognitive architectures* responsible for our acquisition of ideas; rather, it's about the kinds of *developmental processes*

19. This possibility was stressed by Kim Sterelny (private communication).

that underlie those architectures and the relative extents to which those processes are under the control of the environment, as opposed to the genes.

Before explaining why I reject this as an account of the historical nativism–empiricism controversy, let me stress that I think the issue of developmental plasticity is very deep and very important—ultimately more interesting and important, I suspect, than the architectural questions I've been focusing on. Disputes about cognitive architectures are narrow, with few repercussions outside the confines of academic psychology and philosophy of mind. The question of the mind's plasticity, by contrast, is a broad one, having sweeping implications for an enormous variety of social and political issues, ranging from how we should bring up our children (does early and varied stimulation really matter?) to how we should treat criminals (is rehabilitation possible?) to how we should address a variety of social ills and inequalities (is poverty perpetuated, or intelligence created, by the genes or in the environment?). Nonetheless, I maintain, the nativist–empiricist debate as a matter of fact concerns the first, rather boring, question and not the second, more exciting one.

For there is in my view reason to reject the developmental reading of the nativist–empiricist debate. First, the notions of developmental plasticity and implasticity (or 'canalization') themselves are somewhat slippery. Whether or not a process is developmentally robust depends on the measure of environmental autonomy it possesses—the extent to which it is immune to possible changes in the environment. But since immunity to environmental change comes in degrees, developmental processes are more or less (im)plastic, not plastic or implastic, period. That (im)plasticity is a graded notion is not necessarily a bad thing, of course: that a boundary is vague doesn't mean it doesn't exist; and nor does it mean that it cannot be identified with that marking the distinction between nativist and empiricist. What *is* worrying about the concept of plasticity, though, is that the degree to which a certain process counts as (im)plastic depends on what sorts of environmental variability one counts as being relevant to the process at hand. That is, the implasticity of a process is a measure of the extent to which it is robust under possible alterations in the environment. But what counts as a possible environmental manipulation depends on what we take the relevant space of environments to be, and this, in turn, seems to depend on our explanatory interests in using the concepts 'plastic' and 'implastic' in the first place.[20]

Suppose, for instance, that you are interested in the development of our species over evolutionary time. Then you might define the space of 'possible environments' to include, say, all those capable of sustaining hominid life. Against this background, a process like the human fetus's development of normal facial features (to recall our earlier example) looks paradigmatically

---

20. A similar objection was raised by Paul Griffiths in his comments on Ariew (1996) at the Philosophy of Science Association meeting in Cleveland, OH, November 1, 1996.

implastic: in overwhelmingly most possible hominid environments, faces develop unproblematically. But suppose instead that you are an obstetrician
interested in the healthy development of individual babies. Then the space
of possible environments relevant to your concerns will be (say) those in
utero, and facial development will begin to look much more plastic: a much
higher proportion of possible environments will inhibit normal facial development. Neither of these pictures is objectively the 'right' one: viewed from
one perspective, facial development is implastic; viewed another way, it's
not. But if the notions of plasticity and implasticity are relativistic in this
way, then construing the innateness debate in terms of this opposition runs
into the same problem we saw in chapter 1 with regard to the internalist–
externalist interpretation. The conflict between nativist and empiricist seems
like nothing more than a difference in explanatory emphasis or theoretical
orientation: nativists* think that our acquisition of ideas is implastic because
they have in mind a wider space of possible environments than do empiricists*, who in the light of their interests regard acquisition as a highly plastic
process.[21]

To be sure, this relativity in the notion of (im)plasticity is not in itself a
decisive blow against the developmental interpretation of the nativism–empiricism controversy, just as the relativism of the internalist–externalist opposition was not decisive against that interpretation. For, as was noted at
the end of chapter 1, it might be that nativists and empiricists (and their
commentators) are in fact *just wrong* in thinking that there's something
tangible at stake between them. There is, however, another reason to resist
understanding innateness in terms of developmental plasticity or degree of
canalization, namely, that the arguments from the poverty of the stimulus
that nativists use to defend their position do not in fact entail anything about
the degree of plasticity possessed by the processes responsible for our acquisition of ideas and beliefs. For the fact that the outputs of learning might
be thoroughly underdetermined by the available environmental information
(as poverty of the stimulus arguments contend) is quite consistent with any
amount of plasticity in the learning process itself.

Recall, for instance, Plato's argument for the innateness of the slave boy's
beliefs about Pythagoras' Theorem (§1.4.2). As Plato tells the story, the
inputs that gave rise to the boy's knowledge were both impoverished and

---

21. Actually, the situation may be worse even than this. As Kim Sterelny has pointed
out to me (private communication), one usually thinks of a trait as being innate (or even
innate to degree X), period. However, traits cannot usefully be said to be implastic (or
implastic to degree X), *simpliciter*, even when the space of 'possible environments' is fixed.
For a trait may be stable with regard to one kind of environmental change, yet extremely
unstable with regard to another. The development of a bird's normal song repertoire, for
instance, resists huge variations in, say, feeding schedules, yet is extremely sensitive to even
minor variations in the timing and amount of exposure to adult songs. The interesting
question in this case seems not to be "Is the trait implastic? Does it develop in most possible
environments?" Rather, the interesting question is "In *which* possible environments does
the trait develop?"

highly unusual: Meno's slave did not need very much in the way of information to acquire the belief in question; but he did need to be in an environment of a very specific sort (that is, he needed to be asked the right
questions, in the right order, by Socrates). In this case the stimulus is impoverished, yet the acquisition process is plastic: take Socrates' questioning
out of the picture, and the boy will remain happily ignorant of geometry.[22]
As an example of a developmentally implastic (or highly canalized) process
the inputs to which are impoverished, consider language acquisition. Like
acquisition of hearts and teeth, the acquisition of language looks to be a
robust process: it occurs in virtually all human environments. Yet, as we
will see in chapter 8, language acquisition is also claimed to be driven by a
stimulus that is highly impoverished, and language for that reason is held
to be substantially innate. That the output of a developmental process is far
richer than the inputs to it, is consistent with that process's being either
plastic or implastic. So if nativism is what is entailed by nativists' arguments
from the poverty of the stimulus, nativism is not a hypothesis of developmental implasticity.[23]

2.6 Reprise: The Case for Special-Purpose Faculties

In the previous section, I defended the architectural or 'special faculties'
interpretation of the nativist position against a competing developmental
account. I argued not only that the latter interpretation makes the parties
to the controversy seem as if they are talking past each other, but also that
no view about plasticity (or canalization) is entailed by nativists' arguments
in any case. In §§2.3 and 2.4, I showed how the faculties interpretation of
the nativist position receives support from a number of considerations. First,
it enables us to decipher the nativist's claims in such a way as not to fall
into any of the interpretive traps discussed in chapter 1. Second, it enables
us to view nativism as a sensible and reasonable response to the poverty of
the stimulus arguments that are advanced in its support. Third, since the
hypothesis of dedicated learning mechanisms was the one avenue that empiricists *didn't* explore in responding to arguments from the poverty of the
stimulus, reading the nativist in the way I am suggesting enables us to understand why, and despite their many agreements, empiricists and nativists
regarded themselves as being in opposing camps. And finally, the present

22. Or, in Ariew's terms, the process has a very low degree of canalization: in most
possible environments, the trait (knowing Pythagoras' theorem) will fail to develop.

23. In the two examples above, I've tried to keep my notion of what counts as a
possible environment constant: roughly, I take the space of relevant environments to be
those that allow the development of higher cognitive capacities in humans. Intuitively,
many more of those environments support the development of language than support the
development of beliefs about Pythagoras' theorem. Thus the development of language is
much more robust (by this measure) than that of knowledge of geometry.

interpretation allows us to see these two camps as clashing over a real and important issue, namely, the nature of the inborn psychological mechanisms that underlie belief and concept acquisition.

If I am right, an interesting question arises. If this view about cognitive architectures is all there is to nativism, why are empiricists so resistant to it? After all, the nativist's hypothesis of special faculties is not obviously false. Indeed, the postulation of dedicated learning mechanisms is, at least on the face of it, a far better response to the problem of the gap than some of the strategies favored by empiricists. In contrast to, for example, the phenomenalist's contention that there is no world existing independently of our minds, the notion that different cognitive skills are fitted to different tasks is a commonplace. No eyebrows are raised when it is claimed that the psychological and/or neurophysiological mechanisms responsible for our ability to perceive colors differ from those underpinning our ability to perceive pitches. Why does the analogous claim in the case of the mechanisms responsible for ability to *learn* different things meet with such strong resistance?

In my view, at least part of the explanation of empiricists' resistance to the idea of domain-specific learning devices derives from their failure to distinguish the 'modest' enrichment that this hypothesis represents from the more general enrichment—the 'power-learning' hypothesis—that was mentioned in §2.3. Confusion arises because, although the latter hypothesis is *not* supported by the argument from the poverty of the stimulus, it (or something that initially looks very like it) *is* suggested by a second argument commonly found in nativist writings. In the next chapter, I show how nativists' 'impossibility arguments' lead them to suggest a radical enrichment of the organismic contribution to concept and belief acquisition. I suggest that the empiricist is right to dismiss this second strand in nativist thought.

3

What Nativism Is (II)

The Mystery Hypothesis

We saw in chapter 2 how arguments from the poverty of the stimulus grant that the empiricist can succeed in explaining certain central cases of concept and belief acquisition. Their point is just that since some of the items we acquire are beyond the reach of the empiricist's general-purpose learning mechanisms, we must view the mind as inherently containing additional, task-specific learning faculties.

There is, however, another form of argument to be found in nativist writings, one that allows the empiricist not even this much success. Whereas poverty of the stimulus arguments seek to show only that empiricism is partly mistaken, what I call 'impossibility arguments' claim to establish the much stronger conclusion that empiricism is wholly false. On this view, indeed, empiricism could not be true, for the doctrine rests on a picture of mind–world interaction that is fundamentally incoherent or self-undermining. But if that is the case, then the empiricist can explain nothing about how a mind comes to be furnished. And, if *that* is the case, the nativist concludes, everything that is in our minds must be innate.

Endorsed by Descartes, Leibniz, and (at least some of the time) Fodor, this rather extravagant claim begs for elucidation: How could *everything* be innate? In this chapter and part II, I offer an interpretation of what might be meant by such declarations and explore how this radical element in nativist thought is to be reconciled with the more moderate position discussed in chapter 2. As in that chapter, my method will be to approach the nativist's conclusion through examination of his arguments for it: whatever those arguments entail is what 'Everything is innate' must be taken to signify.

As will emerge below, there are deep commonalities in the impossibility arguments of Descartes, Leibniz, and Fodor. However, their quarrels with empiricism differ enough in their particulars to warrant separate treatment. Fodor's argument and the relation of his views to those of his forebears are dealt with in part II. In §§3.1 and 3.2, I outline the cases made by Leibniz and Descartes for their extreme nativisms, then argue in §§3.3–3.5 that the *real* conclusion of those arguments is a kind of anti-naturalism about the mental. Impossibility arguments, I shall show, work to undermine the empiricist assumption that the processes underpinning our acquisition of ideas and beliefs are simply species of natural phenomena, amenable at least in principle to natural-scientific explanation. Hence, I shall suggest, the nativist's claim that everything is innate is not to be interpreted as an attempt to explain the processes of acquisition: it is, rather, an expression of hopelessness and pessimism about that explanatory project itself.

3.1 The Impossibility Argument of Leibniz

As we have seen (§§2.2.2, 2.4.1), Leibniz is sometimes willing to criticize his opponents from within their own empiricist perspective, advancing on the basis of poverty of the stimulus arguments a nativism that is limited to our acquisition of certain sorts of ideas or beliefs. But in fact his own metaphysics, and in particular his view that individual substances have 'no windows,' is deeply hostile to empiricism. So, where he considers them from within a properly 'Leibnizian' perspective, Leibniz argues that empiricist acquisition theories are fundamentally inadequate. He concludes, on these grounds, that everything in our minds is innate.

Everything in the world, on Leibniz' view, is composed of countlessly many 'individual substances,' or 'monads,' each of which evolves continuously through time. This evolution is such that the state of every substance is correlated in a particular way with the state of every other substance in the universe. In virtue of these correlations, Leibniz says, each substance is like a soul, in that it 'perceives' or 'mirrors' or "expresses, however confusedly, all that happens in the universe, whether past, present or future."[1] The correlations between substances' states, however, do not arise from any real action of one substance upon another, being rather the consequence of a preestablished harmony set up by God.[2] For Leibnizian substances are completely independent of each other: they have, as he puts it, 'no windows,' no ability either to act upon or to be acted upon by other substances. Thus, any change that occurs in a substance is entirely a consequence of its own nature, dictated by its own unique 'principle of appetition' or program.[3] As a corollary, all apparent relations among substances are phenomenal: they are not, so to speak, *really* real. For all that is really real are the myriad

1. *Discourse on Metaphysics* §9. All quotations from Leibniz, except where noted, are as translated by Ariew and Garber (Leibniz 1989).

2. In deciding which subset of possible substances to create, God chose the substances whose states are correlated in such a way as to ensure that the actual world is both maximally orderly and maximally diverse. It is in this sense that our world is the best, that is, the most harmonious, of all possible worlds.

3. For a concise statement of Leibniz's metaphysics, see his "Principles of Nature and Grace, Based on Reason" (Leibniz 1989:207–13).

individual substances, each developing along its own predetermined path. Some manifest relations, however, Leibniz holds to be *in a sense* real; realer, as one might say, than others. These relations are what he calls 'well-founded' phenomena, to be distinguished from 'mere' phenomena. A mere phenomenon has no grounding whatsoever in reality and hence is not real in any sense at all: it is an illusion or fantasy. A well-founded phenomenon, by contrast, does have some degree of reality, for our perception of it reflects real modifications in the underlying substratum of monads and their intrinsic properties.[4] Leibniz holds causation to be real only in this latter sense: it is a well-founded phenomenon that reflects changes in the degrees of perfection of substances' mutual perceptions.[5] So although causation is not *really* real (there being nothing more to it than this slight alteration, due to the pre-established harmony, in the way that the internal states of the substances comprising cause and effect are correlated), causation is in a sense real—for there is, after all, at least *this* much to it. The same holds, mutatis mutandis, for the substances and properties adverted to in physics and other sciences: matter, forces, gravitation, and the like are not really real; but they are in a sense real. For to the extent that our scientific theories are good ones, they will reflect real facts about the substances comprising the world.[6]

Leibniz's view that causal relations among substances are not really real has obvious implications for empiricist accounts of concept acquisition. For both human minds and material objects are composed of Leibnizian substances. But if substances cannot act upon each other, whether causally or in any other way, we cannot speak, except in a sense, of an idea's being caused by, or transmitted from, or derived from, external objects through experience. Whatever happens in our minds, including our acquisition of ideas and beliefs, is simply a consequence of our own nature, of the evolution of our 'dominant monad' according to its own preordained program. As Leibniz has it, "each substance is like a world apart, independent of all other things, except for God; thus all our phenomena, that is, all the things that can ever happen to us, are only consequences of our being".[7]

So, while certain mental events may be correlated with certain external events (whether in the world or in our bodies); and while these correlations may even be such that it is appropriate at times to speak of the external events' *causing* the internal events, such talk is not literally true. It is true only in a sense—true, that is, in the sense just outlined. Now Leibniz takes it, rightly I think, that empiricists would not be content with the claim that

4. See, especially, the letters to Des Bosses (Leibniz 1989:197–206).

5. On Leibniz's view (e.g., *Monadology*, §§51–52, and *Discourse on Metaphysics*, §15), we say that a substance C causes some effect in substance E when C comes to express E more perfectly and, at the same time, E comes to express C less perfectly. I set aside the question of what, exactly, this is supposed to mean.

6. This idea is developed in many places. See, e.g., the discussion of mass in the letters to de Volder (Leibniz 1989:171–86) and the discussion of corporeal substance in the letters to des Bosses (Leibniz 1989:197–206).

7. *Discourse on Metaphysics*, §14.

their acquisition theories are true only 'in a sense.' He assumes, that is to say, that empiricists view the idea- and belief-bestowing actions of external objects on minds as 'really' real and regard themselves as providing a literally true, if only partially complete, account of how beliefs and concepts are acquired. Of their theory Leibniz asks rhetorically, "How could experience and the senses provide the ideas? Does the soul have windows?"[8]

Since Leibniz does not accept that anything (except God) can act upon a substance—since he holds that the soul has *no* windows—he cannot accept that experience can provide the soul with ideas or beliefs. On his view,

> when we take things in a certain metaphysical sense [i.e., when we are speaking of what is 'really' real], we are always in a state of perfect spontaneity, and . . . what we attribute to the impressions of external things arises only from confused perceptions in us corresponding to them, perceptions that cannot fail to be given to us from the first in virtue of pre-established harmony.[9]

Hence "all our future thoughts and perceptions are merely consequences . . . of our preceding thoughts and perceptions."[10] So although "the outer senses can be said to be, in a certain sense, partial causes of our thoughts" (1981: 74), the *real* truth, on Leibniz's view, is that "all the thoughts and actions of our soul come to it from its own depths and could not be given to it by the senses" (1981:74): everything in our minds, in short, is innate.

3.2 The Impossibility Argument of Descartes

Like Leibniz, Descartes holds empiricism to be fundamentally flawed because, he thinks, experience cannot cause ideas. However, his reasons for this view are very different from those of Leibniz. Responding in the *Comments on a Certain Broadsheet* to his ex-disciple Regius' contention that "all common notions which are engraved in the mind have their origin in observation of things or in verbal instruction" (CSM I:304; AT VIIIB:358), Descartes argues that not only is the mind clearly capable of thinking some things up for itself but, stronger, that Regius' claim "is so far from being true" (CSM I:304; AT VIIIB:358) that

> whoever correctly observes how far our senses extend, and what it is precisely that can come from them to the faculty of thought, must admit that in no case do they exhibit to us the ideas of things, such as we form them in thought. So much so that *there is nothing in our ideas that is not innate in the mind, or faculty of thinking.* (CSM I:304; AT VIIIB:358; emphasis added)[11]

8. Leibniz (1981:111).
9. From Leibniz's letter to Coste, December 19, 1707 (Leibniz 1989:195).
10. *Discourse on Metaphysics*, §14.
11. Here I use the translation of M.D. Wilson (1991:303). CSM's translation ("we must admit that in no case are the ideas of things presented to us by the senses just as we

Since the senses do not exhibit ideas of things such as we form them in thought, *all* our ideas—not just those of God and mathematics—are innate!

As a preliminary to examining Descartes's argument for this extreme nativism, it's necessary briefly to recall his view on sense perception. In the *Treatise on Man* (CSM I:99–108; AT XI:119–202), he describes the processes by which physical agitations of the sense organs and brain give rise to our perceptions of sensory ideas. In vision, for example, light from bodies strikes the eye and forms images of those bodies on the retina. These images cause the fibers in the optic nerve to be pulled with varying vigors, and the resultant tension in the fibers causes the openings at their other ends (Descartes conceives of the nerves as being like tiny pipes) to dilate. These openings lie on or close to the pineal gland, and animal spirits from the gland (animal spirits are an especially rarefied form of blood) rush to enter them. Different nerves receive spirits from different points on the gland's surface, and this differential flow of spirits from the gland constitutes yet another image of the perceived object. This image forms the proximal input to the generation of ideas in the mind proper: it is what "the rational soul united to this machine will consider directly when it imagines some object or perceives it by the senses" (CSM I:106; AT XI:177).

In the *Comments,* Descartes takes up a puzzle raised by this picture of perception: How can these images in the brain, being simply motions of nerves and vital spirits, give rise to our ideas of light, color, shape, distance, size, and so on? If "[n]othing reaches our mind from external objects through the sense organs except certain corporeal motions" (CSM I:304; AT VIIIB:359), and if "there is no similarity between [the] ideas and the corporeal motions" (CSM I:304; AT VIIIB:359), how could all the myriad ideas we form in our minds *come from* those motions, as the empiricist says? Just as a person with no experience of computers might be bemused by the fact that the sequence of keystrokes he types in at the keyboard is entirely unlike the picture of Notre Dame that subsequently appears on the screen, so Descartes is led by his consideration of empiricism in the *Comments* to ponder the fact that the contents of our ideas are utterly unlike the corporeal motions that precede them.[12]

As we saw in the quotation displayed above, Descartes's ruminations on this subject led him to a conclusion of universal nativism. But how does he get from the observation that the contents of our ideas (their 'objective realities,' as he would say) are unlike the brain states that precede them, to

---

form them in our thinking") misleadingly suggests that what the senses 'present' to us are in fact ideas, Descartes's point apparently being just that they are not the same ideas as those that are formed in the mind proper. This rendering is problematic in light of the scholarly consensus that the mature Descartes did not use 'idea' to refer to the 'corporeal images' of things that are formed in the sense organs and brain consequent upon experience (see Chappell 1986; Schmaltz 1998:5 and n. 13).

12. The computer analogy for Descartes's puzzle in the *Comments* is due to Garber (1992:366ff. and n. 57).

the conclusion that all our ideas are innate? The bridge here is constituted by his views on causation, articulated and developed in a number of works including the *Meditations*, and summarized in what O'Neill (1987) calls the 'Containment Principle':

> THE CONTAINMENT PRINCIPLE: Whatever reality or perfection exists formally in a thing, or objectively in an idea, must be contained formally or else eminently in its total, efficient cause.[13]

This principle reflects Descartes's view of the world—very alien to the modern mind—as being hierarchically structured along several dimensions. First, things in Descartes's universe have different amounts of 'reality,' corresponding intuitively to the extent to which they depend on other things for their existence. God has the greatest degree of reality (since he relies on nothing); substances, such as minds and bodies (which depend on God), come next; and modes or properties of substances come last, since they owe their being to the substances of which they are modifications. Second, there is the more finely grained (and less easily explained) 'perfection' scale. God, being maximally perfect, is again at the top; then come angels; then minds; then (intricate) material things; then (simpler) material things; then, last again, modes or properties of things.[14] Third, qualities (including degrees of reality and perfection) themselves have different modes of being, on Descartes's view: they can be possessed or contained by an object formally, objectively, or eminently. An object possesses F-ness *formally* if it is in fact F; it contains F-ness *objectively* if it represents F-ness; and it possesses F-ness *eminently* if it is higher in the hierarchy of perfections than anything that could possess F-ness formally. Consider, for example, the property *being a man*. Descartes possesses that property formally (because he is a man); my idea of Descartes contains that property objectively (because it represents a man); and God and angels contain that property eminently (because they are higher up the perfection scale than men). So, putting all this together, what the Containment Principle says is that the total, efficient cause of F-ness (whether F-ness be formally contained in an object or objectively contained in an idea) either must be F itself or must be higher up the ontological scale than any possible F thing.

And what this means is that, given Descartes's account of perception, the brain states consequent on experience, being mere corporeal motions of spirits and nerves, could not cause ideas. Consider, for example, my idea BLUE. By the Containment Principle, the cause of an idea containing blueness objectively (that is, one representing blueness) must itself contain blueness ei-

13. O'Neill (1987:230). O'Neill (1987) and Schmaltz (1991) provide insights into Descartes's views on causation that are of especial relevance to understanding the *Comments* argument.

14. This discussion of Descartes's 'reality' and 'perfection' scales is based on that of O'Neill (1987).

ther formally or eminently. That is, it must either (1) be blue or (2) be higher up the perfection scale than any blue thing. But the states of my brain and nervous system aren't blue! Nor are they more perfect than blue things, since brain activities are merely modes of material substance themselves and so lie at the very bottom of the ontological hierarchy. Thus, by the Containment Principle, bodily states could not be the cause of my idea of blueness. Descartes claims in the *Comments* that the same thing goes, mutatis mutandis, for all our ideas. So quite generally the corporeal motions resulting from sense experience could not be the causes of our ideas. Empiricism must be false root and branch. All our ideas must be innate.

Now, Descartes's argument looks invalid as it stands. For if corporeal images are motions and shapes of spirits and nerves in the brain, then they *do* contain formally at least some of the properties—namely, motions and shapes—that are contained objectively in (i.e., that are represented by) our ideas. Thus, by the Containment Principle, corporeal images should suffice to cause at least ideas of motions and shapes, which contradicts Descartes's conclusion of universal innateness. Descartes, however, denies this possibility and the limitation on his nativism implied by it. "[N]either the motions themselves nor the figures arising from them are conceived by us exactly as they occur in the sense organs, as I have explained at length in my *Optics*," he argues (CSM I:304; AT VIIIB:359). Hence "the very ideas of the motions themselves and of the figures are innate in us." (CSM I:304; AT VIIIB:359). And to be sure, he did argue in the *Optics* that not even ideas of primary qualities are like the motions that precede them: when we look at objects, for example, the 'pictures in our eyes,' that is, on the retina, "usually contain only ovals and rhombuses when they make us see circles and squares" (CSM I:172; AT VI:140–41). Thus, he concludes, this apparent exception to his universal nativism is not really an exception: all our ideas are innate.[15]

But what could Descartes mean by such a claim? Is he really denying that experience causes ideas? Is his innateness hypothesis seriously intended as an alternative account of their acquisition? As a preliminary to addressing these questions—and the analogous questions raised by the arguments of Leibniz, discussed above—I want to explore in a more general way what might be the import of the nativist's impossibility arguments. In the next section, I argue that the immoderate conclusions of such arguments cannot simply be accepted at face value as proposing that, rather than coming from our experience, all our ideas are inborn. In §3.4, I return to the views of Leibniz and Descartes, proposing on their basis an alternative reading of the radical nativism that their impossibility arguments give rise to.

15. In the foregoing, I have glossed over the myriad subtleties and problems of interpretation that the *Comments* argument for nativism raises. See M.D. Wilson (1991), and Schmaltz (1998) for further discussion.

3.3 "Everything Is Innate" Is Not an Acquisition Theory

Impossibility arguments are much broader in scope than poverty of the stimulus arguments. The nativist hypothesis proposed in response to them is thus correspondingly broad: if no (or virtually no) concepts could be got from experience, then all (or virtually all) concepts must be innate. As we have seen in this chapter, proponents of impossibility arguments have not been shy to proclaim exactly this. Descartes asserts that "there is nothing in our ideas which is not innate in the mind" (CSM I:304; AT VIIIB:358). Leibniz writes: "I believe indeed that all the thoughts and actions of our soul come from its own depths and could not be given to it by the senses" (1981:74). Fodor's quondam view, to be discussed in Chapter 4, is that "most de facto lexical concepts [i.e., concepts expressed in English by a single word] are innate" (1981b:306). Everything in our minds, in short, is innate. Strong stuff. But, to ask again what we have been asking all along: What does it *mean*?

The claim that everything is innate should, ideally, mean something more than 'Empiricist acquisition theories are false.' That is, the claim should represent some genuine alternative to the empiricist's view of how the mind comes to be stocked with ideas and beliefs. The remainder of this chapter and most of the next three constitute an extended argument for my contention that 'Everything is innate' does not represent a genuine alternative to empiricism. In the present section, I will present a prima facie case for thinking that this assertion does not provide an alternative acquisition theory. For, I argue, it cannot be interpreted so as to be both true and interesting.

First of all, the 'special faculties' interpretation of innateness, defended in the last chapter, is completely inapplicable in this case. Whatever 'everything is innate' means, it obviously can't mean that all our concepts and beliefs are acquired by means of a special-purpose learning device, there being little point in talking of domain-specific faculties when the domain in question is everything. Nor, less obviously, can it mean that there are several different special-purpose faculties that collaborate to produce in us our full complement of ideas. For impossibility arguments work equally, insofar as they work at all, against both domain-specific learning strategies and the more general strategies postulated by the empiricist. Impossibility arguments contend that there is something deeply problematic about the notion that what is in our minds comes to us 'from the outside.' And since domain-specific learning from experience is, after all, still a form of learning from experience, the hypothesis of domain specificity simply does not address the impossibility objection.[16]

16. Though if the nativist had argued for 'everything is innate' by systematically going through our concepts and showing that experience is impoverished with respect to *all* categories of concepts, that *would* license our reading her claim as postulating a bevy of task-specific devices. One of the points I am trying to make in part 1 of this book is that it matters to our interpretation of the nativist hypothesis what argument is used to support that hypothesis: different arguments, I contend, result in very different—and perhaps irreconcilable—nativist theses.

Nor can the nativist's claim be taken to mean that mental items are among those human traits that are not in any real sense *acquired* at all.[17] Legs, brains, hearts—indeed, most bodily organs and parts—are innate in this sense: they are present at birth, inborn, natural. But as Locke made clear, 'everything in our minds is innate' cannot be understood on analogy with 'hearts and legs are innate'; as meaning, that is, that every concept and every belief we ever acquire is literally present in our minds at birth. For although this claim would represent a genuine alternative to the acquisition theory of the empiricist, it is obviously false. By any reasonable criterion of what it is for a concept or a belief to be present in the mind, none of us has all, most, or perhaps even any of our concepts or beliefs in our minds at birth. Our (putatively) innate beliefs are not the sorts of things we are conscious of, or can reason with, or will assent to if asked; and our (allegedly) innate concepts bring with them no ability to refer to or think about or recognize the objects they are concepts of.

Perhaps, then, the nativist means to claim that concepts and beliefs, like teeth, breasts, and body hair, are acquired 'come what may' during the normal course of development. But while there is on the one hand a straightforward sense in which our ideas are like teeth and hairy chests, in that we all reliably acquire a mental life of some kind or another, this is not how we should understand the nativist's radical hypothesis. For no one denies that we all get *some* concepts and *some* beliefs simply in virtue of being human and living in the world! So were this truism all the nativist meant to assert, his proclaiming that 'everything is innate' would be at best disingenuous, and at worst egregiously misleading. On the other hand, though, suppose that the nativist meant instead to assert that *particular* concepts and *particular* beliefs—not just concepts and beliefs in general—are acquired reliably during any normal course of development. This view would be much more appropriately represented by his declaration that everything is innate, for it is emphatically not accepted on all sides that our acquisition of particular beliefs and concepts is simply the outcome of normal developmental processes. On the contrary, as we have seen (§2.1), empiricists hold that very specific sorts of experiences are necessary to the acquisition of particular mental items. So while they'd admit that acquiring beliefs and acquiring concepts are run of the normal developmental mill, they would deny that it's just in virtue of developing normally that one acquires the *belief that p* or *the concept of an F*.

Thus, were the nativist arguing that particular beliefs and concepts are, as it were, 'standard issue,' like hairy chests and teeth, his thesis would represent a real and radical alternative to the empiricist picture of acquisi-

---

17. Terminological note: here and throughout this book I use 'acquire' and cognates to refer in a theory-neutral way to the processes, whatever they are, by which concepts and beliefs become available for general cognitive use. Concepts, for example, may be acquired by learning, or as a result of maturation, or through triggering, or some other way.

tion. The trouble is, however, that this latter claim is rather obviously false. For whatever a 'normal course of development' might be, the claim that an idea or belief is acquired 'in' one surely implies not only that those items are acquired in any environment that falls within the 'normal' range; but also that the character of what is acquired is largely invariant over that range. But while it is true (as we saw above) that normal humans acquire concepts and beliefs in all normal circumstances, it is *not* true that the nature of their conceptual and doxastic repertoires is insensitive to variation in those circumstances. On the contrary, the features of human mental lives show an extreme sensitivity to variations in experience. British convicts transported to New South Wales had, and Australian Aborigines prior to 1788 did not have, concepts of and beliefs about syphilis. This fact is explained straightforwardly by the fact that the convicts, but not the pre-1788 Aborigines, had had experiences of syphilis. Variations in concepts and beliefs are directly tied to variations in experience. Not so with variations in hairy-chestedness or toothedness: unlike a person's acquisition of the concept SYPHILIS, a person's acquisition of chest hair or teeth is not tied (so far as I know) to the presence or absence of any specific environmental factor.[18]

This point is related to my earlier discussion (§2.5) of the 'developmental implasticity' interpretation of nativism (which I called nativism*). As we saw there, there is a continuum of traits, ranging from those that are more or less wholly under the control of our genes (and impervious to most environmental factors) to those that are more or less wholly due to environmental factors (given that we have the kinds of genes we do). Corresponding to this continuum is a graded notion of plasticity (or innateness*). Traits like having hearts and legs and hairy chests and teeth, lying closer to the former end of the continuum and being impervious to most environmental factors, are highly implastic, hence 'very innate*.' Traits like having high cholesterol and having heart disease and being able to run a mile in under 4 minutes look to lie somewhere in the middle. Their presence is due both to specific genetic factors and to specific environmental factors. Whereas traits like having a tattoo or a driver's license or green hair are highly plastic, not 'innate*' at all, for whether or not a person acquires these traits (given, of course, that she possesses the basic sorts of human equipment) depends entirely on environmental factors.

So, first, while *having concepts* and *having beliefs* look to be features located toward the 'very innate*' end of the plasticity scale—up there with teeth and hairy chests—*having a concept of syphilis* and *having beliefs about syphilis* are way down at the other end—on a par with having a tattoo or green hair. That's to say, while everyone gets some concepts and some beliefs

18. There was, no doubt, an amount of toothlessness among the First Fleeters; toothlessness, moreover, that is directly attributable to an environmental factor, namely, the absence of vitamin C in many sailors' diets. But losing teeth as a result of scurvy, like losing concepts as a result of being hit over the head, is not relevant to the developmental point I am making here.

simply in virtue of being human and living in the world, not everyone thereby acquires a concept of, or beliefs about, syphilis. Whether a person acquires those items depends on her having very particular sorts of experiences: the processes responsible for them are extremely plastic. And, second, if the nativist's claim that everything is innate is to hold any interest at all when interpreted in developmental terms, it must be understood as the claim that the acquisition of *particular* beliefs and concepts is, like that of hearts and teeth, highly implastic. It's of no interest whatsoever to be told merely that the acquisition of some kind of mental life is robust (or innate*). For, as I pointed out before, everyone believes this, and no one needs an impossibility argument to be convinced of it. By contrast, it is of interest to be told that the traits *having a concept of syphilis* and *having beliefs about syphilis* are 'innate*.' For this implies something that not everyone believes, namely, that a person will acquire these items more or less regardless of the sorts of experiences she has. Unfortunately, however, this latter claim is false.

So to the extent that the nativist's contention that everything in our minds is innate is to be read as proclaiming that we all have an innate tendency to acquire concepts and beliefs, or that acquisition per se is a robust developmental phenomenon, it is undoubtedly true. But since all of this is perfectly consistent with empiricism, such proclamations are uninteresting as alternatives to the empiricist acquisition theory. And insofar as the nativist's hypothesis is to be read as the claim that specific beliefs or concepts are developmentally implastic (our acquisition of them being analogous to our acquisition of hearts or hairy chests), the nativist's claim, though undoubtedly interesting and a real alternative to the empiricist's story, is false.

None of this, of course, constitutes a proof that 'everything is innate' is not meant to be a substantive theory about how we acquire ideas. My aim has been, rather, to emphasize that it is not obvious how to interpret the nativist's claim such that it *could be* a theory about how our concepts and beliefs are acquired. For there are constraints on such an interpretation that are not obviously jointly satisfiable. First, since this claim issues from an impossibility argument, we are constrained to interpret it such that it cannot be undermined by such arguments. This, as I have suggested, rules out our interpreting the nativist as asserting a generalized form of the domain-specificity hypothesis. Second, since 'everything is innate' is the conclusion of arguments purporting to show that empiricism is fundamentally misguided, we must interpret it such that it represents a genuine alternative to empiricism. This rules out an interpretation according to which 'everything is innate' just means that humans are built such that in normal conditions they acquire an assemblage of concepts and beliefs. For this claim is perfectly consistent with empiricism: it merely states the fact that an acquisition theory must account for, rather than offering any competing explanation of that fact. And finally, since the particular constitution of our minds seems to depend in very specific ways on the precise character of the experiences we have, we need to interpret the nativist's contention such that specific experiences, and not merely experience-in-general, are accorded a special role in our acquisition of particular mental items. And this rules out our interpreting him as claiming that each concept and each belief (like hearts or hairy chests) is acquired pretty much regardless of what experiences we have.

In part II, I continue the arguments of this section, examining in detail, and ultimately rejecting, Fodor's proposals for how to elaborate 'everything is innate' such that all these constraints are satisfied. For the present, I want simply to assert, without further ado, that the nativist's impossibility thesis is not an acquisition theory. This raises the question: If this kind of radical nativism is not an acquisition theory, what *is* it?

3.4 Non-naturalism

The idea that I want to explore is that 'everything is innate' is a statement of non-naturalism. I suggest that, rather than viewing the nativist's hypothesis as being a theory on the same level as the theories he is criticizing, we should view it as embodying a certain *attitude toward* theories at that level. In particular, I will suggest, we should view it as expressing a deep pessimism about our prospects for developing a naturalistic, that is, broadly scientific theory of belief or concept acquisition. By way of introducing this idea, I want to return in the present section to the views of Leibniz and Descartes.

Leibniz is fairly explicit as to how we should construe his nativism. As we saw above (§§2.2.2, 3.1), he explains that his tactic in the *New Essays* is, first, to show that empiricism is false by its own lights (for special-purpose faculties would be needed to explain how experience could cause all ideas) and, second, to argue that it is wholly misguided in its assumption that ideas are caused by experience. Regarding the latter contention, he argues that although the putative causal relations between the substances composing our bodies and those comprising our minds are 'well-founded phenomena,' they are not in the strictest sense real. Whatever happens in our minds derives not from the action of the external world upon it via the senses but is, rather, a consequence of our own individual development, as preordained by God. What this means, metaphysically speaking, is that the bearing that our experience appears to have on our attainment of a mental life is strictly an illusion. Our ideas do not come from without, they come from within. They are, as Leibniz says, innate. And what it means in practical terms is that a full understanding of how acquisition occurs is beyond our grasp. For while we can speculate about God's designs in ordering the world as he did, his will—and the acquisition phenomena that depend on it—remain inscrutable to us. Leibniz's claim that all our ideas are innate to the understanding, therefore, is not merely a denial of the empiricist's causal account of acquisition; it entails also that no such account can be given.

Turning now to Descartes, we saw in §3.2 how his idiosyncratic take on causation, combined with the dissimilarity he detects between corporeal motions and the contents of our ideas, implies that no ideas are got through experience. This denial that experience causes ideas, articulated in the *Comments*, echoes the broader conclusion of a much more familiar argument to the effect that mind–body interaction *tout court* is impossible in the Cartesian world. In my view, Descartes's response to the general problem of mind–body interaction illuminates his radical nativism. As I shall show in the rest of this section, when we see what he makes of body–mind relations in general, we can better grasp what he means in claiming that everything is innate.

As a preliminary, let's recall why mind-world interaction is thought to be problematic for Descartes in the first place. On his view, minds are composed of mental substance and bodies are composed of corporeal substance. The two kinds of substance are essentially different. Mental substances are essentially non-extended and thinking; corporeal substances are essentially non-thinking and extended. With this dualism of substances goes a dualism of properties: a given property may be instantiated either by corporeal things or by mental things, but not by both kinds of thing. For properties or attributes are for Descartes merely modifications of substances, and the ways that a substance may be modified depend on what sort of substance it is. As he puts it in the *Principles* (§53):

> extension . . . constitutes the nature of corporeal substance; and thought constitutes the nature of thinking substance. Everything else which can be attributed to body presupposes extension, and is merely a mode of an extended thing; and similarly, whatever we find in the mind is simply one of the various modes of thinking. For example, shape is unintelligible except in an extended thing; and motion is unintelligible except as motion in an extended space; while imagination, sensation and will are intelligible only in a thinking thing. (CSM I:210–11; AT VIIIA:25)

From the seventeenth century onward, commentators have observed that this dualist metaphysics makes it mysterious how there could be causal relations of any kind between body and mind. For if causation requires that cause and effect either share properties or be at different ontological levels (as the Containment Principle (§2.2.1) asserts), then mind and body, sharing *no* properties and being at the *same* level (at least as regards their degree of 'reality'), seemingly cannot interact in any way at all. As a consequence, not merely concept acquisition, but *all* processes in which we take minds and bodies to act causally on each other, in whatever direction, would appear to be impossible. Descartes himself, however, staunchly resisted this conclusion. He was utterly unwilling to accept the general impossibility of mind–body interaction that this argument entails. As he expresses his view in a letter to Princess Elizabeth, who pressed him mercilessly on this very issue, "There are two facts about the human soul on which depend all the things we can know of its nature. The first is that it thinks, the second is that it is united to the body *and can act and be acted upon by it*" (AT III:663; emphasis added).[19]

Recent scholarship has shown Descartes to be at least partly justified in this last assertion. For the actions of minds on bodies can in fact be accommodated within the Cartesian framework. Although they are equally 'real' as bodies, minds are nonetheless held by Descartes to be more 'perfect' than bodies. Thus, they *eminently* contain modes of material substance and hence (by the Containment Principle) could after all act causally on bodies—as when, for instance, one's desire for a drink causes one's hand to grasp the glass.[20] Actions in the other direction, however, remain problematic. For bodies contain mental properties neither formally nor eminently, and hence apparently could cause no changes whatsoever in mental substances. So it would seem, as Garber (1992, 1983), for instance, concludes, that the disparate elements of Descartes's views cannot be wholly reconciled. Although he can explain how minds affect bodies, "the account of . . . causation that runs through Descartes' writings on physics makes it . . . virtually impossible to understand how he conceived of body–mind causation" (Garber 1983: 17).

Wilson (1978), however, argues that a rapprochement—of a sort—can be forged between the various components of Descartes's position. She argues that Descartes held what she calls a 'Natural Institution' theory of the relation between mind and body. On this conception, the sorts of causal relations between minds and bodies that are evidenced in sense experience and voluntary action are entirely contingent, a contrivance of a beneficent God: "it is only by the natural institution of God, and not by any intrinsic relation, that this particular motion in the inmost part of the brain brings about this particular sensation" (Wilson 1978:207). By God's divine fiat, that is to say, things are so arranged that certain kinds of bodily events give rise to certain kinds of mental events and vice versa.[21] Thus causal relations between mental and corporeal substances exist, but are anomalous. They fall outside the scope of the principles that usually govern such relations and are permitted in the Cartesian world solely by courtesy of God's will. Remnant's (1979) discussion of the union of mind and body in Descartes leads him to a similar conclusion, although one that does not mention God explicitly as the place where the explanatory buck stops. Remnant notes that

19. As translated by Kenny (1970:137).

20. See O'Neill (1987); M.D. Wilson (1991); Schmaltz (1998).

21. See Descartes's account of how changes in the movements of nerves in the brain are "*ordained by nature to enable the soul . . . to know* the place occupied by each part of the body it animates . . ." (*Optics*, CSM I:169; AT VI:135; emphasis added). See also his claim that "it is the movements composing this picture [on the pineal gland] which, acting directly on the soul insofar as it is united to our body, *are ordained by nature* to make it have such sensations. . . . we must suppose our soul to *be of such a nature that* what makes it have the sensation of light is the force of the movements taking place in the . . . brain" (*Optics*, CSM I:167; AT VI:130; emphasis added).

in his correspondence with Princess Elizabeth, Descartes claims, in effect, that the notion of mind–body unity—and the notion of their interaction that depends on it—are primitive. He writes:

> there are in us certain primitive notions which are as it were models on which all our other knowledge is patterned. . . . As regards body in particular, we have only the notion of extension which entails the notions of shape and motion; and as regards soul in particular we have only the notion of thought. . . . Finally, as regards soul and body together, we have only the notion of their union, on which depends our notion of the soul's power to move the body, and the body's power to act on the soul and cause sensations and passions. (AT III:663)[22]

Thus mind, body, and the mind–body union, according to Descartes, each define "an autonomous sphere of knowledge" (Remnant 1979:383), each domain best investigated by very different methods and each domain in principle irreducible to any of the others. According to this 'Complementarity Doctrine,' as Remnant calls it (1979:384), mind–body unities—as distinct from minds and bodies considered individually—engage in "another sort of behaviour, subject to another set of principles" (Remnant 1979:385). Hence,

> [t]o explain the interaction of soul and body would involve regarding the soul as one thing, acting in accordance with *its* laws of nature, and the body as another thing, acting in accordance with the laws of *its* nature, and giving an account of how the activities of the soul modify those of the body and vice versa. . . . But this kind of explanation is ruled out by the fact that when body and soul are considered as acting one upon the other they must be regarded as a single thing—to try to explain their interaction on the analogy of two bodies interacting can only result in confusion and obscurity. (Remnant 1979:384)

Mind–body interaction is thus sui generis and cannot be understood on analogy either with either purely physical causation (as when motions of nerves at our extremities cause motions of spirits in the brain) or purely mental causation (as when one thought leads to another). Whatever understanding we can have of it derives solely from our conception (known through introspection) of the unity of body and mind itself.

What the positions of Wilson and Remnant have in common is their insistence that, for Descartes, although mind–body interactions occur within the natural order, they are inexplicable—inconceivable, really—on any terms but their own. Minds and bodies interact causally, and we know that they do, and that's all there is to be said. But if it is indeed Descartes's view that mind–body interaction is sui generis, a phenomenon unto itself, wholly distinct from any of the other sorts of interactions between substances in the world, then this has far-reaching implications for the attitude he should take

22. Letter to Princess Elisabeth, as translated in Kenny (1970:138).

toward attempts (such as the empiricist's) to develop a naturalistic theory of belief and concept acquisition. If relations between body and mind are at bottom inexplicable, then all that one can properly say about acquisition is that it occurs; or perhaps that it occurs due to God's good graces. Anything further in the way of explication is impossible. So just as it would be an error to ask why the laws of nature are as they are or to demand further explication of a physical primitive like (say) energy, it's a mistake to demand any further kind of model or explanation of the processes underpinning acquisition. Concept acquisition occurs, and we know it does, and that's all there is to it.

This, I submit, is the real import of Descartes's conclusion in the *Comments*. His assertion that everything in our minds is innate is a truism—with a twist. The truism is that experience acts on the inherent structure of our minds so as to produce ideas in us. The twist lies in his refusal—or, rather, his acknowledgment of his inability—to say anything more about the causal processes underlying acquisition than that they occur. So while he was sometimes prepared (as we saw in §2.2.2, for example, in our discussion of the *Meditations*) to play the psychologist's game, offering competing accounts of the processes at work in acquisition, Descartes at heart believed such processes to be impenetrable.

3.5 Nativism as Non-naturalism

Leibniz and Descartes are thus led, albeit by very different paths, to the view that the bearing of experience on our acquisition of ideas is utterly inscrutable. Herein lies a real point of difference between their views and those of the empiricists they criticized. In proposing their acquisition theories, empiricists assume that belief and concept acquisition are simply species of natural phenomena. As such, they think, these processes can be accommodated within a broadly scientific conception of the natural world. Thus, the empiricist provides us with sketches or models of the causal-mechanical processes that, he believes, underpin our acquisition of concepts and beliefs. The nativist, by contrast, views these attempts to provide an explanation of acquisition as wholly misguided. Once the true natures of mind and body are recognized, it becomes clear that our acquisition of ideas and beliefs, and the bearing that experience has on it, is a mystery inaccessible to us. Only confusion and obfuscation can result from pushing science into realms that, by their nature, are beyond its ken. As Descartes puts it: "all human scientific knowledge consists solely in clearly distinguishing these [primitive] notions and attaching each of them only to the things to which it applies. For if we try to solve a problem by means of a notion that does not apply, we cannot help going wrong."[23]

23. Ibid.

The impossibility arguments of Leibniz and Descartes, then, are designed to call attention to the wrongheadedness of the empiricist's explanatory enterprise. Empiricists try to solve the acquisition problem by means of a notion—namely, the action of experience on our minds—that simply does not apply. In calling all our ideas innate, nativists are rejecting the empiricist's overly optimistic attempts to provide causal-explanatory models for the acquisition process. Their hypothesis of universal innateness is not an alternative to such models—for, as we have seen, they believe no alternative to be possible. Instead, it emphasizes the deeply enigmatic character of the phenomena of acquisition themselves.

Two objections may be raised against the reading I am here proposing. First, if Leibniz and Descartes believe that it is impossible to explain acquisition, why do they bother to advance the faculties hypotheses discussed in the last chapter? Why, that is, do they indulge in theoretical sorties that are, by their own lights, completely infeasible? I do not think that this objection need be taken very seriously, it being, after all, a common enough argumentative strategy to attack a disfavored position both on its own terms and on one's own. A second objection, however, is more important. If this kind of anti-naturalistic position is the point of nativists' impossibility arguments, why don't they *just say so?* Why all this talk of innateness? I would suggest that the reasons for this are two. One derives from the historical opposition between nativists and empiricists. As I argued in chapter 2, one real and substantive point of disagreement between nativists and empiricists concerned the nature of the organismic contribution to learning: Are we endowed with very general methods for learning from experience (as the empiricist claims)? Or are we rather (as the nativist maintains) furnished with a bevy of task-specific faculties? This disagreement was framed, for reasons I won't speculate upon, as a disagreement over whether or not certain of our ideas or beliefs are innate: innateness became the bone over which the opposing camps contended. As a result, the term 'innate' acquired a certain symbolic importance and 'nativism' came to stand for any view that opposed itself to empiricist accounts of belief or concept acquisition. Hence, even though there are, as I have argued in this chapter and the last, two quite distinct grounds on which nativists have challenged the empiricist, these arguments have been run together, nativists characterizing their anti-empiricist conclusions in each case in terms of the concept 'innateness.'

But there is, I think, also a deeper reason why nativists play down the nonnaturalistic implications of their impossibility arguments, namely, that if they are right, the only appropriate response to nativism is: gloom. If there really is something deeply problematic about the notion of ideas and beliefs arising in the mind as a result of our interaction with the external world; if natural science really is in principle unable to illuminate the processes by which we acquire a mental life; if the mind really is radically sui generis; if its nature really does lie ultimately beyond the reach of our epistemic capacities—what then? Should we simply give up? It seems that we should. If the nativist is right, mental processes in general, and those underpinning our acquisition of concepts and beliefs in particular, look to be in principle unknowable.

It may be responded, on behalf of the nativist, that things are not quite this grim. For some domain's being beyond the epistemic reach of *natural science* does not entail that it is unknowable. We did not, after all, need science to discover Pythagoras' Theorem or Zeno's Paradox. Nor, it may be claimed, do we need science to learn about the mind. What we need is some other methodology, analogous perhaps to that used in mathematics and logic, or philosophy. If only we could acquire these additional epistemic skills, they would enable us to solve the acquisition problem. But what reason is there to believe either that we can develop some other 'way of knowing' or that we would, if possessed of that 'other' way, be able to solve the acquisition problem? Certainly no grounds for optimisim are to be found in the nativist's own theoretical sorties. There is no obvious analogy between the realm of the mental and that of mathematics or logic that would support the contention that perhaps something like their methods is appropriate to theorizing in the psychological domain. On the contrary, mental events seem to be very much part of the natural world: concept and belief acquisition are contingent processes, occurring in space and time, and bearing relations of various sorts (including, apparently, causal relations) to other nonmental processes and events. The a priori methods characteristic of math or logic seem wholly inappropriate to inquire into this domain. But if neither empirical inquiry nor a priori reasoning is appropriate to understanding concept acquisition, what other method is there? Well, perhaps it's the philosophical method that we need, the method that nativists themselves employ. However, if these are the 'special epistemic skills' at issue, we have no reason to think that using them will enable us to solve the acquisition problem. For as was argued above, the nativist's claim that 'everything is innate,' while presumably a result of philosophical reasoning, does not provide a solution to that problem: all that the nativist's philosophical reflections on the acquisition problem tell us, I suggested, is that that problem is insoluble. In sum, if the methods of natural science are inappropriate to discovering the nature of the acquisition process, then so too, it would seem, are those of philosophy, logic, and mathematics. And as to what other methods there might be that *are* appropriate here, we remain totally in the dark.

The form of nativism issuing from an impossibility argument, I have argued, reflects a deep pessimism as to our prospects for understanding how the human mind is furnished with ideas and beliefs. This element in nativist thought, I surmise, is what is at bottom responsible for empiricists' gut opposition to nativism in any shape or form. Resistance is, in my view, wholly appropriate where 'nativism' denotes the outcome of an impossibility argument. If some argument entails that some familiar and pervasive feature of the world is unknowable, the correct response is not immediately to give up; it is, rather, to take the view that there must be something wrong with the argument. But where 'nativism' denotes the conclusion of an argument from the poverty of the stimulus—where it denotes, that is, a commitment to domain-specific faculties—empiricist resistance to nativism, while perfectly explicable given the association of innatism with nonnaturalism, is inappropriate. The nativist's faculties hypothesis is neither uninteresting nor obviously false. It deserves more serious consideration than it was accorded by historical empiricists. In recent years and thanks largely to the proselytizing of Noam Chomsky, this hypothesis has begun to receive something like the attention it deserves. In part III, Chomsky's nativism will receive further scrutiny.

3.6 What Nativism Is

On the picture that I have urged in part I, there are two independent strands in nativist thought. One component of the nativist's position is a psychological hypothesis, asserting the existence of domain-specific learning devices or mechanisms. The other component is a metapsychological, or more narrowly 'philosophical' hypothesis, intimating that the mind is much more mysterious than is dreamed of in the overly simplistic natural philosophy of the empiricist. Thus the nativist's claim that such and such mental item is innate, or inborn, or part of our biological endowment, is ambiguous. Sometimes it means that that item is acquired by means of a task-specific learning device; other times, it means, rather, that, empiricist boasts to the contrary notwithstanding, we have no idea whatsoever how that item was acquired.

My defense of this interpretation has had four components. First, as I argued in chapter 1, standard accounts of what nativism is do not work. Nativism is neither an epistemological theory nor a solution to the 'genetic' question. We therefore stand in desperate need of an alternative reading.

Second, a concern with the two issues I have distinguished is evident in the writings of historical nativists—at least once you start looking for it. In chapters 2 and 3, I have examined the nativisms of Leibniz and Descartes, arguing that each of these authors can profitably be read in the way that I am suggesting.

Third, and in addition to the direct textual evidence that can be marshaled in its favor, the view that nativism has 'two faces' gains additional indirect support from the fact that it explains two otherwise puzzling aspects of the nativist tradition mentioned at the end of chapter 1. It accounts, in the first instance, for the fact that nativists use both 'poverty of the stimulus' and 'impossibility' arguments to support their position. Worries about how to reconcile these quite different argumentative strategies disappear once it is recognized that each in fact supports a different thesis. Poverty of stimulus arguments, I suggested in §2.4, support claims about domain specificity. Arguments pointing to the fundamental impossibility of empiricism, by contrast, lead to nativist utterances of a kind that, I argued in §3.4, are best interpreted as expressions of metatheoretical gloom.

The bipartite interpretation I defend also explains our conflicting intuitions about the philosophical significance of the nativist doctrine. To the extent that the nativist is making a claim about domain specificity, nativism is a substantive theory of the mind deserving serious consideration. Hence our intuition that there is something real and important at stake in the nativism–empiricism controversy. But to the extent that the assertion of a nativist hypothesis is just an expression of pessimism about the project of domesticating the mind, it is not, or so I argued (§3.5), worth taking so seriously. Hence our other intuition that nativism, as nothing more than a denial of empiricism, is fundamentally uninteresting.

Finally, my interpretation allows us to understand why modern-day theorists as diverse in their arguments and claims as are Jerry Fodor and Noam Chomsky are properly viewed as being a part of a nativist tradition spanning almost three thousand years. The reason being that each beautifully exemplifies one component of that tradition. Fodor's nativism, as I will argue in part II, is of the metapsychological variety. Chomsky's, as I argue in part III, boils down to the claim that language-learning is a product of a highly task-specific learning device. The fact that the present characterization of what nativism is illuminates the contemporary controversy, and establishes a continuity between that controversy and its historical antecedents, is a further point in its favor.

Three small caveats before leaving the past and embarking on a consideration of contemporary nativism. First, it should be emphasized that I have not here been making any kind of *conceptual* claim about what the terms 'nativism' and 'innateness' mean or have meant or should mean. As should be abundantly clear by now, our intuitions as to what these terms signify are singularly unhelpful when it comes to figuring out 'what nativism is.' My aim has just been to show that, as a matter of exegetical fact, the two issues I have distinguished have been foci of nativist concern. Nor, second, do I want to claim that these two issues are the only points over which nativists and empiricists have disagreed. As should also be clear, those whom we call 'nativists' disagree with those denominated 'empiricists' on a bewilderingly wide range of topics. My aim has been simply to bring out two aspects of that disagreement that are, in my view, central to the historical debate and of particular help in understanding the contemporary controversy. Nor, finally, do I mean to suggest that nativists themselves would want to characterize their position in the way I am presently urging. While claims about domain-specific faculties are often fairly close to the surface, the metatheoretic despair that I am attributing to the nativist is heavily disguised—the disguise being, in fact, the nativist's talk of innateness itself.

CONCEPT ACQUISITION

Problem or Mystery?

The Case Against Empiricism

Making explicit the account of the mind that it commits us to may be the best way of showing that our psychology has gone wrong, if, in fact, it has. . . . Some of the things we seem to be committed to strike me, frankly, as a little wild.

(Fodor 1975:ix)

In part I, I distinguished two versions of the doctrine that there are innate ideas. Where it derives from poverty of the stimulus arguments, nativism may be interpreted as the claim that certain kinds of mental items are acquired by means of task-specific faculties. But where it issues from arguments purporting to show that any form of empiricism is fundamentally misguided, nativism is rather to be understood as an assertion of non-naturalism. Now, moving from the past to the present, I shall discuss the modern controversy between nativists and empiricists. I argue that exactly the same issues that fueled the earlier debate are operative today as theorists attempt to come to grips with the acquisition problem—with the question, "How do we come to know the things we do?" My aim now is more evaluative than descriptive. The focus will be not so much 'What is nativism?' as 'Should we believe it?'

In part II, we deal with what I will argue is a modern invocation of the impossibility argument introduced in chapter 3. Impossibility arguments emphasize some fundamental incoherence or self-contradiction in the empiricist position, and issue in the radically nativist claim that "everything is innate." As a twentieth-century instance of this mode of argument, I take the case for nativism first tendered by Jerry Fodor in his (1975) book, *The Language of Thought*, and further elaborated in "The Present Status of the Innateness Controversy" (1981b) and the recent book *Concepts: Where Cognitive Science Went Wrong* (1998). As will be explained in §§4.1 and 4.2, Fodor attributes to the empiricist the view that acquiring a concept is a matter of learning (through hypothesis-testing) what its meaning (or content) is. He contends, however, that since most concepts don't have the sorts of meanings that can be mentally represented (that is, since concepts are typically 'internally unstructured'), most concepts could not, in fact, be learned. The empiricist account of concept acquisition thus claims that most concepts are learned while entailing that most of them are not. Hence empiricism is untenable.

In his (1975) and (1981b), Fodor embraced a thoroughgoing nativism as an alternative to the empiricism he repudiates. A self-described "mad dog nativist" (1984a:39), he argued that humans have an innate representational system that is "as powerful as any language that one can ever learn" (1975: 82) or, as he also put it, that "most de facto lexical concepts are innate" (1981b:306).[1] By this, Fodor meant that concepts are 'triggered by' experience rather than being 'learned from' it. What this claim could mean, and in what sense this theory is nativist, will be the subject of §§4.3 and 4.4.

In his (1998), however, Fodor seems to retract his earlier nativism. His new view, which will be outlined in chapter 5, is that by enriching our metaphysics in certain ways—that is, by viewing many of the properties of which we have concepts as "appearance properties" (1998:135)—we can understand how concepts could be 'primitive,' that is, unstructured and hence unlearnable, without thereby being innate. I will argue, however, that this is mere window dressing. The new Fodor is just as much of a nativist as the old one. Indeed, I shall argue further, there is a strong continuity between both of the positions Fodor has espoused and the mystery-mongering of his nativist predecessors. Implicit in Fodor's earlier writings is the view that there can be no psychological theory of how concepts are acquired. Underlying the arguments of his (1998) is the stronger view that there can be no natural-scientific account of concept acquisition. Thus Fodor's fundamental attitude toward acquisition is anti-naturalistic, just like the attitudes of Leibniz and Descartes.

In chapter 6, I will argue that we need not share Fodor's pessimism. I defend a picture of concept acquisition in which psychological processing plays a central, and necessary, part. To the extent that concept acquisition is psychologically mediated, I claim, we can expect to succeed in developing a scientific (viz., psychological) theory of it. The acquisition problem might be hard. But it is not insoluble.

4.1 Fodor's Argument

Fodor's anti-empiricist argument, presented in his (1975) and (1981b), starts with the claim that our ability to learn language depends on our antecedently

---

1. A 'lexical concept,' in Fodor's usage, is one that is expressed by a word rather than a phrase (1981b:260–61). 'Concepts,' for Fodor (and me), are mental representations considered as entities in their own rights, not the intentional objects that mental representations express. See Fodor (1991a:316, n. 35).

possessing an internal system of representation that is roughly equivalent (in terms of its expressive power) to natural languages. Fodor argues that our best psychology views learning as involving the formulation and testing of hypotheses about the matter being learned, which in turn requires that the learner possess some medium in which to express her hypotheses (and represent data relevant to assessing them). Thus consider an English student of French who is learning *chat*. She formulates and tests hypotheses about that word's semantic properties (*Chat* means rat; *Chat* means stick; etc.), and has succeeded in learning it when she figures out that what *chat* means is cat.[2] Note, however, that in order to grasp the correct hypothesis about *chat*'s meaning, the learner must antecedently understand the English predicate 'cat' used in stating it: our knowledge of our first public language is what enables us to learn a second. But then how is our first public language acquired? Fodor argues that this case is parallel to that just discussed. In order to succeed in learning a first public language, we must antecedently know some other language—obviously a *non*public language—of sufficient power to express the meanings of natural language predicates. This nonpublic language is what Fodor calls 'the language of thought,' or 'Mentalese.' It is the internal system of representation used in the human mind.

The next stage of Fodor's case against empiricism involves arguing that not only must we know Mentalese before we could learn a language, we must know it innately:

> you can't learn a language unless you already know one . . . the language of thought is known (e.g., is the medium for the computations underlying cognitive processes) but not learned. That is, it is innate. (1975:65)

But why couldn't Mentalese be learned? In his (1981b) and again in his (1998), Fodor argues that learning Mentalese is impossible. He targets what he calls (1981b) the "classical" empiricist theory of concept learning, according to which learning a concept is analogous to learning *chat*. That is, when we learn a concept like PLATYPUS, we formulate and test hypotheses as to its meaning, the concept having been learned when we correctly conceive its semantic properties. Fodor argues that this account can be applied only to the acquisition of concepts that exhibit a certain kind of 'internal structure,' namely, the combinatorial structure that is exhibited on its face by a phrasal concept like THE SWAGMAN BY THE BILLABONG and that can be revealed by analysis of some lexical concepts (e.g., BACHELOR). Such internally structured or 'complex' concepts are "logical constructs out of a primitive basis in which they are not themselves contained" (Fodor 1981b:283).

---

2. My use of 'means' here is intended to be neutral on the question of exactly what sorts of semantic properties predicates of natural languages have. Fodor (1975) assumes that predicates have purely extensional semantic properties—his sample hypotheses concerning a predicate F are thus of the form: " 'x is F' is true iff y is G." But since his argument here does not turn on this assumption, I use the more general formulation.

Their semantic properties are a function of the semantic properties of the concepts constituting them.[3]

Fodor claims that while the empiricist's learning theory may suffice to explain the acquisition of complex concepts, it is viciously circular if applied to unstructured (or 'primitive') concepts. For whereas the correct hypothesis as to the semantics of a complex concept can be represented using other concepts (namely, the concepts that it is a combination of), the correct hypothesis about the semantics of a primitive, unanalyzable concept can be represented only by *that very concept*. So while the right hypothesis about BACHELOR's meaning can be stated using the concepts UNMARRIED and MAN, it's impossible to say what an unanalyzable concept like (say) RED means— unless, of course, you're prepared to use the concept RED itself, which clearly you're *not* prepared to do if what you are doing is *learning* RED! In short, if learning RED requires us to formulate hypotheses about its meaning, and if formulating those hypotheses is possible only given that we already possess the concept RED, then RED could not be learned at all. Fodor concludes that if the empiricist's learning theory is applied to the acquisition of primitive concepts, it is circular. It presupposes that we have available the very concepts the acquisition of which it is supposed to explain.

Empiricism, then, can provide no explanation of the acquisition of primitive concepts. Which point, as Fodor grants (1981b:272–75), empiricists have generally recognized, acknowledging that the acquisition of primitive concepts must be explained in another way, as being somehow a direct causal consequence of experience. But what they have failed to recognize, Fodor argues, is that *most of our concepts are primitive*. Whereas empiricists implicitly assume that most concepts are analyzable, like BACHELOR, a Fodorean rationalist argues that virtually no lexical concepts exhibit such internal organization.

According to Fodor, "the empirical evidence overwhelmingly favors the view that most concepts are internally unstructured" (1981b:283). There are several kinds of evidence he invokes in this connection. First, he cites the fact that "attempts at conceptual analysis practically always fail" (1981b: 283ff). It is almost always possible to come up with a counterexample to a proposed definition of a word, the indefinability of words being taken by Fodor as prima facie evidence that the concepts those words express are unstructured.[4] Second, Fodor cites the lack of empirical evidence in support

---

3. Although, following Fodor, I shall speak throughout this discussion of concepts' internal structures, it should be emphasized that concepts' constituents need not be conceived as being actual (physical or syntactic) *parts* of them. Any concept whose content is determined by its relations to other concepts counts as 'internally structured.' So, for instance, conceptual role and description theoretic and 'two-factor' and 'semantic network' theories of content all view concepts as being internally structured, as that term is being used here.

4. Fodor acknowledges (1998:43) that it's possible that words should be indefinable while concepts are complex (e.g., if concepts had nondefinitional structure—see §4.2), and

of the view that entertaining a concept is a matter of entertaining its definition: "[i]t's an iron law of cognitive science that, in experimental environments, definitions always behave exactly as if they weren't there" (1998:46).
For example, although, he says, there is

> some evidence that the state of mind you're in when you hear an expres-
> sion is sometimes in a certain sense close to the one you're in when you
> hear a term that figures in its definition ... [there are no] empirical
> grounds for claiming that the latter state of mind is, as it were, a constit-
> uent of the former: that understanding "cat" involves entertaining ANI-
> MAL. (1981b:288)

Third, Fodor points (1998:46) to the difficulty of giving an account of what
makes definitions, so to speak, definitive. Why should 'unmarried' be part
of the meaning of 'bachelor' whereas 'tends to die younger than married
men' is only 'collateral information'? Quinean arguments against notions
like synonymy and analyticity count as arguments against definitions. To the
extent one takes the Quinean objections seriously, then, one should view
definitions with mistrust. Finally, Fodor argues that intuitions about "intrinsic conceptual connectedness" (1998:75ff.), which some philosophers might
claim to be evidence of the existence of definitions, in fact are evidence of
something else, namely, how our concepts get connected to the world. We
have the intuition that 'is an F' and 'is a G' are analytically connected, not,
according to Fodor, because being an F is definitive of being a G. Rather,
our intuition reflects the fact that our epistemic situation is such that our
main (or even only) way of getting "semantic access" (1998:75ff.) to Gs is
via Fs. Getting semantic access to a G is a matter of getting oneself placed
in the appropriate nomological relations for the reference of one's concept
'G' to be Gs (that is, on Fodor's view, it's a matter of getting 'G' and Gs to
covary in the way that an information theoretic semantics requires—see
§6.1.2). And sometimes, Fodor argues, the only way to do this is by using
one's epistemic access to F-ness. So, for example, LOOKS RED and IS RED
might seem to be analytically connected. According to Fodor this is not
because of any semantic relations (e.g., constituency) between the two concepts. It's just because looking red is the best—probably the only—indicator
we normally have of something's being red. We use the property *looking
red* to mediate our access to *being red*. Thence arises our feeling that LOOKS
RED and IS RED are intrinsically connected.

   In his (1975), Fodor took the indefinability of most concepts to show that
most concepts do not have internal structure, arguing from this that if most
concepts are unstructured, then most concepts could not be learned. Schematically:

hence is aware that the evidence for the lack of structure in concepts provided by the
indefinability of words is not decisive.

1. Only internally structured concepts could be learned.
2. Most concepts are indefinable.[5]
So, 3. Most concepts are not internally structured.
So, 4. Most concepts could not be learned.

And if most concepts are not learned, they must be acquired in some other way—which is to say, according to Fodor (1981b), that they are innate.

4.2 Alternative Accounts of Conceptual Structure

Tacitly in his (1981b) and explicitly in his (1998), Fodor acknowledges that this argument is invalid. It equivocates on two senses of 'internally structured.' While it is true that most concepts are not internally structured in the sense of being definable, the possibility remains that they might have some other, nondefinitional, kind of constitution. So, it seems, one could accept Fodor's (2) and deny his (3), thus blocking his argument to nativism.

Indeed, that concepts have nondefinitional structure is the moral that many in cognitive science and philosophy have drawn from the failures, adumbrated by Fodor, of the definitional account. On the definitional or 'Classical' view, concepts are constituted by their definitions, that is, by specifications of the individually necessary and jointly sufficient conditions for a thing's falling within their extension.[6] Thus PLATYPUS, viewed Classically, is represented by a Mentalese formula specifying the necessary and sufficient conditions for platypus-hood. As the discussion above indicates, however, most concepts are not Classically structured, and in place of the Classical view, a variety of non-Classical accounts of concepts' internal structure have been proposed. According to these theories, of which several different types exist, concepts are represented not by their definitions but by other structures that do not specify necessary and sufficient conditions for membership in the category. According to one type of theory, for instance, concepts are constituted by 'stereotypes' or 'exemplars,' that is, by representations of the 'best example' of the kind. Thus, if golden retrievers are the 'best' example

---

5. Actually, he does not need the modal claim that most concepts are indefinable here: it suffices to show the falsity of the definitional thesis that most concepts are not defined.

6. This view as applied to proper names and general terms (rather than concepts) is familiar to philosophers from the work of Frege and Mill. Putnam (1975) and Kripke (1972) argue against the definitional account as applied to terms of natural language. Variants on the 'description theory,' applied explicitly to concepts, have been proposed by, e.g., Glass and Holyoak (1975) and Katz and Fodor (1963). Collins and Quinlan's 'network model,' which saw concepts as being nodes in a hierarchically structured web of attributes (e.g., BACHELOR is the node dominating the nodes ADULT, UMARRIED, and MALE) was an attempt to implement the classical view in a computational framework (Collins and Quinlan 1969, 1970). However, empirical disconfirmation of the description theory as applied to concepts abounds—see Smith, Shoben, and Rips (1974); Hampton (1982); Medin and Smith (1984); Fodor et al. (1980). Smith and Medin (1981) provide a survey of related findings.

of doghood, then a representation of a golden retriever will be the stereotype or exemplar for DOG.[7] According to another non-Classical theory, often called 'the family resemblance picture' or 'prototype theory,' and associated most closely in psychology with the work of Eleanor Rosch and her colleagues, concepts are represented by a cluster of properties that instances of the concept typically or usually exhibit. Thus, for example, the prototype for PLATYPUS might be FURRY AQUATIC DUCK-BILLED CREATURE LIVING IN A BILLABONG. And other accounts have been proposed as well.[8] What is important about these theories, and what unites them, is their claim that concepts have internal structure, but that that structure is nondefinitional.

There is considerable empirical evidence for the 'psychological reality,' to use Fodor's phrase (1981b:295), of nondefinitional conceptual structures such as prototypes and exemplars.[9] In light of this, many psychologists have concluded that our concepts have nondefinitional structure.[10] If they're right, Fodor's argument against the empiricist collapses. For it turns on the inference from a concept's being indefinable to its being unstructured to its being unlearnable. But if concepts have prototype structure, the move from 'in-

7. This theory resurrects Berkeley's treatment of general ideas in the *Principles*, §§13ff. For more recent treatments, see Brooks (1978); Medin and Schaffer (1978); Putnam (1975); Estes (1994).

8. Cf. Smith and Medin (1981).

9. There is, that's to say, a lot of evidence that the kind of information contained in prototypes plays a role in determining our performance on a variety of cognitive tasks. Indeed, as Fodor says, "you can hardly devise a concept-possession test on which the knowledge of prototype structure fails to have an appreciable effect" (1998:93). Rips, Shoben, and Smith (1973) and Rosch (1973) set the ball rolling when they showed that subjects make distinctions in judging the typicality of instances of a kind: robins, for example, are judged to be 'more typical' birds than are penguins. Since then, evidence has been amassed indicating that such typicality judgments predict performance on a number of other tasks:

1. Categorization times. Rosch (1973) showed that how fast Ss verify that Fs are Gs depends on how typical the individual Fs are as instances of G (see also Smith and Medin 1981; Danks and Glucksberg 1980).
2. Order of item output. Mervis, Catlin, and Rosch (1976) showed that the more typical Fs are outputted first when Ss are asked to list all the Fs.
3. Order of concept attainment. Rosch (1973) showed that children acquire concepts for more typical instances of kinds first.
4. Family resemblance. Rosch and Mervis (1975) found that the more typical an F is, the higher its 'family resemblance score' (this is an objective measure of the number of features it shares with other Fs).
5. Cross-cultural regularities in color judgments. Berlin and Kay (1969) and Rosch (1975) showed that while color vocabularies differ from culture to culture as to how they carve up 'color space,' people nonetheless agree across cultures on what are the most typical instances for the color categories that they do recognize.

10. Some theorists, indeed, think that much more than a prototype (or stereotype) is contained in a concept. Holistic theories such as Johnson-Laird's 'mental models' account (1983) and Lakoff's 'idealised cognitive models' account (1987) view concepts not only as containing structures reflecting properties of their extensions but also as containing features that influence how they function in perception, interact with other concepts, and play a role in determining action.

definable' to 'unstructured' is blocked. And since all that seems to be required for learnability is internal structure of some (not necessarily definitional) kind, the move to 'unlearnable' is blocked too. So if learning PLATYPUS, for instance, were a matter of figuring out a prototype rather than a definition, then the fact that PLATYPUS is indefinable does not count against its being learned. Learning PLATYPUS would be a matter of testing hypotheses about platypuses' typical features, and while this would require that we had some other concepts—AQUATIC, CREATURE, DUCK-BILLED, FURRY, and so on—it would not require, self-defeatingly, that we had PLATYPUS itself. If concept learning does not in fact involve the representation of definitions, in short, the empiricist acquisition theory is immune to Fodor's critique.

Fodor rejects the notion that concepts might have nondefinitional structures (1981b:296–98; 1998:100ff.). On his view, a theory about the nature of concepts must explain how the contents of individual concepts contribute to the contents of the more complex mental states of which they are constituents. For, he thinks (e.g., 1975; 1990a; 1998:94–100), the only way to account for the productivity and systematicity of thought is by developing a combinatorial semantics for concepts. On a combinatorial view, the meaning or content of a complex thought is determined by the meanings of that thought's constituent concepts (and the ways they are put together). This, on Fodor's view, explains why thought is productive: the ability to think that Frank loves Minnie brings with it the ability to think that Minnie loves Frank because the very same concepts that are constituents of the former thought are also constituents of the latter. It also explains why thought seems to be systematic in the sense that a concept usually means the same thing no matter what context it occurs in. Whether I'm thinking that Frank loves Minnie or that Frank lives in Stoughton, Wisconsin, it's *Frank* that I'm thinking about, and this, Fodor argues, is again because the same concept—FRANK—is a constituent of both thoughts and contributes the very same content to each.[11] But if our semantics is combinatorial in this way, then our account of what concepts are must be able to explain how the contents of individual concepts manage to combine to bestow content on the complexes that contain them. It must explain, for instance, how the content of PLATYPUS contributes to the contents of more complex concepts like FEMALE PLATYPUS, and ultimately to the contents of whole thoughts like THERE'S A PLATYPUS IN MY BILLABONG. What's wrong with prototypes and stereotypes, on Fodor's view, is that conceptual contents, so construed, cannot play this explanatory role.

Fodor offers a number of reasons for thinking that prototypes and stereotypes are inappropriate vehicles for conceptual contents. His initial strategy was to argue that concepts' contents could not be prototypes because

---

11. An exception to this rule is idioms. The meaning of the thought that someone should fish or cut bait, for instance, is at best tangentially related to the meanings of its (ostensible) constituents, FISH, CUT, and BAIT.

complex concepts simply do not appear to have them: "there may be prototypical *grandmothers* . . . and there may be prototypical *properties of grandmothers*. . . . But there are surely no prototypical properties of, say, *Chaucer's grandmothers*, and there are no prototypical properties of *grandmothers most of whose grandchildren are married to dentists*" (1981b:297; emphasis in original). But, one might ask, even if no 'mental picture,' so to speak, of grandmothers-most-of-whose-grandchildren-are-married-to-dentists springs to mind, one can surely imagine how that concept might nonetheless have a prototype, that is, a set of associated 'typical features' derived from the prototypes of its constituents. Fodor's dentistic grandma might, for instance, get her tendency to have gray hair from the prototype of a grandmother and her tendency to find her grandsons- and granddaughters-in-law rather boring from the prototype of a dentist. And in fact, proposals abound in the concepts literature for how the prototypes of constituents may be combined to form prototypes for complexes.[12]

In *Concepts* (1998), however, Fodor stands his ground. He reiterates his claim that many complex concepts lack prototypes: "for indefinitely many 'Boolean' concepts, *there isn't any prototype*" (1998:101; emphasis in original). CAT, he allows, might have a prototype, but NOT A CAT doesn't. PINK and SQUARE may have prototypes, but PINK OR SQUARE does not. So whatever it is that concepts contribute to the meanings of complexes in which they occur, it couldn't be a prototype.

But suppose that one were to claim, contra Fodor, that Boolean concepts like PINK OR SQUARE *do* have prototypes. Perhaps, for instance, the prototype of PINK OR SQUARE might be the union (or intersection, or something) of the sets of features associated with PINK and SQUARE. Fodor responds by introducing what he calls the 'pet fish problem' (1998:102). A dog is a typical pet, and a trout (let's suppose) is a typical fish. Suppose we've constructed prototypes or stereotypes for PET and FISH that reflect this fact. (Lassie might be the stereotype for PET; SILVERISH, SCALY, GILLED, SWIMMING ANIMAL ABOUT A FOOT LONG might be the prototype for FISH). Now consider the complex concept PET FISH. As Fodor points out, a goldfish is a pretty typical pet fish. So construct a PET FISH prototype or stereotype to reflect this fact. *And now explain how the PET FISH prototype is constructed out of the FISH and PET prototypes.* The point is that you can't. The prototype of PET FISH (supposing there is one) is no kind (or at least no obvious kind) of construction out of the prototypes of that concept's constituents. So while prototype-combining might be made to work on a few well-chosen examples, it will

---

12. Osherson and Smith (1981, 1982); Smith and Osherson (1984); Smith (1980, 1988); Smith et al. (1988). See Zadrozny (1994) for a proof to the effect that *any* semantics is, trivially, encodable as a compositional semantics, hence that standard notions of compositionality, though intuitively clear, are in fact vacuous. He suggests replacing the notion of compositionality with that of systematicity, which places more substantive constraints on semantic theories and would thus be more useful in distinguishing among them.

not work in general. Or as Fodor puts it, "Prototypes aren't compositional. Conceptual contents, however, must be compositional. . . . So concepts aren't prototypes" (1998:105).

In chapter 6, I will defend the view that concepts have nondefinitional constituents, arguing that even though they play no direct role in a compositional semantics, prototypes (or something like them) should be regarded as part of concepts' content in that they help to secure concepts' references (which *do* play a role in semantics). For now, though, let us grant Fodor his third premise and look at his alternative picture(s) of how concepts are acquired. Originally, he argued as follows. If only internally structured concepts can be learned, and most concepts have neither definitional nor nondefinitional structure, then almost no concepts can be learned. Almost all our concepts must be innate. As I remarked above, Fodor now claims to have found a way to avoid nativism even while holding fast to the premises of his argument. This claim will be discussed in chapter 5. In the rest of this chapter, we will pause to examine his earlier view.

4.3 Radical Concept Nativism

Most concepts are innate.

One might have thought that a provocation like this would cause something of a commotion among philosophers of mind, psychologists, and cognitive scientists generally. But as a matter of fact, Fodor's startling conjecture has been almost completely ignored over the last twenty or so years. This is very puzzling. After all, it's not as if everyone believed him! Nor has there been any general lack of interest in the nativism issue, now or in the past, that would explain the deafening silence with which Fodor's proposals have been met. One suspects that the cognitive science community's avoidance of this issue derives partly from an ostrichlike hope that it will all just go away if only we ignore it hard enough, and partly from the suspicion that Fodor couldn't really be serious in claiming that all our ideas are innate. But serious he certainly is, and serious we should be too, for Fodor's nativism will not go away, however assiduously we might neglect it. Fodor argues that radical concept nativism follows ineluctably from views that are so widely subscribed to in cognitive science circles that they have the status, almost, of platitudes. Since it is far from obvious where, if anywhere, those arguments go astray, Fodor's nativism demands both our respect and our attention. Not only is his view an intrinsically intriguing position, with analogs (as I'll be arguing) in the writings of Leibniz and Descartes, but it presents a formidable challenge to standard computationalist assumptions, a challenge that cannot be simply brushed aside.

My aim in part II of this book, then, will be to un-neglect Fodor's nativism and give the 'mad dog' nativist's bone the kind of chewing over that it has long deserved. In this chapter, I will construct a more detailed account of the nativist picture that Fodor merely sketches in his (1981b). In chapter

5, I will explore its relation to the nativisms of the past. Then, in chapter 6, I will offer some actual arguments in support of doing what most of us apparently did instinctually—viz., rejecting it.

4.3.1 Triggering

One thing that Fodor clearly does not mean to imply, when claiming that most concepts are innate, is that experience is irrelevant to their acquisition. Such a view would be implausible for two reasons. First, as I stressed in §1.5, it is undeniable that both the world and our genetic endowment contribute to our acquisition of a mind, and it's undeniable too, as I argued in §3.3, that what concepts we acquire is dependent on the precise nature of our experience (and not merely on our having 'experience-in-general'). Second, Fodor holds that expressions in the language of thought have extensional semantic properties.[13] His commitment to a referential semantics for Mentalese gives him another motive for emphasizing the experiential contribution to concept acquisition. For arguably a person's genetic code exists 'inside her skin.' Yet, as Twin Earth fantasies show, what is inside a person's skin will not determine what her concepts refer to. Instead, reference is (partly) determined by the relations that that person bears to the external world. Exactly which kinds of relations with the world are needed to fix reference is a matter of considerable dispute among naturalistically inclined philosophers of mind, as is the question of what else (other than these relations' obtaining) may be required.[14] But if a person's concept WATER refers to water (partly) because she bears certain kinds of relations (such as, perhaps, causal relations) to that stuff, then the full explanation of how she acquires WATER must advert to facts about how she is embedded in the world. An explanation that talks only about what happens inside her skin will be at best a partial account of her acquisition of that concept.

In his (1981b), Fodor stresses that head–world interactions must be involved in acquisition, arguing that experience is "causally necessary and sufficient for the availability of all concepts" (1981b:273). Fodor calls the operation by which concepts are acquired through experience 'triggering,' and distinguishes it from learning as follows. Learning a concept is a matter of formulating and testing hypotheses about its content. Our experience in learning bears causally on acquisition to the extent that it confirms or disconfirms those hypotheses. Thus concept-learning is a "rational-causal" (1981b:273) process: the "ambient stimulation" that constitutes the causal input to acquisition "must provide inductive support for the concepts it occasions" (1981b:305).[15] On the Fodorean view, by contrast, acquisition

---

13. Fodor (1975:29–34), (1980), (1981a: part II), (1987), (1990a), (1994), (1997).
14. See Cummins (1989) for a survey of approaches to these questions.
15. I assume that Fodor means here that the stimulation provides inductive support not for the concept per se (how could a concept be inductively supported?) but, rather, for our hypotheses about the concept's meaning.

"requires no rational relation between a concept and its causes" (1981b: 305). In triggering,

> the structure of the sensorium is such that certain inputs trigger the availability of certain concepts. Punkt. Whereas in the case of [learning] there are . . . rational-causal processes: the psychological mechanisms which mediate the availability of such concepts realize an inductive logic, and the experiences of the organism stand in a confirmation relation to what is learned. (1981b:273)

So, on the picture outlined in "The Present Status," concepts are triggered, where triggering, unlike learning, embodies a nonrational, "brute-causal, i.e. 'merely' empirical" (198b1:280) head–world relation.

This sketch raises two related questions about the nature of the mechanism that, on Fodor's view, sustains concept acquisition. We are told that it is not a mechanism of learning, but to know this is to know little. In order to understand Fodor's nativism, we need to know in addition what he means when he calls the trigger–concept relation 'brute- causal' and what is it about a person's initial state or structure that enables her to acquire concepts given only the 'brute' interactions with the world that triggering supplies. The 'brute-causality' of the acquisition process will be discussed in §§4.4 and 4.5. For the present, let's concentrate on the second of these questions.

In asking about the nature of the inborn structures or states in us that triggering stimuli trigger, we are asking for an account of how we have to be, such that a brute-causal interaction with the world could suffice to give us a concept. According to Fodor, one acquires a concept when one gets "nomologically locked to the property that the concept expresses" (1998: 125); "having a concept," he says, "is something like 'resonating to' the property that the concept expresses" (1998:137). And you're a detector for F-ness, on his view, if it's a law that *being an F* causes tokenings of "F!" in minds like yours. So acquiring PLATYPUS, for instance, is a matter of getting nomologically locked to *being a platypus*. You get locked to that property when you become a 'platypus-detector,' that is, when certain states of you come to carry information about platypuses. Your states carry information about platypuses if, as a matter of nomological fact, you'd go into those sorts of states (call them PLATYPUS! states) when (and ideally only when) you come into causal contact with instantiations of platypus-hood.[16] So you are locked to *being a platypus* if your tokenings of PLATYPUS! carry information about platypuses, and your tokenings of PLATYPUS! carry information about platypuses if (1) it's a law that platypuses cause tokenings of PLATYPUS! (in minds of such and such sorts) and (2) your mind is a mind of that sort.[17]

16. The bells and whistles Fodor adds (1990a:122ff) to this account in response to the "Disjunction Problem"—the problem that you get when you token PLATYPUS! as a result of nonplatypus experiences—need not detain us here. But see §6.3.

17. See (1990a:121–22) for a summary of Fodor's information-theoretic account of conceptual content; see his (1990a:51–136) for a more extended discussion of

Given this account of concept possession, our question now becomes, "What properties do we need to attribute to the mind, such that experience of a triggering stimulus will cause it to lock to a particular property?" Implicit in Fodor's (1981b) are two quite different ways of approaching this issue. Sometimes he speaks of an innately specified 'function' from stimuli onto concepts (a function embodied in what he calls the 'sensorium'). This suggests that he is thinking of the organismic contribution as some kind of genetically determined mechanism, a psychological device of some sort that, once triggered by an appropriate stimulus, yields concepts as output. Other times, though, Fodor talks of concepts' becoming 'available,' as if acquisition were the activation by a triggering stimulus of some sort of preexisting, conceptlike object. We come into the world equipped with a stock of 'protoconcepts,' mental structures of some sort that become fully fledged concepts once they are triggered by an appropriate stimulus.

In the next section, I'll argue that this latter picture is seriously confused. For there's simply nothing for protoconcepts to *be*. My view is that the organismic contribution to concept acquisition can be investigated only if it is conceived in mechanistic terms. Concept acquisition is a process, not an event, and even a nativist account of it must provide a theory about the mechanisms that sustain it. I will pursue this project in §4.5.

4.4 Protoconcepts

What are protoconcepts? What properties would they need to have, such that an experience would vitalize them and force them from cognitive inertia into glorious mental activity? What could they be?

An obvious place to start looking for an answer to this query is the computer model for the mind, long championed by Fodor and by now perhaps the dominant source of metaphors, both within science and in the popular imagination, for the mind and its activities. On this view, the human mind is to be compared to a computer. Thoughts are held to be relations to symbols encoded in the machine; thinking is held to be computation, that is, the rule-governed manipulation of these symbols. The advantage of this picture, according to its proponents, is that it enables us to see how thoughts can be both contentful and causal: their contents derive from the contents of the symbols that realize them; and they enter into causal relations in virtue of those symbols' 'formal' or 'syntactic' properties.[18] So perhaps we should

concept possession in particular. It is with some trepidation that I rely on these recent pronouncements in a discussion of Fodor's earlier views, but judging from the (very few) indications he offers in his (1981b) as to the requirements for possessing a concept, I believe that his view there differs little enough from his current picture to justify the anachronism.

18. See, e.g., Fodor (1975, 1981a). See Devitt (1990) for a helpful attempt to disentangle the various claims implicit in the computer metaphor.

think of protoconcepts as being mental symbols with syntactic properties but no semantic properties. Protoconcepts are strings of our 'machine code,' differentiated from each other by virtue of their syntax or 'shape' but acquiring semantic properties only when they are triggered by experience.

It's hard to talk about this proposal, given the convention in the literature of using the same label (e.g., 'PLATYPUS') for mental representations under both semantic and syntactic description. Normally, the fact that we use 'PLATYPUS' to refer indiscriminately to a certain semantic type (the concept PLATYPUS) and a certain syntactic type (mental object with the 'shape' PLATYPUS) doesn't matter much. In this case, however, the ambiguity gets confusing. Accordingly, let me introduce the following terminology: 'PLATYPUS' refers to the semantic type *concept of a platypus* (and to tokens of that type). 'PLATYPUS' refers to mental objects of the syntactic type (whatever it is, maybe a certain pattern of neural activity) that PLATYPUS tokens belong to (and to tokens of that syntactic type). Then the current proposal is that we acquire PLATYPUS when the protoconcept **PLATYPUS** is triggered by an experience (of, as it might be, a platypus). You have innately the ability to token **PLATYPUS**es (those syntactic objects), and that somehow turns into the ability to token PLATYPUSes (the same syntactic objects but now with a semantic interpretation) once you experience, say, a platypus.

I find this suggestion immensely puzzling. On the view we are considering, protoconcepts are supposed to be innately specified. Are we then to think of ourselves as being born with minds containing, literally, a bunch of uninterpreted symbols just waiting for experience to glue an interpretation onto them? Surely not. Think of a Turing machine. The present suggestion is that each protoconcept can be identified with a string of symbols on the machine's tape. Initially uninterpreted, these strings get glued onto their referents by triggering: **PLATYPUS** is glued onto platypuses; **POSSUM** is glued onto possums; **EMU**, perhaps, is never triggered at all, and so on. But this can't be right. It seems implausible to think that the mind at birth has all these uninterpreted symbols actually stored on its 'tape,' that is, in memory. Yet if we attribute to it instead a mere disposition to token **PLATYPUS**es under appropriate circumstances, then it's hard to see how we've said anything of substance about concept acquisition. For on this reading, a protoconcept is simply the output, under syntactic description, of the mechanism (whatever it is) that results in our acquiring a concept given the appropriate kinds of experiences. And the problem is that everyone, including the empiricist, can agree we have innate protoconcepts in this weak sense. That there are internal mechanisms responsible for concept acquisition, and that acquisition results in the production of a syntactically describable entity (that is, a concept), are hardly the points at issue. What needs explaining is what these mechanisms are. An acquisition theory should tell us *how* experience turns syntactic objects—**PLATYPUS**es—into fully fledged intentional objects—PLATYPUSes. *That* this happens is hardly news.

Perhaps, then, we should abandon the attempt to view protoconcepts syntactically, and try for a more intentional characterization. Perhaps we could view them not as uninterpreted Mentalese symbols but as concepts' 'narrow contents.' Unlike 'wide' semantic properties, such as truth or reference, narrow contents supervene on what is 'inside the skin' of the thinker, and as such have been argued by Fodor and others to be indispensable to the provision of psychological explanations of behavior.[19] On this picture, a protoconcept is a conceptlike entity possessing a narrow content but lacking in wide semantic properties like reference. Triggering, then, would supply the external context required for the determination of concepts' wide semantic properties.

On some views, the narrow content of a concept is its conceptual (or functional) role, that is, its causal and/or inferential relations to sensory inputs, other concepts, and behavioral outputs.[20] Conceptual roles, however, clearly cannot do duty as Fodorean protoconcepts. On the one hand, protoconcepts cannot be conceptual roles understood as concepts' *actual* causal/inferential relations within the mind: what relations could concepts we don't have enter into? But nor, on the other hand, can protoconcepts be conceptual roles understood dispositionally as networks of *potential* causal/inferential interactions. For protoconcepts are supposed to be innately specified, whereas the dispositions that our concepts have to interact causally or inferentially with other mental items or behaviors are not. I was not born such that my tokenings of PLATYPUS are disposed to cause tokenings of MONOTREME or ENDANGERED, or utterances of 'platypus.' On the contrary, I learned that platypuses are endangered, that they are monotremes, and that 'platypus' is the word that I, as an English speaker, should use to express my platypus beliefs: most (maybe all) of the causal/inferential dispositions my concepts have, have been fixed by my experiences. If protoconcepts are innately specified, therefore, they cannot be concepts' dispositions to enter into relations within the mind, for those dispositions are not innately specified. Protoconcepts cannot be narrow contents qua conceptual roles.

Fodor himself has always resisted the notion that narrow contents are conceptual roles, and hence would accept the conclusion just reached as to the futility of identifying protoconcepts with them.[21] On his view, narrow

19. In, e.g., his (1980), Fodor argues that the causes of behavior must supervene on what is inside the skin. Hence wide contents, being partly determined by relations with the world, are unfitted to explain behavior. Narrow contents, being by definition supervenient on intracorporeal facts, are by contrast explanatorily appropriate. See also Loar (1981) and Fodor (1991b). See, however, Fodor (1994:27–54), in which he proposes that we abandon narrow content-based psychological explanations in favor of accounts in terms of broad contents and 'modes of presentation.'

20. See Loar (1982); McGinn (1982); Block (1986). In speaking of 'causal and/or inferential relations,' I aim not to take any stand on which functional relations, exactly, constitute concepts' conceptual roles.

21. Fodor rejects conceptual role theories of narrow content because (1) he abhors meaning holism (the view that all of a concept's relations with other concepts and so on are essential to its semantic identity) and (2) he believes that allowing any amount of conceptual role to count toward the narrow content of a concept inevitably leads to holism. For his critique of holism, see Fodor (1987: ch. 2) and Fodor and Lepore (1991). See

contents are merely functions (in the mathematical sense) from contexts onto referents.[22] Thus, if Fodorean protoconcepts are to be identified with narrow contents, it is to these functions that we should look. Suppose, then, that proto-PLATYPUS is a function specifying that PLATYPUS refers to platypuses on Earth, to Martian robots on Twin Earth, and to echidnas (why not?) elsewhere. But if protoconcepts are merely functions from contexts onto referents, then to say that acquisition occurs when experience triggers them is merely to say that the organism instantiates a function such that when experience supplies a context, a reference is determined. (That is, to say that a certain experience triggers proto-PLATYPUS and yields PLATYPUS as a result is to say merely that the organism instantiates a function such that in this particular experiential context, that organism acquires PLATYPUS.) So now the claim that protoconcepts are triggered by experience boils down to the claim that you get certain concepts when you have certain kinds of experiences; and the Fodorean claim that protoconcepts are innate boils down to the claim that our minds are inherently structured such that this is the case. Again, this is hardly news. Appealing to protoconcepts in this sense redescribes, rather than explains, the phenomena that we need an acquisition theory to account for.

In sum, talk of innate protoconcepts doesn't help us much in our quest to understand what the organism contributes to concept acquisition, for it's unclear what protoconcepts could be. They're not plausibly cashed out as uninterpreted Mentalese symbols, whether actually stored in memory or construed as dispositions. Nor can we identify them with narrow contents. If narrow contents are conceptual roles, they couldn't be innate. And if narrow contents are functions from contexts to referents, then they're useless for our purposes. What we were asking is, What property or properties do we need to attribute to the organism such that its interaction with a triggering stimulus suffices for it to acquire a concept like PLATYPUS? Being told that the property in question is that of instantiating a function such that under those circumstances the concept it acquires is one that refers to platypuses is unenlightening. We already know that we instantiate this function. What we *don't* know, and what we need an acquisition theory to tell us, is how this comes about. Talk of protoconcepts is of no help in this connection.

4.5 'Brute-Causal' Mechanisms

The arguments of the preceding section suggest that it is a mistake to conceive concept acquisition as the animation, by experience, of some preexist-

Devitt (1993a, 1996) for arguments in support of allowing a modest amount of conceptual role to be constitutive of narrow contents.

22. At least this was his view prior to (1994)—see note 19. According to it, a narrow content is a function that yields a reference as value, given a context as argument. See Loewer and Rey (1991:xxix). As they note, a similar view to that which Fodor espoused is defended in White (1982).

ing mental object. Concept acquisition is a process, and in order to understand it, we need a theory of it viewed as such. Just as a vending machine is constituted such that putting seventy-five cents in the coin slot causes it to deliver a can of soda, so we are constituted such that certain kinds of stimulation will cause us to acquire certain concepts. The organismic contribution to concept acquisition is not a protoconcept but some sort of causal mechanism that, given appropriate inputs, will deliver concepts as output.

Since this kind of picture is hardly proprietary to the nativist (§1.3), we need to know in more detail what Fodor's proposed acquisition mechanism is like. In exploring this issue, we are subject to a constraint: if Fodor's radical concept nativism is to be a real alternative to empiricism, it must be clear that the acquisition mechanism he proposes is substantially different from its rival, and different, moreover, in a quite specific way. As we saw above (§4.3), Fodor claims that his view is distinguished from empiricism in virtue of the fact that while the empiricist views the processes responsible for concept acquisition as being 'rational-causal,' the nativist sees them as being 'brute-causal.' Indeed, barely a page of his (1981b) goes by without Fodor's emphasizing the 'bruteness' and 'nonrationality' of the causal transactions involved in concept acquisition. So, although it's not yet clear in what sense, exactly, the nativist takes acquiring concepts to be brutely causal, our account of his position should reveal concept acquisition to be in some reasonable sense a process of this sort.

One can try to infer the nature of the Fodorean concept-forming mechanism by looking at the inputs to and outputs of it. Given an account of the inputs and outputs, we can then attempt to describe the processes mediating them. The output, obviously, is concepts. What are the inputs to the mechanism? Here, things are much less clear. As we have seen, Fodor distinguishes himself from the empiricist by stressing the 'nonrationality' of the relation between concepts and their triggers. The empiricist holds that the causally efficacious properties of the inputs are those in virtue of which they confirm or disconfirm our semantic hypotheses. Thus the input–output relations in acquisition, on her view, make a certain kind of sense: there's an epistemic explanation of why it's experiences of platypuses that cause acquisition of PLATYPUS. On Fodor's view, by contrast, there is no such reason why a particular stimulus triggers a particular concept. For the cause–concept relation is "brute-causal" (1981b:280): experience causes concepts *without* inductively supporting any semantic hypotheses.

But there are lots of brute (or nonrational) kinds of causal relations. Which of them is relevant to concept acquisition? Fodor explains that

> the normal relation between lexical concepts and their occasioning experiences is brute-causal, i.e. "merely" empirical. . . . [T]he ethological precedents from other species suggest that such relations may often be extremely arbitrary. There are fledgling ducks for which the operative rule seems to be: if it moves, it's mother. The fact that this experience triggers this concept is surely to be understood on a Darwinian model and not on

the model of concept learning. In particular, the observation that the stimulus moves is surely not functioning as data confirmatory of some universal duckish hypothesis about the internal structure of MOTHERHOOD. The point is that the Nativist view allows for any amount of this sort of arbitrariness that you like. (1981b:280)

Thus, it seems, the Fodorean relation between concept and cause is nonrational or brute-causal in the sense of being arbitrary.

Not, of course, wholly arbitrary. Fodor's claim, as is implicit in his analogy with imprinting, is not that the inputs to the concept-forming mechanism are random, or inexplicable, or undetermined. That movement triggers imprinting and that it's imprinting that movement triggers are none of these things. For there is (as Fodor suggests in the passage displayed above) a plausible evolutionary explanation of why this regularity should exist. Imprinting, presumably, is triggered by movement because movement was a reliable enough indicator of motherhood in the ancestral duck environment for ducklings who imprinted on moving things to imprint, mostly, on their mothers. And presumably it's imprinting that movement triggers because ducklings who imprinted on their mothers were more apt to survive, reproduce, and pass their 'genes for imprinting' to their offspring. Given that ducks evolved, in short, we can understand why imprinting should be under the control of movement, and the input–output relation in this case is not arbitrary in any very strong sense.

But the movement–imprinting connection is arbitrary in at least two other senses that are more germane to Fodor's concerns. First, it is arbitrary *under intentional description* (to borrow terminology from Fodor 1998). Because the empiricist sees an epistemic connection as holding between concepts and their causes, cause–concept relations, described intentionally, on her view make a certain kind of sense. That is, she finds it perfectly obvious why experiences *of emus* should be causally implicated in the acquisition of concepts *of emus*: it's because the experiences that lead to acquisition of EMU must provide evidence for or against the learner's hypotheses about what EMU means. But that an experience *of movement* should cause a concept *of mother*—well, what could be odder, or make less sense, than that? Unlike the emu–EMU connection, there is no (so to speak) intentional integrity about the movement–MOTHER relation. The duckling's experiences of moving things are not "functioning as data confirmatory of some universal duckish hypothesis about the internal structure of MOTHERHOOD" (Fodor 1981b: 280), so there is no intentional-level rationale for the fact that those experiences cause that concept. The causal mechanism underpinning imprinting, then, is arbitrary in the special sense of being intentionally uninterpretable. It is also (and this is a second kind of arbitrariness that the Fodorean might emphasize) historically quite contingent. There are rarely unique solutions to evolutionary design problems, so although de facto it was movement that was recruited by Mother Nature as the cause of imprinting, other properties could have been recruited as triggers for imprinting instead. Natural selection will favor more or less any (heritable) mechanism that tends to enhance fitness. So it's just an accident, contingent on what duckish psychologies happened to be around for selection to act upon, that it was movement (not, say, duck-billedness) that was recruited as imprinting's trigger.

So the cause–effect relation in imprinting is arbitrary in two (related) ways: it is intentionally opaque and it is historically contingent. Similarly, Fodor suggests by his analogy, in the case of us and our concepts. The relations between the inputs to and outputs of the acquisition mechanism, just like the movement–imprinting relation, are arbitrary *sub specie aeternitatis*. If emus do cause acquisition of EMU (and on this view it would seem quite possible that they might not), this fact is just an evolutionary accident, an artifact of the way we were built. Many properties other than those that were actually recruited as triggers for EMU could have been selected instead. That the emu–EMU relation appears to make intentional sense, then, is just an unlucky (because misleading) accident. There is really nothing deep about it, any more than there's anything deep about the movement–MOTHER relation. Both relations, on the Fodorean view, get the same, nonintentional explanation: they exist as they do solely in virtue of brute, 'engineering' facts—facts about the ways we happen to be made.[23]

4.6 Concept Acquisition, Fodor-Style

Let me summarize the picture of acquisition that is emerging here. According to the Fodorean nativist, concept acquisition is subserved by a brute-causal mechanism, where 'brute-causal' means 'not rational-causal', and this, in turn, means that the mechanism embodies an input–output relation that is (1) intentionally opaque and (2) historically contingent. These last two points reveal one central difference between Fodor's story and that of an empiricist. Whereas the empiricist thinks that emu experiences cause the acquisition of EMU because those experiences confirm our hypotheses about what EMU applies to, the nativist gives an explanation in terms of natural selection: emu experiences cause EMU and platypus experiences cause PLATYPUS just because we evolved that way. There's also a second crucial difference between Fodor's story and the empiricist's, this one turning on the kind of processing that goes on when experiences cause concepts. Fodor claims that our experiences are sufficient to occasion acquisition of concepts: "triggering of the sensorium is, normally, causally necessary and sufficient for the availability of all concepts" (1981b:273). The empiricist, by contrast, thinks that though emu experiences might be necessary to acquiring EMU, they're not sufficient. For on the empiricist view, something else is causally implicated in our acquisition of that concept, namely, our formulation and evaluation of hypotheses about its meaning. To put the contrast bluntly but not, I think, inaccurately: Fodor (1981b) thinks that Mother Nature and the

---

23. Thanks to Kim Sterelny for helpful discussions of the arguments in this section.

world do all the causal work in concept acquisition. The empiricist, by contrast, thinks that *we have to do some work as well.* Nature and the world contribute to acquisition, but something else is needed too, namely, our formulation and test of semantic hypotheses.

On this reading, there is a substantive difference between Fodor's theory and the empiricist's. Moreover, it's a difference that makes sense of Fodor's claim that he views acquisition as a 'brute-causal' rather than a 'rational-causal' process. For Fodor, once we're wired up by evolution, experience is causally sufficient for acquisition. For the empiricist, by contrast, it is only experience *together with a bunch of other psychological processing* that suffices for acquisition to occur. This other psychological processing is what gives rise to the 'rational' element in the causal story told by the empiricist, and it is the existence of this element that Fodor, I think, wants to deny.

The adequacy of the Fodorean picture of concept acquisition will be examined in chapter 6. In the next chapter, we will look at Fodor's recent claim to have found a way to avoid this sort of radical nativism while nonetheless retaining his critique of empiricism.

5

The Constitution Hypothesis

"Then you should say what you mean," the March Hare went on.
"I do," Alice hastily replied; "At least—at least I mean what I say—that's
the same thing, you know."
"Not the same thing a bit!" said the Hatter.
                    Lewis Carroll, *Alice's Adventures in Wonderland*

In the last chapter, we surveyed Fodor's arguments against empiricist accounts of concept acquisition and looked at his earliest attempts to fill the
explanatory lacuna left by empiricism's ostensible demise. The empiricist,
according to Fodor, is committed to the view that acquiring a concept is a
matter of formulating and testing hypotheses about what it means (or what
its content is). This, he argued, is impossible, because concepts are internally
unstructured, that is, they simply don't have the kinds of meanings about
which hypotheses can be formulated. If, in light of this, the empiricist per-
versely clings to her insistence that acquisition involves learning, then her
theory is self-defeating: paradoxically, if empiricism is right, a person could
learn the concept of an F only if she already had the concept F-NESS.

In his (1975) and (1981b), Fodor concluded from the falsity of empiricism
that nativism must be true: if most concepts are unlearned, then most concepts must be innate. He made it clear that in claiming this, he was not
denying the role experience plays in concept acquisition. On the contrary,
he stressed repeatedly in his (1981b) that experience is necessary for acquisition to occur, and envisaged (or at least seemed to allow as possible) two
different acquisition models. On one of these models, experience serves to
trigger innate protoconcepts, transforming preexisting mental objects or
structures of some sort into fully fledged intentional objects. I argued that
this way of elaborating the nativist view is unhelpful. However we tried to
elucidate the notion of a protoconcept (and we tried several ways), the as-

sertion that protoconcepts are triggered by experience boils down to the observation, with which no one would disagree, that there's something about our minds such that our experiences lead to our getting concepts. A better model, I urged, is one that sees experience as triggering some kind of inner mechanism, the idea being that we are 'wired up' to get certain concepts, given certain experiences, just as a duckling is 'wired up' to imprint on the first moving thing it sees. Fodor distinguished his mechanism from an empiricist one by stressing that it is a 'brute-causal' device: it involves no 'rational-causal' processing, such as hypothesis-testing. But this, as we will see below, has an undesirable empirical consequence. What that consequence is, and how it gives rise to what Fodor (1998) calls 'The Doorknob/DOOR-KNOB' problem, will be introduced in §5.1. Fodor's proposed solution to this problem, and its relation to both his earlier nativism and the radical nativisms of Leibniz and Descartes, will be discussed in the rest of this chapter.

5.1 The Doorknob/DOORKNOB Problem

On the triggering model, as explained in Fodor (1981b), the relations between experiences and the concepts they occasion are historically contingent and intentionally arbitrary. There is, however, a serious problem with this picture. Discussed at length by Fodor (1998:127ff.), although in fact first raised by Sterelny (1989), the problem is this: If any amount of intentional arbitrariness in the cause–concept relation is indeed possible, why do we see so little of it? If acquisition is like imprinting, that's to say, why are the relations between concepts and their causes typically *not* arbitrary under intentional description? Why is it experiences *of emus* that cause EMU, and experiences *of mothers* that cause MOTHER, and experiences *of doorknobs* that cause DOORKNOB? Fodor (1997:85) calls this the 'doorknob/DOORKNOB problem.' If in principle any old thing could have been recruited as the trigger for the concept F-NESS, why is it usually Fs that as a matter of empirical fact do the trick?

The empiricist, as we've seen, has an explanation of why it's typically emu experiences that lead to acquisition of EMU: experiences of emus are what (dis)confirm our hypotheses about what EMU means. The nativist, by contrast, can apparently appeal in this context only to natural selection. If emus cause EMU because of how we happen to be built, and if we're built how we are because of natural selection, then surely it's to our evolutionary history that we should look for an explanation of the emu–EMU regularity, and of the doorknob/DOORKNOB effect in general. Fodor (1998) argues, however, as did Sterelny (1989), that natural selection does not explain this regularity. On the contrary, and as we saw in discussing imprinting (§4.3), it seems to predict quite the opposite. It predicts that the cause–concept relation, like the movement–imprinting relation, will be arbitrary.

Or does it? There is a way, actually, that the doorknob/DOORKNOB effect might be biologically explicable. As Fodor (1998:128ff.) explains, natural selection presumably brought about the existing relations between experiences and concepts by designing some kind of mechanism that mediates that relation. (Compare: the Coca-Cola Company brings about the seventy-five-cent–Coke relation by designing a mechanism that gives you a Coke when and only when you give it the money.) So, it would seem, natural selection could perfectly well have brought about the emu–EMU, mother–MOTHER, and doorknob–DOORKNOB relations by designing a mechanism that sustains them. A mechanism like, for instance, inductive learning. If Mother Nature designed us so that our concepts get caused by experiences that confirm hypotheses about what they mean, then natural selection *can* explain the intentional non-arbitrariness of concepts and their causes. Which would be fine, were it not for the fact that on Fodor's view there are independent reasons for thinking that concept acquisition could not involve inductive learning.

The Fodorean thus faces a dilemma: if concept acquisition is like imprinting (that is, if it's mediated by a brute-causal, evolved mechanism whose input/output relations need 'make no sense' under intentional description), then the relations between concepts and what cause them should, be arbitrary. But they're not. That's the first horn. And if it is claimed that natural selection evolved a mechanism that accounts for the existence of the many annoying intentional regularities in this domain, then that mechanism could only be something like an inductive learning mechanism. But, as Fodor's arguments as to the impossibility of inductive concept-learning indicate, it's not. And that's the second horn. As Fodor expresses it:

> If concept acquisition isn't inductive, then *how* does Mother Nature contrive to ensure that it *is* instances of F-*ness* (and not of G-*ness*) that trigger the concept F in the course of ontogeny? After all, if Mother N wants to select for the doorknob/DOORKNOB type of relation between concepts and their experiential causes, she has to do so by selecting *a mechanism that produces* that relation between one's concepts and their causes. . . . The obvious candidate to select if one wants to ensure that concept acquisition exhibits the d/D relation is inductive learning. But we have it on independent grounds that primitive concepts can't be learned inductively. There may be a way a conceptual atomist to get out of this dilemma, but waving his hands around about Darwin certainly isn't it. (1998:129)

5.2 The Constitution Hypothesis

In chapter 6, I'll argue that this dilemma is a false one. Inductive learning is involved in concept acquisition, but since what is learned is (1) nondefinitional and (2) not the sort of thing we should expect to play a role in a compositional semantics, the inductive learning hypothesis runs afoul of neither Fodor's arguments against definitions (§4.1) nor his arguments against prototypes and the like (§4.2). But explaining how Fodor's dilemma can be dehorned is a long story. Before we begin it, let's look at how he himself proposes to deal with this difficulty.

Fodor sets up the problem as follows. The empiricist apparently can explain the link between experiences of Fs and acquisition of F-NESS because her "model takes the *content* relation between a concept and the experience it's acquired from to be a special case of the *evidential* relation between a generalization and its confirming instances" (1998:132). But this won't do for Fodor because, he thinks, the empiricist's theory is incoherent. And a Darwinian explanation of the link won't do either, for a Darwinian story rides piggyback on an empiricist one: the only conceivable way that Mother Nature could have brought about the situation that it is usually F-experiences that cause acquisition of F-NESS, is by giving us an inductive learning mechanism of the very sort we've just rejected. Is the ubiquity of the doorknob/DOORKNOB effect just a cosmic coincidence, then? Fodor thinks (rightly, in my view) that it can't be. So he needs an account of the cause–concept relation that, on the one hand, explains why that relation is intentionally nonarbitrary (that is, why it is experiences of Fs, not Gs, that cause acquisition of the concept of an F) while, on the other hand, making no appeal to inductive learning as an account of how this relation came to be so constrained.

What I shall call Fodor's 'Constitution Hypothesis' is intended to provide the required story. On this view, large chunks of the world are constituted by us (in a manner to be explained), and it is this metaphysical fact, according to Fodor, that explains the doorknob/DOORKNOB effect. The fact that experiences of Fs cause acquisition of F-NESS is the consequence of a "*metaphysical* truth about how concepts are constituted, rather than an empirical truth about how concepts are acquired" (1998:133). For "what it is to be a doorknob isn't *evidenced* by the kind of experience that leads to acquiring the concept; [instead] what it is to be a doorknob is *constituted* by the kind of experience that leads to acquiring the concept DOORKNOB" (1998:134). The point being that if being a doorknob *just is* being the kind of thing that causes us to acquire DOORKNOB, then the doorknob/DOORKNOB relation is metaphysically necessary, hence unsurprising.

That doorknobs (and, by implication, a plethora of other things) are mind-dependent in this way is urged by Fodor to be independently plausible. "Look," he says, "there is presumably something about doorknobs that makes them doorknobs, and either it's something complex or it's something simple" (1998:134–35). If what makes a doorknob a doorknob is a complex property (or cluster of properties), then we should be able to figure out what that complex of properties is—either through analysis of 'doorknob' or by doing doorknob science. But 'doorknob' is unanalyzable and "there's nothing for a science of doorknobs to find out" (1998:135). So, he continues, what makes a doorknob a doorknob must be something simple: *being a doorknob* must be a primitive property (though obviously not a *metaphysically* primitive property—doorknobhood is clearly not on an ontological par with fundamental properties like spin or charge!). But "[h]ow could 'doorknob' be undefinable . . . and lack a hidden essence . . . without being metaphysically primitive . . . ?" (1998:135) Fodor's answer is that " 'doorknob' works like 'red.' " (1998:135) "[W]hether a thing is a doorknob is constituted by facts about whether we (do or would) take it to be a doorknob; just as whether something is red is maybe constituted by facts about whether it looks red to us" (1998:141). On his view, doorknobhood is an appearance property. It's "a property that's *constituted* by how things strike us" (1998:136, emphasis Fodor's). In particular, "what makes something a doorknob is just: being the kind of thing from experience with which our kind of mind readily acquires the concept DOORKNOB" (1998:137), where acquiring the concept DOORKNOB, recall, is a matter of getting 'nomologically locked to' or 'becoming a detector for' doorknobhood (§4.3).

Fodor's idea, then, is that by putting the 'secondary quality' account of doorknobhood together with his information-theoretic account of what it is to have a concept, he can solve the doorknob/DOORKNOB problem without appealing either to evolution or to an empiricist-style inductive learning device:

> [if you put it all together] then you get: *being a doorknob* is having that property that minds like ours come to resonate to in consequence of relevant experience with stereotypic doorknobs. That, and *not* being learned inductively, is what explains the content relation between DOORKNOB and the kinds of experience that typically mediates [sic] its acquisition. (1998: 137)

Indeed, the Constitution Hypothesis is more powerful even than this. For "[i]t also explains how *doorknobhood* could seem to be undefinable and unanalyzable without being metaphysically ultimate. And it also explains how DOORKNOB could be both psychologically primitive and not innate" (1998:137).

In short, Fodor's claims in his (1998) are (1) that many of the properties of which we have concepts are mind-dependent (in the same way as *being a doorknob* allegedly is); (2) that the mind dependence of these properties explains why it is typically experiences of instances of the property (not experiences of other sorts) that occasion acquisition of concepts that express that property; and (3) that the mind dependence of these properties also explains how our concepts of them could be unanalyzable (hence unlearnable) without being innate. In §5.3, I'll examine the second and third of these claims, arguing that the kinds of metaphysical maneuvers represented by the Constitution Hypothesis can do neither of these things. In the rest of this section, I will briefly look at the dispositional account of doorknobhood itself. Although my arguments later won't turn on the truth or falsity of that account, I nonetheless want to indicate in a preliminary way the sorts of problems that it faces, independently of what explanatory work it can or cannot be made to do in the philosophy of psychology.

5.2.1 Metaphysical Excursion: Doorknobs and
DOORKNOB Dispositions

Dispositionalism about doorknobhood inherits all the ills that dispositionalism about everything else is heir to. One common complaint about dispositional analyses of colors, for instance, concerns the air of circularity that
pervades them. If something's being red is defined as its causing us to have
certain sorts of experiences, it is natural to ask "What sorts of experiences?"
and it's tempting to answer "Reddish experiences" or "Experiences (as) of
redness." But if we can say nothing about what reddish experiences or experiences 'as of' redness are, other than that they're experiences of the sort
typically caused by red things, then the analysis is circular. Another common
(and not unrelated) allegation against dispositional accounts of colors is that
their explanatory arrows go in the wrong directions. The dispositionalist
says that a thing has the property redness because it has certain characteristic
effects on our minds (it leads to experiences as of redness). On the contrary,
the critic says, things have the characteristic effects that they do on our
minds (they lead to experiences as of redness) *because they are red.* Their
being red explains why some things cause us to sense redly, and not vice
versa.

Analogous worries can be raised against Fodor's dispositional account of
doorknobhood. He wants to say that x is a doorknob in virtue of its having
certain characteristic effects on us. But, one might object, surely those things
have the effects they do on us *because they are doorknobs.* In which case,
the effects don't explain what it is to be a doorknob; instead, *being a doorknob* is what explains the effects. Like dispositional accounts of redness,
Fodor's account might be thought to get the explanatory relations between
our mental states and the properties that cause them back-to-front. It could
also be accused of circularity. Fodor says that *being a doorknob* is a matter
of having certain sorts of effects on us. So, one might ask, what effects,
exactly, are those? As in the case of redness, a dispositional account of
doorknobhood will be vacuous in the absence of some way of specifying the
effects doorknobs have on us that is independent of their being effects *of
doorknobs.*

Fodor adds an epicycle to his analysis that is designed to evade these sorts
of objections. Strictly speaking, on his view, it's not that doorknobs give rise
to the kinds of mental states that *doorknobs* cause. Instead, doorknobs give
rise to the kinds of mental states that *things that satisfy the doorknob stereotype* cause. The doorknob stereotype (or prototype) is a specification of
properties that doorknobs typically have.[1] Perhaps a stereotypical doorknob
is a movable protuberance attached to a door at about waist level. Then the

---

1. Fodor uses 'stereotype' in his (1998) discussion of the doorknob/DOORKNOB problem to mean what is usually meant by 'prototype,' that is, not in the sense of 'exemplar'
but in the sense of 'cluster of typical properties.' I'll follow his usage, as nothing much
turns on it, but the reader should keep this change in mind.

claim would be that being a doorknob is being the kind of thing that has the same effects on our minds as do movable protuberances attached to a door at about waist level. Since this specification of the effects that door-knobs have on our minds appeals not to the property *being a doorknob* but, rather, to the property *being a movable protuberance attached to a door at about waist level*, the charge of circularity is apparently avoided. So while

> maybe this kind of objection shows that an account of *being red* mustn't presuppose the property of *looking red* . . . no parallel argument could show that an account of *being a doorknob* mustn't presuppose the prop-erty of *satisfying the doorknob stereotype*. The conditions for satisfying the latter are patently specifiable without reference to the former, viz by enumerating the shapes, colors, functions and the like that doorknobs typically have. (1998:138)

Running the analysis through the doorknob stereotype seems also to al-low Fodor to avoid the objection that his account gets the explanatory re-lations between us and doorknobs backward. That objection seeks to present the dispositionalist with two, mutually exclusive, explanatory strategies: on pain of circularity, he must choose between his own explanation of a thing's being an F in terms of its having certain effects on us, and the person in the street's explanation of a thing's having those effects on us in terms of its being F. Fodor's choices, however, are not mutually exclusive in this way. He explains a thing's being a doorknob in terms of its causing certain effects in us; and he explains those effects in terms of the thing's satisfying the doorknob stereotype. No obvious circularity attaches to the conjunction of these explanations, so Fodor seems to be immune from this type of criticism.

I suspect, though, that these problems remain despite Fodor's detour through stereotypical doorknobs. While it may be plausible to claim that it's because doorknobs satisfy the doorknob stereotype that they have the effects they do on us, suppose we now inquire, "What effects *do* things satisfying the doorknob stereotype have on us?" Fodor's answer, as we've seen, is that things satisfying the doorknob stereotype typically cause acquisition of the concept DOORKNOB. Now it is true, as Fodor emphasizes, that it appears entirely contingent—surprising, even—that one should get the concept DOORKNOB from experiences of waist-high, movable protuberances attached to doors.[2] There is nothing objectionable about the claim that experiences of things that satisfy the doorknob stereotype cause us to acquire DOORKNOB (or to lock to *being a doorknob*—remember that for Fodor, acquiring a concept just is 'locking to' the property it expresses). There is, however, something objectionable about putting this account of acquiring DOORKNOB together with the Fodorean analysis of doorknobhood.

---

2. While movable protuberances attached to doors . . . (etc.) are pretty good examples of doorknobs, they're even better examples of stereotypical doorknobs. Why, then, do we get the concept DOORKNOB rather than the concept STEREOTYPICAL DOORKNOB? "[W]hat you'd *expect* people reliably to learn from stereotypic examples of X is not the concept X but the X stereotype" (Fodor 1998:140).

To see this, let's run through the steps in Fodor's analysis one more time (with feeling). First, consider a blatantly circular analysis of doorknob-hood—an analysis of the kind Fodor presumably wants to avoid:

x is a doorknob if x has (or would have) the same effects on us as typical doorknobs have (or would have).

Fodor, as we've seen, can remove the second 'doorknob' from the analysis by actually specifying the properties that typical doorknobs have:

x is a doorknob if x has (or would have) the same effects on us as do (/ would) waist-high, movable protuberances attached to doors.

So far so good. But we want to know more. We want to know not just that being a doorknob is a matter of having the same causal powers (with regard to our minds) as waist-high, movable protuberances; we want to know *what those causal powers are*. If your aim is to find out what x's are, it's no good to be told that x's have the same causal powers as y's, if you don't know what causal powers y's have. For an analysis of this kind to be informative, the causal powers shared by x's and y's need to be described, not just ascribed. Well, that's OK, isn't it? For Fodor in fact *does* tell us what the causal powers of stereotypical doorknobs are. He tells us that what stereotypical doorknobs characteristically do is: cause us to acquire the concept DOORKNOB, that is, lock to *being a doorknob*. So we have:

Waist-high, movable protuberances attached to doors cause us to lock to doorknobhood (/acquire the concept DOORKNOB).

But although, as was remarked above, there's nothing wrong with this claim if it is taken in isolation from Fodor's overall analytical project, a rather ugly circularity arises when this account of stereotypical doorknobs' causal powers is plugged back into the Fodorean analysis of doorknobhood:

x is a doorknob if x has (or would have) the same effects on us as do (or would) waist-high, movable protuberances attached to doors, and waist-high, movable protuberances attached to doors cause us to lock to door-knobhood (/acquire the concept DOORKNOB).

Or, in other words,

x is a doorknob if x causes us to lock to doorknobhood.

This is about as circular as an analysis of *being a doorknob* can get. Thus, although Fodor looks as if he can avoid the charge that his analysis is circular (by using the doorknob stereotype to pick out the mental states that doorknobs constitutively cause), and although he looks as though he can avoid the charge that his analysis is uninformative (because he can specify the causal powers that doorknobs share with things satisfying the doorknob stereotype), he cannot do both of these things at the same time. Because he characterizes the causal powers of stereotypical doorknobs in terms of their ability to get us to lock to the property *being a doorknob*, he illicitly imports doorknobhood back into his analysis of that very property.

No doubt there are moves that a friend of the Constitution Hypothesis could make in response to this kind of objection. (After all, dispositional analyses of secondary qualities have survived several centuries of similar demurrers.) I do not, however, propose to anticipate such moves here. Suffice it to note that whatever one might think about the prima facie plausibility of the claim that things are doorknobs (or cats, or trees, or computers, or books, or . . .) just in virtue of our taking them to be so, it's no easy matter to spell out a constitution hypothesis such as Fodor proposes in any detail. Whether it is necessary to try very hard depends, of course, on how eager one is to embrace this kind of metaphysical picture. Fodor clearly thinks that psychologists, at least, should be strongly motivated to adopt the Constitution Hypothesis, for doing so would (he claims) enable them to explain not only why we get the concepts we do from the experiences we do, but also how concepts could be unlearned without being innate. I'll argue in the next section, however, that the metaphysical issue is moot. Even if doorknobs (and trees and cats and . . .) were mind-dependent in the way Fodor suggests, this metaphysical fact would not make any of our psychological problems go away.[3]

5.3 Ontology, Acquisition, and Innateness

Fodor's claim is that the Constitution Hypothesis is both independently plausible and theoretically necessary. It's plausible because it's (allegedly) hard to see what else doorknobs (etc.) could be, given that they're unanalyzable yet not metaphysically ultimate. And it is theoretically well motivated because it "explains the content relation between DOORKNOB and the kinds of experience that typically [mediate] its acquisition. . . . and it also explains how DOORKNOB could be both psychologically primitive and not innate" (1998:137). Let us examine these last two assertions in turn.

Reflection upon the kinds of events that precede our acquisition of concepts raises the question of why it is experiences of Fs, not experiences of Gs or Hs, that typically lead us to acquire the concept F-NESS. As Fodor puts it: "Why is it so often experiences of doorknobs, and so rarely experiences of whipped cream or giraffes, that lead one to lock to doorknobhood?" (1998:127). That this is actually rather a deep question became evident in our discussion of triggering (§4.3). If concept acquisition really were like imprinting, we'd expect to find concepts being caused by more or less arbitrary things—things that during our species' evolutionary past were perhaps reasonable indicators of the properties our concepts express (as

---

3. I am indebted to David Hilbert, Alex Byrne, and Daniel Stoljar for helpful discussions of the material in this section.

movement is a pretty good indicator, for a duck, of motherhood) but that do not necessarily have any more intimate connection with what our concepts mean. But we don't find this. What we find instead is that there is a strong correlation between acquiring the concept of an F and experiencing F things.[4] This constant conjunction is what Fodor calls the doorknob/DOORKNOB effect, and is the first of the psychological phenomena he claims to be able to explain via his Constitution Hypothesis. Since doorknobs *just are* things that typically cause acquisition of DOORKNOB, "the intrinsic connection between the content of DOORKNOB and the content of our doorknob-experiences is metaphysically necessary" (1998:136). That being so, Fodor argues, no further (e.g., psychological) explanation is needed of the fact that experiences of doorknobs cause acquisition of DOORKNOB: thanks to the Constitution Hypothesis, the doorknob/DOORKNOB effect is "not a fact that an inductivist account of concept acquisition is required in order to explain" (1998:137). But, I shall argue, the doorknob/DOORKNOB effect remains unexplained *even if* one accepts that causing DOORKNOB is constitutive of doorknobhood, that is, *even if* one accepts the Constitution Hypothesis. And as to what sort of explanation—inductivist or not—*will* explain the effect, a metaphysics of the kind Fodor is promoting is entirely silent on that point.

Fodor wants to say that experiences of doorknobs (rather than of giraffes) cause one to lock to doorknobhood because all there is to *being a doorknob* is being the kind of thing we lock to in consequence of doorknob experiences. This account parallels the following explanation of the 'sleeping pills/ sleep effect': taking sleeping pills (rather than, say, amphetamines) causes you to go to sleep because all there is to *being a sleeping pill* is being the kind of thing that makes people go to sleep. But the latter is no explanation at all! The problem is not that the explanation is circular (suppose that the circularity is removed by the provision of some other characterization, not mentioning sleep, of what sleeping pills do to us). The problem is, rather, that the explanation is *uninformative*. It simply does not answer the question we are asking. For when we ask why sleeping pills make us go to sleep, we already know that they're sleeping pills and that being a sleeping pill has something to do with making people sleep. These facts are presupposed by our question; they're not the subject of it. Instead, what we want to know when asking this question is: What it is about sleeping pills and/or us that accounts for their reliably having the effects on us that they do? We want to know something about the *mechanism* that sustains the causal regularity in question. For instance, if we want to know why sleeping pills (rather than amphetamines) make people sleep, we're presumably asking for an account of what it is that distinguishes sleeping pills from amphetamines such that the former (but not the latter) have certain causal powers with respect to us. If we want to know why sleeping pills put people to sleep (rather than

---

4. An important qualification to this claim will be made in chapter 6—see the discussion of 'reference borrowing' in §6.3.

waking them up, as do amphetamines), then we're asking for an account of how the causal powers of sleeping pills work their magic on the human brain (which receptors get affected, etc.). But whatever aspect of the mechanism sustaining the sleeping pills/sleep regularity it is, exactly, that arouses our curiosity, that curiosity is not satisfied by a Fodorean Constitution Hypothesis. Being told that it's metaphysically necessary that x is a sleeping pill if x makes us lie down and snore tells us neither what it is about sleeping pills that gives them this miraculous power nor what it is about us that enables sleeping pills to exercise that power. The Constitution Hypothesis is simply beside the point.

The same is true when we ask about the doorknob/DOORKNOB effect. We already know that experiences of doorknobs cause us to acquire concepts of doorknobs. (This, after all, was what led us to see the doorknob/DOORKNOB problem in the first place!) So it doesn't much help us to be told—even if it's true—that doorknobs cause DOORKNOBs because as a matter of brute metaphysical fact they are the kind of thing that causes DOORKNOBs. Again, what we are after when we ponder the doorknob/DOORKNOB effect is an account of what it is about doorknobs, and/or what it is about us, that enables those things to have that kind of effect on us. Maybe we want to know what it is that doorknobs have in common such that they all have the same effects on our minds.[5] Or maybe we want to know exactly how it is that things of that sort bring about the effects that they do.[6] But whatever it is that we want to know about the causal processes underpinning the doorknob/DOORKNOB effect, being told that it's metaphysically necessary that there should be such an effect is of little or no interest to us. For that leaves the question of mechanisms unanswered.[7]

Thus, the questions raised by the doorknob/DOORKNOB effect remain *even if* one accepts the Fodorean claim that doorknobs just are DOORKNOB-causers. For what wants explaining in this case are the mechanisms—psychological, neurological, computational, whatever—that sustain the causal relation in question. Since our need for an explanation of mechanisms remains *whatever* the metaphysical status of that relation happens to be, Fodor is just wrong in claiming that the Constitution Hypothesis accounts for the doorknob/DOORKNOB effect, and that no other (e.g., inductivist) explanation of the effect is required.

---

5. It might turn out that we need several different accounts of the 'categorical bases' of doorknobs' causal powers. Then doorknobs would be like, say, fire extinguishers: doing the same thing by different means.

6. Again, as in the case of fire extinguishers, there may be several different mechanisms to describe.

7. I suppose that it might be of some kind of interest, in that the relation's being metaphysically necessary might constrain the kinds of causal mechanisms that are candidates to implement it. (Although in order to know what kinds of constraints the relation's metaphysical necessity might impose on mechanisms, you would also need to understand what metaphysical (as opposed to logical or nomological) necessity is supposed to be. Which I don't, really.)

Fodor also asserts that a Constitution Hypothesis shows how concepts could be unlearned (because unstructured), but not innate. One might argue that this claim about the Constitution Hypothesis's explanatory powers must be mistaken, and for the much same reasons as was the one just discussed. Nativism about concepts, on the face of it, is a claim about the mechanisms responsible for concept acquisition. So if a Constitution Hypothesis is silent as to mechanisms, as I've just argued, it should have nothing to say about innateness either. I think that this is partly correct: the constitution hypothesis is irrelevant to the nativism issue construed as concerning the mechanisms of acquisition. However, as I shall argue in the rest of this chapter, Fodor's Constitution Hypothesis is *not* irrelevant to nativism viewed in the second way I suggested in part I, that is, as an expression of metatheoretical despondency. For both of the Fodorean accounts of acquisition—the triggering account of his (1981b) and the new, constitution account of his (1998)—reflect his opinion that concept-acquisition cannot be explained in psychological terms. Fodor's view is that, contrary to what the empiricist naively believes, our acquisition of concepts is a phenomenon outside the purview of psychology. His position thus bears a striking similarity to the anti-naturalistic nativisms of Leibniz and Descartes: like them, he takes the view that our acquisition of ideas is in principle inexplicable—if not altogether, at least by a scientific psychology.

5.4 The 'Standard Argument' and the Dialectical Role of the Constitution Hypothesis

There is something very strange about Fodor's claim in his (1998) to have found in the Constitution Hypothesis a way to avoid being a nativist. The Constitution Hypothesis was developed in order to defend an argument, which he calls (1998:123) the 'Standard Argument,' against a possible threat raised by the doorknob/DOORKNOB effect. But the Standard Argument is an argument *for nativism*. How, then, could a metaphysical thesis designed to buttress that argument fail to brace nativism as well? It seems that something very odd is going on. Figuring out what, is the task of this section.

Let's first recall the 'Standard Argument' for innateness (that is, the argument set out in §§4.1 and 4.2) and try to get clear about where the Constitution Hypothesis fits into Fodor's dialectic. The Standard Argument goes like this:

1. Most concepts have no internal structure.
So, 2. Most concepts cannot be learned.
So, 3. Most concepts are innate.

The nativist conclusion (3) of this argument could be blocked by denying either (1) or (2). We've already seen (§4.2) Fodor's case against denying (1). If concepts have internal structure, that structure must be either definitional or nondefinitional (e.g., prototypical) in nature. Virtually nothing, according

to Fodor, has a definition, and prototypes won't do the right kinds of combinatorial work in our semantic theory. So (1) stands. What, then, of premise
(2)? One way to make plausible the denial of (2), Fodor points out, would
be to find some independent reason to think that learning *must* be involved
in concept acquisition. For if there were a really strong argument to the
effect that acquisition must involve hypothesis formulation and testing, then
one would have to assume that there was something wrong with Fodor's
arguments against this possibility. In which case, we should not rely on
Fodor's premise (2) to get us to innateness.

Fodor's (1998) discussion of the doorknob/DOORKNOB effect arose in the
context of his exploration of this last option. He considers the possibility
that the existence of the effect might provide grounds for the denial of (2).
It could provide such grounds, he thinks, if it were to turn out that the only
way to explain why doorknobs cause DOORKNOB were to suppose (in empiricist vein) that concepts are learned from their instances. And it might
turn out like this for the following reason. First, Fodor assumes, the door-
knob/DOORKNOB effect can't be an accident. It demands an explanation of
some kind. But the nativist apparently cannot explain it, since (as we've
seen—§5.1) all he can appeal to in this connection is natural selection, and
natural selection predicts that concepts should have intentionally arbitrary
causes. The empiricist, by contrast, can explain the effect. On her view, the
experiences that bear causally on acquisition are those that provide evidence
for and against learners' hypotheses about what their concepts mean. Doorknobs being a pretty good source of evidence about things in the extension
of DOORKNOB, then, the empiricist would naturally expect to find doorknob
experiences high on the list of things that cause acquisition of that concept.
The empiricist, in other words, says that the doorknob–DOORKNOB effect
exists because concepts are learned from their instances, which directly contradicts the Standard Argument's (2), which asserts that they're not. Absent
some other explanation of the effect, then, premise (2) of the Standard Argument looks to be in serious trouble.

Fodor, however, is exceedingly unwilling to give up (2). For (2) is a corollary of the view—to which he is clearly 110 percent committed—that concepts are internally unstructured. If concepts are unstructured, that's to say,
they *couldn't* be learned. For there's simply nothing to formulate and test
hypotheses *about*. But if Fodor is unwilling to give up the notion that concepts are unstructured, then he cannot give up (2). And if he cannot give up
(2), then he cannot accept that the empiricist's is the only explanation of the
doorknob/DOORKNOB effect. So he has to find an alternative way to explain
that regularity. Enter the Constitution Hypothesis. If there were a *metaphysical* explanation of the doorknob/DOORKNOB effect, then obviously the
empiricist's story about concepts' being learned is *not* the only explanation
of it. In which case, there is no reason to deny (2) after all. In which case,
the Standard Argument stands.

In §4.5, I expressed some doubts about whether a constitution hypothesis
does in fact explain why doorknob experiences cause acquisition of DOOR-

KNOB. I want, however, to set those doubts aside for now and accept for the present the contention that it does. For it's at this point that Fodor's discussion apparently goes off the rails. Premise (2) of the Standard Argument is (we're supposing) safe. So what moral should we draw from this? Well, surely, what a defense of (2) should make us conclude is that "Nativism Rules OK." Defending (2) via the Constitution Hypothesis is a way of defending the Standard Argument, which is a way of defending radical concept nativism. And yet, what Fodor *claims* the Constitution Hypothesis to show is not that most concepts are innate but, rather, that they needn't be!

> [I]t may be that the explanation of the d/D [i.e., doorknob/DOORKNOB] effect is metaphysical rather than psychological. In which case, unless I've missed something, there isn't *any* obvious reason why the initial state for DOORKNOB acquisition needs to be intentionally specified. A fortiori, there isn't any obvious reason why DOORKNOB has to be innate. NOT EVEN IF IT'S PRIMITIVE. (1998:143)

So we have the following conundrum: in his (1975), (1981b), and again in his (1998), Fodor presents the Standard Argument as an *argument for nativism*. Now, having defended both premises of the argument against a variety of actual and possible objections, he claims that nativism is nonetheless avoidable. What could be going on?

It's pretty clear, I think, that at least one of the things that is going on here is a shift in the way that Fodor is using the term 'innate.' In the older works, he counted a concept as being innate so long as it was unlearned, that is, so long as it was acquired in some way other than through the testing of hypotheses. He called that other way 'triggering,' and called a concept 'innate' so long as it was triggered by experience rather than being learned from it. Now, as we saw in chapter 4, Fodor's conception of triggering in his 1981b was susceptible of two different readings. In some moods, he spoke as if triggering involved the activation, by experience, of innately specified 'protoconcepts,' quasi-intentional objects of some sort that become full-blooded concepts when 'switched on' by a triggering stimulus. In other moods, however, Fodor spoke of triggering as if it involved, rather, the activation by experience of some kind of quasi-psychological mechanism, the 'sensorium.' Rather than making available something that was already, in some sense, present in the mind, experience on this account initiates a brute-causal process that results in the addition of a concept to the learner's cognitive stock.

Thus, in the earlier works, Fodor seemed to conceive two ways that a concept could be innate: it could be innate in the sense of existing in the mind as a protoconcept, or it could be innate in the sense of being the product of a nonrational, brute-causal psychological mechanism. In his (1998), however, he resolves this ambiguity. Now, a concept is regarded as innate only if it arises out of an innate protoconcept or, as Fodor expresses it, only if the initial state of the organism whence that concept arises needs to be intentionally specified:

the philosophically interesting question about whether there are innate ideas is whether there are innate *ideas*. It is, after all, the thought that the 'initial state' from which concept acquisition proceeds must be specified in intentional terms (terms like 'content,' belief,' etc.) that connects the issues about concept innateness with the epistemological issues about a prioricity and the like. (1998:142)

"The issue," Fodor says, "isn't whether acquiring DOORKNOB requires a lot if innate stuff; anybody with any sense can see that it does. The issue is whether it requires a lot of innate *intentional* stuff, a lot of innate stuff that has content" (1998:143). So whereas in his (1981b) he was prepared to regard accepting the mechanical or sensorium model as a way of being a nativist about concepts, he now retracts that view:

the 'innate sensorium' model suggests that the question how much is innate in concept acquisition can be quite generally dissociated from the question whether any *concepts* are innate. The sensorium is innate. . . . But . . . the innateness of the sensorium isn't the innateness of anything that has intentional content. Since the sensorium isn't an idea, it is a fortiori not an *innate* idea. So, strictly speaking, the innate sensorium model of the acquisition of RED doesn't require that it, or any other concept, be innate. (1998:142)

The new Fodor, in short, differs substantively from the old one only in that he explicitly rejects the protoconcept model for acquisition: he now comes down firmly in favor of the 'brute-causal' sensorium picture.[8] He differs verbally from the earlier Fodor in that whereas Fodor (1981b) was prepared to call the sensorium model a nativist one, Fodor (1998) is prepared *not* to:

if the locking story about concept possession and the mind-dependence story about the metaphysics of *doorknobhood* are both true, then the kind of nativism about DOORKNOB that an informational atomist has to put up with is perhaps not one of *concepts* but of *mechanisms*. That consequence may be some consolation to otherwise disconsolate Empiricists. (1998: 142)

So, Fodor now feels able to say, "[m]aybe there aren't any innate *ideas* after all" (1998:143).

5.5 Is Fodor a Nativist?

Fodor's view in his (1998), then, is that while concept acquisition requires a lot of innate 'stuff,' it doesn't require that any of that stuff be intentional. He thinks this is enough to allow him to avoid having to be a nativist. Is he

8. As, indeed, he ought, given how hard it is to make sense of the protoconcept idea— §4.4.

right? In a way, of course, it doesn't really matter all that much how one answers this question. 'Nativist' means so much (or, perhaps, so little) to so many that one could make a good case for calling even someone like Locke a nativist—as, indeed, Leibniz did. On the other hand, though, as President Lincoln is credited with observing, calling a tail a leg doesn't make it one, and much of the point of part I of this book was to attach a stable enough core of historical meaning to the term 'nativist' to allow us to say with some confidence whether or not someone counts as a nativist *in that sense*. Of course, I didn't manage to find just one core of meaning for 'nativist.' There were two, since nativist doctrine, I argued, bifurcates into two distinct strands: the hypothesis of domain specificity and the expression of meta-theoretical gloom. Nonetheless, and regardless of what Fodor wants to call himself, the question still arises: Is he a nativist in either of the senses I've distinguished? Is there, in other words, enough similarity between the views he espouses, and the views of defenders of innateness in the past, such that we're justified in placing him within the nativist tradition?

My view is that Fodor is now, and has been since 1975, a nativist in the second of the senses articulated in part I. His position, then and now, is that since concept acquisition is not a properly psychological process, no psychological theory of it is possible. I'll argue that both his earlier triggering hypothesis and his later Constitution Hypothesis are ways of elaborating a metatheoretical view as to the unlikelihood of our developing a natural-scientific understanding of how a mind comes to be furnished. To this extent, I'll suggest, his view is continuous with the non-naturalisms of Leibniz and Descartes. Whether it is actually identical with their anti-naturalistic pictures will emerge below, as I make the case for Fodor's being a 'metatheoretical pessimist' in more detail.

The view that I want to defend is that Fodor's position is of a kind with the mystery-mongering of Descartes and Leibniz. Both his earlier appeal to triggering as an 'explanation' of how concepts are acquired and his later appeal to the Constitution Hypothesis are just different ways of saying the same, pessimistic thing, namely, that we can expect no psychology—and perhaps even no science at all—of concept acquisition. In his (1998), Fodor makes it admirably explicit that his "bottom line" (1998:141) on concept acquisition is that acquiring concepts is a psychologically inexplicable process:

> there isn't *any* obvious reason why the initial state for DOORKNOB acquisition needs to be intentionally specified. . . . The moral of all this may be that thought there has to be a story to tell about the structural requirements for acquiring DOORKNOB, intentional vocabulary isn't required to tell it. *In which case, it isn't part of cognitive psychology.* (1998:143, emphasis added)

What, though, of Fodor's earlier position? Much of his (1981b) was devoted to a consideration of the mechanisms by which concepts might be acquired, and it is tempting to read his talk there of triggering and the sensorium, his analogy with imprinting, his discussion of the 'hierarchy of triggers' and the 'mental chemistry' view (see §6.4) as being psychological in character. It is tempting, that's to say, to read "The Present Status" as offering an alternative psychology—a *nativist* psychology—in place of the ousted empiricist account. I believe, however, that it's a mistake to read Fodor (1981b) as indulging his usual predilection for psychological speculation. The theory he offers there is not a competitor with the psychological accounts that he rejects. Instead, it is an expression of the same view that he makes explicit in his (1998), namely, that explaining concept acquisition is none of the psychologist's business.

Recall the Classical empiricist, described in §3.1. Her view was that there are two different sorts of operations responsible for concept acquisition: one for the acquisition of primitive concepts; the other for the acquisition of complex concepts. About the latter kind of process, which she took to be operative in the majority of cases, the empiricist had a theory to offer: complex concepts are acquired either by abstraction from, or by recombination of, primitive concepts. About the former process, however, she had nothing to tell us: in her view, the mechanisms responsible for our acquisition of primitive concepts are something of a mystery. Now look again at Fodor's (1981b) argument. His central disagreement with classical empiricism—and he is quite explicit on this point—is that *the class of primitive concepts is much larger than the classical empiricist thought*. Rather than there being very few primitive concepts, as Locke et al. opined, there are, on Fodor's view, lots of them: most lexical concepts are primitive.[9] Which means that rather than there being a small mystery at the bottom of our psychology of concept acquisition, there's a big mystery permeating all of it. If there's a puzzle about our attainment of primitive concepts, and if most of our concepts are primitive, then concept acquisition is, more or less *tout court*, a puzzling matter.

Puzzling in what way? According to Hume, the origins of our primitive ideas are utterly unfathomable. The acquisition of primitive ideas is "perfectly inexplicable by human reason,"[10] and the most we can say is that they derive from impressions that "arise in the soul originally from unknown causes."[11] Sometimes Locke expresses a similar despondency. For example, he writes that since the

> mechanical affections of bodies [have] no affinity at all with those *Ideas*, they produce in us, (there being no conceivable connexion between any impulse of any sort of Body, and any perception of a Colour, or Smell, which we find in our Minds), we can have no distinct knowledge of such

9. And that's a lot of primitive concepts. If each word in English expresses a different lexical concept, then, since there are between 50,000 and 250,000 English words (depending on how you count—see Aitchison 1987:15), there are presumably about the same number of lexical—hence primitive—concepts.

10. Hume, *Treatise*, I.3.v (1978:84).

11. Ibid., I.1.ii (1978:7).

Operations beyond our experience; and can reason no otherwise about them, than as effects produced by the appointment of an infinitely Wise Agent, which perfectly surpass our Comprehensions.[12]

In his less dramatic moods, however, Locke occupies a more moderate position, arguing not that our acquisition of primitive concepts is altogether inexplicable, but only that the question of how they arise is beyond the scope of his current inquiry. The etiology of simple ideas, he writes, is "an enquiry not belonging to the *Idea*, as it is in the Understanding; but to the nature of the things existing without us."[13] And this latter enquiry into the nature of things Locke has already set aside as being outside the scope of his project in the *Essay*: "I shall not at present . . . trouble myself to examine . . . by what Motions of our Spirits, or Alterations of our Bodies, we come to have any . . . *Ideas* in our Understandings. . . . These are Speculations, which, however curious and entertaining, I shall decline as lying out of my Way, in the design I am now upon."[14]

Classical empiricists, then, vacillated somewhat in their metatheoretical attitude toward primitive concepts: sometimes they recommend that since the matter is beyond our ken, we should give up our search for an explanation of how primitive concepts arise in the mind; other times, they advocate only that we set this issue aside as being not properly the concern of the psychologist. Which perspective should Fodor accept? If he were to adopt the resigned stance that Hume and (sometimes) Locke recommend, his position should be exactly on a par with the non-naturalisms of Leibniz and Descartes! If most concepts are primitive, and if our acquisition of primitive concepts is inexplicable, then concept acquisition on the whole will prove unfathomable. But it is difficult for the thoroughly modern natural philosopher to look with equanimity upon this bleak prospect.[15] Surely concept acquisition could not altogether surpass our comprehension. The compass of the human understanding has expanded tremendously in the last three hundred years. We have developed new tools, both theoretical and practical, for investigating the world—tools that Hume and Locke could not have even begun to imagine. Science has revealed to us the inmost corners of the atom and the outmost edges of the universe and much else in between. Surely we, who have achieved so much, could not be stumped by so thoroughly mundane a phenomenon as our own acquisition of concepts?

Fortunately for Fodor (1981b), who is as naturalistically inclined as anyone, there appears no need for him to accept this sobering conclusion. For, unlike the anti-empiricist arguments of Leibniz and Descartes, which asserted the impossibility of world–mind causation and thus struck at the heart of any science of concept acquisition, Fodor's arguments in his (1975) and

---

12. *Essay*, IV.3.xxviii (Locke 1975:559).
13. Ibid., II.8.ii (Locke 1975:132).
14. Ibid., I.1.ii (Locke 1975:45).
15. And, as Locke's ambivalence reveals, this vision is hard too on the eyes of the thoroughly *early*-modern natural philosopher!

(1981b) undermine only the attempt to give a *psychology* of concept acquisition. He argues that concept acquisition could not involve hypothesis-testing; and he asserts that the hypothesis-testing model is the only conception of learning available to the psychologist. And all that follows from this, is that our acquiring concepts is inexplicable *using the theoretical apparatus of cognitive psychology*. Nothing whatsoever follows from Fodor's argument about whether or not some other science might succeed where psychology must fail. Fodor is thus at liberty, or so it seems, to follow Locke in his more moderate moods, and conclude only that we should set concept acquisition aside as being outside psychology's ambit.

There are several further strands of evidence suggesting that Fodor took an anti-psychology stance on the acquisition question as early as his (1981b). First, the position he defends in "The Present Status" is based on exactly the same argument, namely, the Standard Argument displayed above, as is the anti-psychologism of his (1998). Second, the Standard Argument is strikingly similar, structurally, to the impossibility arguments of Leibniz and Descartes, discussed in chapter 3. Like them, Fodor's argument makes no appeal to the poverty of the stimulus, aiming rather to ensare the empiricist in a contradiction. Just as Leibniz and Descartes argued, in effect, that the empiricist both must and cannot view acquisition as involving causal interactions between minds and what lies outside them, so Fodor argues that the empiricist both must and cannot view acquisition as involving hypothesis-testing.[16] This supports the view that Fodor's purpose, like that of Leibniz and Descartes in their 'impossibility modes,' is not to exhibit some superficial or cosmetic problem with the empiricist theory. It is not to pave the way for a triumphant presentation of his own variation on the psychological theme. Rather, Fodor's aim, like that of his predecessors, is to make the point that the empiricist's psychological program is flawed at the most fundamental level.

A third indication that even in his (1981b) Fodor was reaching toward his (1998) line that acquisition is nonpsychological is the fact that nowhere in that paper does he ever refer to concept acquisition in such a way as to suggest that it is a computational process. Yet all psychological processes, on Fodor's view, are computational processes: they involve the rule-governed manipulation of mental representations.[17] So if the processes responsible for acquisition are not computational, then they aren't psychological either. Hence, I think, his talk in "The Present Status" of the 'brute-causality' of concept acquisition is meant not only to repudiate the 'rational-causal' account of the empiricist but also to suggest the more sweeping claim that the concept-forming mechanism is not a computational mechanism—hence not a psychological mechanism—of any kind at all.

16. The empiricist must accept the inductivist account of concept-learning because it's the only account on offer; yet she cannot accept that account because it entails that virtually no concepts are learned.

17. See, e.g., his (1975) and (1980).

And finally, it is striking too, to anyone familiar with Fodor's scornful rejection of 'Pop Darwinian' appeals to evolution in the philosophy of mind, that "The Present Status" is replete with references to biology, ethology, natural selection, Mother Nature, and so on. If I am right in my interpretation of Fodor's 1981 position, such talk is not inconsistent with his current view regarding the bearing of evolutionary theory on matters within the purview of cognitive science. Rather, Fodor's talk of imprinting, triggering, evolution, innately specified functions from stimuli onto concepts, brute-causal mechanisms, and what-have-you should instead be construed as constituting a hint as to where we might hope to find a solution to the acquisition problem. Given that none will be forthcoming from psychology, we should look to biology or ethology to unravel this conundrum for us. As Fodor himself puts it, in what I think is the key to interpreting "The Present Status" paper, "[o]ur ethology promises to be quite interesting even if our developmental psychology turns out to be a little dull" (1981b:315).

5.6 How Low Can You Go?

This chapter discussed how Fodor's Constitution Hypothesis is supposed to explain both the doorknob/DOORKNOB effect and how ideas could be primitive (hence unlearned) without being innate. I argued that the Constitution Hypothesis does not explain the doorknob/DOORKNOB effect because it is silent as to the mechanisms by which that effect is sustained. That being so, I suggested, one wouldn't think it would have much to say about nativism either, since nativism about concepts seems prima facie to be a hypothesis about how concepts are acquired, that is, a hypothesis about mechanisms. If the Constitution Hypothesis can tell us nothing about the mechanisms that are responsible for concept acquisition, surely it can tell us nothing about the propriety of a nativist, as opposed to an empiricist, account of those mechanisms.

But recall the arguments of part I: there are two nativisms. In some cases, I agreed, nativism is a substantive hypothesis about psychological mechanisms. Where it derives from arguments from the poverty of the stimulus, the claim that certain ideas are innate is best understood as meaning that the ideas in question are acquired by task-specific learning devices. But in other cases, I argued, what the nativist is offering is *not* properly viewed as a conjecture about mechanisms. Where an innateness hypothesis stems from an impossibility argument pointing to some fundamental incoherence or contradiction in empiricist accounts of acquisition, it is rather to be read as a metatheoretical claim about the psychologist's explanatory project itself. When Descartes and Leibniz argued that all ideas are innate because no ideas could be caused by experience (either because causation requires a resemblance between mind and body that does not exist or because monads have 'no windows'), what they were doing, I suggested, was expressing pessimism about our prospects, qua natural scientists, for taming the mental. Concept acquisition and the mind–world interactions that appear to sustain it are so deeply weird, on their view, that there is reason to think that we can never achieve a proper understanding of them.

In the latter part of this chapter, I've been arguing that the position defended by Fodor in both his (1998) and his (1981b) is of a kind with the radical nativisms propounded by Leibniz and Descartes three centuries ago. Like theirs, Fodor's view—whether disguised as an innateness hypothesis or not—is indicative of a certain degree of pessimism as to our prospects for understanding how a mind comes to be furnished. But is Fodor's gloom as profound as was his forebears'? Leibniz and Descartes, recall, took the view that since mind–body causation is so deeply problematic, there can be no scientific account whatsoever of how our experiences give rise to ideas. Their nativism was in fact an expression of a profoundly anti-naturalistic attitude toward the acquisition problem. As we've seen, however, Fodor does not go this far—at least not in his (1981b). While he there denies the possibility of a psychological theory of how concepts are acquired, he seems perfectly comfortable with the notion that some other science—biology or ethology or whatever—might succeed where psychology must fail.

In his most recent work, however, there are indications that he is moving even closer than this toward the position of the eighteenth-century nativists. In his (1998), replacing the sanguine references found in "The Present Status" to the explanatory powers of biology and ethology, are arguments *against* the possibility of attaining an evolutionary explanation of concept acquisition. As we saw in §5.1, Fodor's current view is that, contra the hopes he expressed in 1981, an appeal to natural selection cannot satisfactorily explain how experience causes concepts. Because evolutionary theory (sans an inductivist hypothesis, which Fodor takes to be out on independent grounds) predicts that there should be an arbitrary relation between experiences and concepts, and because that relation is not in fact arbitrary, no explanation of how concepts arise will be forthcoming from the biologists. But if neither biology nor psychology can explain how we get concepts, what can? Fodor's answer is, it seems, that philosophy can! In his (1998), he argues that it's the metaphysicians who (thanks to the Constitution Hypothesis) can explain why doorknobs cause DOORKNOBS. Which suggests that it is the metaphysicians—and not the scientists—who get to explain concept acquisition as well! Which looks awfully akin to the non-naturalism of a Leibniz or a Descartes to me.

6

Prospects for a Psychology
of Concept Acquisition

To be sure, there remains something about the acquisition of DOORKNOB
that wants explaining.

Fodor (1998:136)

In the last chapter, we saw what an embarrassment it was for the Fodor of
1981 that the relations between concepts and their causes typically make a
good deal of intentional sense. The fact that we get EMU from emus and
PLATYPUS from platypuses and DOORKNOB from doorknobs has an 'intentional integrity' about it of exactly the kind that should not exist, were Fodor
(1981b) right about the arbitrariness of the inputs to the concept-forming
mechanism. In his (1998), fielding a barrage of heavy ontology, Fodor
charges to the rescue of his earlier self—sort of. The fact that it is experiences
of FS that cause concepts of F-NESS is no cause for alarm, he argues, for it is
metaphysically necessary that this should be the case. FS *just are* things-that-
cause-concepts-of-F-NESS, so the intentional integrity of the cause–concept
relation is about as unembarrassing as anything can be! Further, since metaphysically necessary connections are the province of philosophers, explaining
the relations between our concepts and the experiences we get them from is
not something that a mere psychologist (such as Fodor [1981b] might claim
to be) need worry about. Of course, the older, wiser Fodor acknowledges,
the younger Fodor's nativism may have to go. And maybe his naturalism as
well. But at least his brute-causal/nonrational/noninferential/nonempiricist
picture of concept acquisition is safe.

I'll argue that this picture is untenable. Whatever one makes of Fodor's
apparent flirtation in his (1998) with rank non-naturalism (see §5.6), his
basic contention—and the one I propose to hold him to—is that concept

Parts of this chapter have been published as Cowie (1998).

112

acquisition is not a psychological process, and hence is not the kind of thing about which a psychological theory can or should be given. In this chapter I will show that, on the contrary, psychological processing is absolutely essential to the acquisition of most concepts, and I will argue that, to the extent this is so, we can and should expect cognitive psychology to provide a theory of it.

The argument will have three parts. I'll argue, first, that the Fodorean contention that concepts are 'brute-causally' acquired cannot be sustained (§§6.2–6.3). The kind of mechanism that Fodor proposes can account neither for concepts acquired ostensively nor for those got through reference-borrowing. What this indicates, I'll suggest, is that concept acquisition must be 'psychologically mediated.' In the vast majority of cases, our acquisition of concepts requires the presence in our minds of certain other mental states.

Then (§6.4), I'll sketch an account of how this cognitive mediation might be achieved. On the view I urge, the acquisition of a concept in most cases requires the possession of some kind of recognitional capacity, a capacity that, I'll suggest, may be implemented in a variety of ways—by definitions (though this, as Fodor showed, is rare), by prototypes or stereotypes, even by what Fodor (1994:37) characterizes as "policies" to "use experts as instruments." Some of these recognitional capacities may well be inborn, I allow; most of them, however, must clearly be learned through experience. Thus, learning is frequently involved in concept acquisition, and what is learned must be intentionally described. Contra the Fodorean, then, acquisition requires psychological explanation.

The third part of the argument in this chapter involves defending this conception of acquisition against some objections, including in particular Fodor's criticisms of nonclassical theories of conceptual contents, and the charge of verificationism. The latter bullet, I am prepared simply to bite (§6.5.2). As to the former, I argue (§6.5.1) that Fodor's (1981b, 1998) case against prototypes' and the like being learned during acquisition turns on a mistaken conception of the role that prototypes are playing in a semantics of the kind I suggest. The sense in which they are (on this view) to be regarded as concepts' contents or meanings is not the sense of 'meaning' that matters to the provision of a compositional semantics. What concepts need to contribute to complexes of which they are a part is their 'Fregean meaning,' their meaning in the sense of whatever-it-is-that-fixes-their-reference. Prototypes, however, are what I'll call *non-Fregean* meanings: they may be necessary for the fixation of reference but they are not sufficient, so it is unsurprising that they cannot do the compositional job all by themselves. Compositionality, I urge, is no bar to prototypes and the like being involved in the acquisition of concepts. Which, I conclude, is a jolly good thing, since something like prototypes *must* be involved in that process.

6.1 The Sterelny–Loar Objections

I remarked in chapter 4 that Fodor's innatist agitations gave rise to surprisingly little in the way of commentary or criticism from the broader philosophical community. Two notable exceptions to this generalization are Sterelny's (1989) and Loar's (1991) critiques of Fodor's nativism. In this section, I shall survey their criticisms and discuss how Fodor might try to disarm them. In the next section, I show that the nativist's victory is pyrrhic.

6.1.1 Three Objections

Fodor's contention is that the mechanism by which concepts are acquired is a 'brute-causal' one. Triggering by experience is sufficient for concept acquisition to occur in the sense that there is no contribution made by further psychological states or processes to the acquisition process. We have already seen (§5.1) one of the objections made by Sterelny (1989) against this picture as presented in Fodor (1981b). There, Fodor had compared acquisition to imprinting, implying that the triggers for concepts are arbitrary under intentional description. Sterelny pointed out that (as Fodor 1998 was to realize) it is simply untrue that any old thing will suffice to make PLATYPUS available. Only platypuses[1] will do, and it is therefore false that we can "allow for any amount of arbitrariness that [we] like" (1981b:280) in the cause–concept relation. Fodor (1998) grants this objection and retracts his claims about the arbitrariness of the trigger. He agrees that concepts of F-NESS tend to be caused by Fs, and argues that this regularity stems from a constitutive connection between *being an F* and *being a cause of acquisition of F-NESS*. In this way, he hopes to retain the brute-causal picture of acquisition while accepting the de facto non-arbitrariness of the relations between the acquisition mechanism's inputs and outputs.

Sterelny (1989), however, has another criticism up his sleeve. He confronts the Fodorean with what he calls 'the *Qua* Problem,' posed originally (in Sterelny 1983) as a difficulty for what Devitt and Sterelny (1987) call 'pure-causal' theories of reference. According to a pure-causal theory, the reference of a concept is fixed by the causal connections that obtain between it and its referent. In the paradigm (that is, ostensive) case, EMU refers to emus because those things cause tokenings of that concept.[2] Sterelny points out that any tokening caused by an emu is also caused by a bird, a vertebrate, an animal, and so on. So why does the concept that emus cause refer to *emus*, rather than to birds, or vertebrates, or . . . ? If EMU refers to emus because it is caused by emus, there must be something that determines that

---

1. More or less—the mechanism of 'reference-borrowing,' where we get concepts not from experiences of their instances but from representations of their instances, will be discussed in §6.3.

2. See Devitt (1981). Pure causal theories contrast with, e.g., description theories, according to which the reference of a concept is determined by an associated description.

it is *qua emu* that those animals cause that concept. The *Qua* Problem is the problem of specifying what that 'something' is.

In his (1989), Sterelny applies the *Qua* Problem to Fodor's nativism. Fodor must admit that F-experiences are what typically cause acquisition of the concept F-NESS: emu-experiences cause acquisition of EMU, cat-experiences cause acquisition of CAT, doorknob-experiences cause acquisition of DOOR-KNOB, and so on. But, Sterelny points out, any experience of an emu is also an experience of a bird, a vertebrate, an animal, a thing. . . . So how does the concept-forming mechanism 'know' to output a concept that refers to emus rather than one referring to birds, or vertebrates, or . . . ? If emus cause acquisition of EMU, then it must be *qua emu* that emus are triggering the acquisition device. In virtue of what, he asks, is this the case? He suggests that it may be a prototype or stereotype that we associate with the concept that determines which of its many causes is the one that fixes its reference. It is something about our background psychological state that makes it the case that a given emu is experienced *as* an emu, and hence that the concept-forming mechanism is determined to output the concept *of* an emu.

A third problem for Fodor, discussed by both Sterelny (1989) and Loar (1991:122ff.), arises out of the existence of an important and systematic class of exceptions to the doorknob/DOORKNOB regularity. Many concepts are not acquired ostensively. Some people may have gotten PLATYPUS through experience of platypuses, but most people outside of Australia (indeed, most people inside of Australia too, if my own attempts to locate a platypus in the 'animal friendly' platypus enclosure at Taronga Zoo in Sydney are any guide) get their PLATYPUS concepts through hearing someone talk about platypuses, watching TV shows about platypuses, reading books about platypuses, browsing the World Wide Web, whatever. Devitt (1981) calls this 'reference-borrowing': in case we are not directly acquainted with the referent of a concept, we can nonetheless acquire a concept with that reference by being connected (in the right way) with someone who *is* so acquainted. Loar calls concepts acquired through reference-borrowing 'deferential' concepts: we "implicitly take [their] reference to be determined by the language [we] speak" (1991:120).[3] Whatever you call it, nonostensive acquisition is a problem for Fodor. How could a brute-causal mechanism such as he postulates 'know' to output the concept PLATYPUS, and not THE SOUND /PLATYPUS/ or WORD MEANING PLATYPUS, or the like, in response to a trigger comprising someone's uttering 'platypus'? Both Sterelny and Loar again argue that further mental states must be involved in selecting the first referent over the others. Sterelny surmises that it is an intention to borrow reference that determines that, rather than picking the 'obvious' causal chain

---

3. Loar's conception is thus narrower than Devitt's (and Sterelny's, incidentally), for whereas the notion of reference-borrowing applies in cases where the occasioning experience is neither ostensive nor linguistic (as when I see a picture of a platypus), Loar's main concern is with concepts acquired through linguistic experience.

linking the acquired concept with its trigger (viz., /platypus/), the acquisition mechanism selects as the determinant of reference the more complex and socially mediated causal chain connecting that concept with platypuses. For Loar, it is a 'guiding conception' or, roughly, an intention that that concept refer to whatever 'platypus' refers to, that does the trick. While neither of these proposals has been fleshed out, they share an insistence that nonostensive acquisition must be psychologically mediated. Acquiring 'deferential' or 'borrowed' concepts is not a brute-causal matter. It is eminently 'rational-causal,' or psychological, in nature.

6.1.2 Historical versus Counterfactual Contents

Sterelny's formulations of these objections suffer from a polemical defect. They tacitly assume what I'll call a 'historical' conception of reference. That is, they assume that the reference of a concept is fixed by its *actual* relations (e.g., causal or informational relations) with things in the world. As a corollary, then, they suppose that if what is acquired as a result of a triggering experience is the concept of an F, then it must have been an F that triggered the acquisition mechanism. For if a concept were triggered by something that is not F, that concept could not refer to Fs, in which case it would not be the concept F-NESS.

The historicist intuition that concepts must be triggered by their referents is what lies behind Sterelny's *Qua* Problem. If a given triggering experience is going to cause acquisition of EMU, then it must be qua emu that the experience is doing the triggering. For if it is not qua emu that an emu triggers the acquisition device, then the concept acquired could not refer to emus. Similarly, it is what lies behind his worries about reference borrowing. A historical semantics implies that concepts refer to their triggers. So on this view it is mysterious how concepts could, as in the case of reference-borrowing, refer not to their triggers (words, pictures, etc.) but, rather, to what their triggers represent. Thus, Sterelny concludes, since something more than mere brute-causal interactions with the world is needed to secure concepts' reference, concept acquisition could not be a brute-causal process.

However, it is one thing to explain how reference gets fixed and it's another to explain how concepts are acquired. Theories of reference, or of representation more generally, seek to explain in virtue of what a particular object (word, concept, picture, other symbol) means what it does. What makes the English 'cat' refer to cats? In virtue of what does my concept PLATYPUS represent platypuses? Why is this photo a picture of the Notre Dame? Theories of reference thus seek to answer a metaphysical question: What makes it the case that a certain thing is *about* something else?

Theories of concept acquisition address a rather different question. Rather than asking: In virtue of what does PLATYPUS refer to platypuses?, theories of concept acquisition ask: In virtue of what do we come to have PLATYPUS, a representation of platypuses, in our heads? This is an etiological question about (ostensibly) psychological processes: What are the processes responsible for our heads' coming to contain objects with the sorts of representational properties that it is the job of theories of reference to explain?

Herein lies Sterelny's polemical problem, for the fact that explaining reference and explaining acquisition are in principle distinct theoretical tasks offers a loophole through which the Fodorean can slip to evade his objections. For although historical semantic theories entail that the conditions under which concepts are acquired are also those that fix reference, there are other theories of reference, including the counterfactual theory proposed by Fodor, that do not have this consequence. Hence Fodor is at liberty to agree with Sterelny (and Loar) that reference-fixing is not a brute-causal matter while maintaining nonetheless that concept acquisition is.

Historical semantic theories suggest that reference is fixed by whatever causes acquisition of a concept. Pure-causal theories of the kind propounded by Kripke (1972/1980), Putnam (1975), Devitt (1981), and (with modifications) Devitt and Sterelny (1989), for example, see the reference of a term (or concept) as being fixed by the causal connections holding between it and the object in the presence of which it is introduced. Thus, if triggers cause the first tokenings of concepts, concepts must refer to their triggers. Co-variational causal (or 'causal-informational') theories, of the sort defended by Dretske (1981) and explored at one time by Fodor himself (1984b, 1990b), hold that the reference of a term is a matter of what it carries information about, where a term carries information about whatever its tokening is de facto causally correlated with. Since concepts covary with their triggers, they must carry information about, and therefore refer to, the triggering property.

By 1987, however, Fodor had come to reject historical semantics such as these on the grounds that they fall prey to what he calls 'the Disjunction Problem.'[4] Suppose, the argument goes, that one night you glimpse a skunk slipping through the garden, and think 'There's the cat!' We want to say that your thought was mistaken: you thought that it was the cat when it was really a skunk. Given a historical account of what CAT means, however, we can't say this. For if concepts refer to what in fact causes them (or to what they in fact covary with), then if your concept was caused by (or covaries with) a skunk, it must refer to skunks. So, assuming that tokens of that type are also caused at times by cats, what tokens of CAT refer to is cats-or-skunks. So you did not think mistakenly that a cat was before you. Instead, you thought, correctly, that a cat-or-skunk was there. Perceptual error, it would seem, is impossible.

Fodor holds, not unreasonably, that if a theory of reference entails omniscience, that theory must be false.[5] So, he urges, instead of focusing on concepts' actual causal (etc.) relations with the world in developing our se-

4. See Fodor (1987; 1990a:51–87).

5. The disjunction problem works best against the simplest versions of historical theories. Unsurprisingly, proposals abound in the literature as to how to deal with misrepresentation. I leave to others the task of evaluating them.

mantic theories, we should focus instead on their counterfactual relations. If we could somehow make the counterfactuals count, then what would be important to the reference of CAT is not that concept's actual relations—be they with cats, skunks, or cats-or-skunks—but rather the relations it *would have with cats* (in certain ideal semantic circumstances). If CAT's reference were fixed by what tokenings of CAT would (under ideal circumstances) be caused by—namely, cats—then it wouldn't matter one whit that in some circumstances—or even in most circumstances—CAT tokens are caused by non-cats. So long as the concept satisfies the relevant counterfactuals, its reference to cats is secure, and the disjunction problem is defanged.

The counterfactuals that, on Fodor's view, fix conceptual contents are sustained by a network of natural laws connecting the property that the concept refers to with tokenings of that concept. Schematically,

> A representation R expresses the property P in virtue of its being a law that things that are P cause tokenings of R (in, say, some still-to-be-specified circumstances C). (Fodor, 1998:12).

That is, CAT refers to cats because there exists a nomic relation between the property *being a cat* and the property *being a cause of CAT tokens*—and not because of any actual, historical connections between that concept and the world.

This basic picture needs elaboration if it is to deal with the disjunction problem (and, as we'll see, Loar and Sterelny). For if skunks can cause CAT tokens (as in the story above), then there must be laws permitting this too: there must be laws connecting CATs with *being a skunk* in addition to the laws connecting CATs with *being a cat*. In which case, by the schema above, CAT refers to skunks as well as cats, and the disjunction problem remains unsolved. Elaborating the basic counterfactual story, however, has proven somewhat tricky—so tricky, indeed, that Fodor tends now to leave the semantic details more or less to their own devices.[6] But we can still get an idea of what kind of explication is needed by looking at one of his older formulations of the counterfactual theory.

In his (1990a:93ff.), Fodor responded to the disjunction problem by postulating an asymmetry among the laws governing tokenings of CATs. He maintained that whereas the ability of cats to cause CATs is independent of any ability that skunks might have to cause CATs, the converse is not the case: skunks cause tokenings of CAT *only because cats do*. This suggests that if there are nomic relations between other properties and tokenings of CAT, then those other relations 'asymmetrically depend' on the cat–CAT relation:

---

6. See his account of informational semantics in his (1998:12): "Meaning is information (more or less). . . . what bestows content on mental representations is something about their causal-cum-nomological relations to things that fall under them: For example, what bestows upon a mental representation the content *dog* is something about its tokenings being caused by dogs. . . . Just how this works depends, of course, on what sort of causal-cum-nomological covariation content is and what sorts of things you think that concepts represent."

the skunk–CAT law exists in virtue of there being a cat–CAT law, but not vice versa. This asymmetry, Fodor argues, is semantically significant. For reference depends only on the counterfactuals sustained by the independent (cat–CAT) law. Dependent laws (such as the skunk–CAT law) are beside the semantical point. Thus you did make a mistake when you saw the skunk and thought CAT! Your CAT token referred to cats, and not to skunks-or-cats, because skunks cause tokenings of CAT only because cats do, that is, because the cat–CAT law is, as I'll say, 'semantically primary.'

Now I have my doubts about asymmetric dependence and, judging by the conspicuous absence of asymmetry talk in his recent writings, so has Fodor. But we do not need to pursue those doubts here.[7] The importance of the asymmetric dependence story was that it offered Fodor a way of picking out some of the nomological relations enjoyed by a concept as being semantically primary. It offered, that is to say, a way of distinguishing those laws which supply the counterfactuals that are relevant to the fixation of reference from the 'semantically secondary' laws—those that are irrelevant to reference. And this is what gets him out of the disjunction problem. Although there are presumably lots of laws subsuming the myriad causal relations entered into by a concept like CAT, only one of those laws—the cat–CAT law—is relevant to fixing what CAT means.

This alone, Fodor thinks, is reason enough to accept that, contra the historical picture, it's the counterfactuals that fix content. But a counterfactual semantic theory offers more than the hope of dissolving the disjunction problem; it offers also to save Fodor's acquisition theory from the depredations of Loar and Sterelny.

6.1.3 Answering Sterelny and Loar

The distinction between semantically primary and semantically secondary laws has the effect of divorcing concepts' reference from their etiology. This, in turn, allows Fodor to insist that there is a distinction between explaining reference and explaining acquisition. And this allows him to grant that triggers do not fix reference while nonetheless retaining his view that they brute-cause concepts. That is, given a counterfactual semantics (plus a story about certain laws' being semantically primary), the causal factors implicated in a concept's arising in the mind need have nothing to do with how its reference is determined. For the causal process under which a concept arises may be covered by a semantically secondary law, in which case that causal process is irrelevant to the concept's identity. Reference is secured by the semantically primary law, and that the acquisition process happens to be covered by a secondary law is thus of no semantical interest.

So, first, it doesn't matter to the identity of the concept attained whether triggers are arbitrary or not. So long as the law connecting, say, doorknobs

---

7. It is (putting it mildly) unclear what it is for one law to be 'dependent' on another; and it's unclear too why we should take Fodor's word for how the putative dependencies go.

with DOORKNOBs is primary, anything at all could cause tokenings of that concept. A fortiori, anything could cause the first tokenings of that concept. Fodor (1981b) was right after all: on a counterfactual semantics, the triggering stimuli for concepts can in principle be 'as arbitrary as you like'—even if, in practice, they're not.

Nor, second, does it matter qua what a trigger causes the acquisition of a concept. Sterelny thought that it was important that it should be qua platypuses that platypuses trigger PLATYPUS, for otherwise, he asked, how could that concept succeed in referring to those animals? On the counterfactual view, though, PLATYPUS refers to platypuses in virtue of the platypus–PLATYPUS law: the laws connecting monotremes, vertebrates, and so on with PLATYPUSes are semantically secondary. So platypuses could trigger PLATYPUS qua the things that wowed the Royal Society in 1779 and, so long as the platypus–PLATYPUS law is primary, that concept's reference to platypuses is secure.

Nor, finally, does reference-borrowing constitute a problem. So long as the ability of /platypus/ or TV shows or *National Geographic* articles to cause tokenings of PLATYPUS is secondary to the ability of platypuses to do so, then any of these things could trigger that concept. What concept is acquired depends not on what the trigger is, but rather on what the primary laws governing tokenings of that concept happen to be.

So Fodor can apparently evade the Sterelny–Loar objections to his acquisition theory. Which is not to say that those objections are uninteresting. On the contrary, the points made by Loar and Sterelny have a significance that goes far beyond the assessment of Fodor's particular position. For what their arguments show is that you cannot be both a nativist about concept acquisition and a historicist about semantics. That is, if you take the view (as many do) that the conditions under which concepts are acquired are also those under which their references are fixed, then you cannot *also* take the view that acquiring concepts is a brute-causal matter, for brute-causal interactions between the mind and the world do not suffice to determine concepts' references. Sterelny and Loar thus rule out completely one way of being a nativist about concepts. What we have seen in this section, though, is that there remains another option for the nativist to explore. By eschewing a historical semantics, one can deny the assumption, upon which the Sterelny–Loar arguments turned, that "meaning is method of acquisition." One can claim that the reference of a concept is determined by the relations (actual or possible) between concepts and objects that are described in the primary laws. This means that a nativist may agree with Sterelny (and Loar) that the brute-causal processes he describes do not determine reference, yet maintain that this in no way impugns his claim that they are the processes by which concepts are acquired.[8]

8. The arguments of this section were inspired by certain of Fodor's remarks in his (1990a) and (1991a). In his (1990a), he lauds Skinner's semantics because for Skinner, all that matters are relations of "[nomic covariance] between symbols and their denotations. It doesn't matter how that covariance is mediated; it doesn't matter what mechanisms

In what follows, I will grant for the sake of argument that reference is taken care of in (more or less) the way Fodor suggests. The question still remains: Is the acquisition mechanism 'brute-causal' rather than 'rational causal'?

6.1.4 The Issue Recast

The Fodorean nativist claims that, given how we have been 'wired up,' experience is both necessary and sufficient for the availability of all concepts. The necessity of experience implies that you cannot get a concept like ECHIDNA in your head in the absence of any experience. Its sufficiency implies that experience is *all* you need for the acquisition of that concept. No additional 'top-down' or psychological processing (such as the formulation and testing of semantic hypotheses) is implicated in ECHIDNA's attainment.

In explicating the 'brute-causality' of the acquisition mechanism, Fodor claimed that the experiences occasioning acquisition of a concept 'can be as arbitrary as you like.' While this may be true in principle, the experiences that as a matter of fact give rise to concepts are of two broad types. Some concepts (I suspect a minority) are acquired ostensively. In this case, it is experiences of Fs that cause acquisition of the concept F-NESS. Many others, though, are acquired through reference-borrowing. In this second kind of case, the concept F-NESS is acquired not from experiences of Fs but, rather, from experiences of *representations of* Fs. Giving a nativist account of concept acquisition, therefore, divides into two subtasks. First, one must explain how Fs brute-cause acquisition of F-NESS. Second, one must explain how representations of Fs brute-cause F-NESS. I'll argue in the next two sections that the Fodorean can succeed in neither of these endeavors.

6.2 Ostension

Envisaging a nativist account of ostensive acquisition requires that we conceive a brute-causal mechanism such that seeing (or otherwise coming into sensory contact with) an echidna suffices to cause it to deliver ECHIDNA to the mind. The mechanism's being brute-causal entails that it does not require for its functioning the input of any particular psychological states or processes. It is an innately specified, stimulus-driven kind of device that, given an echidna experience, causes us to 'lock to' or 'resonate to' echidnas. The

sustain the covariation" (1990a:56). He argues that just because the covariance is mediated, this doesn't mean that the mediation helps to determine the meaning. In his (1991a) response to Loar, Fodor writes: "Ostensive definitions, 'guiding conceptions' and the like may be among the mechanisms that occasion or sustain such nomic relations [i.e., those definitive of reference]; but they aren't constitutive of semanticity; only the nomic relations themselves are" (1991a:287).

task, then, is to explain how, in virtue merely of having an echidna experience, our minds become echidna detectors.

Providing the required explanation might at first seem straightforward. In ostensive acquisition, it is an echidna that triggers ECHIDNA. Thus, the process of ECHIDNA acquisition instantiates the semantically primary law and we, by implication, must be echidna detectors before acquisition occurs. That is, our minds must somehow be structured such that they inherently have the capacity to resonate with *being an echidna*. Concept acquisition takes place when the resonations begin. What of the Fodorean claim that acquisition is brute-causal? This, as we've seen, implies that there is nothing psychological going on when echidnas make us think ECHIDNA. Our ability to resonate to echidnas is unmediated by any intentional states or processes. This seems unproblematic too. There is nothing inherently odd in supposing that just as a Coke machine is designed such that the property *being coins of a certain size and weight* causes delivery of a Coke, so we were 'designed,' that is, we evolved, such that *being an echidna* causes tokenings of ECHIDNA.

But anything that has the property *being an echidna* also has the property *being a vertebrate*. This raises the question: Is the acquisition mechanism *also* brutely sensitive to *that* property? Here the nativist faces a dilemma. Answering "No" would imply that the concept VERTEBRATE could not be acquired through ostension. For if the concept-forming mechanism were not brutely sensitive to *being a vertebrate*, then the process by which VERTEBRATE is acquired, and subsequently tokened, could not be subsumed under a primary law relating *being a vertebrate* to *being a cause of VERTEBRATE tokens*. VERTEBRATE acquisition would have to be subsumed under one or other of the dependent laws involving VERTEBRATE, which is to say that VERTEBRATE could be acquired only through reference-borrowing. Since this would seem to be false, the Fodorean had better say "Yes," admitting that the property *being a vertebrate*, as well as the property *being an echidna*, can trigger the acquisition mechanism. But if both echidna-hood and vertebrate-hood can trigger acquisition, then we need an account of what it is that determines which of these is the causally efficacious property in a given instance. We need an account, to put it in more Fodorean terms, of what determines *which law* subsumes the acquisition process in case we are experientially connected with an echidna. Is it the primary law relating *being an echidna* to *being a cause of ECHIDNA tokens* (in which case the mechanism should output ECHIDNA)? Or is it the primary law relating *being a vertebrate* to *being a cause of VERTEBRATE tokens* (in which case the output is VERTEBRATE)?

A variant of Sterelny's *Qua* Problem thus arises to plague the nativist: Either (1) it is false that we're born such that we can resonate selectively to both echidnas and vertebrates (in which case we need another account of how VERTERBATE is acquired), or (2) if the nativist claims (as perhaps he should, given that we do seem to be able to get both VERTEBRATE and ECHIDNA ostensively) that we *can* resonate selectively to both kinds of thing, then there must be something that determines that, in a given instance, we're resonating to an echidna qua an echidna, and not qua a vertebrate, and hence that we acquire ECHIDNA, rather than VERTEBRATE. What could this 'something' be?

In addition to denying outright that *being a vertebrate* can trigger the acquisition mechanism (a move I suppose to be an option of last resort), there are three ways Fodor might go here. First, he might claim that *all* the properties of an input are causally efficacious, thus implying that a single echidna experience occasions acquisition of concepts for all the kinds of which echidnas are members. This is unacceptable: people routinely acquire concepts of particular kinds without thereby acquiring umpteen others as well.

Second, he might claim that it is a matter of chance which properties of the input engage the acquisition mechanism: nothing determines whether it's *being an echidna* or *being a vertebrate* that is the causally salient property, hence nothing determines which concept is outputted given an echidna experience. Some concept is acquired; but which concept this is, is entirely up for grabs. This would imply that we should expect to find people who have acquired, say, VERTEBRATE and MAMMAL but not DOG; ARMCHAIR but not CHAIR; MISOGYNIST but not MAN. Typically, though, we first acquire concepts for middle-sized physical objects like CHAIR and DOG, only later acquiring concepts for sub- and superordinate kinds like ARMCHAIR and VERTEBRATE, and later still acquiring abstract concepts like MISOGYNIST. If it truly were a random matter which concepts are acquired given what experiences, in short, we'd expect to find a lot more variability in the course of acquisition than, in fact, we do. So this response looks untenable as well.

In his (1981b), Fodor has a story about why we see the trends we do in concept acquisition. In explaining why we acquire DOG before acquiring either more general concepts like VERTEBRATE or more particular concepts like POODLE, he suggests that "the triggering structure of the mind is *layered*, the attainment of some . . . concepts being the effect of (hence never prior to) the attainment of others" (1981b:308). Thus, DOG is acquired prior to VERTEBRATE and POODLE because in the latter cases, "triggering . . . is mediated by the previously attained conceptual repertoire" (1981b:313): the structure of the acquisition mechanism is such that the acquisition of DOG is a causally necessary condition for the triggering of VERTEBRATE or POODLE; hence VERTEBRATE and POODLE are acquired after DOG. So, "while all primitive concepts are ipso facto triggered, there is nevertheless a hierarchy of triggers, and it is this hierarchy . . . which predicts the observed order of concept attainment" (Fodor 1981b:301).

The triggering hierarchy represents a third way the nativist might take out of the difficulties raised in this section. If the concept-forming mechanism operates according to a rule like "Given an echidna-ish input, output ECHIDNA unless ECHIDNA has already been acquired, in which case output MONOTREME; and if MONOTREME has already been acquired, output MAMMAL, VERTEBRATE, . . . , etc.," then we can see why experiences of instances of a kind should sometimes be insufficient to occasion concepts of that kind.

For according to this rule, if MAMMAL and MONOTREME have not yet been acquired, VERTEBRATE will not be triggered by an echidna experience, even though that experience is in fact an experience of a vertebrate.

6.2.1 A Dilemma

The triggering hierarchy represents perhaps Fodor's best shot for solving the present difficulties while at the same time retaining the idea that acquisition is brute-causal. However, postulating an inborn triggering hierarchy also confronts him with something of a dilemma. Suppose that the structure of the hierarchy were relatively simple. Then we would expect to see a lot more *in*variance in the order of concept attainment than, arguably, we do. Since mechanisms that vary widely from individual to individual are in general poor candidates for innateness, the claim that the hierarchy is innately specified strongly suggests that it is common to most or all members of our species. Such commonality, indeed, is assumed by Fodor himself when he invokes the hierarchy to account for a relatively stable, species-wide feature of concept attainment, namely, the fact that most children acquire concepts like DOG before they acquire VERTEBRATE or POODLE. However, apart from this 'concepts-for-middle-sized-objects-first' rule, regularities are the exception rather than the norm in concept formation. In contradiction to the rule proposed above, it is simply not true that once a person has ECHIDNA, further echidna experiences will trigger MONOTREME; and if MONOTREME has already been acquired, will trigger MAMMAL, VERTEBRATE, and so on. There were, after all, plenty of Australian Aborigines who experienced plenty of echidnas without acquiring MONOTREME, MAMMAL, and VERTEBRATE.

This is evidence against a triggering hierarchy, at least of the simple sort we're currently envisaging. For if there were an innately specified triggering hierarchy, and if it were what determines whether a person acquires ECHIDNA or MONOTREME or MAMMAL or VERTEBRATE from a given echidna experience, then we would expect to see the same kinds of regularities in this case as are found in the case of DOG and POODLE, just discussed. That is, if the Fodorean postulates an inborn triggering hierarchy to solve the current version of the *Qua* Problem wherever it arises—and that is virtually everywhere—then the specific order in which particular concepts are acquired should be highly invariant from person to person, and from culture to culture. But it is not, and that it is not, I suggest, constitutes the first horn of a dilemma, to wit: postulating a simple triggering hierarchy implies interpersonal and cross-cultural developmental regularities that simply do not exist.

In response, the Fodorean might argue that we don't see such regularities because the hierarchy is much more highly structured than the simplistic rule discussed in the previous section suggests.[9] The acquisition of MONOTREME,

9. David Hilbert and Jim Woodward both suggested this response.

for example, might require not just the previous acquisition of ECHIDNA but also of EGG-LAYING, MAMMAL, and AUSTRALIAN. Thus echidna-experiences did not trigger MONOTREME in Australian Aborigines, not because there is no inborn triggering hierarchy but, rather, because the Aborigines did not possess the other concepts—like AUSTRALIAN, a much later construction of European imperialism—that the hierarchy specifies as being necessary to MONOTREME's acquisition. The point is quite general. *Any* empirical facts about who has what concepts, in what order, in what circumstances, can be accommodated, so long as we're prepared to build enough complexity into the triggering hierarchy.

For that very reason, though, this enrichment strategy also looks suspiciously ad hoc: the more bells and whistles we add, the more the hierarchy smells of the explanatorily vacuous 'whatever-it-is-that-explains-concept-acquisition,' familiar from part I. It also looks suspiciously like a step away from brute-causation and back toward rational-causation. For one thing, postulating a hierarchy of any kind means that we are putting intentionally specified necessary conditions on the operation of the acquisition mechanism. If you need to possess the concepts AUSTRALIAN and EGG-LAYING and MAMMAL in order to acquire MONOTREME, then acquisition *does* require input from other psychological states and is not quite as brutely causal as we have been led to believe. For another thing, postulating a rich inborn hierarchy gets whatever plausibility it has from a tacit acceptance of a picture of acquisition that is, from a Fodorean perspective, illicit. Why do we find it plausible, if we do, to say that prior acquisition of MAMMAL, EGG-LAYING, and AUSTRALIAN is necessary for attainment of MONOTREME? I suppose it's because having those concepts is in some intuitive sense necessary for grasping MONOTREME's meaning. But to find such enrichment plausible for this reason is to enjoy intuitions stemming from a rational-causal picture of acquisition. From Fodor's perspective, after all, it might just as well have been XYLOPHONE, CONTRAPUNTAL, and ROMANIAN that turned out to be necessary for getting MONOTREME. Of course the nativist could claim now that it is an empirical question what the structure of the hierarchy is. And of course he'd be right. Still, I suggest, the notion that possessing other concepts is *biologically* necessary for the attainment of MONOTREME gets whatever plausibility it has through being conflated with the rational-causal idea (which, in fact, I will be defending below) that having some concepts is *psychologically* necessary for the attainment of others.

But what is most worrying about this move, and what leads most directly, I think, to the second horn of the nativist's dilemma, is that there is an undeniable tension between viewing the mechanism of acquisition as richly structured and viewing it as inborn. If you're going to be a nativist about the mental, then, if you keep the inbuilt stuff relatively simple, you can get away with issuing a promissory note (or notes) on the biology. You can wave your hands around, claiming either that the mechanism in question was shaped in some relatively straightforward way by natural selection or else, perhaps, that it arose fortuitously through some non-Darwinian process. The more you enrich the hypothesized inbuilt structure, though, the less trustworthy such notes appear. As nativists about language, among others, have begun to recognize, inborn complexity demands an explanation, or at least an explanation sketch, in terms of natural selection.[10] Absent an account of how they could have evolved, highly complex triggering hierarchies are just somethings-we-know-not-what, postulated to "explain" acquisition when, really, we have no explanation of acquisition on hand at all.

In explaining the nature of the allegedly brute-causal mechanisms mediating the ostensive acquisition of concepts, the nativist is caught between the rock of complete randomness (nothing but chance determines what concept a given experience causes us to acquire) and the hard place of innate overdetermination (the triggering hierarchy is the determining factor). Neither of these pictures is in line with what we know to be true about concept acquisition: there is a certain amount of regularity in the order in which concepts are got; but these regularities occur within a sea of variability. Enriching the hierarchy might explain the observed order-within-disorder of concept attainment. But, I have argued, it is implausible to think that there could be a biologically specified hierarchy with the kind of structural complexity that would be required to explain the empirical facts. In short, a simple hierarchy will not account for the facts of acquisition; but a complex hierarchy is evolutionarily implausible. The triggering hierarchy does nothing to illuminate the mechanism of ostensive acquisition.

There is, of course, another way of explaining the facts of concept acquisition. This is to suppose that acquisition is psychologically mediated, that there is something external to the acquisition mechanism (e.g., your state of background knowledge and/or your current desires and interests) that determines which concept you get from a given experience. If some concepts were acquired 'brutely' in virtue of the way our 'sensorium' is innately structured, and others were derived through some collaboration of this 'primitive base' with both our further experiences and our surrounding beliefs, needs, and interests, then it wouldn't be surprising to observe both some commonalities and a lot of variability in the conceptual history of different individuals. But, while I shall urge this picture in §6.4, it is an account that the Fodorean cannot accept. To view ostensive acquisition as psychologically mediated is to admit that it is not an innately specified, brute-causal, stimulus-driven process. It is to admit that the radical nativist's acquisition theory is inadequate.

6.3 Nonostensive Acquisition

There is a puzzle about the mechanism for reference-borrowing's being brute-causal too. I acquired PLATYPUS through hearing someone say 'platy-

---

10. See Oyama (1985); Pinker and Bloom (1990); Pinker (1994:332ff.).

pus.' You acquired it through watching a nature program on TV. An Italian acquires it through reading the word *ornitorinco*. A speaker of American Sign Language (ASL) acquires it through seeing a certain sequence of hand movements. Assuming that each of us possesses roughly the same kind of genetically specified acquisition device—assuming, that is, that each of us could, in a different environment, have got PLATYPUS in some way different from that in which we did—we must conceive of a mechanism such that any of these types of experiential input suffices to cause the delivery of that concept. The mechanism, in other words, must be built such that any of the following properties—*being a token of the sound /platypus/; being a token of a TV show about platypuses; being a token of the written word 'ornitorinco'; being a hand movement of kind . . . ;* and so on—is enough to brute-cause the output of a mental symbol occupying the place in the nexus of causal–nomological relations that (on the counterfactual theory) determines that concept's reference to platypuses.

But how could a brute-causal mechanism be sensitive to such a diverse range of inputs? It is possible to imagine a machine that is brutely sensitive to *being a platypus*. But it is very much harder to conceive of a brute-causal mechanism that is sensitive to the huge class of properties that on this view are triggers for PLATYPUS. For the properties in question are an extremely motley bunch: the written symbol *ornitorinco* shares no obvious intrinsic properties with the spoken sound /platypus/, which shares no properties with a picture of a platypus, which shares no properties with the ASL sign meaning *platypus*. What kind of brute-causal mechanism could it be that managed to recognize and respond to just these things? And how, as Sterelny (1989) asks, could such a mechanism have evolved? Recall that on the nativist view, it is just because of Nature's whim that we are wired up to acquire PLATYPUS when stimulated by platypuses. But how could Nature have 'known' that in the eighteenth century, a certain series of sounds would be introduced to refer in English to platypuses, or that a certain sequence of squiggles on a page would in Italian designate those animals, or that in the twentieth century, a very particular arrangement of hand movements would be introduced in ASL to mean *platypus*—and thus have known to make our minds such that hearing this sound or seeing those squiggles, or witnessing those movements would cause a concept that covaries *with platypuses?*

6.3.1 Possible Responses

There are again three ways that a nativist might respond. First, he might emphasize that the fact that we cannot imagine such a mechanism does not mean that there isn't one. Nor does the fact that we can't imagine how it might have been built entail that Mother Nature didn't build it. Indeed, he might continue, his argument shows that there must be and she must have; and all our failure of imagination should do is remind us that there are more things about the place than we (if not Fodor) ever dreamed of. To make this sort of response, however, is to admit that Fodorean nativism is just a redescription of the problem about how we acquire concepts, not a solution to it.

Second, the nativist might agree that PLATYPUS triggers do not share any obvious intrinsic properties for the mechanism to respond to, and maintain instead that it is sensitive to some other, less obvious property uniting them. However, it seems that there are only two properties shared by the triggers for PLATYPUS. One is the property *being triggers of PLATYPUSes*, which is clearly a non-starter in this context. The other is *representing platypuses*. But as Fodor argues in his (1987:33–41)—plausibly enough, I think—relational properties of things can affect their causal powers only if there is some natural law or other mechanism that explains how this effect occurs.[11] If we look for a mechanism by which to relate *representing platypuses* to PLATYPUS, however, we are back where we started: a mechanism would ground the causal powers of *representing platypuses* by responding to some intrinsic property or properties shared by things possessing that relational property. But, as we have just seen, no such intrinsic property is available in this case. Perhaps, then, it's a matter of natural law that *representing platypuses* causes PLATYPUS? But to claim solely on the basis of the present difficulty concerning nonostensive acquisition that there is a special law of nature in virtue of which the property *representing platypuses* causes tokenings of the concept PLATYPUS is outrageously ad hoc. In any case, it does not really solve the problem at hand. For what we want to know is how there could be a brute-causal mechanism that outputs PLATYPUS given any of the diverse experiences that de facto lead to the nonostensive acquisition of that concept. We've seen that there are no shared intrinsic properties that the machine could respond to. So then we asked how a machine could respond 'brutely' to the one (relational) property that the inputs do share. And to be told just that there is a special law of nature in virtue of which that mechanism can respond to that property is, its flagrant ad hockery aside, entirely beside the point. What we want to know, when we are talking about acquisition mechanisms, is how the laws of nature are implemented. Merely insisting on there being a law, then, is to skirt the problem altogether.

A third way in which the nativist might try to explain the mechanism for nonostensive acquisition is by again invoking his 'hierarchy of triggers.' As described above (§6.2.1), the hierarchy explained why experiences of instances of concepts are insufficient for acquisition to occur. What needs explaining, though, in case a concept is acquired through reference-borrowing, is not why experiences of instances are sometimes insufficient for acquisition; it is why they are sometimes unnecessary. The question is: How can you get MONOTREME from a nonmonotreme trigger? and not (as before): How can you fail to get MONOTREME despite (like the Aborigines) experiencing lots of monotremes?

---

11. E.g., the relational property *being a Sagittarius* has no causal powers because there is no law or causal mechanism explaining how the positions of the planets at one's birth affect the subsequent course of one's life.

A possible elaboration of the hierarchy that might serve to answer this difficulty is suggested by Fodor's discussion of what he calls the 'mental chemistry' view of concept acquisition.[12] On this view, according to Fodor, concepts can be 'triggered' by other concepts alone: "if entertaining A and B is causally sufficient for acquiring C, then . . . [a]ll that's required to learn C is *the previous acquisition of A and B.* That's to say, in effect, that some simple concepts may be triggered by other concepts" (1981b:303–4). While it is somewhat unclear whether Fodor meant to endorse this view, it does imply not merely that possession of one concept may be necessary for the acquisition of another, but also that possession of one concept may be sufficient for the attainment of another. So if Fodor were to adopt the mental chemistry picture, he could argue that something like the following two-stage process occurs in nonostensive acquisition. Hearing the sound /platypus/ brute-causes acquisition of the concept /PLATYPUS/, which in turn, and with no further experiential input, brute-causes PLATYPUS.[13]

But while it may not be so odd to think that hearing /platypus/ could brute-cause THE SOUND /PLATYPUS/, it surely is bizarre to suppose that we evolved such that THE SOUND /PLATYPUS/ could brute-cause PLATYPUS. It's bizarre, that is to say, to think that once you have a mental representation of the noise someone makes when she says 'platypus,' *this is all you need* to acquire the ability to think thoughts about platypuses. So if it you find it questionable on evolutionary grounds to attempt to skirt the *Qua* Problem by holding that our minds are structured such that attainment of MAMMAL and EGG-LAYING (let alone XYLOPHONE and CONTRAPUNTAL) are necessary to the acquisition of MONOTREME, you're going to find it even more implausible to think that we evolved such that acquisition of /PLATYPUS/ is sufficient for acquisition of PLATYPUS itself.

It is not, of course, so implausible to think that we evolved such that acquisition of /PLATYPUS/ *together with some other psychological processing* could enable us to think thoughts about platypuses. If you had /PLATYPUS/, for example, then you could form the intention to use a certain other mental symbol—it might be PLATYPUS—to mean whatever /platypus/ means. But to think that nonostensive acquisition involves the deployment of such "guiding intentions" (Loar 1991:122) is to admit that that process is not brute-causal. It is to admit, again, that the Fodorean picture of acquisition is inadequate.

6.3.2 Fodor on 'Deferential' Concepts

Before exploring further the notion that concept acquisition is, after all, a thoroughly psychological process, we should look at one final possibility that

---

12. See Fodor (1981b:299ff.). Briefly, the idea of mental chemistry seems to be that concepts may be composed out of other concepts without containing them as parts.

13. Note that what /platypus/ etc. causes cannot be PLATYPUS REPRESENTATION, for it's hard to see how one acquires the concept REPRESENTATION OF A PLATYPUS prior to possessing a concept of the thing, the platypus, that the representation is a representation of.

remains open to the nativist in dealing with his troubles to do with reference-borrowing, viz., denial. Fodor might choose to insist that the only route to acquisition is ostension, in which case the brute-causality (or not) of reference-borrowing is moot. Now, denying outright that reference-borrowing is a way of getting concepts seems on the face of it too high a price to pay to save radical concept nativism. If the only route to acquisition is ostension, then it follows that most of us do not have many of the concepts we thought we did. Nonetheless, Fodor in his (1990a) seemed to be inclining in this direction. There, he agued against the existence of deferential concepts à la Loar,[14] writing:

> ... [t]he application of mental representations can't be deferential in [Loar's] sense for at least two reasons: first, we have no policies with respect to our concepts (only with respect to our words); and second, we think in a de facto private language, a policy of deference to other speakers of which would verge on incoherence. Fodor (1991:285–86)

This may be a way of denying that reference can be borrowed, for a deferential concept (as we saw in the last section) looks like an obvious candidate for what one acquires through that process.

By 1994, however, Fodor had changed his mind on this issue. In *The Elm and the Expert*, he argues that if deference is understood to be a matter of adopting a certain policy, namely, the policy of using other people as instruments, then there can be deferential concepts. For Fodor, having a concept is a matter of having your mental states covary in the right kinds of ways (actually and counterfactually) with properties in the world. One of the ways that you can secure the requisite correlations, he argues, is by using others' thoughts as guides for your own. So, to take Fodor's example (1994: 34–36), one way you might manage to get your ELM and BEECH thoughts to covary in the right kinds of ways with elms and beeches is by making "the character of the correspondence between [your] thoughts and the world *a matter of policy*" (1994:35). That is, if you really care about having ELM thoughts (rather than ELM-OR-BEECH thoughts), you can make it a point to find yourself a botanist. Then, by assuming that her ELM thoughts are reliably correlated with elms, and that her utterances of 'elm' are reliable guides to her ELM thoughts, you can use her as an instrument with which to correlate your mental states with elms. You can acquire the ability to think about elms, in other words, by making it a policy (roughly) to think ELM iff an expert says 'Yup, it's an elm.'

Herein is another mechanism by which reference-borrowing could be sustained. You can acquire the concept ELM by getting your ELM thoughts to covary with elms, and you can do that by listening to what experts tell you about elms. Note, however, that this way of getting the concept of an elm,

---

14. See §6.1. See also Loar (1991:121–22): "Suppose my concept 'horse' is deferential, that I implicitly take its reference to be determined by the language I speak, that I intend to refer in my thinking to whatever 'horse' refers to in that language."

like Loar's way, is not brute-causal. Adopting policies with regard to one's thoughts, and adopting policies with regard to the thoughts and words of others, requires considerable cognitive sophistication. It is an eminently *un*-brute thing to do. So if reference-borrowing works like this, then even on Fodor's own view, acquiring concepts nonostensively could not be a brute-causal matter.

6.4 Concept Acquisition Is Psychologically Mediated

Fodor's (1994) account of deferential concepts underscores the points that I have been stressing in the last two sections. We have seen repeatedly that when you try to describe in any sort of detail how concept acquisition works, you cannot do it without doing psychology as well. The arguments of §6.3 showed that if one insists that the mechanism of nonostensive acquisition be described nonintentionally, one ends up with no borrowed concepts at all. Since it is impossible to imagine how Nature could have designed a machine that would output PLATYPUS in response to any of the myriad experiences that can lead to our acquiring that concept nonostensively, no Fodorean brute-causal borrowing mechanism exists. The arguments in §6.2 tend to the same conclusion vis-à-vis ostension. If ostension were brute-causal, then either we ought to get virtually all our concepts at once (which we don't); or we ought to get them in a completely haphazard and inexplicable order (which, again, we don't); or everybody ought to get them in the same order (which they don't). More than a genetically bestowed predisposition to respond to the things that we perceive around us is involved in acquiring concepts. A person might be 'wired up' to respond to *those creatures* (and here I point to a platypus), but what concepts she gets from an interaction with a platypus—what she starts 'resonating to' as a result of that experience—is not a brute-causal matter. It is instead highly sensitive to a variety of other factors, such as what she knows, what she is interested in, whether she gives a damn, and so on. It is possible, as we saw in §6.2, for a nativist to dig in his heels and simply insist that there is enough inbuilt structure in our minds to explain away the vagaries of acquisition. But where that structure came from, and why we should believe in it when there is a more plausible—that is, psychological—account of acquisition in the offing, remains a mystery.

Concept acquisition is not a brute-causal process. Instead, it is thoroughly psychologically mediated. This raises substantive questions: What kind of psychological mediation is required? How do the mediating structures arise in the mind? In what follows, I shall sketch some tentative answers to these questions. I assume that some kind of causal-informational story about content will be made to work; that having the concept of an F will involve states of you carrying information about F-ness; and hence that acquiring the concept of an F is a matter of getting yourself into a position whereby states of you *can* carry information about F-ness. Following Fodor, I shall say that to acquire a concept is to get oneself 'locked to' F-ness, that is, to acquire the ability to respond selectively and reliably (in appropriate circumstances) to nearby instantiations of the property *being an F.* Against this background, the two questions just raised can be reformulated as follows. First, what does a person need to be like, what sort of mind does she need to have, in order that she can 'lock to' F-ness? Second, how does a person come to have a mind like that? Let us turn to these questions.

6.4.1 Concept Possession: What Kind of Psychological Mediation Is Needed?

I take the arguments of this chapter to have shown that resonating or 'locking' to F-ness usually involves more than merely having one's genetic endowment interact brute-causally with the world. Being an F detector is usually not something one *is*; it is something one *does.* Having concepts, in most cases, involves using one's mind. But using one's mind how? Much of the discussion about concept acquisition seems to assume that there is just one kind of thing that a person needs to do in order to have a concept. Debate rages about whether she needs to know a definition of F-ness, or to have encountered an F triggering stimulus, or to represent a prototype or a stereotype of F-ness, or to know a lot, or a little bit, or everything, or nothing at all about Fs, in order to possess the concept F-NESS. It seems to me, however, to be very unlikely that there will turn out to be just one way to have a concept. Having a concept is a matter of resonating to the property that the concept expresses, and there are many different mechanisms, some of which will be more appropriately employed in some circumstances than in others, whereby such resonations could be sustained.

One way that a person could lock to a property is by knowing its definition. You can start resonating to *being a bachelor,* for instance, by learning that bachelors are unmarried men. So long as you are already locked to the properties *being unmarried* and *being a man,* that is to say, you can use your abilities to detect those properties in your attempts to spot bachelors. This, I believe, is the truth in the 'Classical' theory of concepts: one way of having a concept, or of locking to the property that that concept expresses, is by knowing its definition.

As Fodor showed, however, knowing a definition is not, and indeed could not be, the only way that a person locks to a property. Another way to be in a position to detect Fs is to know the prototype or stereotype for F-ness. As we have seen in chapter 5, one can get oneself locked fairly well to *being a doorknob* by responding selectively to waist-high, movable protuberances attached to doors. Or one can get oneself locked to *being a dog* by responding differentially to things that look more or less like Rover. This is what is right about non-Classical theories of concepts: one of the ways you can become a detector of Fs, is by knowing the F prototype or F stereotype, and responding selectively to things that satisfy that prototype or are relevantly similar to the stereotype.

There is another means by which people get themselves locked appropriately to properties of interest. We can make our words and states of mind resonate with the world by making use of the mental states and words of others. One may 'borrow' reference (Devitt 1981) from an expert, or 'defer' to an expert (Loar 1991), or, as Fodor (1997) has it, 'adopt a policy to use an expert as an instrument.' By so doing, one brings one's own thoughts about Fs into harmony with the experts' thoughts about Fs. Since experts' thoughts about Fs are apt to covary nicely with F-ness, harmonizing one's own F thoughts with experts' F thoughts is a way of resonating to Fs. This is the truth in theories that stress our reliance on what Putnam (1971) called the 'linguistic division of labor.' This is a mechanism (better termed, perhaps, the 'semantic division of labor,' in view of its application to the semantics of both natural languages and mental states) whereby the recognitional burden that is a concomitant of concept possession is shared out among the different members of the community, with the consequence that each individual's conceptual repertoire extends well beyond the limits of her own discriminative capacities.

Finally, one can be locked to a certain property by virtue of how one is built. One's brain and perceptual apparatus can simply be structured such that they react reliably and characteristically to that property: one's concept for that property can be inborn. Indeed, one's brain and perceptual apparatus *must* be so structured, in at least some cases. For it is our ability to resonate with these basic properties that presumably enables us to come to detect the rest. This is the truth in classical empiricism. There are some properties we are born able to detect; there are some concepts we possess innately.

Given a broadly information-theoretic account of conceptual content, in short, there appear to be a number of ways in which one can have a concept. One can detect F-ness by knowing its definition, or by knowing a prototype or stereotype for F-ness, or by relying on the recognitional abilities of others, or simply by being built that way. I will discuss some objections to this picture of concept possession in §6.5. For the moment, however, I just want to emphasize that it is a corollary of the informational approach to concepts that possessing the concept of an F will usually involve one's knowing something about Fs.[15]

Usually, but not always. We saw above that one can be an F-detector simply in virtue of how one is built. Consider now how a person might be born such that she is locked to, or able to respond selectively and characteristically to, a given property. Two models suggest themselves. One is the physiological reflex. It may be that, just as we are born such that our pupils contract involuntarily when a light shines in our eyes, so we are born such that we respond *cognitively*, but again characteristically and involuntarily,

---

15. I.e., having some beliefs about Fs. I use 'know' in the psychologist's broad sense rather than the philosopher's narrow sense.

to certain sorts of sensory transductions. Imagine that a light shining in the eyes causes not only pupillary contractions but also, and simply by virtue of what one might call a 'cognitive reflex,' tokenings of the (syntactic) item LIGHT! Tokenings of LIGHT! would thus, and solely in virtue of our physiology, be apt (in appropriate circumstances) to covary with nearby concentrations of photons. In virtue of this, such tokenings would be tokenings of the concept LIGHT. Note that in this case, nothing that could plausibly be called 'knowledge about light' is involved in our possessing that concept. Here, I think, we find the truth in Fodorean nativism. Fodor is right to insist that there must be some concepts that are both unlearned and psychologically primitive. There must be some properties that we are born to detect—and born to detect, moreover, in a purely brute-causal and non-intentionally-mediated manner.

But the Fodorean or 'reflexive' picture of inborn resonance is not the only possible model for unlearned concepts. It may be that we also have capacities to resonate to F-ness that are both unlearned and psychologically complex. An example might be our ability to recognize faces. It appears that recognizing something as a face involves the deployment of stored knowledge about faces.[16] Suppose that we compare the current visual input with a stored 'face template' and token, if the match is close enough, FACE, a syntactic object which (thanks to the information it carries) means *face*. It appears also, however, that infants are born with the ability to detect human faces: they are born with the concept FACE.[17] This could be explained if knowledge of what typical faces look like is supplied by our genes rather than being abstracted from our experience, that is, if some face templates were innately specified. If this were the case, then we would have a concept, FACE, that is on the one hand innate in the sense of unlearned, but on the other hand psychologically structured or nonprimitive. That this latter possibility exists indicates one of the falsehoods in Fodor's nativism. Fodor supposes that the class of innate concepts (i.e., the class of unlearned recognitional capacities) is coextensive with the class of primitive or unstructured concepts (i.e., the class of non-intentionally-mediated recognitional capacities). But this is not necessarily so. While some concepts (like LIGHT in the example above) must be both unlearned and psychologically unstructured, or 'reflexive,' there may also be concepts, like FACE, that are unlearned, yet complex in their internal structure.

16. Though what kind of stored knowledge is involved is, putting it mildly, an open question. See Serjent (1989) and Bruce, Burton, and Craw (1992) for further discussion.

17. See H.D. Ellis and Young (1989:4–10) for a survey of the literature on neonatal face perception. H.D. Ellis (1992b) shows that minutes-old infants respond selectively to faces and that two-day-old babies can reliably discriminate their mother's face from those of strangers. See Carey (1992), and H.D. Ellis (1992a) for discussion of how the interaction of these inborn capacities and learning result in adult competence. See also §11.5.

6.4.2 Concept Acquisition: How Is That Mediation Achieved?

What the discussion of §6.4.1 shows is that, given an informational account of concepts, possessing a concept in most cases will involve having knowledge of some kind about its object. The only exception is concepts that we possess in virtue of our 'cognitive reflexes.' In all other cases, concepts appear to be 'internally structured.'

This has implications for one's picture of concept acquisition. The nativist maintains that acquisition is brute-causal, that is, that it is not psychologically mediated. Against the present account of what it is that one acquires when one acquires the concept F-NESS, this amounts to the claim that nothing intentional is going on when we acquire the ability to detect Fs. This, in turn, amounts to the claim that all our concepts are like LIGHT and FACE: they are based on recognitional capacities grounded either in 'cognitive reflexes' or, in case the concept is internally structured, on knowledge about Fs that does not need to be learned. The nativist must in effect claim that for every value of F, our ability to recognize Fs is inborn. But this is not credible. I shall argue that in many cases where concept possession involves knowledge, that knowledge is more plausibly held to be acquired through learning.

First, though, let me stress again that I am perfectly happy to admit two kinds of cases in which learning is *not* involved in concept acquisition: one can be born (hence not have to learn how to be) a detector of Fs by having an F-sensitive cognitive reflex, or by having genetically encoded knowledge about F-ness that one can use to recognize Fs with. In the former case, no knowledge about Fs is required for possessing the concept; in the latter, knowledge is required, but is not acquired through a process of individual learning.

And let me stress, second, that I am prepared also to countenance the existence of *many* unlearned concepts of these two sorts. For all I know, we could have hundreds or thousands or tens of thousands of unlearned recognitional capacities. I'd not be surprised, for example, if many of the representations deployed in early perceptual processing turned out to be predicated on cognitive reflexes. Concepts like LIGHT, DARK, CONTRAST BOUNDARY, DARK SPOT, LINE, CHANGING PITCH, TICKLE, ITCH, PAIN, ACRID SMELL, SWEET SMELL—whatever concepts are employed by our perceptual 'input modules' in computing higher-level representations of inputs for the use of the cognitive system more generally—will, I expect, turn out to be unlearned. Similarly, I suspect that there will prove to be a lot of innately specified prototypes, stereotypes, dispositions—maybe even definitions!— that bestow upon us, again without our needing to learn anything, recognitional capacities (hence concepts) for more abstract properties. One can imagine, for instance, how selective pressures on ancestral hominid populations might have favored organisms who knew (without having to learn) that where there are two dark dots with a couple of darker lines underneath them in a certain configuration, there's likely to be a conspecific's face. Or that when there's a dark squiggly line in the lower portion of one's visual field, there's likely to be a snake. If an organism had a genetically specified face template or snake template, ready for use by the visual system from birth onward, then she would have an inborn or unlearned ability to resonate with faces or snakes—she would have (without having to learn) the concept FACE or SNAKE. And maybe HUNGER, REDNESS, MOMMY, PREDATOR, FOOD, THING, WORD, SENTENCE, TWO, MORE and LESS, AGENT and CAUSE are also concepts of this sort.

But whereas the nativist, I've argued, can retain his nativism only by claiming that *all* our concepts, structured and unstructured, are unlearned, I say that, on the contrary, many structured concepts are learned. I'm happy to think that MOTHER and AGENT and FOOD are innate—indeed, I'm happy to agree that *any* recognitional capacity that may have affected our ancestors' fitness is innate. But I draw the line at PLATYPUS and QUARK and CONTRAPUNTAL and DOORKNOB and TRIANGLE and BACHELOR and most of the other concepts that we have. There is, so far as I can see, absolutely no evidence whatsoever that we are born with abilities to respond selectively to these sorts of things. On the contrary, there is every reason to think that we have to learn how to lock to these properties. So, while I am prepared to acknowledge that many (or even all) of the representations that are involved in the transduction of sensory information are reflexive, and while I am prepared to acknowledge that many other perceptual concepts may be unlearned as well, I think that most of our 'higher-order' concepts are acquired through learning.

Consider, for example, how one might acquire the concept DOORKNOB. Acquiring the concept is a matter of coming to resonate to *being a doorknob*. Resonating to *being a doorknob*, recall, requires that one respond selectively to waist-high, movable protuberances attached to doors. Now, either one is born such that one responds selectively to waist-high protuberances, or one has learned to respond selectively to such things. The nativist says that we are born that way, whereas I think that it is much more plausible to suppose that responding selectively to waist-high movable protuberances is a skill that we learn. First, responding selectively to waist-high protuberances requires a certain level of attention and motivation. You have to care enough about doorknobs to bother attending to them at all, and I doubt that we're born caring about doorknobhood: why should we be? Second, responding selectively to things satisfying the doorknob stereotype requires a certain amount of perceptual and cognitive sophistication: you have to be able to distinguish the waist-high protuberances from the chest-high indentations (keyholes), from the eye-high indentations (peepholes), from the eye-high protuberances (door knockers), from the knee-level indentations (mail slots). Performing these sorts of discriminative tasks is not something we're born able to do, any more than pecking the red disk only when the light is on is something that a pigeon is born able to do. Instead, responding to doorknobbish things, like pecking only when the light is on, is something that one must learn how to do. To the extent that knowledge of what typical doorknobs are like is involved in being a detector of doorknobs, learning must be involved in acquisition of the concept DOORKNOB.

The point is even clearer when one considers a concept like QUARK. In order to acquire QUARK, one needs to become a (reliable enough) quark detector. In order to do that, one must either borrow reference from a physicist or become a physicist oneself. Both of these are things that one must learn to do. To borrow reference from a physicist, one must form an intention to think as the physicist does: one could form the intention, for instance, to token QUARK! when and only when Murray Gell-Mann says "Yup, it's a quark." But not only are we not born with any intentions vis-à-vis our QUARK!-tokenings; we're also not born knowing that Gell-Mann is a good prospect as a reference lender in this context; or that tracking his utterances of "Yup, it's a quark" is a way of tracking quarkhood. Intentions to think like experts are not inborn; they're acquired through experience. Similarly unhardwired, I take it, is the process of becoming a physicist oneself. Becoming a quark detector requires that one spend about ten thousand years in graduate school, working extremely hard at figuring out how to use and interpret a variety of hugely complex and artificial extensions of one's perceptual and cognitive apparatus, such as computers, particle accelerators, and so on. People aren't born with the ability to detect quarks, any more than they are born with desires or intentions to think like Gell-Mann. The psychological states that undergird a person's ability to resonate to *being a quark* are learned, not inborn.

And the same is true, or so I wager, in lots of cases. A few moments' reflection on what might be required to get oneself into the position whereby one's mental states carry information about platypuses, dogs, triangles, bachelors, xylophones, books, and echidnas strongly suggests that acquiring the requisite recognitional capacities is in many cases a highly sophisticated psychological process. It is comparatively seldom that we have the recognitional capacities that ground locking from birth. On the contrary, definitions, prototypes, stereotypes, and policies to think like experts are things that we acquire through and because of our ability not merely to experience the world but to *learn from* that experience.

6.4.3 Fodor's Failure of Nerve

Throughout most of his (1998), Fodor runs the same, nonpsychological line about concept acquisition that he defended in his (1981b) and that we have discussed in this chapter:

> To be sure, there remains something about the acquisition of DOORKNOB that wants explaining. . . . certainly, it's got to be something about 'our kinds of minds' that this explanation adverts to. But, I'm supposing, such an explanation is *cognitivist* only if it turns on the *evidential* relation be-

tween *having the stereotypic doorknob properties* and *being a door-knob.* . . . Well, by this criterion, my story isn't cognitivist. (1998:136–37)

Here, although Fodor admits that explaining how we lock to doorknobhood will involve talking about 'our kinds of minds,' he denies that the required explanation is cognitivist, that is, that it involves talk about evidence, hence learning, hence (more broadly) intentionality. For, he thinks, he has already given the requisite explanation—and given it, moreover, in nonpsychological (that is, in metaphysical—§5.2) terms. The above quotation continues:

My story is that what doorknobs have in common qua doorknobs is the property of having the property that our kinds of minds do or would lock to from experiences with instances of the doorknob stereotype. (Cf. to be red just is to have that property that minds like ours [do or would] lock to in virtue of experiences of typical instances of redness. Why isn't that ok? (1998:137)

Well, we have seen in this chapter what is *not* OK about Fodor's 'explanation' of locking. To explain how how minds like ours lock to doorknobhood requires more than telling a metaphysical story about doorknobs; it requires also that one tell some kind of story *about us,* and in particular about the processes by which we come to be doorknob detectors. Fodor denies, and I have defended, the claim that learning is an important process by which such recognitional abilities are acquired.

What's odd is that in the final chapter of his (1998), Fodor almost admits all of this. He almost recognizes that on his (informational) account of what possessing a concept amounts to, learning must frequently be involved in concept acquisition. He argues that in order to acquire a natural kind concept like WATER, we need to do some science. Back "in the Garden" (1998: 150), before humankind had the ability to distinguish water from the look-alike substance xyz, we had merely the concept WATER-OR-XYZ. Then, though, we started doing science, and got the ability to tell water from xyz (or to defer to others who had that ability). And it was only then, on Fodor's view, that people acquired the natural kind concept WATER. But this *just is* the kind of picture that was sketched above as following naturally and plausibly from an information-theoretic account of concept possession. In order to have a concept, on that view, you need to be able to distinguish its referent from other things well enough that you can resonate selectively to that referent. Getting that ability, I argued, frequently involves learning. It is not something one is born with. Given that 'doing science' is simply another name for learning, then, Fodor here seems to be agreeing with me—at least as regards concepts for natural kinds.

Now admittedly, the final chapter of Fodor's (1998) is written in a somewhat tongue-in-cheek and allegorical mode. So perhaps Fodor does not really want to endorse the picture he sketches there. But that, of course, is something I cannot determine. So let me conclude simply by setting out two questions that his (1998) discussion of kind concepts raises. First, how does

Fodor reconcile this account of the acquisition of WATER (as necessitating that one learn, through science, how to tell water from xyz) with the picture, defended elsewhere in the work, that concept acquisition is a brute-causal, non-intentionally-mediated process? Second, why does he think that this kind of story is appropriate only for concepts of natural kinds? Surely much the same thing goes on with many of our concepts—of individuals, artifacts, abstractions, and so on. Most of the time, we are not born with the ability to tell instantiations of F-ness from instantiations of properties that are its near relatives. Most of the time, fortunately, this doesn't much matter to our being in the world. In cases where it does matter, though, there are mechanisms by which our F-detecting abilities can be improved. Mother Nature can improve our ability to detect F-ness where that ability bears on our survival and reproduction: we can acquire more finely tuned F-detecting abilities through the process of natural selection. And we can improve our F-detection ourselves, where it really matters, for whatever reason, to us. If we really care about making the distinction between water and xyz, or elms and beeches, or platypuses and ducks, we can find experts to defer to or become experts ourselves. We can (and do) acquire more finely tuned F-detecting abilities *through learning*.

6.5 Objections

In the preceding section, I defended a view of concept possession and acquisition that overall looks something like the following. We are born with certain recognitional capacities—born with concepts of edges and color boundaries and faces and things and pains and food. These unlearned concepts, whether structured or unstructured, comprise a 'primitive conceptual base' and constitute the tools with which we proceed to acquire further concepts. Once a person has some basic recognitional abilities, she can use them to acquire others. She can use the concepts she has to help her to lock to new properties, in much the same way as a wine taster uses the discriminations she can already make to bootstrap her way to still further and finer oenological distinctions. These new concepts, in turn, are used to construct prototypes and stereotypes and definitions for still further properties, and so on.[18] At some point, we'll have acquired the kind of cognitive sophistication that will enable us to start using instruments other than our own perceptual apparatus in our discriminative enterprise. We'll be able to start learning how to use other people and words and pictures and web browsers and particle accelerators as instruments, thus continually expanding our detecting abilities—and our conceptual repertoires.

In this final section, I shall try to rebut two objections to this picture.

18. Exactly which concepts are structured and unstructured, which are innate, and which are learned is, of course, an empirical matter.

6.5.1 Verificationism

One objection to the kind of theory I've been sketching here concerns its verificationist overtones. On my story, one has the concept of F-ness to the extent that one is (in ideal circumstances) a reliable detector of that property. To the extent that one would fail to discriminate Fs from Gs, even in ideal circumstances, one's concept will not be the concept of an F, but, rather, the concept of an F-or-G. But the idea that what you can think about is limited to what you can detect is a brand of verificationism, and verificationism (as everyone knows) is a thoroughly bad thing.

In response, I'd like to stress, first, that what is really bad about verificationism is verificationism *about truth*. This is the view that the proposition (or belief) expressed by (say) 'platypuses are duck-billed' is true if and only if we can verify (or know, or detect, or are prepared to assert, etc.) that platypuses are duck-billed. And verificationism about truth is a bad thing because the proposition (/belief) that platypuses are duck-billed is true or false regardless of what you or I can verify (know, detect, will assert, etc.). But the view I have been defending is a theory about the meanings of semantic atoms (concepts or, derivatively, words). Truth is a semantic property of semantic complexes (beliefs or, derivatively, sentences). One can be a verificationist about the semantic properties of the atoms while refusing to be a verificationist about the complexes, that is, while denying the verificationist theory of truth. Say that a person's concept PLATYPUS refers to whatever property (or properties) it is, instantiations of which reliably cause her to token PLATYPUS! Say that her concept DUCK-BILLED refers to whatever would cause her to token DUCK-BILLED![19] Then, using the normal Tarskian methods, one can derive the following truth condition: that person's belief PLATYPUSES ARE DUCK-BILLED will be true if and only if all of the things that have the property instantiations of which reliably cause her to token PLATYPUS *also* have the property instantiations of which reliably cause her to token DUCK-BILLED. And whether or not this is so—whether or not things having the first of these properties also have the second—is an objective fact about the world that is quite independent of what that person knows or can tell or is prepared to say. The truth of one's belief that platypuses are duck-billed depends on what the world is like, and not on what the believer can discover about what the world is like. Verificationism about meaning does not entail verificationism about truth.

Verificationism about meaning does nonetheless entail that one can think about something only to the extent that one could, in ideal circumstances, detect it. This would appear to be a problem, for it seems to indicate that there may be a lot more semantic indeterminacy in our thoughts than we might previously have suspected. I think that your PLATYPUS thoughts are

---

19. I leave out the 'in ideal circumstances' qualifications here since they don't bear on the points I'm making.

thoughts about platypuses, and not thoughts about platypuses-or-clever-Martian-simulacra. But if it were to turn out that you couldn't tell the difference, even in ideal circumstances, between the real thing and the Martian fake, then your PLATYPUS thoughts would have the disjunctive content instead.

To which I respond: so be it. If you really could not tell the McCoys from the decoys, even in ideal circumstances, then your PLATYPUS thoughts don't distinguish them either. By way of mitigation, though, let me stress the following. First, what is at issue here are not a person's *actual* detecting abilities but those she *would* have *in ideal circumstances*. Now, admittedly no one knows exactly how to cash out 'ideal circumstances' for the purposes of an information-theoretic semantics, and I certainly do not propose to make an attempt to do it here. But the fact that a semantics of the kind I've been working with has the counterfactuals to play with offers some hope that the theory can be articulated in such as way as to prevent all our thoughts from ending up with madly disjunctive contents. Maybe you cannot actually distinguish the real platypuses from the Martian simulacra, but maybe you could if circumstances were more favorable. If so, that would be enough to ensure that in your mind, PLATYPUS means *platypus*.

Second, it's worth stressing also that not all the work in getting around the disjunction problem here is being done by the counterfactuals. Some of it may be done by you. One way you can improve your circumstances vis-à-vis the detection of platypuses (and hence improve the odds that your thoughts are about platypuses) is by learning. You could go to grad school in zoology and acquire the sorts of knowledge (about, as it might be, platypus DNA) that would enable you to pick out the real thing from the mock-ups. Some of the work may also be done by others in the community. As we've seen before, you can improve your platypus-detecting abilities by deferring to an expert. Let someone else go to grad school in zoology and learn all about platypus DNA. Then you can use that person as a means of distinguishing a real platypus from an ersatz. If an expert can tell the difference, you could tell the difference too. For you could use that expert as a platypus-sensitive instrument.[20]

---

20. Indeed, I suspect that deference is potentially of great use in dealing with the disjunction problem generally. Suppose that, as a matter of fact, we all have a default policy of deference with regard to our thoughts. Suppose that we've all adopted the policy that where it really matters to us that we are thinking determinately about Fs (not indeterminately about Fs-or-Gs), we will conform our thoughts to those of an expert in F-ness. So, for instance, suppose that we've all adopted the policy that in cases where it really matters to us, we will rely not on our own meager platypus-detecting abilities but, rather, on those of experts. This would mean that it'd be true of all of us that (when it really matters) we'd be excellent platypus detectors, for (when it really matters) we'd get an expert on the job. Let 'ideal semantic circumstances' include circumstances where it really matters, and hey presto! it turns out to be true of all of us that in ideal circumstances, we would be able to distinguish platypuses from the Martian fakes, and hence that we are now thinking PLATYPUS thoughts that are thoughts *about platypuses!*

6.5.2 Systematicity and Productivity

A second objection to the account I've defended runs as follows: Look, Fodor has already shown that non-Classical theories of concepts can't be adequate because they cannot explain the productivity and systematicity of thought. So the theory sketched here, being in large part non-Classical, cannot be right either.

Fodor urged, recall (§4.2), that there is a constraint on the kinds of meanings or contents that we can attribute to concepts. In order that we can construct a compositional semantics for thoughts (and doing this is necessary if we're to explain thought's productivity and systematicity), concepts must have the kinds of meanings that they can contribute to the meanings of complexes in which they occur. But prototypes and stereotypes aren't the kinds of meanings that concepts can contribute to complexes. For composing conceptual contents so construed gives the wrong answers about the complexes' contents. Since there is no way to put together the prototypes and/or stereotypes for PET and FISH so as to generate the correct meaning for PET FISH, prototypes and/or stereotypes could not be the meanings of PET and FISH. And since prototypes and stereotypes aren't meanings, it couldn't be that you need to have knowledge of prototypes or stereotypes in order to have concepts. Which is directly contrary to what I have argued in this chapter. Which would seem to be a problem for me.

As a preliminary to explaining how this problem is to be resolved, I want to make three points. First, what compositionality really requires is that concepts contribute *their references* to complexes in which they occur. For what really matters to the explanation of productivity and systematicity is that the references of complexes depend in regular ways on the references of their constituent concepts, or, more broadly, that the truth (or satisfaction) conditions for whole thoughts be a function of the references of the thoughts' constituent concepts (and the ways those constituents are put together). That is, what compositionality demands is that concepts contribute to complexes whatever semantic property is is, in virtue of which they have the references they do. So, when Fodor says that concepts must have the kinds of meanings they can contribute to complexes, he's using 'meaning' in the narrow, technical sense of 'what fixes reference.' Call these reference-fixing semantic properties 'meanings-in-the-technical-sense.'

Second, there is another way in which the term 'meaning' (or 'content') is used in the philosophy of mind and psychology. In addition to talking of meanings-in-the-technical-sense we also talk at times of meanings in a more intuitive sense, as being whatever it is that one must 'grasp' when one has a concept. Call these 'meanings-in-the-intuitive-sense.' The arguments of §6.4.1 suggest that it follows from an information-theoretic theory of content that what one needs to know in order to possess a concept is something that gives one the ability to 'resonate' or 'lock' to its referent. 'Meanings-in-the-intuitive-sense,' therefore, can be prototypes, stereotypes, intentions to use experts as instruments, and so on. They are constituted by whatever it is that one needs to know if one is to possess that concept.

And third, although one long-standing and popular tradition in semantics—what one might call the Fregean tradition—identifies meanings-in-the-technical-sense with meanings-in-the-intuitive-sense, there is in fact a good deal of evidence that that tradition is misguided. According to the Fregean view, the two (ostensibly different) kinds of semantic property picked out by the two uses of 'meaning' identified above are, in fact, the same semantic property. For on this view, what you need to grasp when you have a concept just is what determines the reference of the concept (and vice versa). The model for the Fregean is a concept like BACHELOR. Arguably, you cannot have the concept of a bachelor unless you know that bachelors are adult, unmarried males, hence ADULT & UNMARRIED & MALE is the-meaning-in-the-intuitive-sense of BACHELOR. By a stroke of luck, though, it turns out that a thing satisfies BACHELOR iff it also satisfies ADULT & UNMARRIED & MALE, which means that the meaning (in the intuitive sense) of the concept can also function as its meaning-in-the-technical (that is, reference-fixing) sense! So BACHELOR doesn't have two sorts of meaning: it has, rather, a single meaning—namely, the semantic property of being associated (in our heads) with the representation ADULT & UNMARRIED & MALE. That single semantic property, though, performs two different roles in our semantic theory: it explains what fixes BACHELOR's reference, and it also accords with our intuitions about what you need to know to have that concept. The Fregean expectation (or hope) is that virtually all our concepts will turn out to be like this.

There is reason, however, to think that a Fregean semantic synthesis will not work in general. For there is reason to think that concepts' meanings-in-the-technical-sense—the fixers of reference—often cannot be identified with their meanings-in-the-intuitive-sense—with what you need to know to have the concept. For one thing, it turns out on many modern semantic theories, that what fixes a concept's reference isn't the kind of thing that you can grasp, so the meaning-in-the-technical-sense cannot function as the meaning-in-the-intuitive-sense. On a causal-historical semantics, for example, what determines the reference of a concept are facts about what its tokenings are caused by. It is because tokenings of BIRD have, historically, been caused by birds that that concept refers to those things. But if those causal links are the fixers of reference—if they are the meaning of BIRD in-the-technical-sense—then clearly they couldn't also be the meaning of BIRD in-the-intuitive-sense. For although one can certainly be a term in such causal relations, the actual historical-causal relations between oneself and the world aren't the kinds of things one can grasp when one has a concept.[21] And the

---

21. It's not, on this story, that you need to *know that* such links exist in order that your concept BIRD refer to birds—it's preposterous to suggest that a person cannot have the concept BIRD unless she knows that she's causally connected to birds! Instead, it's the

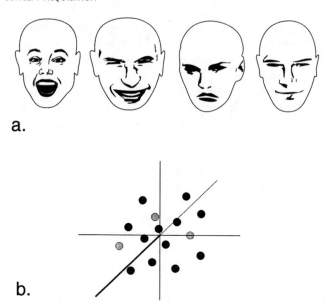

Figure 6.1 Prototypes
a. Prototypical faces. b. Prototypical faces as they might be represented in the mind, namely, as points toward the center of a multidimensional feature space. *Source*: After Ellis and Young (1992:7).

same is true, mutatis mutandis for other 'externalist' theories of mental content: if reference is fixed by the relations that hold between one's concepts and the world, then there must be a distinction between conceptual contents qua fixers of reference (meanings-in-the-technical-sense) and conceptual contents qua things you must grasp in order to have the concept (meanings-in-the-intuitive-sense).

The exact same anti-Fregean point can be made from the opposite direction, so to speak. For it often turns out that what you need to know in order to have a concept (the meaning-in-the-intuitive-sense) will not determine what that concept refers to: it won't function as a meaning-in-the-technical-sense. So, for example, while it might be plausible to claim that in order to have the concept FACE—that is, to 'resonate' or 'lock' to faces—one needs to know that typical faces look something like those in figure 6.1.

It would be a grave mistake to think that the mental representations of schematic faces corresponding to figure 6.1 also fixes the reference of FACE. For it simply is not true that a thing is a face iff it resembles (to some

mere fact of those relations' obtaining that secures that concept's reference—hence it's the mere fact of those relations' obtaining that comprises that concept's meaning (in the technical sense). See Devitt (1996:49–54 and n. 4) for criticism of what he calls 'Cartesianism' about content.

appropriate degree) this stereotype. Similarly for many other concepts: even if one is tempted to claim that you can't have the concept of a bird—you cannot resonate to *birdhood*—unless you know that birds typically have feathers, fly, and sing, it would be wrong to take this meaning-in-the-intuitive-sense to be BIRD's meaning-in-the-technical-sense, for there are things in the extension of FLYING & FEATHERED & SINGING that don't belong in the extension of BIRD, and vice versa.

Thus the beauty of externalist semantic theories is that they offer you a way of denying the Fregean picture of meaning. The Fregean says that the meaning that you grasp or know when you possess a concept is also the meaning that fixes that concept's reference. The externalist can deny that what you know when you possess a concept fixes the concept's reference, because on an externalist view, it is that concept's (causal, nomological, whatever) relations with the world that fix reference. The externalist can deny, in other words, that concepts' meanings-in-the-intuitive-sense function also as their meanings-in-the-technical-sense.

Now, denying this is not so crucial if you cleave to a Classical theory of concepts' internal structure (§4.2). For in these cases, the Fregean and non-Fregean pictures give the same semantic result. That is, BACHELOR ends up referring to bachelors regardless of whether its reference is fixed by an associated description (as the Fregean claims) or by its causal (nomological, etc.) relations with the world (as the externalist might claim). Making a distinction between meanings-in-the-intuitive-sense and meanings-in-the-technical-sense is, however, of the utmost importance if you adopt a non-Classical theory of concepts' internal structure. On a non-Classical account, what is associated with the concept (its meaning-in-the-intuitive-sense) won't fix reference because it falls short of specifying necessary and sufficient conditions. Something else must be fixing non-Classical concepts reference—and for an externalist, that something else is, of course, the concepts' relations with the world. Putting it only mildly tendentiously: you cannot be a Fregean about meaning and a non-Classicist about concepts. For part of what it is to be a non-classicist about concepts is to deny the Fregean assumption that what you need to know is what determines reference. [23]

The point is that if the Fregean identification of meanings-in-the-technical-sense with meanings-in-the-intuitive-sense is misguided in the case of non-Classical concepts—if non-Classical concepts in fact have two kinds of meaning—then from the fact that prototypes cannot be concepts' meanings-in-the-technical-sense it does not follow that they are not meanings-in-the-intuitive-sense.

Fodor argues that prototypes are useless in developing a compositional semantics. I noted that the important semantic properties, so far as compositionality is concerned, are concepts' meanings-in-the-technical-sense—their reference-fixing properties. Hence, another way to express Fodor's anti-prototype point is as follows: prototypes and stereotypes are no good to the project of doing compositional semantics because they don't fix reference. They are not concepts' meanings-in-the-technical-sense. I quite agree—indeed, I suggested, this result follows almost by definition from a non-Classical theory of concepts. Where I disagree with Fodor is in the conclusion he wants to draw from this fact. He wants to conclude that because prototypes (etc.) are not concepts' meanings-in-the-technical-sense, they are not semantic properties of concepts *at all*. Hence, he argues, they are not the sort of thing that we need to learn during concept acquisition. But this conclusion follows only on the Fregean assumption that concepts have just one kind of meaning that both fixes reference and is what you need to grasp. A non-Fregean approach to semantics leaves open the possibility that prototyeps and stereotypes might be what you must know or grasp in order to have a concept *even though* what you grasp will not fix that concept's reference, and hence are (as Fodor rightly points out) inappropriate vehicles for compositional contents.

That a non-Fregean approach to semantics leaves open this possibility is, I think, a rather good thing. For, as I have argued through most of this chapter, an informational semantics entails that recognitional abilities are involved in concept possession. There would seem to be only three possibilities for how those recognitional capacities might be realized. They could be altogether unmediated—cognitive reflexes—though as I argued, this is comparatively rare. They could be mediated by definitions—but as Fodor showed, this is rare too. The only remaining possibility is that they are mediated by knowledge that falls short of definitions: knowledge represented by prototypes, stereotypes, beliefs about who the experts are, and so on. So if concept possession entails that one possess an ability to recognize its instances, and if those abilities are not brutely reflexive (my claim) and not dependent on one's knowledge of definitions (Fodor's claim), then they *must* be dependent on one's knowledge of (something like) prototypes and stereotypes, that is, on nondefinitional knowledge about the things in the concept's extension. Grasping prototypes and stereotypes sometimes *is* constitutive of having concepts.

6.5.4 Nativism Rejected

What does all this have to do with nativism? Fodor's nativism is the view that concept acquisition is brute-causal, that is, that it is unmediated by any psychological (i.e., intentionally described) states and processes. I argued in §§6.1–6.3 that this view can explain neither how concepts are acquired ostensively nor how they are acquired through reference-borrowing or deference. I concluded that there must therefore be something wrong with the Fodorean picture and suggested that its fault lies precisely in its denial that learning is a part of concept acquisition. The fact that concept acquisition cannot be explained in brute-causal terms, I suggested, is evidence that concept acquisition is a 'rational-causal,' or psychologically mediated, process instead.

In §§6.4 and 6.5, I have attempted to provide an independent line of support for this contention, developing and defending a positive account of concept acquisition that explains exactly how it is that the Fodorean story derails. Fodor's denial that anything like learning is involved in the acquisition of concepts depends on his being able to show that concepts are internally unstructured: if concepts are unstructured, there's nothing *to* learn in concept acquisition. To this end, he argued against both Classical (that is, definitional) and non-Classical (e.g., prototype) accounts of conceptual structure. In response, I urged that an information theorist has good reason to think that concepts must be internally structured, for on this view there must be something that mediates your recognition of the concept's object. Thus, there seems to be a direct conflict between the information theory's requirement that concepts be structured, and the Fodorean contention that they are not. I showed that the conflict is only apparent: Fodor's anti-prototype arguments do not in fact preclude concepts' having prototypical structure, and to think otherwise is mistakenly to extend the Fregean view in semantics into areas where it should not go. Hence there is nothing to stop us from taking the view that concepts have non-Classical (e.g., prototypical or stereotypical) structure.

And here we are back to the issue of nativism. If concepts are internally structured, then acquiring a concept is a matter of acquiring the appropriate structure. How do we do this? The nativist says that no learning is involved in concept acquisition. I say that, on the contrary, if acquiring concepts is a matter of acquiring knowledge of prototypes and stereotypes (or definitions, or intentions to think like experts, or whatever), then learning will frequently be involved in acquiring concepts. For it is implausible to think that we are equipped from birth with the kinds of finely tuned recognitional abilities that our possession of concepts requires.

So what of Fodor's (1975) argument that concept-learning is impossible? That argument, recall, showed only that Classically structured concepts are unlearnable (§4.2). It is only in case what must be learned are necessary and sufficient conditions for a thing's falling under the concept, that learning a concept requires that one already have it. What I've defended here is an account of concepts according to which they have a variety of non-Classical structures. And while learning the prototype or stereotype for F-ness will of course require that we possess other concepts, it will not require, self-defeatingly, that we have the concept F-NESS itself.

In sum, what I've tried to show is that there is no bar to concepts' having nonclassical structures; hence there is no reason to deny the possibility of concept-learning; and hence there is no reason to insist that psychology be silent on the acquisition process. There is no reason to deny that a psychological theory of the concept-learning process will be forthcoming. Hence the Fodorean nativist's pessimism as to the scope and eventual success of the sciences of the mind is unwarranted.

III

THE FATE OF THE FACULTIES HYPOTHESIS

7

Language-Learning

From Behaviorism to Nativism

I now turn to what I argued in part I to be a second strand in the nativism–empiricism debate, namely, the controversy over the existence of task-specific faculties for the acquisition of particular kinds of knowledge. According to the empiricist, all learning is to be explained in fundamentally the same way: we are possessed of certain very general strategies, applicable in all domains, for learning from experience. The nativist, by contrast, maintains that some of our knowledge cannot be explained on the domain-neutral empiricist model. He employs arguments from the poverty of the stimulus to support his view that, in certain cases, we must regard what is in our minds as being the product of task-specific learning mechanisms supplied by our innate endowment.

As a modern instance of this line of thought, I take the views of Noam Chomsky. His claim, in the early 1960s, to have shown that human beings possess innate knowledge of natural languages reignited philosophers' and psychologists' interest in the phenomenon of learning generally, and in the doctrine of innate ideas in particular. In this chapter, I give an overview of Chomsky's account of language acquisition and recall its rise from the ashes of psychological behaviorism and American Structuralist linguistics. Although much of this material will be familiar, I believe that it is territory worth covering once again. For it will enable us to limn a taxonomic framework within which the case for linguistic nativism will be examined in subsequent chapters.

7.1 Chomskyan Nativism: The Core Claims

Chomsky's thinking about language acquisition is rooted in a remarkable fact: by about age eight, all normal children have mastered the language of their community. Setting aside limitations in their vocabulary, they are able to understand virtually any sentence spoken to them and to construct for themselves novel sentences of a high degree of complexity. This is quite a feat. Natural languages are vast and elaborate entities: vast in that each contains infinitely many sentences; elaborate in that sentencehood is an extremely complex property for a sequence of sounds to have. Yet, before they are able to do much else, human children learn to speak and understand a language. They do so, moreover, without apparent effort or instruction, simply on the basis of their exposure to a smallish sample of the sentences their language contains. So easily and smoothly do children learn language, indeed, that it is easy to let the ordinariness of language acquisition—the fact that overwhelmingly most children do it with so very little fuss—overwhelm one's sense of its extraordinariness. Chomsky, though, has never suffered from this particular problem; if he suffers at all, it is from its converse. From the time of his earliest writings, he has emphasized the "remarkable capacity of the [learning] child to generalize, hypothesize, and 'process information' in a variety of very special and apparently highly complex ways" (1959:43), and has insisted that one of the primary tasks confronting the linguist is to explain how language is acquired.

Chomsky contends that such an explanation must be nativist. On his view, the facts of language acquisition cannot be explained unless we postulate an inborn 'language faculty'—unless, that is, we suppose that humans are innately possessed of a highly specialized cognitive mechanism, incorporating a rich stock of detailed information about natural languages, the function of which is to enable or facilitate language learning. Chomsky is notable in that he does not rest content with the general claim that a domain-specific device for language-learning exists. Instead, he regards the description of the language faculty as the central theoretical task of modern linguistics and has advanced detailed hypotheses as to the character of the language-learning mechanism.

In his earlier writings, Chomsky defended what has come to be known as a 'hypothesis-testing' model of learning, analogous to the one sketched in §4.2.[1] According to this conception, the child is like a 'little linguist,' unconsciously projecting hypotheses about the syntactic and semantic structure of her language and testing them against the data provided by her experience. Here the similarity of the learner to the linguist ends, however. The ease and rapidity with which children learn language, as contrasted with the slow and painful labor that is the lot of the practicing linguist, show, according to Chomsky, that the child's theorizing about language must be constrained by principles that go beyond the sorts of general considerations of explanatory power, simplicity, generality, and so on that figure in theory construction in science (including linguistics) and are invoked in empiricist models of learning. These extra elements, he argues, are defined by a Uni-

---

1. Chomsky himself has rejected the 'hypothesis-testing' label on the (unelaborated) grounds that it is misleading (1991a:21).

versal Grammar (UG) that specifies the language to be used for the formulation of linguistic hypotheses, constrains the form of those hypotheses, and
provides an 'evaluation metric' to legislate the degrees of acceptability of
competing hypotheses. The constraints set by UG on the learning function
instantiated by the learner are built into the mind at birth. Like Leibniz's
veins in the marble, they are innate.

Since the early 1980s, the hypothesis-testing model has been superseded
in the linguistics literature by a 'parameter-setting' theory of language-
learning. Rather than comparing the child to a theoretical linguist, proponents of the parameter-setting approach favor an analogy with the growth
of bodily organs. Just as the heart, for example, develops in largely predetermined ways so as to perform its biological function of circulating the
blood, so the language faculty is a mental 'organ' that develops, again in
largely genetically determined ways, so as to fulfill its biological function,
viz., enabling us to speak and understand a natural language. As Chomsky
has recently expressed the idea: "The child's language 'grows in the mind'
as the visual system develops the capacity for binocular vision, or as the
child undergoes puberty at a certain stage of maturation. Language acquisition is something that happens to a child placed in a certain environment,
not something the child does" (1993:29).[2]

The 'growth' of the language faculty is not, of course, altogether uniform
across individuals: people do, after all, end up speaking different languages.
These 'phenotypical differences' are regarded as being due to *parametric
variation*. The principles of Universal Grammar encoded in the language
faculty contain a limited number of variables, thus allowing that faculty a
small amount of 'choice' as to how it will develop. At certain crucial points,
the learner's linguistic experience will 'set' a parameter, different parameter
settings resulting in competencies in different languages. So, for example,
one 'choice' the language faculty is believed to make concerns whether or
not to allow the subject of an utterance to be omitted. That is, while Universal Grammar requires that all sentences must have subjects, some languages (such as Spanish and Italian) allow the speaker to leave the
grammatical subject out of the spoken string. If the language faculty is exposed to a language, like Spanish, where subjects may be omitted, the 'Null
Subject Parameter,' as it is called, is set one way; whereas exposure to a
language, like English, where subjects must be phonologically realized, will
cause it to be set differently (Chomsky 1990:644ff.).

7.1.1 Five Core Claims

The norm, in much of the discussion that these proposals have provoked,
seems to have been to treat Chomsky's nativist approach to language acquisition as an organic whole, to be accepted in its entirety, or not at all.

---

2. See also Chomsky (1990:633ff.), Lightfoot (1991:2).

Thus Chomsky himself, and many of his defenders, at times speak and write as if to resist some element of the Chomskyan weltsanschauung—say, the parameter-setting model for the acquisition process, or the claim that Universal Grammar describes the language faculty—were to fail in some monumentally idiotic way to understand the wealth of evidence and arguments for linguistic nativism. I'll argue, however, that Chomskyan nativism embraces a number of partially independent theses concerning language-learning, and thus that it is possible rationally to reject some elements of the Chomskyan position while accepting others. Indeed, I'll ultimately suggest, since Chomsky's "core" claims as a matter of fact possess different degrees of evidential support, picking and choosing among them is exactly the right thing to do.

In this section, I articulate what I take to be the 'core' claims of Chomskyan nativism and use them to articulate a framework within which various attitudes toward language acquisition can be located. In the rest of this chapter and those following, I will demonstrate how distinguishing these claims, elucidating their logical relations, and considering separately the grounds for each will enable us better to understand and evaluate the Chomskyan position and its rivals.

Both the hypothesis-testing and the parameter-setting models of the mechanism of language acquisition, as well as Chomsky's conception of linguistic competence as involving knowledge or 'cognizance' of grammar, embody his commitment to

(R) Representationalism
Explaining language mastery and acquisition requires the postulation of contentful mental states and processes involving their manipulation.

(R) reflects Chomsky's endorsement of a representational theory of the mind. As we will see below (§7.2), Chomsky may with justice be regarded as the father of modern representationalism. For in the middle years of the twentieth century, it was he who instigated the drive to relieve the mental of the opprobrium with which it had been invested by positivist philosophers and psychologists prior to the 1960s. In his justly famed (1959) attack on Skinner's *Verbal Behavior*, Chomsky initiated a crusade to 'make the mind safe for science' (or, perhaps, vice versa), arguing emphatically that no serious human psychology can afford to ignore the fact that contentful mental states play a role in the production and explanation of behavior, linguistic behavior in particular.

Most representationalists, Chomsky very much included, are also committed to some or another version of

(B) Biological Boundedness
In virtue of the inborn structure of the human mind, there are constraints on the space of thinkable thoughts. (In particular, there are constraints on the possible hypotheses about language that learners may entertain during the course of language acquisition.)

Arguably, at least a weak form of (B) is entailed by Representationalism, if only because of the de facto finitude of our lives and brains: we cannot, for instance, entertain a proposition (whether about language or anything else) that would take more than a lifetime for a human brain to represent to itself. Representationalism may also imply a somewhat stronger Boundedness thesis, namely, that there are in principle restrictions on the kinds of contents our thoughts can have. For most representational theories hold that minds contain a finite stock of simple ideas that are combined to form other, more complex thoughts. Thus, depending on exactly how these 'conceptual atoms' and the rules for combining them are characterized, it will frequently be plausible to think that the precise nature of the representational system used by the mind will circumscribe not just the possible forms, but also the possible contents, that our thoughts can have. Simply in virtue of his Representationalism, then, Chomsky must and does acknowledge the existence of biological bounds on our cognitive capacities. Endorsing Popper's supposition that our biology limits our ability to achieve full understanding of the world, Chomsky writes that "since [our cognitive capacities] have definite structure—otherwise they would achieve nothing in any problem situation—they will have scope and limits" (Chomsky 1991b:40). However, in fact he holds our biology to constrain our thinking much more closely than (B) alone would suggest. His view that the mind inherently contains a special faculty dedicated to the task of theorizing about language implies that the limits on the hypotheses children can entertain during language learning are both biologically specified and proprietary to the linguistic domain. Our lack of liberty in thinking about language thus derives not (or not just) from whatever restrictions nature might impose on human cognitive capacities in general; rather, it is the result of biologically determined limitations, deriving from the structure of the language faculty, on our thinking about natural languages. Hence we have

(DS) Domain Specificity
Learning a language requires that the learner's thoughts about language be constrained by principles specific to the linguistic domain.

and

(I) Innateness
The constraints on learners' thoughts during language learning are in some manner innately encoded.

Together, (R), (B), (DS), and (I) constitute what I shall call *Weak Linguistic Nativism*. Weak Nativism is the view that the mind inherently contains a special faculty dedicated to the task of learning a language. It is a "bare" architectural hypothesis, analogous to the hypotheses of domain-specific learning devices endorsed (as I argued in chapter 3) by Leibniz and Descartes to account for our knowledge about God, mathematics, and necessities. While it offers few clues (beyond what is implied by (R)) as to the precise psychological mechanisms responsible for language-learning, Weak Nativism nonetheless asserts that that mechanism must be task-specific, and that its special characteristics are inherent, not acquired.

Chomsky's nativism, of course, comprehends more than than this. As we saw above, he is unusual among proponents of special faculties in not merely affirming that a task-specific faculty for language exists. He goes beyond the commitments of the Weak nativist and defends in addition a hypothesis about the nature of the postulated language faculty. On Chomsky's view, the operations of the language faculty conform to the principles articulated in the Universal Grammar.

Universal Grammar (or 'Linguistic Theory'), as Chomsky understands it, is distinct from grammars for particular languages. Rather than specifying the particular rules governing, say, English or Walpiri, Universal Grammar is a theory about those features that natural languages have qua natural languages. It describes the class of 'linguistic universals,' the properties that are common to all natural languages. In his (1965:28ff.), Chomsky distinguishes two broad kinds of linguistic universal. 'Substantive' universals delineate what may be thought of as the 'natural kinds' of linguistics (sentence, adverb, subject, fricative, etc.), thus suggesting a proprietary vocabulary for the statement of both linguistic generalizations and grammatical rules. 'Formal' universals specify in more abstract terms the defining properties of natural languages, thus constraining the forms particular grammars may take and delimiting the contents of particular rules. "Substantive universals . . . concern the vocabulary for the description of language; formal universals involve rather the character of the rules that appear in grammars and the ways in which they can be interconnected" (Chomsky 1965:29).

While Chomsky's conception of what the universals of language are has evolved substantially over the years, he has nonetheless held fast to the notion that the principles of Universal Grammar both derive from and are descriptive of the initial state of the language acquisition device.[3] He reasons

---

3. The general trend in Chomskyan linguistics has been toward the provision of an ever more general and abstract account of what the language universals are. In his (1965: 29ff.), Chomsky offered as examples of universals a few fairly low-level generalizations about language, such as Jakobson's theory that all phonemes are definable in terms of a small, fixed number of acoustic-articulatory features and his own principles that grammatical rules are structure-dependent and that grammars include transformations. In his (1981), where he first articulated the 'Government-Binding' or 'Principles and Parameters' approach to syntax, he argued that natural languages evince many more, and much deeper, regularities than hitherto realized. The Government-Binding view that natural languages are merely variations on a single linguistic theme spurred the articulation of more abstract universals such as the 'Subjacency Principle' (which restricts the distance that elements of a phrase marker may be moved to satisfy other conditions imposed by the Universal Grammar) and the 'Case Filter' (which rules out constructions where an N is not assigned a Case). As an "extreme variant of this approach" (1991a:22), Chomsky envisaged the possibility of formulating universals of such generality that one could deduce "the 'apparent rules' [of particular languages] from general principles in the sense that the interaction of these principles would yield the phenomena that the rules were constructed to describe. The rules postulated for particular languages . . . would then be shown to be epiphenom-

(sometimes on empirical grounds, sometimes on more 'conceptual' grounds, as we'll see in chapter 10) that if all languages have a certain feature F, it is because the language faculty itself incorporates F-ness (or some other property productive of F-ness). He thus adds to the weak linguistic nativism comprised by (R), (B), (DS) and (I), the further hypothesis (U):

(U) **Universal Grammar**

The constraints and principles specified in (DS) as being required for language learning are to be identified with the principles of the Universal Grammar.

These five claims—Representationalism, Biological Boundedness, Domain-Specificity, Innateness, and Universal Grammar—together constitute what I will call *Chomskyan Nativism*.

I said above that failing to distinguish carefully between the 'core' claims of Chomskyan nativism, and consequently among the arguments appropriate to establishing each of them, has led to a situation whereby criticism of some strand in Chomsky's view is frequently taken, by nativist and censor alike, to be tantamount to the rejection of all elements in the Chomskyan position. This, in turn, has contributed to the development of something of a rhetorical impasse, incredulous stares and mudslinging denunciations of opponents' views having to some extent usurped the role of reasoned argument and provision of evidence in this debate. This is not to deny, however, that the core claims do form something of a natural cluster when viewed from the Chomskyan perspective. The conjunction of (U) and (I), for example, entails (DS), (B), and (R). Thus, reasons to accept (U) and (I) are ipso facto reasons to accept (R), (B), and (DS); and arguments against (R), (B), or (DS) are correctly construed by Chomskyans as undermining the conjunction of (I) and (U). But while there is a "trickle down" of evidential support from (U) and (I) to the other elements of the Chomskyan core in virtue of these logical relations, there may be no corresponding "trickle-up" effect. For few of these entailments hold in the other direction. Hence, although arguments aimed at establishing the conjunction of (U) and (I) are ipso facto arguments for the other core claims, arguments for (R), (B), (DS), or (I), or for some combination thereof, are not necessarily arguments for the full Chomskyan position.

For example, while (U) straightforwardly entails (DS), (DS) does not entail (U). Since the theory of Universal Grammar is a theory of the properties essential or common to all natural languages, the constraints on our thinking

---

ena ... that is, eliminable, perhaps entirely" (1991a:22). Now, with the advent of the Minimalist Program (Chomsky 1992/93), linguistics moves toward this end, and we find principles such as the 'minimal link condition' (Chomsky 1995:401ff., also known as 'Shortest Move,' Marantz 1995:355), which requires that constituents 'check off' their features (e.g., move to acquire Case) in the most economical way possible, and entails a number of conditions on movement that were captured in earlier Linguistic Theories only by several distinct principles.

about language will of course be domain-specific constraints if they are those identified in (U). Thus, any argument or evidence for (U) will tend to support (DS) as well. However, a commitment to (DS) does not by itself require acceptance of (U), for it is possible that there are domain-specific constraints on language-learning that do not conform to the principles of Universal Grammar.[4] So, and this will be one of my central contentions in what follows, one may accept (DS) while reserving judgment on Chomsky's (U) and the specific models of language acquisition that are based on it.

Similarly, and this will be another point that I will emphasize below, although both the conjunction of (DS) and (I) (and the conjunction of (U) and (I)) entail (B), and although (B) entails (I), (B) does not entail (I)'s conjunction with either (DS) or (U). That is, if Universal Grammar (or some other linguistically specific principles) are innately encoded in some manner in the language-learning mechanism (whether as constraints on hypothesis formation or as parameters to be set by experience), then clearly our biology sets limits on what thoughts we can entertain during the course of language-learning. However, the mere fact that there may be (or even must be) biological constraints on how languages are learned does not entail that those constraints are specific to the language-learning task, nor, a fortiori, does it entail that those constraints, if domain-specific, are as characterized by the Universal Grammar.[5]

And finally, (DS) does not entail (I). As I shall argue in chapters 8 and 9, one may have reason to believe that there must exist domain-specific constraints on the learning mechanism, without thereby having reason to believe those constraints to be innate. (DS) and (I), in other words, are logically independent components of the nativist position, and each must be provided independent support.

In sum, the relations among the elements of Chomskyan nativism, and its relation to the evidence, are more complicated than is often recognized. Failure to appreciate this fact has had unfortunate consequences. In particular, it has led to a perceived shrinking of the space of possible positions on the acquisition problem. Because Chomskyan nativism seems so often to be regarded as an indivisible whole, the denial of some element of Chomsky's position has been taken to undermine the entire nativist project, and to leave one with no alternative but to embrace some naive form of empiricism, such as behaviorism. In his (1990:638–39), for instance, Chomsky favorably com-

---

4. See the learning theory that Bresnan bases on her Lexical Functional Grammar (Bresnan 1978; Bresnan and Kaplan 1981). The theory makes appeal to a domain-specific language faculty while denying that the Chomskyan universals accurately describe its properties.

5. One might, for example, hold that our thoughts are biologically bounded, and that these bounds are set by our innate endowment, while denying that language-learning requires that those bounds be domain-specific. Putnamian empiricism, to be defined below, holds something like this.

	(R)	(B)	(DS)	(I)	(U)
Chomskyan Nativism	✓	✓	✓	✓	✓
Weak Nativism	✓	✓	✓	✓	
Putnamian Empiricism	✓	✓		✓	
Enlightened Empiricism	✓	✓	✓		?
Behaviorism					

Figure 7.1 A partial taxonomy of possible acquisition theories for language.

pares his approach with an alternative view according to which "knowledge of language . . . is a system of habits, dispositions and abilities . . . acquired . . . by conditioning, training, habit-formation or 'general learning mechanisms' " (1990:638). But while Chomsky claims that this naive view is "still widely held . . . by philosophers influenced by Wittgenstein and Quine" (1990:638), what distinguishing the core claims enables us to see is that not all criticisms of the Chomskyan position are criticisms of the entire nativist paradigm. Not all ways of rejecting Chomskyan nativism are ways of being a behaviorist. As figure 7.1 indicates, there are a number of different positions that can be taken on the acquisition question, corresponding to the different stances one might take regarding the various core claims. And while some alternatives to Chomskyan nativism (very much including behaviorism) are indeed just silly and deserve to be dismissed, I'll argue that others, such as Weak Linguistic Nativism and Enlightened Empiricism, are on the face of it quite sensible, and deserve to be taken more seriously as potentially viable alternatives to the Chomskyan view.

In the next section, we will recall Chomsky's (1959) case against behaviorism (that view being represented here as involving the denial of all five core claims). I will argue that Chomsky's defeat of behaviorism was decisive in that it succeeded in establishing (R). However, I will contend, his (1959) arguments fail to discriminate among the other four positions displayed in figure 7.1. In subsequent sections, we will look at Chomsky's later arguments for nativism, and attempt to determine their import for those remaining possibilities.

7.2 Chomksy's Review of Skinner: The Case for Representationalism

Chomsky's nativist revolution began with his highly influential attack on behaviorism (Chomsky 1959). In a scathing review of B. F. Skinner's *Verbal Behavior*, he effectively demolished the behaviorist model of human linguistic behavior. Chomsky rejected as explanatorily and predictively worthless the behaviorist's anti-mentalistic conception of linguistic competence, that is, the inner processes and structures underpinning language mastery. In its place, he proposed a thoroughly cognitivist and representationalist account thereof. He also anticipated his famed argument from the poverty of the stimulus (see §7.4 and chapter 8) in criticizing the behaviorist's conception of language acquisition. In so doing, he set the scene for a nativist explanation of language-learning.

The behaviorist view is that the ability to speak and understand a language consists in nothing more than a complex of 'dispositions to verbal behavior' that is instilled in the mind of the speaker as a result of childhood training. This system of linguistic habits, forged by conditioning, allegedly serves to bring aspects of our verbal and nonverbal behavior under the 'control' of particular environmental conditions. So, for example, you utter 'Fox!' because you have been conditioned in such a way that that behavior has come to be controlled by nearby instantiations of the property *foxhood*; and I turn and gaze toward the fields upon hearing your utterance because I have been conditioned to expect that the utterance of 'Fox!' will be an "occasion upon which turning and looking about is frequently followed by the reinforcement of seeing a fox" (Skinner, quoted in Chomsky 1959:48).

Chomsky rejects this picture of what language mastery consists in. Our ability to use and understand a language cannot be reduced to a congeries of habits or dispositions, he argues, for linguistic behavior is both *stimulus-independent* and *productive*.

Our use of language is stimulus-independent. What we say and how we react to the utterances of others is not merely a reflexive response to the external world. Far from being under the 'control' of environmental factors such as our current state of sensory stimulation and our history of reinforcement, our verbal behavior is determined by a complex of factors, most of them internal and many of them cognitive in nature. Since the behaviorist eschews all talk of the mental, Chomsky argued, his attempt to explain and predict linguistic behavior is bound to fail.

Our use of language is also productive. People routinely display a capacity for linguistic innovation, an ability to use language in original ways and to respond appropriately to the novel utterances of others. Moreover, innovations do not occur unconstrainedly. They are governed by an immensely complicated system of semantic, pragmatic, and syntactic rules. Chomsky argues that speakers' conformity to these rules cannot be explained without taking seriously the idea that "there are, behind the overtly expressed sequences, a multiplicity of integrative processes" (1959:55), and concludes that "no approach to language that fails to take these deeper processes into account can possibly achieve much success in accounting for actual linguistic behavior" (1959:54).

Chomsky's first point against Skinner is thus that the behaviorist underestimates the complexity, and misrepresents the nature, of linguistic competence. A second, equally damning criticism leveled against the Skinnerian program in his (1959) is that it can provide no satisfactory account of how linguistic competence could be acquired.

On the behaviorist's view, linguistic habits are established in speaker–hearers during childhood as a result of conditioning, that is, as a result of training by other members of their linguistic community. Chomsky argues, however, that it is false that a "careful arrangement of contingencies of reinforcement by the verbal community is a necessary condition of language-learning" (1959:39). Not only is it in general unclear what the technical notion of reinforcement might amount to in the context of learning sophisticated 'behaviors' like language, but the claim that anything even remotely like operant conditioning is involved in language-learning is rather obviously untrue.[6] Even superficial observation of children learning a language reveals that explicit and prolonged training, such as generations of lucky rats and pigeons received during the heyday of behaviorist experimentation, plays at most a minor role in the language-learning process. Chomsky points out, for example, that children learn much of their vocabulary and 'feel' for sentence structure from reading, watching television, and passively listening to adults; that immigrant children learn a second language, to native speaker fluency, merely through associating with other children; and that even very young children are capable of linguistic innovation, saying things that they have never been 'trained' to say. He concludes:

> it seems beyond question that children acquire a good deal of their verbal and nonverbal behavior by casual observation and imitation of adults and other children. It is simply not true that children can learn language only through 'meticulous care' on the part of adults who shape their verbal repertoire through careful differential reinforcement. (1959:42)

Since the 1960s, Chomsky's contention that explicit teaching or reinforcement is largely irrelevant to the task of learning language has garnered a certain amount of empirical support, especially vis-à-vis the acquisition of syntax. Frequently cited in this connection are the landmark studies of Roger Brown and his colleagues (e.g., Brown, Cazden and Bellugi 1969; Brown and Hanlon 1970). Over a period of years, they recorded sample conversations between three children and their mothers, finding, in support of Chomsky's argument, that children's progression through various stages of syntactic knowledge is unrelated to parental expressions of approval or disapproval.[7] While parents do tend to correct their children's semantic errors,

---

6. E.g., reinforcement, held by the behaviorist to be necessary to all learning, is explained in terms of drive reduction: a piece of behavior will be positively reinforced (and eventually learned) if it is followed often enough by an event, such as the delivery of a food pellet, that satisfies some basic need or 'reduces a drive' in the organism. But what 'drives,' Chomsky asks (1959:39–42), are being 'reduced' when we learn more complex behaviors, such as speaking a sentence? One could in principle postulate additional 'basic needs,' such as 'communication' or 'problem-solving drives,' in order to explain how reinforcement is involved in the learning of complex behaviors. However, Chomsky contends, invoking pseudo drives such as these renders the concept of reinforcement explanatorily vacuous in these cases.

7. Meaning by 'disapproval' here not just explicit correction but also requests for clarification or failures to comprehend the child's utterance (Brown and Hanlon 1970).

syntactic errors go almost wholly unremarked. Thus, contrary to the behaviorist's contention, training by caregivers is not necessary for children's acquisition of adult syntax.[8] Nor, it seems, does training or correction by adults suffice to bring about changes in children's speech. Anecdotal evidence (see Braine 1971; Pinker 1989:12ff., 1994:180–82) suggests that children are unable to modify their speech in the ways demanded by an adult teacher. Children's speech errors may persist in the face of steady parental correction for weeks or months before disappearing apparently of their own accord.[9]

Chomsky's second point against Skinner, then, is that training such as the behaviorist conceives it is neither necessary nor sufficient for the acquisition of syntactic knowledge. Or, to put it another way, the stimulus to language-learning is much more impoverished than the behaviorist's picture requires. The behaviorist views the learning mechanism as a relatively simple device that modifies the strength of the association between stimulus–response pairs in line with the contingencies of reinforcement: the more frequent the reinforcement, the greater the strength of the association; and the greater that strength, the greater the disposition to emit that response, given that stimulus. But for the learning mechanism, so conceived, to deliver the range and variety of linguistic dispositions that (on the behaviorist analysis) underpin linguistic behavior, the learning child would have to be barraged, constantly, with help and guidance from her linguistic mentors—help and guidance that children do not, in fact, receive. So even if we were to grant the behaviorist his dispositional account of the outputs of learning, it is nonetheless the case that he can 'explain' our acquisition of those dispositions only by supposing that the input to language-learning is very much richer than we have any reason to think it to be.

Chomsky's arguments against Skinner thus established two things: the negative point that the behaviorist cannot explain how language is acquired, even on his own dispositional conception of linguistic competence, and the positive point that the behaviorist's anemic conception of linguistic competence needs to be replaced by a more robustly mentalistic account. Language mastery involves a wealth of syntactic, semantic, and pragmatic knowledge, and language use is shaped by a host of beliefs, desires, and intentions. Dealing adequately with the phenomenon of language, Chomsky made clear, requires the admission of mental states, in particular representational states, into the ontology of psychological theory. It requires endorsement of (R).

As Chomsky's (1959) showed him to be well aware, to adopt Representationalism in the domain of language is immediately to confront two further tasks. First, one must provide a characterization of the postulated mental states underlying linguistic behavior. What is the content of the knowledge

---

8. But see §9.5.3 for further critical discussion of these results and the conclusions based on them.

9. See §9.5 for further discussion of the role of parental feedback in language acquisition.

states or belief states constituting linguistic competence?[10] What are the psychological processes that determine language use and understanding? Second, one must grapple with the fact that the adoption of a representationalist conception of the mind deepens still further the mystery of language acquisition. As Chomsky showed, Skinner could not explain how speaker–hearers acquire even a linguistic competence as attentuated as the behaviorist conceived it to be. How much less adequate, then, must his learning theory be to deal with acquisition of the rich cognitive structures that are entailed by a representational theory of the mind! But beyond emphasizing, throughout his review, the fact that children learn remarkably much about language in a remarkably short time from remarkably few data; and besides hinting at the end of his article that linguistics might one day be able to "provide a precise account of [the] integrative processes, imposed patterns and selective mechanisms [underlying language use]" (1959:55), he offered little in the way of concrete proposals for how the mental states underlying language-learning and language mastery were to be characterized. It was only later that he began to focus explicitly on the problems of elucidating linguistic competence, and explaining its acquisition.

7.3 Generative Grammar: A New Approach to the Psychology of Language

By the early 1960s it was clear that in order to deal with the phenomena of language use and understanding, one must abandon the behaviorist's myopic focus on the 'observable' facts of stimulus and response, and knuckle down to the task of characterizing the mental processes that mediate between them. But how to proceed? After decades in which psychology had been shackled by the methodological and philosophical commitments of behaviorism, the rout of behaviorism left a serious, if exhilarating, void. Into the breach, however, Chomsky strode. Not content with demolishing the Skinnerian theory, he was ready with a new theory and a new methodology. The theory was transformational generative grammar. The methodology was that of the 'new' linguistics.

7.3.1 The 'New' Linguistics

In the late 1950s, Chomsky's generative approach to syntax began to replace the taxonomic paradigm of the American structuralists.[11] The structuralists

10. Recall that I use 'knowledge' and cognates in the psychologist's sense of, roughly, a system of beliefs.
11. Leonard Bloomfield and Zellig Harris were leaders of the American structuralist movement. See Harris (1951: chs. 1, 2) for a statement of the structuralists' aims and methods.

had aimed, not unreasonably, to construct grammars providing general, systematic descriptions of the syntactic features of sentences in a language. But their descriptive enterprise was hampered by their positivistic scruples as regards both the form and the subject matter of their theories. Formally, they held themselves to be constrained by the requirement that theoretical terms (such as 'noun phrase') be definable in terms of observable features of utterances (conceived, ultimately, as sequences of sounds). Ontologically, their distrust of the unobserved led the structuralists to conceive of natural languages as being merely collections of actual utterances, or 'corpora,' the grammarian's task being to catalogue regularities among the sentences in a given corpus.

While not rejecting altogether the descriptive task as a goal of linguistic theories, Chomsky urged a radically different picture of what describing a language entails. He argued, first, that it was a mistake to insist that the linguist's central theoretical terms be definable in terms of observable properties of sound sequences. Linguists must acknowledge the autonomy of syntax from phonetics, he argued, and should address the task of characterizing natural languages with whatever theoretical tools it takes.[12] Chomsky argued, second, that linguists should not be restricted in their descriptive endeavors to the systematization of regularities in sets of actual utterances. Natural languages, he observed, contain infinitely many sentences that will never be uttered by anyone. To describe a language in its entirety, then, one must look for theories that not only succeed in describing the sentences contained in a corpus but also go beyond the data, accurately predicting the existence and properties of new sentences.[13] To these ends, Chomsky urged the development of generative grammars. A generative grammar is a set of rules or procedures that will generate all and only the sentences in a language, spoken or unspoken, together with their structural descriptions. Such a grammar will both characterize the sentences already in the corpus and predict the existence and properties of new sentences. To the extent that it succeeds in fulfilling these dual aims, a generative grammar is, in Chomsky's parlance, 'observationally adequate.'

In his groundbreaking early book *Syntactic Structures* (1957), Chomsky had argued that a certain simple kind of generative grammar, called a 'phrase-structure' grammar, was inadequate to the task of characterizing a natural language. Phrase-structure grammars contain only 'rewrite rules,' that is, rules that specify a method for constructing a variety of sentences by systematically replacing certain syntactic categories with other categories (and, ultimately, words). The sequence of steps taken in the derivation of a sentence—its 'derivational history'—is taken to reflect its underlying syntactic structure, and is represented by a 'phrase marker,' that is, a labeled brack-

---

12. Chomsky (1955, 1975a).
13. Chomsky (1957).

eting or 'tree.'[14] Phrase-structure grammars, Chomsky argued, are observationally inadequate because natural languages display 'unbounded syntactic dependencies.' That is, what a symbol can be rewritten as often depends on other things in the sentence that are arbitrarily far away from the symbol of interest, and hence cannot be captured in simple rewrite rules. He argued that although additional syntactic categories could in principle be introduced so as to allow phrase-structure grammars to account for such dependencies, the explosion of strange categories and proliferation of rules that would ensue would render the grammar, as he put it, "clumsy," "*ad hoc*," and "unrevealing" (1957:35).[15]

A better approach, he suggested, is to enrich generative grammars with another kind of rule: transformations. Transformational rules specify mappings not from syntactic category to syntactic category (as do phrase-structure rules), but from phrase markers to phrase markers.[16] In a transformational grammar such as Chomsky advocated, the generative task is shared between several distinct syntactic components or modules. Phrase-structure rules are employed by the Base component of the grammar to

14. E.g., the first step in deriving a sentence like 'John kissed Mary' involves using the rule S → NP VP to rewrite the sentence symbol 'S' as the symbols 'NP VP.' This step is represented in a tree by the first branch from the root S to the nodes NP and VP

and reflects the fact that English sentences have a fundamentally bipartite (subject–predicate) structure: $[_S[_{NP}\text{———}][_{VP}\text{———}]]$.

15. E.g., a verb symbol 'v' may be rewritten as either 'kiss' or 'kisses,' depending on whether the subject noun phrase of the sentence—which may be separated from the main verb by indefinitely many embedded clauses—is singular or plural. One could try to capture this dependency between subject and verb by using two different phrase structure rules, such as 'S → NP_{sing} VP_{sing}' and 'S → NP_{plur} VP_{plur}' (with corresponding distinctions all down the line) for the generation of sentences with singular and plural subjects. But, Chomsky's objection runs, to do this would be to say, in effect and orthography notwithstanding, that singular and plural NPs (and VPs) are distinct syntactic categories and hence be unable to state such important generalizations as that all English declarative sentences consist of a noun phrase followed by a verb phrase. It's worth noting that this objection to phrase-structure grammars has been met by modern proponents of phrase-structure grammars (e.g., Gazdar et al. 1985). The basic strategy is to take syntactic categories like NP and VP as being partial functions defined over various lower-level features (e.g., an NP has the value + for the feature N and − for the feature V, whereas a VP has − for N and + for V). Dependencies like subject–verb agreement can then be captured by rules defined over the features without losing the ability to state generalizations like 'S → NP VP.' See Soames (1989:556–60) for a brief and nontechnical overview of the 'generalized phrase-structure grammar' approach to syntax.

16. E.g., one early transformational rule specified how to turn an active sentence into a passive one. Given a phrase marker of the form NP–*Aux*–V–NP, one rearranges the elements X_1–X_2–X_3–X_4 of that phrase marker as follows to generate a passive construction: $X_4 - X_2 + be + en - X_3 - by + X_1$. Thus, *John hit Mary* becomes *Mary hit* (+ *was* + *en*) *by John*. (Further transformations operate to change *hit* (+ *was* + *en*) into the passive verb form *was hit*.) From Chomsky 1957:112.)

generate a set of 'initial phrase markers,' termed at various times 'kernel sentences,' 'deep structures,' or 'D-structures.' The output of the Base then serves as input to a second, Transformational component, where transformational rules generate a further set of 'derived phrase markers.' The final output of the Transformational component (a 'surface structure,' or 's-structure') then serves as input to other postulated modules dealing with aspects of morphology, phonology, and, later, semantic interpretation.[17]

7.3.2 The 'New' Psychology of Language

This classical picture of a transformational generative grammar is now seriously outdated. It is nonetheless important. For, at some time in the late 1950s, it occurred to Chomsky that the usefulness of such a theory might not be exhausted by its ability to characterize natural languages, conceived of merely as sets of sentences in abstraction from those who speak them. Perhaps a grammar might also be of help to psychologists in characterizing the competencies of speakers of natural languages, thus providing a timely replacement for the ousted behaviorist account. After all, the grammatical intuitions of speakers, that is, their considered judgments as to what is and is not a well-formed sentence of their language, form the data and ultimate court of appeal for a grammatical theory. A grammar is 'descriptively adequate' only to the extent that it generates just those sentences that speakers do or will count as grammatical and assigns them appropriate structures.[18]

---

17. Chomsky's thinking about the modular structure of the grammar has undergone many changes. In his (1957), he proposed a three-component grammar: the Base, containing phrase-structure rules; the Transformational component, containing transformations; and a Morphophonological component (now called Phonological Form, or PF), whose job was to take surface structures as input and deliver as output representations of sentences for use by the articulatory systems. He later postulated a fourth component, Semantic Interpretation (now called Logical Form, or LF), for semantic interpretation (Chomsky 1965). With the advent of the 'Government and Binding' or 'Principles and Parameters' approach to syntax in the early 1980s, the distinction between the Base and Transformational components of the grammar became blurred, for many of the structural constraints and constraints on movement articulated in that theory applied at both derivational levels. In his most recent writings (e.g., Chomsky 1995), Chomsky has repudiated the Base/Transformational distinction (and the corresponding the D-structure/s-structure distinction). According to his new 'Minimalist Program,' grammars contain just one syntactic component, C_{HL}, where the lexical properties of words and a variety of constraints on movement and tree structure interact to generate, at an 'interface level' called 'Spell Out,' representations Σ_p and Σ_l of the sentence, which serve as inputs to the morphophonological (PF) and semantic (LF) systems, respectively.

18. Actually, the real situation is more complicated than this, since sometimes a speaker's intuitions about well-formedness may be rejected if they conflict with the deliverances of the theory. "Garden path" sentences like *The horse raced past the barn fell* are a case in point, as are multiply center-embedded sentences like *The man the boy the cat the dog bit scratched hated died.* Both are counted as grammatical even though some speakers may well regard them as unacceptable. See Chomsky (1965:11–15) for more on the distinction between '(un)acceptability' and '(un)grammaticality.'

In some sense, then, a grammar is descriptive of speakers' knowledge of what is and is not a sentence of their language. And from this, it seems but a short step to the revolutionary claims that competent speakers know the grammar of their language and that theories in linguistics are descriptive of that knowledge.

It is unclear exactly when this 'psychological' interpretation for grammars occurred to Chomsky. He claims, in his Introduction to the 1975 edition of *The Logical Structure of Linguistic Theories*, that although he already had the idea in 1955, when that work was originally written, it seemed too outrageous a suggestion to make at the time. Katz (1981), however, disputes this claim on the grounds, first, that "[i]t is hard not to be skeptical about Chomsky's claim that timidity prevented a thought of his from becoming known" (1981:40) and, second, that the 1955 manuscript of *The Logical Structure of Linguistic Theories* contains several anti-mentalist diatribes, the positivist tenor of which would seem antithetical to his later position. Katz's skepticism as to Chomsky's dating of his epiphany is supported by the fact that in *Syntactic Structures* (1957), Chomsky comes very close to denying that grammars have any psychological relevance, explaining there that

> grammars [are] devices for generating sentences. . . . Actually grammars of the form we have been discussing are quite neutral between speaker and hearer. . . . A grammar does not tell us how to synthesize a specific utterance; it does not tell us how to analyze a particular given utterance. In fact, these two tasks which the speaker and hearer must perform are essentially the same, and are both outside the scope of [transformational] grammars. *Each such grammar is simply a description of a certain set of utterances, namely, those which it generates.* (1957:48, emphasis added)

But, as we've seen, Chomsky had clearly recognized grammars' psychological potential by the time his review of Skinner was written. There he wrote: "[a]lthough present-day linguistics cannot provide a precise account of these integrative processes, imposed patterns and selective mechanisms [underlying language use], it can at least set itself the problem of characterizing them completely" (1959:55). And by 1965, when the transformationalist manifesto *Aspects of the Theory of Syntax* was published, Chomsky had settled on the view, to which he still subscribes, that "[o]bviously, every speaker has mastered and internalized a generative grammar that expresses his knowledge of his language" (1965:8), with the consequence that "[n]o doubt, a reasonable model of language use will incorporate, as a basic component, the generative grammar that expresses the speaker–hearer's knowledge of the language" (1965:9).

By co-opting grammars to serve as an account of the mental states constituting linguistic competence, then, Chomsky appeared not only to have provided a much-needed alternative to the behaviorist's account of language mastery. He seemed also to have found a new methodology for the psychological study of language and created a new job description for linguists. In developing theories about natural languages, linguists, on Chomsky's view, were at the same time characterizing speakers' 'mastery,' 'internalization,' 'cognizance,' or 'tacit knowledge' of the grammar of their language. Linguists, in other words, were elucidating the nature of the representational states, postulated in (R), that constitute linguistic competence.

7.3.3 Hypothesis-Testing: Chomsky's LAD

The notion that grammars characterize the cognitive states underpinning language use and understanding threw into particularly stark relief the question of how language is acquired. As even the most cursory glance at the linguistics of the period reveals, transformational grammars were immensely complex and subtle theories, employing, as time went by, theoretical constructs that were increasingly remotely related to ordinary experience. How, then, are these rules of grammar learned? Recall that it was only by greatly *under*estimating the complexity of linguisitic competence, and massively *over*estimating the information that serves as input during its acquisition, that the behaviorist was able to make do with a relatively simple account of the mechanism mediating learning. In his review of Skinner, Chomsky had shown that the inputs to the learning function are much less rich than the behaviorist imagined. By deploying grammars as accounts of the outputs of learning, he vastly increased the complexity of the end state of the learning process as well. Under pressure from his arguments, then, the gap between what we know about language and the information about it that we receive from the environment suddenly widened, and the problem of explaining language acquisition became acute.

In line with the dictates of representationalism, which was rapidly gaining adherents, and in place of the behaviorist's noncognitivist, associationist learning theory, a more sophisticated conception of language-learning emerged. Learning, on the view that Chomsky refined and elaborated in the years following his vanquishing of Skinner, is a process of hypothesis formulation and testing, analogous to theory construction in science. Just as the scientist makes hypotheses about the nature of the world and tests them against experimental data, so children learning a language make hypotheses about its semantic and syntactic structure and test them against the data provided by their linguistic experience. So rather than being a nonrational by-product of organism–environment interaction (as the behaviorist believed), acquiring a language, on Chomsky's conception, is an essentially rational process involving highly sophisticated, albeit unconscious, information processing.

By 1965, Chomsky had come to the view that in order to account for language acquisition on a hypothesis-testing model, the learner must have available to her at least the following (based on Chomsky 1965:30–31):

1. *A technique for representing input signals* (e.g., a system for representing the incoming acoustic signal).

2. *A way of representing structural information about these signals* (e.g., a system for the representation of grammatical categories like S, NP, VP, phrase boundaries, thematic relations, etc.).

3. *A highly restrictive specification of a class of possible grammatical hypotheses*, G_1, G_2, ...

4. *A method for testing hypotheses*, that is, for determining what each hypothesis implies with respect to each sentence.

5. *An evaluation metric*, that is, a method for selecting one of the hypotheses that are allowed by 3 and are compatible with the primary linguistic data.

In viewing the learner as a hypothesis tester, this theory straightforwardly requires that she possess the conceptual resources necessary for the formulation of her grammatical hypotheses and for the representation of evidence for and against them. Since the incoming data are in the first instance nothing more than streams of sounds, the child must be able to form a preliminary representation of those sounds via the symbol system postulated in (1). But since the grammatical hypotheses themselves, and the evidence bearing on them, are framed not in terms of sound sequences but, rather, in terms of syntactic categories like NP, S, VP, and the like, the child must also possess the syntactic concepts adverted to in (2). Thus, adopting the hypothesis-testing model commits one to the view that the child, as a prerequisite for the acquisition of language, has available the resources of at least two representational systems. It also entails (4), that one attribute to her whatever inferential resources are necessary for determining the epistemic import of a given piece of evidence upon a given grammatical conjecture. The remaining elements of the learning theory, (3) and (5), are postulated to ensure that language-learning be tractable. Given mastery of syntactic concepts like S, NP, and VP (and of basic logical operators like 'and' and 'or'), the child could in principle formulate infinitely many hypotheses about the syntactic structure of her language. As Chomsky argues, though, the comparative speed with which children acquire language makes it clear that they do not test every logically possible grammatical hypothesis against the data: many of them must be ruled out a priori as unworthy of consideration. Hence the need for (3), which places constraints on the kinds of hypotheses that the learner will entertain, and (5), an evaluation metric, which determines which hypothesis should be accepted in case more than one grammar is compatible with the available data.

On Chomsky's view, the representational systems postulated in (1) and (2), the constraints on grammatical hypotheses postulated in (3), and the evaluation metric postulated in (5) are both domain-specific and innate.[19]

---

19. While Chomsky, like everyone else, presumably holds the inferential procedures specified in (4) to be innate, it's unclear whether he thought them to be domain-specific also. For beyond noting the learner's need to be able to evaluate hypotheses in the light of the data, he had little to say about the nature of the reasoning involved in language

That is, he holds not just that the learner possesses whatever conceptual resources are necessary to her theorizing about language, but also that she possesses them innately, as a consequence of her biology. And he holds also that the learner's initial formulation of hypotheses, and her subsequent choices among competing hypotheses, are shaped not (or not only) by general canons of theory construction like "Prefer simpler, more general, more powerful hypotheses." On Chomsky's view, they are constrained instead (or as well) by her innate knowledge of the principles of the Universal Grammar—domain-specific principles like "All grammatical rules are structure-dependent," "Natural languages are governed by both phrase-structure and transformational rules," "No transformational rule may move a constituent over more than one NP or S boundary," and so on. Thus, endorsement of a 'language acquisition device' or 'LAD' such as Chomsky conceives entails an expansion of one's commitments to embrace all five of the Chomskyan core claims.

It's worth stressing, however, that while accepting Chomsky's vision of the LAD involves accepting his nativism also, supporting a hypothesis-testing conception of learning per se does not necessitate adoption of all five core claims. For example, a Weak nativist could agree that domain-specific constraints such as are postulated in (3) and the metric postulated in (5) are required for language-learning, and she could argue that they are innate while denying that they are as characterized by the Universal Grammar. Accepting such a model would be to embrace Chomsky's (R), (B), (DS), and (I) while repudiating his (U). Alternatively, an empiricist might maintain that hypothesis-testing is implicated in language-learning, and accept that the hypothesis-testing mechanism is a natural feature of human psychology while denying that it is domain-specific (and, a fortiori, that its operations are governed by principles of Universal Grammar). Putnam (1971), for instance, argues that the constraints on grammatical hypotheses postulated in (3), and the evaluation metric posited in (5), flow from whatever domain-neutral principles regulate theoretical reasoning in general. Both hypothesis formulation and hypothesis evaluation, on his view, are governed by such general-purpose principles as "Look for underlying regularities," "Choose powerful hypotheses," "Prefer simpler hypotheses to more complicated ones," and so on. No special constraints or rules need be invoked to explain how languages are learned. In allowing that there are innate principles that both constrain the space of hypotheses and aid in selecting among competing hypotheses while denying that those innate principles are domain-specific,

---

acquisition. It seems reasonable to speculate, though, that at the time in question, Chomsky conceived the learner as applying very general logical rules such as *modus ponens* and *modus tollens* in some fairly straightforward way to her linguistic theorizing. Certainly, much of the work in formal learning theory, which offers more precise characterizations of the learning function, makes use of domain-neutral inferential procedures in determining the import of a given datum for a given hypothesis. See, e.g., Gold (1967); Pinker (1979); Wexler and Culicover (1980); see also chapter 9.

then, the Putnamian Empiricist endorses Chomsky's (R), (B), and (I), and denies his (DS) and (U). Yet another way to embrace the hypothesis-testing model while eschewing the full Chomskyan slate would be to agree with Chomsky that domain-specific constraints are required to narrow the range of possible grammatical hypotheses or to rank competing hypotheses, while denying that those constraints are innately specified, and/or that they are as characterized by Universal Grammar. An Enlightened Empiricist could, for example, maintain that the constraints on the learner's grammatical hypotheses (or on what will count as the best hypothesis) at a given time t' are not fixed by her innate endowment—not by properties possessed by the language faculty ab initio—but are fixed, rather, by her experience, being a function of her state of opinion regarding language at some earlier time t. The Enlightened Empiricist thus accepts Chomsky's (DS) while denying (I) (and, depending on the details, possibly (U) as well).

Similarly, a range of positions can be taken regarding the genesis and nature of the representational systems postulated in (1) and (2) of Chomsky's learning model. On Chomsky's view, the specialized phonetic and syntactic vocabularies mandated by the Universal Grammar as being required for the representation of data and the statement of grammatical hypotheses are known innately. A Weak Nativist might argue instead that although the representational system(s) required for learning language are both specialized and innate, the linguistic categories used by the mind during language acquisition differ in important respects from the categorial structures employed by theoretical linguists in the Chomskyan tradition, and are thus not accurately characterized by the Universal Grammar. He would thus reject Chomsky's (U). An empiricist, to take another possibility, might agree with Chomsky's (DS) that specialized representational systems are required for language-learning, and may even agree that they are related to the systems linguists use (thus accepting (U)), while denying their innateness, (I). On this view, the child learning language generates the necessary syntactic concepts 'on the fly,' abstracting them from her experience and/or compounding them from other concepts in her repertoire as necessitated by the demands of the language-learning task.

No doubt other variations on the hypothesis-testing theme are possible as well. The point here is not to attempt to delineate them all, but rather to emphasize that the rejection of behaviorism and the adoption of a hypothesis-testing model of language-learning does not by itself force acceptance of any of Chomsky's (DS), (I), or (U). There are many ways to elaborate the hypothesis-testing model, and Chomsky's is only one of them. While it will turn out, as we'll see below, that not all of these alternatives are equally plausible, any of them might, for all we have seen so far, prove to be adequate. Further argument is required to get beyond hypothesis-testing to nativism. In the rest of this chapter, I will outline Chomsky's arguments for the remaining core contentions. In the chapters following, I will turn to the task of evaluating them.

7.4 The Poverty of the Stimulus: From Hypothesis-Testing to Nativism

In §7.3, I argued that the hypothesis-testing model for language acquisition, although representing a radical departure from the behaviorist account it superseded, is not necessarily a nativist model. The idea that language is learned by hypothesis-testing, in and of itself, is neutral with regard to the other three (nonbehaviorist) stances on the acquisition question displayed in figure 7.1. In this section and the next, we will examine Chomsky's reasons for insisting that the hypothesis-testing model be elaborated in a properly Chomskyan manner. His arguments for the remaining 'core' claims derive from two sources. First, there are his celebrated 'poverty of the stimulus' arguments for (DS) and (I), to be introduced in this section. Second, as we'll see in §7.5, there is his argument for (U), which derives from his broader views about the relation of theories in linguistics to theories in the psychology of language.

Chomsky's case for nativism (that is to say, for Weak Nativism, the 'bare' architectural hypothesis represented by the conjunction of (DS) and (I)) rests on a series of arguments from the poverty of the stimulus. Similar in structure to the classical poverty of the stimulus arguments discussed in §3.2, the basic form of Chomsky's arguments is captured in the following passage from *Aspects:*

> It seems plain that language acquisition is based on the child's discovery of what from a formal point of view is a deep and abstract theory—a generative grammar of his language—many of the concepts and principles of which are only remotely related to experience by long and intricate chains of quasi-inferential steps. A consideration of . . . the degenerate quality and narrowly limited extent of the available data . . . leave[s] little hope that much of the structure of the language can be learned by an organism initially uninformed as to its general character. (Chomsky 1965: 58)

This argument, which is frequently presented through detailed discussion of particular cases (see chapter 8), depends on three empirical premises. The first is a claim about the outputs of language-learning. It is a hypothesis about what is in the mind of the competent speaker–hearer. According to Chomsky, as we've seen, the speaker's mind contains, among other things, tacit knowledge or 'cognizance' of a grammar for her language. Hence his view that learning a language is, at least in part, a matter of discovering "what from a formal point of view is a deep and abstract theory—a generative grammar . . .".

The second premise concerns the inputs to language-learning. It is a hypothesis about the amount and kinds of information, relevant to the task of learning a grammar, that are available to the learning child. The contention is that only a comparatively tiny amount of relevant information is available in the "primary linguistic data," for the input to language learning is of "degenerate quality and narrowly limited extent." The input's degeneracy derives from the fact that ordinary speech, such as the child hears during language-learning, is sometimes ungrammatical. 'Umms,' 'Aahhs,' hesitations, incomplete or mangled sentences constitute 'noise' in the data, noise that the child must somehow filter out in order to learn the grammar of her language correctly. In addition, the inputs to language-learning are impoverished, of 'narrowly limited extent,' in regard to both quantity and kind. Comparatively few data are available to the learning child: the sentences to which a child has access constitute only a small, finite sample of the infinitely many sentences that a natural language contains. And the kind of information to which a child has access is restricted also. Information about ambiguities, paraphrase relations, other languages and ungrammaticality, which constitutes critical data in the professional linguist's construction of grammars for a language, is claimed to be in general unavailable to children embarked upon the same enterprise. The linguist knows what sentences are ungrammatical, or which are synonymous, or which are ambiguous, for she already knows the language she is theorizing about. Hence, she can use her own competence to supply additional data that may be crucial in distinguishing among competing grammatical hypotheses. But the child, ex hypothesi, knows no language at all and so cannot use his competence as a source of information about his language. And since, as we saw in §7.2, he is rarely offered such information by caregivers, his access to these kinds of data must be extremely attenuated. (But see §§9.3–9.5.)

How, then, do children learn so much (the grammar of their language) from so little (exposure to a stream of noise)? The third premise of Chomsky's argument asserts the inability of nonnativist acquisition theories to answer this question: "The child who acquires a language . . . knows a great deal more than he has 'learned.' His knowledge of language . . . goes far beyond the presented primary linguistic data and is in no sense an 'inductive generalization' from those data" (1965:32–33). There is "little hope," as Chomsky says, that "much of the structure of the language can be learned by an organism initially uninformed as to its general character." Hence we should conclude that language-learning organisms such as ourselves are, on the contrary, initially very well informed about the characteristics of natural languages. The explanation of language-learning requires the assumption of Chomsky's (DS) and (I).

Thus Chomsky's poverty of the stimulus arguments point to a discrepancy, a 'gap,' between the meager input to the language-learning mechanism in the child and its torrential output; between, on the one hand, the information about language to which the child has access during learning and, on the other, the knowledge of grammar that constitutes, on Chomsky's view, the successful learner's linguistic competence. The claim is that this discrepancy is just too great to be accounted for by an appeal, empiricist-style, to some kind of 'general inductive learning strategy.' There must exist in us a special faculty for language-learning, incorporating innately specified linguistic information.

7.5 Linguistics as Psychology: From Weak Nativism to
Chomskyan Nativism

It seems plain on the face of it that, as I suggested in §7.2, the case presented in the previous section for (DS) and (I) falls short of establishing Chomsky's (U). That is, to argue that chilren must have *some* innate knowledge about natural language in order to learn one would seem to be one thing; and to make a case for a particular conception of what that knowledge is would seem to be another. Just as Mendel's postulation of genes—mechanisms of inheritance with certain functional characteristics—did not entail that it was DNA that realizes those mechanisms, so the postulation of a language faculty would appear to be consistent with any number of particular theories about its operation.

Chomsky sometimes appears to grant this point, especially in his more recent work. In the retrospective paper, "Linguistics: A Personal View" (1991a), for instance, he writes as if his claim (U), that Universal Grammar characterizes the language faculty, were simply an empirical hypothesis the adoption of which has been validated by its track record in illuminating the acquisition problem, or 'Plato's Problem,' as he often refers to it. Everyone agrees, he says, that "the basic properties of cognitive systems are innate to the mind, part of human biological endowment" (1991a:15). But, he continues, not everyone thereby agrees what those innate properties are, for that is a further, empirical question: "There are specific hypotheses about what is innate, and these may be considered on empirical grounds: hypotheses of universal grammar, or the theory of vision and so on" (1991a:15). And it is on empirical grounds, he goes on to imply, that one should accept (U): "[t]he most productive approach has been to try to 'factor out' certain general principles that govern rule application and assign them to the initial state of the language faculty" (1991a:22). What Chomsky appears to be saying here, then, is that it's (U)'s 'productivity,' its empirical fruitfulness, that justifies its adoption—and hence that justifies the move from Weak Nativism to the full Chomskyan position.

However, arguments like this are the rare exception, not the rule, in Chomsky's writings. Typically, he appears to give little, if any, credence to the possibility that (U) might not be true—that the language faculty might turn out to be governed by principles other than those identified in the Universal Grammar—and often writes as if acceptance of the hypothesis of a domain-specific language faculty were tantamount to the acceptance of his particular hypothesis, (U), about the nature of that faculty. Chomsky thus tends to collapse (or ignore) the distinction I have urged between Chomskyan and Weak Nativisms. Why? Part of the explanation for his tendency to run (DS) and (U) together is doubtless that (U) was established as a keystone of his research program long before it had had time to produce any real empirical fruits. But a better explanation, I think, lies in his conception of what the domains of theories in linguistics really are. On Chomsky's view, as we saw in §7.3, particular grammars are descriptive of what speakers know about their language. They are theories of competence, or what Chomsky was later to call the 'internalized language' or 'I-language,' language as represented in the heads of its speakers.[20] Their domain is thus the psychology of individual speaker–hearers. What then, of Universal Grammar, the theory of linguistic universals? Well, if theories of particular languages are theories about what is in the heads of speakers of those languages, it makes sense to think of theories of languages-in-general, such as Universal Grammar, as being theories about what is in the heads of speakers-in-general. Theories of speaker–hearers in general must be theories of what all speaker–hearers have in common, and since what all speaker-hearers have in common is, in the first instance, the biological capacity to learn whatever particular language they happen to be exposed to, it seems natural to regard Universal Grammar as a theory of that capacity. In exactly the same way as Chomsky took grammars to be theories of what speakers know about their language, then, he took Universal Grammar to be a theory of what speakers know prior to learning their language. He took it, in other words, to describe the language faculty.

Thus we find a happy convergence. The Weak Nativist postulates a language faculty. In so doing, she raises the question of what its nature is. The Chomskyan linguist 'psycholgizes' the study of language. In so doing, he apparently has ready to hand the perfect solution to Weak Nativism's problem. For the Weak Nativist to insist, in the light of the Chomskyan synthesis, that the nature of the language faculty remains up for grabs looks mulish in the extreme. Small wonder, then, that that position has been ignored.

One of the aims of part III will be to remedy this neglect. Over the next few chapters, we will look in more detail at the arguments that have been put forth in favor of Chomskyan nativism, and attempt to determine the extent to which they support that view as against the more moderate Weak nativism and various forms of empiricism. While I will ultimately be defending a Weakly nativist approach to language acquisition, I shall argue that neither the case for Chomskyan nativism, nor the case against the various kinds of empiricism, is anywhere near as overwhelming as is commonly supposed.

20. The term 'I-language' and the related 'E-language' (for externalized language, language considered in abstraction from those who speak it) were introduced in Chomsky (1986). See §10.2 for further discussion.

8

The Poverty of the Stimulus

In chapter 7, I argued that Chomsky is committed to the following theses about language acquisition and mastery:

(R) **Representationalism**
Explaining language mastery and acquisition requires the postulation of contentful mental states and processes involving their manipulation.

(B) **Biological Boundedness**
In virtue of the inborn structure of the human mind, there are constraints on the space of thinkable thoughts.

(DS) **Domain Specificity**
Learning a language requires that the learner's thoughts about language be constrained by principles specific to the linguistic domain.

(I) **Innateness**
The constraints on learners' thoughts during language-learning are innately encoded.

(U) **Universal Grammar**
The constraints and principles specified in (DS) as being required for language-learning are to be identified with the principles characterized in the Universal Grammar.

We saw in §7.2 how Chomsky (1959) defended (R) (and with it a form of (B)), thus establishing the falsity of behaviorism and paving the way for the development of a more properly mentalistic conception of linguistic competence and language-learning. We saw also, though, that a defense of (R) and (B) does not suffice to establish the rest of the 'core' claims. The falsity of behaviorism is compatible with the truth of a variety of different theories, for the other elements of Chomskyan nativism are substantially independent from each other and can thus be accepted or rejected severally.[1] I distin-

---

1. (U), (DS), and (I) are not completely independent because (U) entails (DS), and (I) entails (B). See §7.1.

guished three (nonbehaviorist) alternatives to Chomskyan nativism. Assuming henceforth that (R) and (B) are accepted on all sides, we have Weak nativism, which is the conjunction of (DS) and (I); Enlightened empiricism, which accepts (DS) and denies (I); and Putnamian empiricism, which accepts (I) and denies (DS).[2] In §7.4, I introduced the arguments from the poverty of the stimulus that have formed the mainstay of Chomsky's case for his position. In this chapter and the next, we will subject them to further scrutiny, the aim being to establish the extent to which the poverty of the stimulus supports the Chomskyan position rather than one of the other three views identified above.

As I mentioned in chapter 7, there have been two kinds of poverty of the stimulus argument used in defense of Chomskyan nativism. First, there is a form of argument, employed by Chomsky himself, that I call the a posteriori poverty of the stimulus argument. This argument, to be discussed in the present chapter, is thoroughly empirical and seeks to show that since language could not in fact be learned from the evidence available in the 'primary linguistic data,' the principles of Universal Grammar must be known innately. The other form of poverty of the stimulus argument, which has recently gained great currency in the literature and will be the subject of chapter 9, makes a more a priori case for nativism. Relying on comparatively minimal empirical assumptions about language competence and learning, this argument, often called the 'Logical Problem of Language Acquisition' or the 'No Negative Evidence Problem,' seeks to show that language could not in point of logic be learned from the available data, and hence, again, that knowledge of Universal Grammar must be innate.

I shall argue that both of these arguments fall far short of their goals. The a posteriori argument from the poverty of the stimulus (hereafter, 'APS') is impotent to establish any form of nativism about the faculties responsible for language learning. For as we will see in this chapter, it is based on empirical assumptions that are at worst outright false, and at best highly dubious. The argument from the Logical Problem, I shall suggest in chapter 9, succeeds only in making plausible (DS). Thus, I aim to show, the strongest kind of nativism with regard to language-learning that can be defended on the basis of the poverty of the stimulus is: Enlightened empiricism! The poverty of the stimulus, in either of its incarnations and contrary to what is invariably assumed in the literature, is completely unable to support *any* form of nativism about language-learning. Nativists' obsession with such arguments has therefore been a mistake. Whether or not nativism is a mistake as well, will be discussed in chapter 11, where I shall look at what other kinds of evidence might be appealed to in order to decide among the possible positions on the acquisition question.

2. See figure 7.1.

8.1 The A Posteriori Argument from the Poverty of the Stimulus

The a posteriori argument from the poverty of the stimulus (APS) takes as an example some specific rule of grammar and argues that the data to which the child is exposed during learning—the 'primary linguistic data' (or '*pld*')—are insufficient to enable a learner, endowed only with a general-purpose learning ability, to infer that rule. The other rules of the grammar being assumed to be the same in this respect, the argument is generalized to apply to the grammar as a whole, and hence to support the conclusion that language-learning is subserved by a special faculty incorporating the linguistic information specified in the Universal Grammar.

The most famous instance of the APS, repeatedly invoked by Chomsky and rehearsed by many others, concerns the child's learning how to form yes–no questions (or 'polar interrogatives') from declarative sentences.[3] Suppose that the child had heard sentences like the following:

(1a) Ali is happy.
(1b) Is Ali happy?
(2a) That man can sing.
(2b) Can that man sing?[4]

What rule for question-formation would she project on the basis of these data? Here are two possibilities:

(H_1) Find the first occurrence of 'is' ('can,' 'will,' etc.) in the sentence and move it to the front of the sentence. [A Structure-independent rule.]
(H_2) Find the first occurrence of 'is' ('can,' 'will,' etc.) following the subject NP of the sentence and move it to the front of the sentence. [A Structure-dependent rule.]

H_1 is adequate to account for the examples (1) and (2) above, but founders when applied to more complex sentences such as (3) and (4):

(3a) The man who is happy is singing.
(3b) *Is the man who happy is singing?

---

3. See, e.g., Chomsky (1975b:30–33, 1986:7–13; 1988:41–47); Chomsky in Piattelli-Palmarini (1979:114–15); Friedin (1991:618–19); Lightfoot (1991:3–4); Pinker (1994: 233–34).

4. It is known that children do hear many yes–no questions and simple declaratives like these in parental speech. Brown and Hanlon (1970:39) give the following figures (frequency of utterance type per seven hundred utterances, averaged across several years and families):

Simple active affirmative declarative (e.g., *John is crying*) = 139
Simple active declarative negative (*John is not crying*) = 56
Simple active affirmative interrogative (*Is John crying?*) = 53

Truncated forms of these types (*He is, He's not, Is he?*), negative questions (*Isn't the baby crying?*) and truncated negative questions (*Isn't he?*) were considerably less frequent, averaging about 5 occurrences/700.

(4a) The book that is on the table is blue.
(4b) *Is the book that on the table is blue?

Sentences like these falsify H_1 and reveal that the structure-dependent aux-iliary fronting rule H_2 is the better hypothesis. When applied to (3a) and (4a), H_2 delivers the grammatical sentences (3c) and (4c):

(3a) $[_{NP}$The man [who is happy]] is singing.
(3c) Is $[_{NP}$The man [who is happy]] singing?
(4a) $[_{NP}$The book [that is on the table]] is blue.
(4c) Is $[_{NP}$The book [that is on the table]] blue?

Now clearly, since no English speaker ever makes errors like (3b) and (4b), we have all managed to learn the correct rule. Chomsky claims repeatedly that one can explain how we do it only if one accepts his nativism.

But supporting Chomskyan nativism, as we've seen, is a matter of pro-viding support for each of (I), (DS), and (U). These are three very different claims, and arguing for each would appear to be a different task. In this chapter, we will see how, by stressing different elements of the APS, we can interpret it as an argument for (DS) and for its conjunction with (I). I'll claim, however, that these arguments are unsuccessful. Even if one accepts the basic pictures of learning and competence that underlie the Chomskyan argument, the APS does not license the Chomskyan position. What happens when these basic pictures themselves are subject to critical scrutiny will be examined in chapter 10, where we look at the Chomskyan case for (U).

8.2 The Case for Domain Specificity: The APS versus Putnamian Empiricism

In one of the earliest philosophical examinations of Chomsky's nativism, Putnam (1971) criticizes Chomsky's postulation of an innate, domain-specific learning mechanism on the grounds that it is both premature and unmotivated. It is premature, Putnam thinks, given how little is known about the possible alternatives to it:

> In the absence of any knowledge of what *general multipurpose learning strategies* might even look like, the assertion that such strategies (which absolutely must exist and be employed by all humans) cannot account for this or that learning process, that the answer or an answer schema must be 'innate,' is utterly unfounded. (Putnam 1971:138)

And it is unmotivated, in Putnam's opinion, because the evidence Chomsky cites in support of his position can either be dismissed outright or else ac-counted for on a domain-neutral learning model. Putnam sketches a picture of acquisition according to which language-learning is a product of the same general-purpose learning strategies as are used in other domains. While granting that "human 'innate intellectual equipment' is relevant to language learning" (1971:134), he insists that we have reason to accept an "innateness hypothesis" only in the "trivial sense that memory capacity, intelligence, needs, interests, etc., are all relevant to language learning" (1971:134). Putnam thus urges that we accept (I), the notion that whatever it is that we use to learn language is innate, while denying (DS), the further claim that what we use to learn language is a special faculty distinct from "the strategies that make general learning possible" (Putnam 1971:139).[5]

Putnam supports his position by arguing that it is compatible with the Chomskyan evidence. He contends, for instance, that the existence of linguistic universals, which Chomsky had claimed to reveal the existence and nature of the innate language faculty, is to be expected on any theory. Obviously, on his view, languages will be shaped by the minds that use them, but there is no reason to think that the properties languages exhibit must derive from minds structured in the way that Chomsky suggests. Any organism with a limited memory capacity, for instance, will use recursive rules to characterize potentially infinite domains like language; any organism with a preference for simpler grammars over more complex ones will prefer grammars containing both phrase-structure rules and transformations; any organism with an interest in others of its kind will have a language containing nouns and proper names; and so on. Linguistic universals, in short, can be attributed to such facts as "[h]uman brains are computing systems and subject to some of the constraints that affect all computing systems [and] human beings have a natural interest in one another" (1971:135). No language faculty need be postulated to account for their existence.[6] Similarly unsurprising, Putnam contends, is the fact that language-learning proceeds without the need for reinforcement. Since "the evidence today is slim that *any* learning requires reinforcement" (1971:137), language can hardly be taken to be distinctive in this regard.

Other alleged evidence for nativism Putnam discounts altogether. The apparent speed and ease of first language acquisition, which Chomsky had taken to indicate that children possess a 'head start' in the linguistic domain, are claimed by Putnam to be artifactual. College students, he claims, can master a second language in much less time and with much less practice than a child puts into first language acquisition, so it's in fact unclear that children learn language either easily or quickly. He also questions the much-touted independence of language acquisition from overall level of intelligence

---

5. Sampson (1989) similarly urges a domain-neutral conception of language learning, which he calls a 'Popperian' conception, arguing that "human language, and the cognitive achievements which depend on languages, are . . . constrained only in trivial ways by the nature of our genetic endowment" (1989:205). On his view, "[w]hat is fixed from birth onwards . . . is the urge to seek maximally strong and simple hypotheses logically compatible with experience, but not any aspect of the content of one's hypotheses" (1989: 207).

6. Putnam also speculates that linguistic universals might be due to all languages' having evolved from a single ancestral language. There is, however, no uncontested linguistic or historical evidence for the existence of a common Ur-language. Rather, the consensus seems to be that language has probably evolved separately in a number of different places.

or IQ, which Chomsky had taken to show that language-learning is subserved by a distinct faculty of mind. Putnam argues that there are significant interpersonal differences in language skills, and that to the extent that people share linguistic competence, all this shows is that "[e]very normal adult learns what every adult learns" (1971:137)—again, hardly a reason to be a nativist.[7]

The one kind of argument for nativism that Putnam does not pick up on in his (1971), however, is the argument from the poverty of the stimulus. This may be because Chomsky's earliest discussions of nativism did not accord much status to the APS, statements of which were made more or less in passing until the 1970s (see the passage from *Aspects of the Theory of Syntax* (1965) displayed on p. 172). Whatever the reason for it, though, Putnam's failure to discuss the APS constitutes a serious lacuna in his (1971) critique, and it is tempting to read Chomsky's later refinements and elaborations of the APS as being, in essence, a response to Putnam's omission.

What Putnam (1971) had demanded, in effect, was that the nativist provide him with a reason to think that language-learning was special, that is, to think that language acquisition demands anything more than the common-or-garden general-purpose learning skills with which, Putnam assumed, we are all equipped. And what Chomsky's more careful and systematic formulations of the APS post-1971 seem to be aimed at doing, is to provide the required rationale. The (1975b) version of the argument, for instance, explicitly targets the Putnamian position, contending that anyone who (like Putnam) denies (DS) will make false empirical predictions about the course of language acquisition. In this version of the APS, Chomsky uses the Putnamian thesis that the learner's formulation of hypotheses is constrained only by general considerations of simplicity, parsimony, explanatory power, and the like to generate empirical predictions that are, he argues, false.

Again using the rule for question formation as his exemplar, Chomsky (1975b) argues as follows. If the learner were as Putnam suggests, that is, if her theorizing about language were governed only by domain-neutral principles of theory construction, she would a priori prefer the structure-independent H_1 to the structure-dependent H_2. But a child who entertained H_1 would presumably use the rule in her own speech and consequently make grammatical errors like (3b) and (4b).

(3b) *Is the man who happy is singing?
(4b) *Is the book that on the table is blue?

As a matter of fact, though, no child ever makes errors like these. So either H_1 must have been falsified by the *pld* and rejected by the child quite early on in the learning process; or else the child must never have entertained H_1 at all. The *pld*, however, are too impoverished to provide evidence that would falsify H_1. Sentences like

7. But see §11.2.1, where a version of this argument is defended.

(3c) Is the man who is happy singing?
(4c) Is the book that is on the table blue?

which were employed in §8.1 to show that H_1 is incorrect, are unlikely to appear in the data to which the child has access during learning. So it is not the case that the child first entertained the false hypothesis and later rejected it because of its inconsistency with the data. So it must be the case that the child never entertained H_1 at all. Since this is contrary to the Putnamian prediction, the learning mechanism in the child is not a general-purpose one. Hence, according to Chomsky, we must accept (DS): "The only reasonable conclusion is that . . . the child's mind . . . contains the instruction: Construct a structure-dependent rule, ignoring all structure-independent rules" (Chomsky 1975b:33). The Putnamian contention that language can be learned via a general-purpose learning strategy is false.

Or is it? There seems to be nothing in this argument that rules out the possibility that a child might have acquired knowledge of the principle of structure dependence *through learning*. It's implausible to think that the learner was told that grammatical rules are structure-dependent. But it is certainly possible that she may have had other experiences that would lead her to seek deep rather than surface regularities in language. Chomsky's argument (if sound) supports the conclusion that the child must know the principle of structure dependence in order to learn how to make polar interrogatives. But it doesn't support his further conclusion that "the principle of structure dependence is not learned, but forms part of the conditions for language learning" (Chomsky 1975b:33). This version of the APS can buttress (DS), but not its conjunction with (I). It can sustain at most an Enlightened empiricism.

8.3 The Case for Weak Nativism: The APS Versus Enlightened Empiricism

Pullum's (1996) discussion of the APS provides an account of how the argument might be interpreted to support both (I) and (DS)—that is, to support Weak nativism as against Enlightened empiricism. Pullum presents the argument as a disjunctive syllogism:

    a. Human infants learn their first languages either by data-driven learning or by innately-primed learning.
    b. If human infants acquire their first languages via data-driven learning, then hyperlearning will never be observed in this domain.
    c. Hyperlearning does in fact occur in the domain of first language acquisition by infants.
    d. Human infants do not learn their first languages by means of data-driven learning.

e. Therefore, human infants learn their first languages by means of innately-primed learning. (Pullum 1996:500)[8]

Innately-primed learning "involves the learner being primed *ab initio* with special information about language" and "[b]y definition . . . proceeds in a way that does not rely solely on a corpus of observed utterance tokens" (Pullum 1996:499). The proponent of innately primed learning, in other words, is at least a Weak nativist, accepting both (I) and (DS). On this view, the learner possesses information about language ab initio, that is, from birth. *Data-driven learning*, by contrast, is any method "that relies on attention to evidence [and is such that] the learner is assumed *not* to be in prior possession of any information about what languages are like" (Pullum 1996:499). Thus, anyone who denied (I) or (DS) (or both) would be a proponent of data-driven learning. *Hyperlearning* occurs when "some knowledge about language structure is acquired by children on a basis that does not involve evidence" (1996:498).

So, according to Pullum, the argument for the conjunction of (I) and (DS) goes like this. The hypothesis of data-driven learning (that is, the denial of (I) and/or (DS)) implies that children should never acquire knowledge of language that is not evidenced in the *pld*. However, children do acquire knowledge of language that is not evidenced in the *pld*: in particular, they acquire knowledge of the structure-dependent H_2. Thus, the data-driven hypothesis is false, and since the only alternative to data-driven learning is innately primed learning, language-learning must be innately primed. Both (DS) and (I), in other words, are true.

Pullum, as we will see below, attacks this argument on the grounds that the alleged instances of hyperlearning appealed to in premise (c) are not, in fact, instances of hyperlearning at all. There are, he contends, plenty of data around that would allow a child to infer that H_2 is the correct rule for question formation. However, there is another problem with the APS as Pullum formulates it, namely, that its conception of data-driven learning collapses a number of positions that I have argued (in chapter 7) are better kept distinct. Data-driven learning is the denial of Weak nativism, that is, the denial of the conjunction of (I) and (DS). As we saw in §7.2, however, there are three ways to deny this conjunction: you can deny (I) but not (DS), making you an Enlightened empiricist; you can deny (DS) but not (I), making you a Putnamian empiricist; or you can deny both (DS) and (I), making you some kind of behaviorist. Pullum, following the nativist, assimilates these three positions. This represents a real concession to the nativist, for it acquiesces in his polemical strategy of tarring all forms of empiricism with the same, behaviorist brush. And this, as we will see in §8.5.2, is what makes premise (b) of the argument seem much more plausible than it really is.

---

8. I have omitted Pullum's explications of the logical structure of the argument.

8.4 Children's Errors and the Primary Data

In §§8.2 and 8.3, we have seen how the APS can be elaborated so as to make a case for the two crucial elements, (I) and (DS), of linguistic nativism. These arguments clearly stand or fall with the truth of their empirical premises. Yet for many years, Chomskyans made no serious attempt to provide empirical validation of their claims about what information is and is not available in the *pld* and what errors children do and do not make. Instead, such claims were defended, if at all, solely on the basis of linguists' intuitions as to what is and is not likely to occur during language acquisition.

> Children make many mistakes in language learning, but never mistakes such as exemplified in [*Is the man who happy is singing?*] (Chomsky 1975b:31)

> A person may go through a considerable part of his life without ever facing relevant evidence, but he will have no hesitation in using the structure-dependent rule, even if all of his experience is consistent with [H₁]. (Chomsky 1975b:32)

> It is certainly true that children never make mistakes about this kind of thing [i.e., whether the rule for yes–no question formation is structure-dependent]: no child ever tries [H₁] first, then is told that is not the way it works and subsequently goes to the other hypothesis. [This is despite the fact that] the more complex cases that distinguish the hypotheses rarely arise; you can easily live your whole life without ever producing a relevant example to show that you are using one hypothesis rather than the other one. (Chomsky in Piattelli-Palmarini 1980:114–15)

> Numerous facts of this sort, falling under what is now generally called "binding theory," are known without relevant experience to differentiate the cases. . . . this is known without training or relevant evidence. (Chomsky 1986:8)

> We know these facts without instruction or even direct evidence, surely without correction of error by the speech community . . . no one taught them to us or even presented us with evidence that could yield this knowledge by any generally reliable procedure. This is knowledge without grounds, without good reasons or support by reliable procedures in any general or otherwise useful sense of these notions. (Chomsky 1986:11–12)

> Children do come to know these things, and this knowledge is indeed part of the output of the language acquisition process, but it is not part of the input, not part of the "evidence" for the emerging system. (Lightfoot 1989:322–23)

> [N]one of this [our knowledge of various grammatical principles] is the result of training or even experience. These facts are known without training, without correction of error, without relevant experience. (Chomsky 1990:640)

> Also, in a child's normal experience, there is no real evidence for the structure-dependent formulation: children are not systematically told that

[a sentence like *Is the man who happy is singing?*] does not occur, least of all that it is "ungrammatical." Nonetheless, despite lack of an environmental stimulus for structure-dependence, and despite the simplicity of the structure-independent formulation, children use the structure-dependent operation when first uttering questions of this kind; questions like [*Is the man who happy is singing?*] do not occur and are not among the "errors" made by children. (Lightfoot: 1992:67–68)

A number of writers have complained that assertions like these are lamentably undersupported by evidence. Sampson, for instance, objects that "there is no suggestion in any of Chomsky's writings that he has empirical evidence to support his claims about non-occurrence of given constructions in a typical child's data" (1989:222). Pinker (1986:58ff.) similarly bemoans the fact that "we do not have anything like the degree of documentation on children's possible but non-occurring errors that we would need to evaluate the conservatism hypothesis fully" (1986:58).[9]

Now, more than twenty years after the APS first began to work its magic for the nativist, some of the essential evidence has begun to trickle in. Crain and his colleagues, for example, have begun to collect systematic data on whether children make quite a wide variety of syntactic errors. In a study that is particularly pertinent to the APS, Crain and Nakayama (1987) confirmed that, as Chomsky predicted, children do not make errors of the sort that would be generated by their adoption of the structure-independent rule H_1. They found in their tests of thirty children between the ages of three and five years that "[c]hildren never produced incorrect sentences like [*Is the man who singing is happy?*]" (Crain 1991:602). While one may ponder the fact that Crain and Nakayama's subjects had had at least three years of linguistic experience prior to the study in which to unlearn any incorrect rule they might have entertained, the fact that very young children know the correct rule does show either that they didn't need to make use of any linguistic evidence in acquiring it; or else that the evidence in the *pld* disconfirming any incorrect rules (and/or indicating the correct one) must be plentiful enough, and obvious enough, for extremely young children to be able to make use of it. On the further assumption that the required evidence is unlikely to be forthcoming in a form that is usable by a toddler, what Crain and Nakayama's results seem to indicate is that children have succeeded in hyperlearning a fact about language. They have knowledge (of the structure-dependent H_2) that can be accounted for only on the supposition that innately primed learning—learning that makes use of inborn knowledge about the linguistic domain—has taken place.

---

9. According to the conservatism hypothesis, which Pinker rejects (see §9.5.2), children do not adopt new rules until the old ones are explicitly falsified in the data. Although Pinker's complaint here concerns the resolution of a specific dispute within the nativist ranks, I take it to be indicative of the 'data drought' that has plagued discussions of language-learning more generally.

What, then, of the nativist's further assumption that no evidence exists that would enable a three-year-old to unlearn an incorrect rule? Sampson (1989) was one of the few linguists who dared to pit his intuitions against the Chomskyan's on this point, arguing, contrary to the APS, that children likely hear plenty of sentences that would disconfirm the structure-independent hypothesis. And indeed, a moment's thought suffices to suggest many such examples: *Is the milk that's in the jug fresh? Is that mess that's on the floor in there yours? Was that book that you were reading any good?* and so on. But intuition is as intuition does. What we need are some hard data—data with which, according to one researcher, "we are woefully underprovided at present" (Pullum 1996:505).

Sampson (1989:223) had noted that Blake's popular poem "The Tyger" contains the line *Did he who made the Lamb make thee?*, which straightforwardly falsifies the incorrect H_1, and that in a list of 'Wonder Questions' in a children's encyclopedia, the eleventh yes–no question is one that would decide between H_1 and H_2. Pullum (1996) continues Sampson's quest to find evidence of the existence of relevant data, searching another two corpora for sentences that would provide evidence against H_1. Ideally, he argues, one would determine the actual frequency with which forms relevant to the rules discussed in the APS arise in the *pld* by searching a large computer-readable corpus containing all or most of the sentences to which an actual child is exposed during language-learning. No such corpus is available, however, so Pullum carried out some "preliminary testing" (1996:505) on the forty-million word *Wall Street Journal* (WSJ) corpus (available on CD-ROM) and on the text of Oscar Wilde's *The Importance of Being Earnest*. He found that in the *WSJ* corpus, out of 23,886 lines containing question marks, the fifteenth question in the corpus is one that disconfirms the structure-independent rule, namely, *How fundamental are the changes these events portend?* And "several other" (1996:505) disconfirmatory tokens occur within the first five hundred questions in the corpus, including (at line 180) a question that is exactly analogous to Chomsky's examples: *Is what I'm doing in the shareholders' best interest?* In *The Importance of Being Earnest*, a much shorter text, Pullum found another counterexample to H_1 in Lady Bracknell's question, *Who is that young person whose hand my nephew Algernon is now holding in what seems to me a peculiarly unnecessary manner?* (1996:507).

While acknowledging that "Lady Bracknell is not an ideal exemplar of modern everyday colloquial speech" (1996:507) and that "children do not get their main exposure to English through being read to from the *Journal*" (1996:505), Pullum argues that these sources may nonetheless be considered representative of the *pld*. Not only is it known that many of the statistical properties of texts do not vary much from one text to another,[10] but the

---

10. Pullum cites in this connection Hudson's rather surprising finding that 37 percent of words in a piece of running text are nouns, "regardless of genre, style, modality, source, or even language" (1994:8).

WSJ in any case contains enough syntactically simple material (including ordinary journalistic English and quotations from actual speech) that

> [w]e have no reason to assume that we will get an unrepresentative sample of the syntactic types of questions that would come up in natural contexts in front of children if we simply look for question marks in the *WSJ* corpus. Speakers of English simply do not have enough conscious control over the syntactic properties of the questions they ask to make such a source unrepresentative. (Pullum 1996:507)

And as for Lady Bracknell, Pullum claims that "What is really at issue here is how often in everyday life we can expect situations to arise in which questions like this are asked" (1996:507). What's revealing, Pullum suggests, is not how she asks it, but that she had cause to ask a question with this kind of structure at all.

Extrapolating from his findings, Pullum argues that "the utterance tokens that could provide the crucial data apparently make up something between 1% of interrogatives and over 10% of polar interrogatives in running text" (1996:508), and since "a child would hear hundreds of thousands of questions during the language acquisition period," she "thus must hear thousands of examples that crucially confirm the structure-dependence of auxiliary fronting" (1996:508). He charges that Chomsky's "assertion that 'you can go over a vast amount of data of experience without ever finding such a case' is unfounded hyperbole" (1996:508), and concludes that the Chomskyan "claim that many people will *never* hear any [questions like this] is surely much weakened by finding attested examples so easily in any kind of English one takes the trouble to search" (1996:508).

I myself am inclined to accept Sampson's and Pullum's claims: it has always struck me as just bizarre to suppose that children encounter *no* sentences of the kind that would disconfirm H_1 in all their years of language-learning. If these claims are valid, then absent some decisive reason to think that children under age three are unable to make use of the available evidence, there need be no mystery about how a data-driven or general-purpose learner would learn the correct rule for forming yes–no questions. Were she to hypothesize the incorrect rule, her experience would soon inform her of her mistake: at any given time, if Pullum's right about the frequency of the appropriate forms, there's a good chance that one of the next hundred or so questions the learner hears will be a sentence that can do the trick.[11] But these sorts of findings are merely suggestive, and not, alas, definitive. We still lack the data we need to settle this question once and for all. It thus

---

11. This claim is not necessarily inconsistent with the finding of Crain and Nakayama (1987) that children do not speak as if they held H_1. First, they studied children three years and older: it's surely possible (especially given what Pullum says about the likely frequencies) that a child would have found data falsifying H_1 (if she had entertained it) before the age of three years. In addition, children's comprehension of complex syntactic forms outruns their capacity to produce them spontaneously: this could account for the anecdotal evidence that not even very young children make H_1-type errors.

behoves us to consider how well the APS might fare on the offchance either that the requisite data do not occur in the *pld*, however often they might occur in other corpora, or that young children lack the sort of cognitive sophistication that would enable them to make proper use of them.

8.5 The Predictions of Empiricism

Suppose, then, that the primary linguistic data do not contain sentences, like *Is that mess that's on the floor in there yours?*, that would falsify H_1. This, together with the fact (evidenced by their failure to make certain sorts of errors) that children know that H_1 is false, is enough to put paid to empiricism. Or so says the APS. On my reconstruction of the argument (§8.2), this is because empiricism predicts that learners would prefer H_1 to H_2, thus leaving it mysterious how learners nonetheless manage to acquire H_2. On Pullum's reconstruction of the argument (§8.3), children's learning of H_2 in the absence of data like *Is that mess that is on the floor in there yours?* is an instance of hyperlearning, and empiricism forbids hyperlearning's occurrence. In this section, I will examine the question of whether empiricism does, in fact, have these consequences.

8.5.1 The Putnamian's Predictions

The Putnamian empiricist denies (DS). In particular, he denies the Chomskyan contention that learners' grammatical hypotheses are constrained by their knowledge that grammatical rules are structure-dependent. In consequence, Chomsky claims, the Putnamian learner would prefer the structure-independent H_1 to the structure-dependent H_2, and hence should be expected, eventually, to make errors of a sort that de facto no one ever makes.

Why, though, should we accept that Putnamian empiricism implies that the learner would prefer H_1 to H_2? Chomsky (1975b) gives two arguments for this contention. The first is based on the fact that H_1 is simpler than H_2, and would thus be preferred by a general-purpose learning device. Chomsky argues that one "would have to be driven by evidence . . . to postulate [H_2] in place of the simpler and more elementary [H_1]" because "[b]y any reasonable standards, [H_2] is far more complex and 'unlikely' than [H_1]" (1975b:32) But why think that the empiricist's simplicity metric would regard H_2 as less simple than H_1? Because, Chomsky argues, H_2 is structure-dependent, whereas H_1 is not:

> [H_1] holds that the child is employing a "structure-independent rule"—
> that is, a rule that involves only analysis into words and the property
> "earliest" ("leftmost") defined on word sequences. [H_2] holds that the
> child is employing a "structure-dependent rule," a rule that involves analysis into words and phrases, and the property "earliest" defined on se-

quences of works analyzed into abstract phrases. The phrases are "abstract" in the sense that neither their boundaries nor their categories (noun phrase, verb phrase etc.) need be physically marked. Sentences do not appear with brackets, intonation boundaries regularly marking phrases, subscripts identifying the type of phrase or anything of the sort. (1975b:32)

But while a positivist might automatically rank structure-independent rules above structure-dependent ones (on the grounds that they advert to more 'observable' properties of sentences, such as word order), there is no obvious reason for anyone else to do so. As Chomsky himself pointed out in his critiques of American Structuralism and behaviorism, grammatical hypotheses that advert merely to observables tend to be less simple, less elegant, and all round less desirable on general theoretical grounds than those framed in terms of unobservables (cf. §§7.2, 7.3.1). So a nonpositivist proponent of domain-neutral learning, taking Chomsky's lesson to heart, would surely endow her learner with a bias toward seeking out the 'hidden springs' (and not the superficial regularities) in the world, a bias that in the domain of language would manifest itself as a preference for rules stated in terms of unobservables over those stated in terms of observables—that is, for H_2 over H_1! Properly conceived, then, a general-purpose hypothesis-generating mechanism such as Putnam postulates need not rank the structure-independent H_1 above the structure-dependent H_2, and the question of whether or not H_1 can be falsified in the data is moot.

As is implicit in the long passage just displayed, however, Chomsky has another argument up his sleeve to suggest that an empiricist learner would perforce choose H_1. The correct rule, H_2, is structure-dependent. So, in order to learn this rule, the child needs to be able to represent to herself facts and hypotheses about sentences' underlying syntactic properties. Chomsky insinuates, however, that since syntactic concepts are "only remotely related to experience by long and intricate chains of quasi-inferential steps" (1965:58), they are unavailable to an empiricist learner. For, being "abstract" (1975b: 32), syntactic categories are not 'given' in experience. But neither (as he had argued in 1955) are they analyzable in terms of the properties (e.g., acoustical properties) that are 'given.' But if syntactic properties are not given— if they are not, as it were, sensible properties of sentences—then they could not be acquired 'brute-causally' from experience. And if they're not analyzable in terms of sensible properties, then they couldn't be compounded out of other concepts that are learned from experience. The syntactic concepts that the learner must use to express the correct, structure-dependent hypothesis must therefore be innate—somehow built into the learning mechanism itself. Thus, since the Putnamian empiricist denies that anything specifically linguistic is innate, his learner would be unable to formulate the correct rule.

The Chomskyan suggestion that syntactic concepts are unlearnable, however, has long been controversial. An early and influential move in the direction of explaining how children could learn such concepts from their experience was the "Motherese" hypothesis, according to which mothers' speech to their children exhibits a number of distinctive features that facilitate the child's earliest attempts at linguistic analysis.[12] It was claimed, for example, that unlike normal speakers, a speaker of Motherese will pause between words, phrases, and (especially) sentences, thereby helping the child to segment the acoustic signal into syntactically salient portions. She will exaggerate the rising terminal intonation on questions and imperatives, thus enabling the child to distinguish these sentences from declaratives. Her utterances of open class words, such as nouns and verbs, will be of much longer duration than in normal speech, this emphasis serving to direct the child's attention toward instances of the most important and basic syntactic categories. The claim here is not that high-level syntactic concepts may be analyzed in terms of concepts like RISING INTONATION or LONG DURATION. It is, rather, that these features of mothers' speech serve to impose some initial order on the 'blooming buzzing confusion' of the linguistic environment encountered by the child, and that by attending to these features, the child may take the first steps toward abstracting the syntactic categories she will need in order to learn the language she is exposed to.

Although the Motherese hypothesis seems now to be generally out of favor, its importance lies less in its claim that mothers' speech to their children is tantamount to a separate language, than in its assumption that children can use statistical information about the input stream in order to abstract syntactic concepts from it. This insight, that abstract concepts may be learned from statistical information about the acoustical properties of language without being reducible to those acoustical properties, has since fueled other attempts to explain children's acquisition of syntactic categories. Wanner and Gleitman (1982), for instance, argued that children are able to identify individual content words in a stream of noise by attending to the stressed portions of the acoustic input: open class words (nouns, verbs, adjectives, etc.) tend to be heavily stressed in speech, whereas closed class words (pronouns, auxiliaries, affixes, etc.) tend to be unstressed. Their claim was not that WORD can be *defined* as STRESSED SIGNAL PORTION; it was, rather, that regularities in stress patterns provide children with important information about word boundaries. Read and Schreiber (1982) found that seven-year-olds are quite good at picking out subject NPs from heard sentences unless the NP consists of a single word, such as a pronoun or a generic nominal, in which case they are hopeless. Read and Schreiber argue that this is because single-word NPs do not exhibit the characteristic intonation patterns (falling tone, lengthening of final vowel) of longer NPs and suggest that intonation patterns also may be relevant to children's learning to perceive noun phrases. Maratsos (1982), to take another example, proposed that

---

12. See Newport (1977) and the papers in Snow and Ferguson (1977), especially Newport, Gleitman, and Gleitman (1977).

syntactic concepts like NOUN PHRASE and VERB PHRASE are acquired by means of a statistical analysis of the distribution of words in simple sentences. Hearing the sentences *Daddy is walking* and *The dog is walking*, the child begins to group together into a single category the words *Daddy* and the *dog*, for both occur in the same context, namely, ____ *is walking*. As the child's analysis becomes more sophisticated and the sample more representative of the language, Maratsos suggests, her groupings will come to converge on the syntactic categories NP, VP, and the like.

Dramatic experimental confirmation of the notion that the statistical properties of the inputs are used by children in order to abstract higher-level concepts for apparently 'unobservable' syntactic properties has recently been provided by Saffran, Aslin, and Newport (1996). In a stunning series of experiments, they demonstrate that children as young as eight months can determine where word boundaries occur in a stream of speech by attending to the statistical features of the input to which they are exposed. Accounting for how children might learn to segment speech into words is a particularly difficult problem for the empiricist, for (pace the theories just discussed) there is no very reliable acoustical indicator (such as a pause in the speech stream or a regularity in the stress pattern) of where word boundaries occur. Saffran, Aslin, and Newport note, however, that there are certain subtle statistical regularities in streams of speech that can be used to distinguish between the recurring sound sequences that form words and those that span word boundaries. In particular, the transitional probability of two sound sequences that form part of a word in a given language is in general higher than that between sounds that span word boundaries.[13] Using a speech synthesizer, Saffran, Aslin, and Newport generated inputs from artificial (but, to an English speaker, natural-sounding) languages such that the only difference between the sound sequences constituting words and those spanning word boundaries within those languages lay in their pairwise transitional probabilities: the transitional probability of two sounds X#Y was 1 in 'languages' where X and Y occurred together as part of a word, and 1/3 in 'languages' where X and Y occurred in different words. They found that eight-month-old infants had learned to distinguish the words in these artificial languages from the non-words after a mere two minutes' exposure to the synthesized inputs. Although conceding that "[i]t remains unclear whether the statistical learning we observed is indicative of a mechanism specific to language acquisition or of a general learning mechanism" (1996: 1928), they suggest that it is nonetheless plausible that "this same general mechanism could be used to find an object, such as a human face, in the environment" (1996:1928, n. 22), and conclude that at the very least, their

---

13. The 'transitional probability' of a sound sequence X#Y is the conditional probability of Y given X. In English, for instance, the transitional probability of /pre/#/ty/ is greater than that of /ty/#/ba/, which reflects the fact that the former pair of sounds occurs within words more often than the latter, which typically spans word boundaries (*pretty baby*) (Saffran, Aslin, and Newport 1996:1927.)

results show that "it is premature to assert a priori how much of the striking knowledge base of human infants is primarily a result of . . . innate knowledge" (1996:1928).[14]

In addition to providing experimental proof that children are both sensitive to, and can make use of, the statistical or distributional properties of linguistic inputs during language learning, Saffran, Aslin, and Newport's findings raise the possibility that they might be able to make use during that process of other subtle linguistic cues as well. Many theorists have complained that Chomsky gives no credence to the idea that, in learning syntax, children make use of semantic information.[15] Whereas Braine (1971), for instance, had argued that children's first 'syntactic' concepts are in fact semantic ones (e.g., ACTOR, ACTION, OBJECT) that are acquired on the basis of contextual information, and that then form the basis from which children abstract the categories of adult syntax, Chomskyans have long held that contextual information is unlikely to play any role in the acquisition of syntactic knowledge.[16] For, it is maintained, the relation between semantic categories (like action words) and syntactic categories (like verbs) is in general highly complex, and is thus an unsuitable source of information about syntax for babies and young children. As evidence for such a view, Maratsos (1982), for instance, cites the prevalence in natural languages of syntactic devices like nominalization, which can apparently turn any 'action phrase' into a noun phrase with the same semantic content. Since both *to cut the bread* and the nominalized version *the cutting of the bread* arguably refer to the same action, Maratsos contends, semantic information could not be used by children as a means of inferring syntactic distinctions. Again, however, the finding of Saffran, Aslin, and Newport that even very young babies

---

14. Friederici and Wessels (1993) show that nine-month-olds are sensitive to the distinction between legal and illegal combinations of phonemes in their language (e.g., Dutch infants orient longer to sounds like /kn/, which is legal in Dutch, than they do to /dw/, which is legal in English but illegal in Dutch), and can use this sensitivity to distinguish word boundaries. Anticipating the hypothesis tested by Saffran, Aslin, and Newport, Friederici and Wessels surmise that "frequency of occurrence is the first ground upon which to build up initial language-specific knowledge, on the basis of which rule governed language knowledge will develop later" (1993:294). See Jusczyk (1997) for an overview of the evidence that humans are highly sensitive to information about relative frequencies.

15. See Putnam (1971); Braine (1971); Sampson (1989). See also §8.6.3.

16. Braine supports his view by noting that children's earliest two-word or 'telegraphic' utterances seem to conform to the rules of "grammars" couched in terms of these sorts of semantic categories:

actor–action (Children will say *Daddy walk* but not *walk Daddy*)
possessor–possessed (*Daddy car /*car daddy*)
object–location (*cup floor /*floor cup*)

Additional evidence for Braine's emphasis on the role of contextual information in language-learning is provided by the fact that caregivers' speech to young children seems designed to facilitate children's use of contextual information. Speakers of 'Motherese' tend, for example, to talk about salient features of the child's environment, and to use many gestures and other cues to direct the child's attention to those features—see Snow and Ferguson (1977).

are sensitive to statistical information throws doubt on the Chomskyan's blanket rejection of the idea that semantic information is implicated in the attainment of syntax. Even very slight variations in the kinds of contexts in which nominalized and unnominalized forms are used might suggest to a child that they are of different syntactic kinds; and certainly such differences, when combined with other distributional information about the two types of phrase and their constituents, would constitute strong evidence of their syntactic distinctness.[17]

In sum, there is no reason to believe that even a Putnamian empiricist would necessarily get hung up on the false (and allegedly unfalsifiable) rule H_1. Not only might empiricist learners be inclined toward the postulation of structure-dependent rules in virtue of their innate bias toward hypotheses with the greatest explanatory power; there also is good evidence that they are perfectly well able to acquire the 'abstract' syntactic concepts that they need to form such hypotheses through statistical analysis of the speech they hear around them.[18] Putnamian empiricism does not entail the proposition that the APS contradicts; so *even if* all its empirical premises were true, the APS would fail to demonstrate the falsity of that position.

8.5.2 The Predictions of the Enlightened Empiricist

Pullum's version of the argument (§8.3) casts a wider net than mine. His premise (b) asserts that hyperlearning is prohibited by *any* form of empiricism, and concludes from the alleged instance of hyperlearning represented by children's learning of H_2, that no form of empiricism is tenable. Is it true that *no* kind of empiricist theory can account for hyperlearning, that is, for the child's acquiring "a piece of knowledge p during a time interval t without being exposed at any time during or before t to any evidence that could establish p by ordinary methods of learning from examples" (Pullum 1996: 498)? This depends entirely, of course, on which kind of empiricism one has in mind, and on what counts as "evidence" and "ordinary methods of learning from examples." If statistical inference, for instance, didn't count as an

---

17. Saffran, Aslin, and Newport's results also put into question certain elements of Chomsky's earliest arguments against behaviorist accounts of language-learning. In his (1959), he had argued that the statistical or 'distributional' analyzes of the sort Skinner had relied on to explain children's acquisition of 'grammatical frames' are an insufficient basis for the acquisition of concepts for syntactic categories. A learner who relied on distributional regularities in learning syntax, he argued, would need a *pld* that contained vastly many 'minimally differing sentences' in order that the correct syntactic distinctions be made. (E.g., it seems that both *The man loved the fish* and *The fish loved the man* would need to occur in the data in order that the child recognize *the man* and *the fish* as being of the same category.) Saffran, Aslin, and Newport showed that children are sensitive to extremely subtle statistical cues, which is suggestive of the possibility that even very slight variations in the distributions of linguistic items may well be enough to enable children to learn to categorize them correctly.

18. I assume that the methods of statistical analysis themselves are domain-neutral.

'ordinary' method for learning from examples, then children's ability to learn where word boundaries are, demonstrated by Saffran, Aslin, and Newport (1996), would count as an instance of hyperlearning and (on the assumption that the statistical methods at issue are domain-neutral) would straightforwardly falsify Pullum's (b). If, on the other hand, statistical inference were regarded as an 'ordinary' learning strategy, then (b) would stand. In the absence of any further account of what hyperlearning is supposed to be, then, the APS as interpreted by Pullum would not even get off the ground.

On behalf of the nativist, Pullum does provide a fuller explication of hyperlearning, explaining that the 'ordinary' methods at issue in this argument are those "that are the object of study for formal learnability theory" (1996:498). Formal learning theory is a branch of mathematical linguistics that is concerned to investigate the capacities of various idealized learners under various assumptions about the available evidence. Pioneered by Gold (1967), formal learning theories conceive of language learners as functions that enumerate the possible grammars for a language L and test each grammar against a corpus of evidence. In Gold's 'text' condition, the corpus consists of a sample of sentences of the target language. In his 'informant' condition, the corpus contains both sentences and non-sentences (tagged as such). New sentences (and non-sentences) are added one by one to the sample, and a given grammar G is retained by the learner until it fails to generate a sentence in the sample (or generates a non-sentence). At that time, a new grammar is adopted for testing, and the procedure is repeated until the correct grammar is identified. A class of languages (where language classes are defined in terms of the formal properties of the rule systems governing them) is said in this literature to be learnable if it is the case that, for any language within that class, a learner can be guaranteed in some finite time to hypothesize the correct grammar for that language and thereafter never be forced by further data to change her mind.

What Gold proved in his seminal (1967) paper was that a learner who is utterly unconstrained as to possible grammatical hypotheses could only be guaranteed to learn languages of finite cardinality (that is, languages containing a finite number of sentences) from text. If the class of natural languages contained even one infinite language, it would be unlearnable.[19] This

---

19. Gold's proof of this is quite easy to grasp intuitively. You can learn a finite language from text in a finite time if, at every step of the learning process, you simply hypothesize that the language you are supposed to be learning is just the set of sentences you've so far encountered in the data. Since the language contains finitely many sentences, there'll come a point at which you'll have encountered all of the sentences in the language, and no further data will lead you to modify your hypothesis. The class of natural languages, however, contains both finite and infinite languages. So if the learner sticks with the conservative strategy just described, then, if the language she's trying to learn is in fact an infinite one, she'll be changing her mind about the grammar of the language (i.e., the set of sentences it contains) ad infinitum. If, on the other hand, she at some point hypothesizes an infinite grammar, then, if the language she is trying to learn is in fact finite, she'll

is of interest in discussions of language-learning because the class of natural languages does include infinite languages (such as English), and yet children can learn any natural language despite being in a situation approximating Gold's text condition. That is, they are rarely told about the strings of words that are not sentences of their language, relying instead for the bulk of their information about language on the sample of sentences comprised by others' utterances. What this shows is that children are not Gold-style learners: they do not test every logically possible grammar against the data. In order to succeed in learning language from text, therefore, they must possess prior knowledge that will constrain their choice of grammatical hypotheses so as to predispose them in some way toward choosing the correct grammar.

Now, the assumption in the learnability literature has been that the kinds of constraints that should be placed on learners' theorizing in order to enable them to learn language from texts such as the *pld* are domain-specific ones.[20] However, as Demopoulos (1989) has stressed, nothing in fact follows from Gold's proof as to the kinds of constraints that are needed in this connection. While domain-specific constraints have proved more amenable to formal treatment, and may have been preferred by mathematical linguists for that reason, it's nonetheless the case that, for all Gold has shown, general-purpose constraints such as 'Prefer more general hypotheses,' or 'Make a tentative universal generalization that all Fs are Gs if you've encountered *n* instances of Fs that are Gs,' would do the trick to ensure the learnability of natural languages. So while it may indeed be the case that no empiricist-style learner could learn a language from text—that is, while I certainly don't have a proof to the contrary on hand—this conclusion cannot be drawn from anything in the learnability literature.

What this means for the APS is that the assumptions about learners and evidence that are made in the learnability literature do not support Pullum's premise (b). On those assumptions, it would seem that *any* learner who succeeds in learning an infinite language from text will have (in Pullum's terms) hyperlearned that language. For in Gold's paradigm, the class of sentences comprising the data is always finite. Yet a learner who succeeds in learning a natural language has managed to figure out how to generate an infinite number of sentences. So at any time *t*, there will be sentences that the successful learner knows to be sentences of L, but that have not yet appeared in the data sample. Since there's no support in the learnability literature for the claim that no empiricist-style learner could succeed in learning a language, there's no argument to be found there either for the nativist's claim that no empiricist-style learner could exhibit hyperlearning.

---

never be able to discover her error from future inputs. Hence the class of natural languages is unlearnable: there's no guarantee that a learner will be able to find the correct grammar in finite time.

20. Some of the work carried out in this tradition will be discussed in chapter 10. See Pinker (1979) for a helpful survey of formal learning theories post-Gold.

The same point can be established more intuitively by reflecting on the implications of the different sorts of empiricism that I distinguished in Chapter 7. While it may be obvious that the behaviorist has problems in accounting for learning that goes beyond the data, and while the version of the APS discussed in §8.2 contends that the Putnamian empiricist may likewise have difficulty in accounting for hyperlearning, it is not clear that an Enlightened empiricist is similarly afflicted. It is not clear, that is to say, that someone who conceded that learners must know, say, the principle of structure dependence, while denying only that that knowledge is inborn, need have problems accounting for children's ability to learn the correct rule for polar interrogatives even in the absence of decisive data favoring that rule. By running together (what I claim to be) three quite different empiricist positions under the rubric 'data-driven learning,' Pullum's nativist illicitly makes his premise (b) seem much more tenable than it is. There is no reason to think that an Enlightened empiricist must be fazed by children's ability to hyperlearn the correct rule for question formation (if hyperlearning it in fact is). So there's no argument from the existence of hyperlearning to the falsity of empiricism, nor to the truth of (DS) and (I).[21]

8.6 Other Versions of the APS

In §§8.2–8.5, I examined two versions of Chomsky's argument from the poverty of the stimulus. The argument asserts the inability of a nonnativist learner to learn the correct rule for the formation of yes–no questions from the available data. I have challenged these arguments on two fronts. I've argued first, and following Pullum and Sampson, that the stimulus is not in fact as impoverished as Chomsky would have us believe. For there is good reason to think that sentences relevant to the choice of rule are plentiful in the primary linguistic data. And I've argued, second, that the APS would fail to support nativism even were this not the case. By failing to distinguish the various different ways of being an empiricist (i.e., of not being a nativist), the APS fails to recognize the explanatory potential of the nonnativist position. While some versions of empiricism might entail that a learner would project the false, structure-independent rule, other (and I've suggested, more plausible) elaborations of the empiricist position do not have this consequence. A learner who was inclined to seek out deep rather than surface regularities in the world might well prefer structure-dependent over structure-independent rules, and so might a learner who had found out from her previous linguistic experience that structure-dependent rules work best

---

21. I want to stress that although this discussion may read as a criticism of Pullum, it is intended to be a criticism of the nativist. Unfortunately for the staunchly anti-Chomskyan Pullum, his version of the nativist's argument is so much more clearly and forcefully stated than nativists' own versions of the APS tend to be that it makes an irresistible target.

in the linguistic domain. If the principle of structure dependence is indeed what's guiding the language learner's theorizing, in short, there is no reason to be found in the APS for thinking that it is innately known.

There is, however, something deeply unsatisfying about both the preceding discussion and the vast literature that provoked it. No nativist is going to be convinced that nativism is false just because the rule for auxiliary fronting turns out to be learnable after all from the *pld* by general-purpose inferential methods, just as no empiricist was ever convinced that nativism is true on the basis of the APS's claim that it is not. So, while the learnability of the auxiliary fronting rule looks as it if is playing the role of an *experimentum crucis* in the nativism literature—judging, at any rate, by the obsessional attention accorded it by theorists on both sides of the nativist/empiricist divide—its failure to settle the issue decisively reflects the fact that there *are* no crucial experiments in science. If recent history and philosophy of science have taught us anything, it's that theories are never falsified or verified (or even significantly confirmed or disconfirmed) by a single predictive or explanatory success or failure. While a solitary success or failure of a theory may serve to trigger the theory's more wholesale acceptance or rejection (as Eddington's measurement of the deflection of light by gravity is sometimes said to have done for Einstein's General Theory of Relativity), a theory needs to do more than account for a single, well chosen example. Although it's never been clear (and still isn't) exactly what else it takes for a theory to triumph over its rivals, theoretical success surely has something to do with a theory's ability to explain a wide range of phenomena and demonstrate that it is overall more plausible and powerful than its competitors.

To this end, nativists have responded to criticisms of the auxiliary fronting version of the APS by constructing other cases, involving different grammatical rules and principles, that are again claimed to be unlearnable from the *pld*. Pinker's work on the acquisition of verb argument structures (1984, 1989) is within this tradition, although it concerns the learning of the lexicon rather than syntax strictly speaking. Crain (1991) also offers a rich vein of nativist argumentation from which several other poverty of the stimulus arguments, including those to be discussed in the next two sections, can be extracted.

8.6.1 The APS and Constraints on *Wanna* and Rightwards Contraction

Many speakers of American English find irresistible the urge to contract *want to* to *wanna*, as in *I wanna banana*. Nevertheless, there are situations where such contractions are alleged to be forbidden by the grammar. In particular, contraction to *wanna* is often claimed to be prohibited where the words *want* and *to* are separated by a Wh-trace, that is, an element, symbolized by *t*, that has been left behind in the phrase marker by the movement of an earlier constituent through the syntactic process known as Wh-raising. In

Wh-raising, questions beginning with a *Wh* word (*Who* . . . ?, *Which* . . . ?, *What* . . . ?, etc.) are formed when the element *wh* is moved out of its post-verbal object location at D-structure into its S-structure location at the beginning of the sentence, leaving a 'trace' of itself behind in its old location. Thus, as Crain (1991) explains, the underlying representations (5a, 6a) are transformed by Wh-raising into the surface forms (5b, 6b):

(5a) You want to kiss *wh*
(5b) Who$_i$ do you want to kiss t_i?
(6a) You want *wh* to kiss you
(6b) Who$_i$ do you want t_i to kiss you?

Given the locations of the traces in these sentences, *wanna* contraction is permitted only by (5); in (6), the contraction is prohibited by the existence of the element *t* between *want* and *to*:

(5c) Who do you wanna kiss?
(6c) *Who do you wanna kiss you?

Similarly prohibited is *is*-contraction in cases where a Wh-trace intervenes between *is* and the material to its right.[22] Thus, the *is* in (7a) can be contracted as in (7b), whereas that in (8a) cannot be contracted as in (8b):

(7a) Do you know what that is doing *t* up there?
(7b) Do you know what that's doing up there?
(8a) Do you know what that is *t* up there?
(8b) *Do you know what that's up there?

Crain (1991) reports that Crain and Thornton (1991) found that children as young as two years old reliably respect these constraints on contraction. While one child in their study consistently violated the constraint on *wanna* contraction, none of the rest did, and "there was not a single instance of [rightward] contraction where it is ruled out in the adult grammar" (Crain 1991:604). These results lead Crain to argue that

> . . . it is difficult to see how knowledge about the ungrammaticality of sentences like [(6c), (8b)] could have been acquired through exposure to environmental input at any age. It is accordingly important to ask when children know that a trace blocks contraction. The logic of the situation would suggest they must know it innately. Otherwise they might make the wrong generalization. . . . If corrective feedback is not available to children who err in this way, however, children who make the false generalization

---

22. Bresnan (1978) had argued that unlike *wanna* contraction, in which case *to* is run together in speech with the word *want* immediately preceding it, *is* attaches to the material following it when contracted. That is, and conventional orthography notwithstanding, the contracted form of *What do you think t is in the box?* is really *What do you think t 'sin the box?* (Otherwise, *is*-contraction in a sentence like *What do you think t is in the box?* would have been a counterexample to the 'Wh-trace blocks contraction' rule just discussed.) This is why *is*-contraction is prohibited by traces *following* the *is*, whereas *to* contraction (as in *wanna*) is prohibited by traces *preceding* the *to*.

would not be informed of their mistake, and would not attain the adult grammar. Because . . . everyone does achieve the same, correct final state . . . it seems that children never make this error. The only way this could be possible, given the absence of relevant experience, is if they know that Wh-trace blocks contraction. Here, then, is a partial syntactic generalization of grammar that clearly calls for assistance from innate linguistic principles. (Crain 1991:603)

8.6.2 The APS and Binding Theory's Principle C

There are also rules governing the coreference of noun phrases, pronouns, and other referring expressions ('r-expressions') within sentences. These constraints are described (in the Principles and Parameters approach) by Binding Theory's Principle C, stating that a pronoun and an r-expression cannot have the same reference if the former bears a certain structural relation—c-command—to the latter. As Crain notes (1991:605), the exact definition of c-command is controversial, but the general idea is that a pronoun c-commands an r-expression if there is a route from that goes from the first branching node above the pronoun down to the r-expression. (See Figure 8.1.)

This prohibition leads to a number of constraints on the possible interpretations of sentences containing pronouns. For instance, it explains why the sentence *Steve thinks he should go* can have both meanings (9a) and (9b), whereas *He thinks Steve should go* can only have the meaning (10a). *He thinks Steve should go* cannot mean (10b) because in that sentence, as figure 8.1 shows, the pronoun *he* c-commands the noun *Steve*. In *Steve thinks he should go*, the pronoun does not c-command the r-expression; hence coreference is permitted.

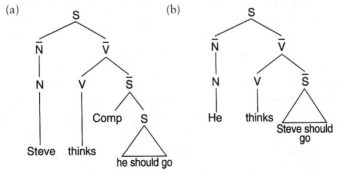

Figure 8.1 C-command. a. No C-command: There is no route from the first branching node above the pronoun (i.e., the embedded S) down to *Steve*; hence, coreference is permitted. b. C-command: There is a route from the first branching node above the pronoun (i.e., the root S) down to *Steve*; hence, coreference is prohibited.

(9a)   Steve$_i$ thinks he$_j$ should go   [*Steve* and *he* have different reference]
(9b)   Steve$_i$thinks he$_i$ should go   [*Steve* and *he* co-refer]
(10a)   He$_i$ thinks Steve$_j$ should go   [*Steve* and *he* have different reference]
(10b)   *He$_i$ thinks Steve$_i$ should go   [Coreference prohibited]

Principle C is invoked also to explain the constraints on coreference in certain types of Wh-questions. *Who did he say has big feet?* can mean (11b) but not (11a), whereas *Who said he has big feet?* can mean either (12a) or (12b). Chomsky (1986) explained this phenomenon of 'strong crossover' (so called because in these sorts of sentences coreference is blocked when the Wh-phrase 'crosses over' the pronoun in moving to its surface position—see figure 8.2) again in terms of Principle C: while the pronoun in *Who did he say has big feet?* does not c-command the Wh-expression, it does c-command its trace, and hence prohibits co-indexing.

(11a)   *Who$_i$ did he$_i$ say t_i has big feet?
(11b)   Who$_i$ did he$_j$ say t_i has big feet?
(12a)   Who$_i$ said he$_i$ has big feet?
(12b)   Who$_i$ t_i said he$_j$ has big feet?

Crain and his colleagues performed a series of experiments to test children's knowledge of Principle C. Subjects were presented with various sorts of anaphoric sentences and one- and two-clause crossover sentences in contexts that strongly favored a certain interpretation. In the crucial conditions, the contextually indicated interpretation was one that Principle C disallows. If children rejected the sentence as false despite its being true under the disallowed interpretation, this was taken as evidence that they had knowledge of Principle C.[23] Crain (1991) reports that Crain and McKee (1985) found that children rejected sentences violating the backward anaphora constraint 87% of the time, indicating, he says, that "[e]ven 2- and 3-year olds prohibit backwards anaphora only when Principle C dictates that they should" (Crain 1991:606). He reports also that Crain and Thornton (1991) found that children "were steadfast in their adherence to Principle C in both one-clause and two-clause crossover questions" (1991:608), correctly rejecting the multiple-reference interpretation 95% of the time in cases (like (9)) when it is prohibited, and correctly accepting the multiple reference interpretation 87% of the time when it is allowed (and contextually appropriate). Crain uses these findings as the basis for further reflections on the poverty of the stimulus:

23. See Crain (1991:605ff.) for accounts of these really very beautiful experiments. The experimental design basically involved the children's watching various hand puppets saying and doing various things, and commenting upon each others' thoughts and actions. In case one of the puppets uttered a falsehood, the children were encouraged to 'punish' it by making it "eat a rag." Crain and his colleagues inferred the grammatical rules that children were following by examining the conditions under which they would punish a puppet for saying something false.

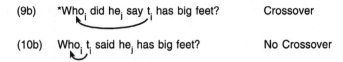

(9b)   *Who$_i$ did he$_j$ say t$_i$ has big feet?   Crossover

(10b)   Who$_i$ t$_i$ said he$_j$ has big feet?   No Crossover

Figure 8.2 Wh-movement over pronoun prohibits coreference. *Source*: From Crain (1991:606).

It is worth asking again whether children could have learned to prohibit coreference in crossover sentences. This would require them to have access to the right kind of linguistic experience. In the present case, this would presumably be information about what sentences cannot mean . . . it is highly unlikely that this source of data is available to children in sufficient abundance to explain their early acquisition of the constraint. This underscores the contention of universal grammar that linguistic constraints are not something children must learn . . . knowledge of the constraint on coreference is built into the human biological blueprint for language acquisition. (Crain 1991:608–9)

"In the broadest terms," Crain concludes, "this research was concerned with testing the hypothesis that linguistic knowledge of considerable complexity emerges in child grammars without decisive evidence from experience" (1991:611). His and his colleagues' findings being merely a few among the increasing "number of empirical demonstrations of children's mastery of syntactic facts for which they have little if any corresponding experience" (1991:611), they can, in Crain's opinion, only "reinforce the view that syntactic knowledge is in large part innately specified" (1991:611).

8.6.3 The APS: A Many-Headed Hydra

As the Peer Commentaries accompanying Crain's (1991) article attest, however, his invocations of the APS are subject to exactly same kinds of criticisms as were leveled against Chomsky's original version in the earlier parts of this chapter. First, Crain is faulted for underestimating the amount of information about language that is available to children, and hence for overlooking the potential of alternative learning theories to account for acquisition of the constraints he discusses. Berman (1991:613), for example, questions his assertions about the unavailability of relevant linguistic data. Referring to earlier work of her own, she argues that "close examination of parental input to 2-year-olds, presumably not unlike what was available to the children in Crain's studies, shows this to be 'neither so depleted nor so uniform as has been suggested' " and maintains, contra Crain, that "children [have] ample opportunity to work on a complicated syntactic issue." Dodd and Fogel (1991:617) point out that children have access also to nonlinguistic information (e.g., contextual information) that could aid them in learning to conform their usage to that of the community. Powers (1991:

630) makes an argument that is identical to the one leveled against Chomsky in §8.4:

> [t]here is no evidence for "children's early knowledge of a linguistic prin-
> ciple for which they have no corresponding experience." To make that
> "stick" it is necessary to show that the subjects had never heard contrac-
> tion of this sort—not only never in an identical context, but also never in
> an analogous context. . . . The problem of proving that language rules
> cannot be or have not been learned from the available input . . . requires
> an analysis of all input (and its order of presentation) and a formal result
> that no learning of language from these data is possible, given an accurate
> characterization of the restrictions of natural language and allowable
> learning mechanisms.

So although Crain goes one better than Chomsky in providing empirical support for his claims about what children know and do not know about language, his claims about the poverty of the available evidence are com-pletely unsubstantiated, and hence vulnerable to the sorts of objections just discussed.

Not only is Crain criticized for failing to provide evidence for this crucial empirical premise, he also is faulted for failing to take note of further data that cast doubt upon his conclusion. A common theme in the Peer Com-mentaries involved pointing out that even if it's legitimate to infer (DS)—the claim that children have task-specific linguistic knowledge that may aid them in language acquisition—from their knowledge at age three of Principle C and the fact that Wh-trace blocks contraction, it's surely premature to infer also from this fact the further claim (I), that that knowledge is possessed innately. Samet and Tager-Flusberg (1991:632) raise the question "How can this simple nativist hypothesis be harmonized with the often tortured path of cognitive development?" They criticize as unrealistic Crain's assumption that "the child has the full resources of UG available at the outset." Sokolov and Snow (1991:635) emphasize that in many of Crain's studies, some chil-dren did in fact make the supposedly impossible errors, thus casting doubt on the universality, and hence innateness, of the constraints in question. Pierce (1991), though himself a supporter of nativism, nonetheless notes that two-year-olds make many errors that three-year-olds do not, indicating that *something* happens to the child's state of knowledge during the learning period—be it learning, maturation, or whatever. Thus Crain's inference not just to (DS) but to (I) in addition is too quick: "it would be unfounded to jump from the observation that children know certain things at age 3 . . . to the conclusion that they know most other things at or before age 2" (Pierce 1991:629).

Crain's arguments, and the peer responses to them, illustrate the perennial difficulty one faces in trying to evaluate a posteriori arguments from the poverty of the stimulus. The nativist—say, Chomsky—articulates a version of the argument. The empiricist counters it by pointing to its evidential short-falls and/or its failure to do justice to empiricism's explanatory potential. But no sooner is one rendition of the APS cut down than myriad other variations on the same argumentative theme spring up to take its place. For every nonobvious rule of grammar (and most of them are nonobvious), there's an argument from the poverty of the stimulus standing by to make a case for nativism. And for every such argument (or at least for all the ones I've ever seen), there are empiricist counterarguments of exactly the kinds we've reviewed in this chapter, waiting, swords at the ready, to take it on.

The great virtue of the a posteriori argumentative strategy, at least to the naturalistically minded, is its insistence that the truth or falsity of nativism about language learning is a thoroughly empirical matter. Ironically, though, it is precisely because the APS is so willing to stand hostage to the vagaries of empirical fact that it remains polemically impotent. The data on which the APS is based are as impoverished as it alleges the data for language-learning to be. So, powerful though this argument has been in guiding the course of theorizing in linguistics and elsewhere, it in fact fails—or so I have argued in this chapter—to establish anything solid as to the relative merits of nativism and empiricism about language learning. Given our current ignorance as to the nature of the learning process and the information on which it is based, one cannot draw any conclusions at all from nativists' argument from the poverty of the stimulus.

9

The Logical Problem of Language Acquisition

Chapter 8 discussed the a posteriori argument from the poverty of the stimulus (APS) in several of its incarnations. I contended, first, that the ability of the APS to establish its conclusions about how languages are learned is seriously undercut by its proponents' failure to provide convincing empirical support for their claims about the sorts of linguistic evidence that are available in the *pld*. Although steps have recently been taken to document more carefully children's knowledge of the rules that are appealed to in statements of the argument, the APS is still badly weakened by nativists' reliance on their own unsupported intuitions as to whether or not children could infer this knowledge from the data that are available to them. These intuitions, I suggested, should be taken with a grain of salt, particularly in light of arguments, like Pullum's (1996) and Sampson's (1989), to the effect that the data are nowhere near as impoverished as nativists' estimates suggest. Until a large-scale study of the *pld* is undertaken, and the presence or absence of relevant forms is established, the APS is doomed to be inconclusive.

A second criticism that I made of the APS concerned its bleak assessment of the prospects for an empiricist explanation of how children could learn language from the data that are supposed to be available. In its tendency to regard any denial of nativism as a return to naive associationism or behaviorism, the APS persistently underestimates the resources available to the empiricist learner and overestimates the difficulty that such a learner would have in acquiring knowledge of syntactic rules. In particular, I argued, the APS fails to appreciate the explanatory power of the Enlightened empiricist's position. Unlike the Putnamian, who in denying (DS) seems to be committed to the implausible view that *no* knowledge about language, however ac-

Parts of this chapter have been published as Cowie (1997). I am grateful to William Demopoulos and Stephen Pinker for their helpful referees' reports on that paper.

quired, plays a role in children's choice of specific hypotheses, the Enlightened empiricist concedes that learners' grammatical decisions at a given moment will be strongly conditioned by their prior linguistic knowledge. She can therefore accept the most plausible of the nativist's contentions (e.g., his insistence that something like a principle of structure dependence is constraining the learner's choice between the two rules for question formation discussed in §8.2) while denying only his further claim that these constraints on hypotheses are innately known. On the empiricist's view, the structure-dependent hypothesis is preferred *not* because children are biologically incapable of entertaining structure-independent grammatical rules (which is, after all, what the nativist view implies) but rather because they have discovered, through their previous linguistic experience, that structural hypotheses tend to work best in the linguistic domain. So, even if there were no data available that bear directly on the learner's choice of H_1 over H_2, the empiricist is not necessarily stumped by learners' acquiring the auxiliary fronting rule. That ability may still be explicable on an empiricist model as arising out of their earlier experiences, linguistic and otherwise, and the cognitions based thereupon.

I also remarked, however, that a posteriori arguments from the poverty of the stimulus are peculiarly unsatisfying. Is the empiricist's insistence that her position has more explanatory power than the nativist credits, a legitimate attempt to elaborate her theory in response to the nativist's objections? Or doth she rather protest too much? Is the nativist's production of new versions of the argument, involving different rules and different claims about the *pld*, an appropriate reaction to the suspicions that empiricists voice about the old ones? Or are these maneuvers just desperate attempts to save his theory from empirical disconfirmation? It is very hard for the disinterested observer to say. Viewed from the trenches, the battle looks interminable.

Perhaps in the hopes of averting a potentially endless war of attrition over its merits, nativists have recently shifted their argumentative emphasis away from the APS and toward another type of poverty of the stimulus argument. Called variously the 'Projection Problem' or the 'Negative Evidence Problem' or the 'Logical Problem of Language Acquisition,' this argument derives not from any particular conception of the nature of linguistic knowledge or view as to the frequency of specific forms in the *pld*, but rather from the logical structure of the language-learning task. It seeks to show that the primary data are impoverished not just in fact but in principle, and that they are impoverished not merely with respect to the acquisition of some particular grammatical rule but with respect to the acquisition of *any* grammar powerful enough to generate a natural language. This more a priori variant of the poverty of the stimulus argument thus seeks to cut through the miasmic uncertainty surrounding the outcome of the a posteriori argument and to establish decisively that nativism about language learning must be true.

The Logical Problem is alleged to arise because there is an almost total dearth of 'negative evidence'—evidence as to which strings of words are *not* sentences of the language being learned—in the primary linguistic data. As a consequence, certain sorts of plausible but false grammatical hypotheses, particularly overgeneral hypotheses, would appear to be experientially incorrigible. So, for example, suppose that on hearing the sentences *It is likely that John will leave, John is likely to leave,* and *It is possible that John will leave,* the learner predicted that **John is possible to leave* is a sentence of English. Then, absent some concrete reason to think that this last is *not* a sentence—absent negative evidence—she should continue in her erroneous belief that the string is allowed by the language. The mystery is why, given that few if any speakers have been told or otherwise informed that **John is possible to leave* is not a sentence, competent speakers of English universally judge that construction to be ungrammatical.

The challenge posed by the Logical Problem is to explain why people do not make these sorts of errors, given that there is apparently nothing in their experience to prevent their doing so. How could language acquisition occur successfully in the face of such massive evidential deprivation? The nativist's advocacy of (I) and (DS) (or (I) and (U)) is a response to this conundrum. By supposing that much of the information about language we possess is supplied by our genes, and not by the world, one can see how acquisition could occur under such conditions. Insofar as it "takes the burden of explaining learning out of the environment and puts it back in the child" (Pinker 1989: 15), nativism—of either the Weak or the Chomskyan stripe—shows how in principle to account for acquisition in the near-total absence of relevant linguistic inputs. On this view, it is learners' inborn knowledge of language that prevents them from making hypotheses the truth or falsity of which cannot be ascertained from their experience.

In its most extreme form, the nativist view would seek to rule out *all* errors of overgeneralization: the learning mechanism is so tightly constrained that learners literally cannot make hypotheses that are too broad. As Pinker (1989:18–30) has argued, however, this draconian position, which he calls the 'conservatism hypothesis,' is untenable: children do, after all, overgeneralize during language-learning.[1] Thus, the nativist's aim must, strictly speaking, be to develop a theory of the constraints on the language faculty such that those constraints are strong enough to prevent most errors, yet not so strong as to rule out those that we know do occur. Nonetheless, the extreme position remains for nativists a kind of ideal in responding to the Logical Problem, and since nothing I will say in the following will turn on this issue, I too will sometimes speak as if the nativist sought to prevent overgeneration altogether. The reader should, however, keep the qualification just mentioned in mind.

In this chapter, I will argue that, contrary to what appears to be the received opinion, reflection on the Logical Problem does little to motivate

---

1. An oft-cited example being their tendency to apply the rule for constructing past tenses of regular verbs to irregular verbs, generating, e.g., the incorrect **goed, *swimmed,* and **runned* in addition to the correct *walked, hurried,* etc.

either Weak or Chomskyan nativism. On the view I shall defend, this argument does support (DS): it does suggest that a learner's theorizing about language must be constrained by certain prior views about the task domain.[2] However, I contend, it provides no support whatsoever for (I), the claim that those prior views are innately encoded. The Logical Problem of Language Acquisition, like the APS, supports at most an Enlightened empiricism.

In §9.1, I give the argument from the Logical Problem as it is typically presented in the literature. In §§9.2 and 9.3, I articulate some obvious empiricist challenges to the argument so formulated and reconstruct it so as to circumvent these objections. This version of the argument, which I take to be the strongest, does make (DS) seem plausible. As I argue in §§9.4 and 9.5, however, it does not legitimate (I). Hence, it gives no support to nativism over empiricism about language.

9.1. The Logical Problem

The argument from the Logical Problem notes that there is in principle a gap between what is known about language and the information about it that is available during language-learning.[3] Take some stage in the learning process at which the child has acquired a theory as to the nature of her language—a grammar, in other words. Call the language generated by her current grammatical hypothesis H. Call the language generated by the correct grammar—the target language—L. Then the learner is in one of five possible situations (figure 9.1).

Situation (5) represents the end point of the learning process: the child's grammar generates all and only the sentences of the target language. The question is how, supposing she is in any of the other situations, she can use the primary linguistic data to get there. In cases (1), (2), and (3), the learner will be forced to revise her hypothesis if she hears a sentence in L that is not a sentence of H—one that is not generated by her grammar. That is, she can move toward the correct grammar by exposure to 'positive evidence,' evidence (as is provided by someone's uttering a sentence) that a given string is a sentence of the target language. Crucially, however, if she is in the situation represented by (4)—if her grammar generates all of L and also some strings that are not in L—she will never be able to discover that she errs just by exposure to further sentences of the target language. For every sentence of L is equally a sentence of H. What she needs is the information that a

---

2. The question of whether those views are accurately described by the Universal Grammar (i.e., the question of whether (U) in addition to (DS) is true) will be the subject of chapter 10.

3. What follows is a synthesis of the many statements of the argument to be found in the literature. See, e.g., Braine (1971:157); Baker (1979); Hornstein and Lightfoot's Introduction to their (1981); Matthews (1984); Lasnik (1989:89–90); Pinker (1986:55–56; 1989:5–6). My presentation is particularly indebted to Pinker.

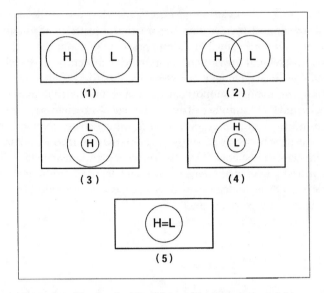

Figure 9.1 The Logical Problem of Language Acquisition

string that is generated by her grammar—a string in H—is *not* a sentence of L: only then can she 'shrink' her hypothesis and bring it back in line with that of the linguistic community. This latter kind of evidence, that a string is *not* in the language, is called 'negative evidence.' And the Logical Problem arises because children apparently have no systematic access to it: information as to what strings are not sentences of the language they are learning is in general unavailable.

First, they are certainly not given lists of ungrammatical strings! And they are rarely corrected when they make syntactic errors.[4] Worse, the primary linguistic data contain a proportion of ungrammatical utterances that are not flagged as such.[5] Worst of all, however, is the fact that there are infinitely many strings of (say) English words that the child will *never* encounter in the data. Some of them she will not hear because they are not, in fact, English sentences; others, however, are perfectly good sentences that are absent from the data for the simple reason that no one has gotten around to uttering them. What this means is that the mere non-occurrence of a string in the data cannot by itself constitute negative evidence. So even if she were always corrected when she made a mistake, and even if her interlocutors invariably spoke impeccably, there would always remain an infinity of

4. Brown and Hanlon (1970).
5. E.g., incomplete sentences, sentences containing 'Umms,' 'Uhhs,' etc. Note, however, that according to one estimate (Newport, Gleitman, and Gleitman 1977), an astonishing 99.7 percent of sentences spoken by mothers to their children are grammatically impeccable.

strings, some of them English and some of them gibberish, that the child has no information about one way or the other.

Hence, if a child's hypothesized grammar were to overgenerate, there'd be no data that would force her back toward the correct theory. So, since children do eventually converge on the right theory, they must never be in situation (4): they must never hypothesize a grammar that is 'too large.' Indeed, since cases (1) and (2) will eventually collapse into case (4),[6] children must never project *any* hypothesis implying statements of the form 'String s is a sentence of L' where s is not in fact a sentence of L. In other words, their theorizing must be constrained such that they are only ever in situation (3). The Logical Problem of Language Acquisition is the problem of explaining how this desideratum is achieved.

Nativists argue that (DS) and (I) are the solution to the Logical Problem.[7] First, let us take the hypothesis that domain-specific information is required for language-learning. The argument is that it is only by invoking her fore-knowledge about language that the learner is prevented from making wild and incorrigible overgeneralizations. The empiricist's requirement that the learner prefer simpler, more general, more elegant (etc.) hypotheses provides little in the way of guidance: too little, surely, to prevent a learner's falling irretrievably into the myriad possible pitfalls revealed by the Logical Problem. Language is so strange, its workings so abstruse, that a learner utterly uninformed as to its character surely *must* go wrong. The Logical Problem thus illuminates, in a particularly vivid and intuitively compelling way, the need for a task-specific helping hand in the linguistic domain.

What of (I), the contention that the requisite information about language is not only known, but known innately? Pinker (1984:33–37) canvasses an argument to the effect that (I) should be accepted on grounds of parsimony. While recognizing that considerations of simplicity could in principle go either way—depending on the details, a single, general-purpose learning mechanism might well turn out to be simpler than a bevy of task-specific ones—Pinker claims that "a conclusion of task-specificity of the learning mechanisms quickly leads one to a tentative conclusion of nativism because of certain parsimony considerations" (1984:33). He argues (1984:34–35) that although the nativist hypothesis that the principles specified in (DS) are known innately is not more parsimonious than any *possible* rival hypothesis,

6. Take case (2) in figure 9.1, for example. Positive evidence will force the child to expand the boundary of H rightward (so to speak) so that it converges with the rightmost boundary of L. But negative evidence is still required to deal with the leftmost, over-generating, portion of H.

7. As I've remarked before, nativists don't tend to distinguish between (DS) and (U), so they often write as if the Logical Problem argument supported (I) and (U), not the Weaker position ((DS) and (I)) mentioned here. Since it doesn't matter to my arguments in this chapter which version of nativism you take the Logical Problem to be supporting, I will usually consider only the Weaker conclusion. The relation between Weak and Chomskyan nativisms will be discussed in chapter 10.

it *is* more parsimonious than any *plausible* rivals, and is therefore to be preferred, pending further empirical findings (1984:36 and n. 10). It seems to me, however, that it is a mistake to propose, even tentatively, as Pinker does, that "the innateness debate in the study of language acquisition be recast as a parsimony debate concerning rival acquisition theories for language and other cognitive domains" (Pinker 1984:36). First, neither the nativist's theory nor its competitors would seem to be sufficiently well articulated at this time to be reliably evaluated in terms of parsimony. Second, it is far from obvious that simplicity is in fact the correct criterion of theory-choice in the cognitive domain. For it is by no means clear that the brain, an evolved organ cobbled together over millennia by Mother Nature, operates according to principles that we find maximally parsimonious.

There are, however, other arguments for (1) available. One of them will be discussed in §9.2. Another goes as follows: Suppose that domain-specific information is required for language-learning to occur. Suppose, for example, that as the Chomskyan nativist asserts, what is required is knowledge of Universal Grammar. Then, we have two choices. Either the principles of UG are learned or they are innate. If they are learned, then the Logical Problem simply arises all over again: the child attempting to infer the Universal Grammar from the data faces exactly the same difficulties with regard to the paucity of available evidence and the danger of overgeneralizing as does the child attempting to infer the grammar of a particular language. Claiming that UG is learned simply pushes the Logical Problem back a step. At the risk of an infinite regress, then, we must conclude that UG is innate.

So, it seems, the argument from the Logical Problem mandates a nativist approach to language acquisition. Further, it mandates nativism while making comparatively minimal empirical assumptions: (1) that speakers learn by some form of hypothesis-testing; (2) that what they learn is some kind of generative grammar; and (3) that the primary data consist overwhelmingly of positive data. As a consequence, the present argument is not hostage to the vagaries of fact and theory to quite the same extent as are the versions of the APS discussed in the previous chapter. And, while its assumptions may be—indeed, have been—challenged, that is not my strategy here.[8] Although I will raise some questions of detail in §9.4, I will argue that even if we accept the basic picture of learning and competence that the argument from the Logical Problem assumes, it *still* fails to support nativism about language-learning.

As a preliminary to my argument, it is necessary to clarify and reformulate the nativist's case so that it resists some obvious empiricist ob-

---

8. Proponents of connectionist-style language-learning models (e.g., Rumelhart and McClelland 1986), for instance, have challenged the view that learning is a matter of hypothesis-testing. Soames (1984a) and Devitt and Sterelny (1989) have questioned whether there is any interesting sense in which speakers know grammars. And linguists themselves have speculated that there might be unrecognized sources of indirect negative evidence in the primary linguistic data—see especially Lasnik (1989). See also §9.5.

jections. That is the task of the next section. Armed with what I take to be the strongest statement of the Logical Problem of Language Acquisition, I shall then turn, in §9.3, to a consideration of its merits.

9.2 Guaranteeing Learnability

An empiricist will immediately counter the argument presented above with the following. First, in defending (DS), the nativist asserts that no general-purpose learning device could sufficiently constrain the child in her choice of hypotheses. He has not, however, established that there is *no possible* empiricist model that could explain how a child could learn a language merely through exposure to a sample of sentences.[9] Second, the empiricist will note, the arguments for both (DS) and (I) proceed as if there were *no* negative data available to the learner, when, in fact, there are sources of both direct and indirect negative evidence in the primary linguistic data. Direct negative evidence—explicit information to the effect that string *s* is not a sentence of the target language—may be comparatively rare, but it nonetheless exists. And indirect negative evidence is surely even more plentiful, being provided, perhaps, by a parent's failure to understand an utterance of the child, or by the repeated failure of certain forms predicted by her grammar to appear in the data. Thus, the nativist's motivation for claiming that overgeneration must be prevented by the incorporation of domain-specific information into the learning device is inadequate. And so is his attempt to iterate the argument from the Logical Problem in establishing that that incorporation is achieved by nature rather than by learning. The argument from the Logical Problem is inconclusive. It fails to establish either (DS) or (I).

The argument, however, can be restated so that it represents a formidable challenge to the empiricist. The reformulated argument turns on the need of a learning theory to *guarantee language learnability*. Normal children are virtually certain to master a language given even minimal exposure to it. An

---

9. The results of Gold in his seminal (1967) paper have, I think, have been misunderstood in this connection. Pinker (1979:232), for example, claims that Gold's proof to the effect that the learner's hypothesis set must be constrained means that we are "committed to at least a weak form of nativism, according to which 'the child approaches the data with the presumption that they are drawn from a language of an antecedently well-defined type' (Chomsky 1965:27)." That is, we are committed to nativism's (DS): the child must be constrained by prior views about language. However, as we've already seen (§8.5.2), what Gold in fact proved was that a learner who is utterly unconstrained as to possible hypotheses will fail to learn a language from positive data. He did not show that no learner constrained merely by general-purpose constraints (such as 'Prefer simpler hypotheses,' etc.) must fail in that task. Since nativist and empiricist agree that there must be *some* constraints on the hypothesis space—since their dispute concerns not the need for constraints per se but, rather, the nature of the constraints needed—Gold's results are irrelevant to their dispute. See also Demopoulos (1989).

acquisition theory must account for this fact. It must explain how learners are equipped such that, *if* they go wrong, they go wrong *only* in ways that turn out to be corrigible on the basis of the evidence available to them. What the Logical Problem underscores is that explaining this is no easy matter. The linguistic evidence available to learners is radically impoverished. Negative data rarely occur. When they do, they occur haphazardly. How, then, can the child be guaranteed only to make errors that are corrigible given precisely the data she happens to stumble upon? And not only do we need to account for the individual case. All children in (say) an English-speaking community learn English despite their being exposed during learning to arguably very different samples of English sentences. How do we guarantee that everyone gets exactly the evidence he or she needs to arrive at the same grammatical hypothesis as everyone else?[10]

Clearly, a learner who *never* overgenerates would be unfazed by the scarcity and sketchiness of negative evidence in the primary linguistic data. The theorist, therefore, should seek to construct a model that approximates, as closely as is consistent with the developmental facts, this conservative ideal. In this endeavor, the nativist is at liberty to impose domain-specific constraints on the hypothesis-generating mechanism. By adopting (DS) or the stronger Chomskyan (U), he may hope to ensure that learners do not project hypotheses requiring negative evidence for their disconfirmation, thus rendering the learnability problem in the individual case tractable. And, by adopting (I) as well—by supposing that the task-specific information required to guarantee learnability is available as a consequence of human biology—the nativist can also explain how it is that we all learn the grammar of our language.

The empiricist, by contrast, appears at a loss. His view is that the mind, ab initio, is equipped only with certain domain-neutral injunctions concerning learning from experience: "Look for similarities," "Prefer simpler hypotheses to more complex ones," perhaps "Seek out underlying regularities," and so on. But, the nativist argues first, there is no reason to think that these sorts of principles, even if coupled with some 'mechanism of inductive inference' (whatever that is), could constrain the learner so that she *never* needed a negative datum to evaluate a grammatical hypothesis. On the contrary, there is every reason to believe that a child employing only general-purpose principles of theory construction will frequently overgeneralize. Second, and supposing that the empiricist's learner does overgeneralize, there is no reason to expect that she will chance upon just the negative evidence

---

10. The necessity that our acquisition theory guarantee learnability is emphasized in, e.g., Pinker (1989:11); Wexler (1982:291–92); Hornstein and Lightfoot (1981:viiff.). What is new in my presentation is the drawing of a clear distinction between this point and the much more general point (discussed in §9.1) that a dearth of negative evidence in some domain makes it difficult for a learner to recover from overgeneralizations. The distinction matters because the two points suggest quite different arguments for (I) that deserve to be treated separately—see below §§9.4–9.5 and chapter 10.

she needs to discover her mistake. Unlike the linguist, who already knows the language she is theorizing about and who can, therefore, construct negative data relevant to her hypotheses, the child learning a language must take her negative data when and as she finds them. Since the empiricist can provide no guarantee that the child will find just the data she needs, when she needs them, he can provide no guarantee of language learnability.

Thus the point of the argument from the Logical Problem, on this reconstruction, is to underscore the difficulty of the empiricist's task: he must explain how it is that learners manage to err only in ways that turn out to be rectifiable on the basis of the paltry and haphazard data that they have access to. Certainly no empiricist model proffered to date has managed to do this; and there are no grounds, the empiricist's protestations notwithstanding, to expect any future attempt to succeed. Of course one cannot rule out the *logical possibility* that some or other brand of empiricism might be true. But, as Hume has put it: " 'Tis impossible to refute a system, which has never yet been explain'd. In such a manner of fighting in the dark, a man loses his blows in the air, and often places them where the enemy is not present."[11] So unless and until the empiricist delivers a theory worth fighting against, the argument from the Logical Problem indicates that we should pursue the nativist paradigm.

9.3 The Case for (DS)—and the Case Against (I)

I think that it should be conceded that the argument of the previous section establishes (DS). Although the nativist's reasoning is not apodictic, the need to guarantee the learnability of language from the primary linguistic data strongly suggests that domain-specific information is implicated in the formulation of learners' linguistic hypotheses. Without the guidance it provides, there are just too many ways to go wrong about the grammar of one's language and too few data around to guarantee that one's mistakes will be rectifiable. The fact that the adoption of (DS) offers at least the hope that learnability can be ensured, where no such hope existed before, is a powerful pragmatic argument in its favor. Thus, while some influential empiricists, for example Putnam (1971) and Sampson (1989), have expended considerable energy in contesting (DS), those energies have, in my view, been misplaced. Indeed, it being something of a commonplace in the philosophy of

---

11. *Treatise* III.1.i (1978:464). Or, as Wexler and Culicover (1980:9) trenchantly put it: "it is perfectly possible logically that the purported linguistic constraint is a special case of, or follows from, a more general cognitive constraint, that is, a constraint that applies to all cognitive systems . . . but the cognitive domains that are referred to . . . are not for the most part subject to any kind of reasonably well specified theory, so it doesn't even make sense to assert the existence of a constraint that applies to these domains. One might almost as well suggest that the linguistic constraint applies to black holes, which would make the constraint even more general."

science that induction cannot work in the absence of a prior theoretical framework, one should on those grounds alone have been suspicious of the Putnamian position.[12]

The Logical Problem argument, then, militates strongly against Putnamian empiricism. But one cannot read into this a mandate for nativism. For recall the arguments of chapter 7: Putnam's is not the only way of being an empiricist. There is a second, more 'Enlightened' form of empiricism, one that grants the nativist's (DS), denying only his (I). On this view, the task-specific information needed for the acquisition of grammatical knowledge is itself acquired through experience, rather than being encoded in the genes. Thus, the anti-empiricist (or pro-nativist) force of the argument from the Logical Problem must come, if it comes at all, from its power to establish (I), the contention that the information specified in (DS) is innate.

In §§9.1 and 9.2, I outlined two arguments from the Logical Problem to this conclusion. The first claimed that the information specified in (DS) could not be gleaned from experience, for learning the highly abstract and unintuitive principles of UG from the data is an even more difficult and error-prone enterprise than that of learning the grammar for a particular language. The contention that the child learns UG simply raises the Logical Problem all over again, so UG must be innate. This 'iterated' argument from the poverty of the stimulus, to be discussed in chapter 10, contains a suppressed premise, namely, that the information posited in (DS) as being necessary to language-learning *is the information specified in the Universal Grammar.* But while many linguists hold that to theorize about UG *just is* to theorize about the information needed for language-learning, I shall argue in chapter 10 that the claim that UG is implicated in learning is an empirical claim in need of empirical defense. Furthermore, I shall suggest, it's an empirical claim that in fact lacks any sound empirical basis. There is no good reason to believe that the knowledge posited in (DS) is knowledge of UG. Hence, I will contend, the learnability or otherwise of UG is inconclusive with respect to establishing the nativist's (I).

In this chapter, we will take up the second of the nativist's arguments for (I), outlined in §9.2. This argument turned on the need for guaranteeing not just the individual's ability to learn language but also that of the entire species. An individual might by chance encounter just the information she needs to keep her grammatical theorizing on track. Yet although everyone exposed to English will learn English, we cannot all be assured such luck: not everyone can be guaranteed access to those vital data. The only way our collective success in language-learning can be accounted for is to suppose that the 'luck' is built in. No matter what the information needed for learning language turns out to be, that information must be biologically encoded. The argument from the Logical Problem entails not only (DS) but (I) as well.

---

12. Thanks to Jim Woodward for this point.

The nativist's case here seems compelling. Nonetheless, I contend, it is flawed. For the Logical Problem is a completely general problem arising for all learning involving projection beyond our experience. There is, that is to say, a dearth of negative evidence not just in the domain of language but in every domain in which people learn. So, if the need to guarantee learnability in the absence of negative evidence is indeed a reason to adopt (I) as well as (DS), we should 'go nativist' about everything. But this is untenable. The nativist's argument, therefore, must be invalid.

9.3.1 A Curry Is Itself and Not Another Thing

Consider, to take a mundane example, learning about food. Given some minimal gastronomic experience, virtually all normal humans are guaranteed to acquire 'culinary competence,' the ability to recognize and distinguish a variety of foods from each other and from non-foods. Yet, when learning about curries, say, no one ever systematically informs us that Irish stews, tacos, and quiches—let alone boats and babies and bison—are not curries. There are infinitely many things that *might* be curries, but that are *not* curries, and that we have no information about one way or the other. Yet, and despite the dearth of negative evidence, we all manage to converge on the view that a curry is itself and not another thing. We all, that is to say, manage more or less to converge in our intuitive judgments as to what is and is not an instance of the kind curry.[13]

What follows from this, for reasons identical to those given above in our discussion of language acquisition, is (DS). General directions to the effect that we should choose simple, elegant, powerful (etc.) hypotheses allow too much room for overgeneralization: "All the world's a curry." Since the data needed to correct such errors seem unavailable, domain-specific information—perhaps some idea to the effect that curries are a kind of food, or that they have a characteristically spicy taste—must be constraining our choices of curry hypotheses.

But what surely does *not* follow from consideration of this case is (I). Although it is not the case that everyone can be guaranteed access to the same curry samples, all normal people exposed to a curry or two arrive at more or less the correct view about what curries are. In the case of language, the nativist urged us to accept (I) as an explanation of this kind of convergence: we all learn the same language because the information we need is built in. Are we then to accept the same inference here? Surely not! It is just absurd to suppose that the domain-specific principles required for learning about curries are innate, biologically encoded in a special 'culinary faculty'!

---

13. It's perhaps worth stressing here that the task at issue is not that of learning the meaning of the word 'curry.' It's rather that of leaning *what curries are.* Compare language-learning: the problem is not learning how to apply the words 'grammatical' and 'ungrammatical' to strings; it's that of learning *what the sentences of one's language are.*

But, and this is the point of this example, if we are reluctant to posit a 'culinary faculty' as guarantor of our ability to acquire curry competence, we should be equally reluctant to accept (1) as the conclusion of the precisely parallel argument offered by the nativist in the linguistic case.

My aim here is emphatically not to suggest that nativism about language is implausible in the way that nativism about curries is: my argument is not an attempted reductio of linguistic nativism. Instead, my purpose is to show that the truth of (1) in the linguistic domain cannot be established by the argument set out at the beginning of this section, any more than the truth of (1) in the culinary domain can be established by the argument in its latter part. Humans learn an awful lot, about a bewildering variety of topics, from sketchy and largely positive data. That they can do so—that they are virtually guaranteed to do so, given some minimal degree of information and motivation—is miraculous and mysterious. It is not, however, a reason to accept a nativist explanation of the miracle or solution to the mystery. To put the point another way, the curry case shows that, contrary to the argument given above, (1) *could not be* the only explanation of how we are all be guaranteed to master a certain domain from the (largely positive) data available. That the 'Logical Problem' in *this* instance is so clearly a sham suggests that the Logical Problem of Language Acquisition may be something of a pseudo-problem too. I shall argue that this is indeed the case. Arguments from the Logical Problem are based on conceptions of the learning task that are seriously inadequate. Once those inadequacies are recognized, the nativist's case loses much of its force.

9.3.2 Four Bones of Contention

The first thing that the curry case makes clear is that there is much more negative evidence around than a proponent of the Logical Problem would allow. What makes learning here possible is the vast quantity of indirect or implicit negative evidence about curries available. For example, the fact that we call hamburgers 'hamburgers,' not 'curries,' is surely evidence—not explicit evidence, but evidence nonetheless—that hamburgers are not curries.

A second and related point raised by this example is that learning is a gradual and piecemeal process. Our theories about curries are constantly being updated and modified in the light of the evidence, both positive and negative. This is important because it means that the child can use the hypotheses she has already formulated to find new sources of negative evidence. Once she has decided, for example, that curries are a kind of food, then the fact that we do not typically eat babies, whereas we do eat curries, is negative evidence: if we don't eat them, babies likely aren't curries. The relation between theories and their evidence, in other words, is holistic: what can count as evidence for or against a hypothesis depends on what else we believe.

That relation is also, to draw a third moral from the curry case, probabilistic. Assessing the bearing of incoming data on our theories is a complex (and poorly understood) matter of mutual accommodation and adjustment. A single piece of evidence may not suffice either to verify or to falsify a theory. Cherished hypotheses may be retained in the light of apparently falsifying data, and many pieces of evidence, each in themselves inconclusive, may have to combine their individual weights to overthrow them. Thus, whereas one experience of a bland and tasteless curry may not be enough to make you give up your hypothesis that all curries are spicy, repeated experiences of that kind may lead you to change your view.

A final point raised by our consideration of the curry connoisseur concerns the nature of 'culinary competence,' the end point of the learning process. First, there probably is no such final point: we never stop learning about curries. Second, it is likely that none of us has *exactly* the same theory about curries as anyone else. You and I may disagree, for example, about whether mulligatawny soup is a curry. On the one hand, it's a delicious concoction of meats, vegetables, and spices with that characteristically subcontinental taste; on the other, though, it's a soup, not a stew, and is not a part of indigenous Indian cuisine, having originated in the kitchens of the British Raj in the nineteenth century. The fact that such disagreements can occur indicates that peoples' curry theories are subtly different—as is to be expected, given their different experiences. But, and this is what is crucial, this fact is completely consistent with their agreeing, as surely they do, on the vast majority of cases. What needs to be explained, then, is not how we all manage to converge on the exact same theory but, rather, how we converge exactly enough to make both communication and disagreement about curries possible.

Thus the Logical Problem, as it pertains to curries, makes four serious errors about the learning task. It fails to recognize the many sources of indirect or implicit negative evidence in the data. It fails to recognize the piecemeal nature of theory construction. It ignores the holistic and probabilistic relations of evidence to theories. And it assumes that what needs explaining is how we all arrive at the same theory when the existence of disagreements about curries shows that we don't. Once these misconceptions about learning are made explicit, the 'Logical Problem' in the curry case simply dissolves. Of course the problem of explaining *learning* does not dissolve. But the task of building a bridge between what we learn and the data we learn it from *without* the help of a biologically specified culinary faculty looks, as it should, much more tractable.

9.4 Some Morals for Language Learners

I contend that the Logical Problem of Language Acquisition is flawed in exactly these ways. In this section, I shall argue that it misconceives the nature of the language-learning task and, in so doing, makes the nativist position look far more inescapable, and an Enlightened empiricist approach far more implausible, than either of them is. In §9.5, I show how, by making more realistic assumptions about the language learner and her environment, we may find rich sources of negative evidence in the *pld*.

9.4.1 The Idealization to Instantaneous Learning

Let's begin by seeing how the general points made above about theory construction and confirmation apply in the case of language-learning. Chomsky has argued (e.g., 1986:51ff.) that in elucidating the nature of the acquisition device, it is legitimate to make a number of idealizations about the manner in which children's linguistic theories are constructed. In particular, he argues that in developing an account of the learning mechanism, one may suppose that the "order of presentation of data is irrelevant, so that learning is 'as if it were instantaneous,' as if S_0 maps the data directly onto S_s" (1986: 52; S_0 is the 'initial state' of mind of the linguistic neophyte; S_s is the 'steady state' of linguistic knowledge achieved by the mature speaker). Thus, he claims, we should define "a certain model of language acquisition and also a model of explanation" (1986:52) according to which the initial state S_0 of the acquisition device is viewed as a function that directly maps the totality of available data E onto the steady state S_s.

What the curry example suggests, I think, is that this idealization to instantaneous learning is in fact a very unrealistic and misleading one. Just as the child learning about curries used her intermediate hypotheses ('Curries are a kind of food') the better to exploit her experience as a source of relevant evidence, so may the child learning language make use of intermediate linguistic hypotheses in bootstrapping her way up to full linguistic competence. Indeed, I'd put it more strongly than this and predict that language-learning will prove explicable only on the assumption that it is *not* an instantaneous process. Trying to explain how a child could learn a language 'as if instantaneously' from a perusal of all the linguistic data is like trying to figure out how Democritus might have discovered quantum mechanics, had he been handed another two thousand years' worth of experimental results. The insights, clues, and even misinformation provided by the theories that came between the Democritan and quantum mechanical conceptions of the world were essential to the development of modern physical theory. Discovering quantum mechanics required that one solve problems (e.g., the wave–particle duality of light) that Democritus could not have formulated; it required that old data (e.g., the phenomenon of blackbody radiation) be reinterpreted in the light of new theories in order that their significance might become clear; it required that old concepts (e.g., 'elementary particle' or 'energy') be gradually reconfigured so as to fit the world better; and so on. If one tried to understand the process of scientific discovery without taking into account its having occurred over centuries and by degrees, one would get nowhere fast. Similarly, I suggest, in the case of language acquisition. MacWhinney (1989:90) puts it like this:

> What we see when we look at language acquisition is a gradual development. Mastery of the phonological contrasts of the language is a step-

by-step process. During the second and third years, each week sees the
acquisition of new sounds, patterns of sounds, or refinements in the articulation of existing sounds in particular words. For years, each day sees
the learning of several new words. Each day the child sharpens his or her
use of old words and acquires new meanings for old words. Syntactic
patterns also emerge in a gradual way. New patterns such as auxiliary
inversion for questions are applied first to a few words and then a few
more. . . . [T]his gradualism [is] an important indicator of the true course
of development. Contrary to the claims of nativist theory, the child seems
to be proceeding in a bottom-up fashion, acquiring the language system
brick-by-brick.

Language acquisition is not an instantaneous process, any more than scientific discovery is an instantaneous process, and it's simply a mistake to
attempt to model it as if it were one.

In denying that the Chomskyan idealization to instantaneous learning is
appropriate, I do not mean to deny his further assumption that, in the case
of language, the order of data presentation is pretty much irrelevant to the
final state attained. For although the order of data presentation has been
argued critically to affect the outcome of a learning process in some cases,[14]
the notion that this is an especially important variable in language acquisition is given the lie by learners' ability to converge on (more or less) the
same final state despite arguably being exposed to different samples of sentences during learning. Chomsky, however, seems to suggest that the idealization to instantaneous learning *follows from* the idealization to unordered
data: the "order of presentation of data is irrelevant, *so that* learning is 'as
if it were instantaneous,' as if S_0 maps the data directly onto S_s" (1986:52,
emphasis added). His idea seems to be that if the order of data presentation
doesn't matter to the success of the learning process, then intermediate hypotheses could not be part of that process either. For in order to be sure to
recover from errors made in intermediate stages, the learner would have to
be guaranteed access to particular pieces of evidence—a guarantee that cannot, it seems, be given if the data are presumed to be unordered. I think,
though, that the two idealizations are independent. For something like the
requisite guarantee can be provided when one reflects on the sheer size of
the data sample to which a language learner has access. Assuming that there
is a goodly amount of redundancy in the data (that is, assuming that there
are many strings that could serve to disconfirm a given hypothesis), the
learner is likely eventually to find the evidence she needs to reject a false
intermediate hypothesis. The order of data is irrelevant to language acquisition not because learners never stand in need of particular kinds of data

14. For example, Pinker and Prince (1988) argue that it was only because the network's trainers presented data in a particular order that the much-touted PDP model of
Rumelhart and McClelland (1986) was able to mimic the child's learning of verb past
tenses. They show that on different assumptions about the order of data presentation, the
network would have failed (e.g.) to overgeneralize the past-tense rule for regular verbs,
and hence would have failed to mirror children's generation of *goed, *swimmed, etc.

at particular times (as when they entertain and subsequently evaluate an intermediate hypothesis) but, rather, because there is so much redundancy in the data that the needed evidence can be assumed to turn up at some point or another.

9.4.2 The Nature of Confirmation

This last claim is strengthened by the reflection that theory confirmation and disconfirmation are holistic and probabilistic. As Duhem and Quine have taught us, any datum may be taken to bear evidentially on any theoretical statement, given the right background assumptions. Moreover, the acceptance or rejection of a hypothesis is rarely an all-or-nothing decision, but rather a probabilistic judgment as to the likelihood of its truth or falsity. In failing to take account of the holistic and probabilistic nature of confirmation, Chomsky (and most theorists in the learnability tradition too) make the mistake of thinking that the only way a dubious grammatical hypothesis may rationally be rejected is by being explicitly falsified in the data. (Thus, for example, Chomsky's original version of the APS, discussed in §8.2, depended on the assumption that a learner could establish the falsity of the structure-independent rule for question only formation by finding in the data sentences, like *Is the man who is singing happy?*, that directly contradict its predictions.) But a learner who employed a 'softer,' stochastic learning strategy need not retain a rule until it is explicitly falsified. As I've argued before (§8.4), a learner would be quite within her rights provisionally to reject a structure-independent rule simply on the grounds that structure-dependent rules have tended to work better for her in her previous attempts to model English syntax. Her reasoning in this case would not, of course, be demonstrative: there can be no guarantee that the structure-dependent rule will turn out to be correct in this case too. But given her theoretical findings to date, the learner can nonetheless rightly surmise that a structure-dependent hypothesis is more likely to be correct than a structure-independent one. Hence a learner who can exploit probabilities in addition to brute certainties in her theorizing about language might well be in a position to learn the auxiliary fronting rule even if there were no direct evidence in the *pld* against the structure-dependent alternative.

9.4.3 The Assumption of Complete Convergence

An objection to the notion that language learners reason probabilistically and holistically might be thought to arise as follows. If different learners are exposed to slightly different data samples, and/or if they assign slightly different prior probabilities to particular hypotheses, and/or if they make slightly different choices as to how to accommodate particular pieces of data within their overall 'web of belief,' then one would predict that their theories about language might evolve in potentially very different ways. In which case, it would be utterly mysterious how all English speakers (say) manage to acquire the same language, that is, to converge on the very same (correct) grammar for English. The fact that we all acquire the same language, therefore, shows that the learning process is nowhere near as idiosyncratic as the present proposal implies.

But the Chomskyan assumption that the 'final states' of language learning are the same in all learners is dubious. Although we all agree about the grammaticality or not of many, probably most, sentences, there are none-theless cases where people's grammatical intuitions conflict. Is *Colorless green ideas sleep furiously* ungrammatical (as current grammars would suggest) or merely semantically anomalous (as it seemed to Chomsky in his *Aspects* days)? Is *Who do you believe the rumors about?* ungrammatical (as Lightfoot (1982:114) maintains)? Or is it, as I think, grammatical (though rather inelegant)? Is it really the case that no speaker of American English would say *Who do you wanna kiss you?* Chomsky himself is now prepared to admit that, strictly speaking, everyone speaks her own 'idiolect,' and that the grammarian's invocation of an 'ideal speaker–hearer' as arbiter of inter-personal disputes about grammaticality is, indeed, an idealization away from the actual facts of the matter.[15] But while idealizing away from individual differences in linguistic competence may be appropriate for the purposes of constructing a grammar of standard English, the assumption that different speakers do not differ in their state of linguistic knowledge is surely very misleading when the issue is language learnability. For it implies a problem, viz., that of explaining complete convergence among different speakers, where none may in fact exist. Now, it *may be* that there will turn out to be more convergence among speakers than can be accounted for on the sort of statistical learning model I am urging here. But this remains to be shown. The nativist may assert all he likes that speakers converge so much that one needs to postulate innate knowledge of language to account for it. But pending evidence to that effect, it seems to me to be at least as plausible to maintain instead that the amount of divergence-within-convergence in speakers' 'final states' is exactly what one would expect given the vagaries of their experience and the 'softer' constraints that a statistical learning algorithm places on their construction of grammatical theories.[16]

In sum, while idealization is a necessary part of any scientific inquiry, not all idealizations are created equal. Indeed, it is surely a part of the scientist's task to determine which idealizations are innocuous and which obscure vital features of the systems under consideration. I have argued that the nativist's idealizations—to instantaneous learning, to complete convergence, to a Popperian conception of the learner's methods of theory construction—although probably perfectly sound in case one's concern is to theorize about lan-

15. See Chomsky in Piattelli-Palmarini (1979:174ff).

16. Sampson asks: "What reason have we got for believing that these differences [in grammaticality judgments] are smaller than would be predicted from the limited size and non-identity of children's data sets?" (1980:228)

guages, can lead us badly astray in our thinking about language acquisition. In particular, as I will argue in the next section, these idealizations blind us to the myriad sources of negative evidence in the *pld*, and hence make the Logical Problem of Language Acquisition appear far more difficult than it really is.

9.5 Substitutes for Negative Data

The points raised in the previous section bear crucially on the issue of negative evidence, wherein the crux of the learnability problem for languages resides. The argument from the Logical Problem asserts that a learner who believes that all Fs are Gs, when in fact only some (or, indeed, no) Fs are Gs, will need negative data—the information that some Fs are *not* Gs—in order to shrink her hypothesis and arrive at the correct theory. But, as the argument goes on to point out, explicit information to the effect that Fs are not Gs is typically unavailable. Children are not told which strings are ungrammatical, and nor are they corrected when they utter ungrammatically. How, then, do they manage to acquire a grammar that not only generates all the sentences of their language but fails to generate all the non-sentences as well? The nativist insists that the learner's hypotheses be so strictly constrained by domain-specific innate information that she never (or very rarely) entertains a hypothesis that is too large.

Now linguists do pay lip service to the idea that there are indirect sources of negative evidence in the linguistic data: the possibility is typically mentioned, only to be set aside. The arguments in §§9.3 and 9.4, however, show that this possibility should not be ignored. Just as there are many sources of negative evidence in the data concerning curries, so there must be substantial sources of negative evidence in the data concerning language.

As a preliminary to exploring some of these sources, let me introduce some terminology. Hitherto, I have been using 'data' and 'evidence' interchangeably. Let me now stipulate that by 'data' I shall mean the facts as they are presented to experience, and by 'evidence' I shall mean those facts as they bear on the (dis)confirmation of some theory. The point of this—admittedly vague but, I think, serviceable enough—distinction is to underscore the fact that positive data can constitute *both* positive *and* negative evidence for a theory—and similarly for negative data. The positive datum that *a* is G can be positive evidence for (i.e., confirm) a theory T if, for instance, T predicts that *a* is in fact G; conversely, if T predicts that *a* is not G, then that same positive datum will be negative evidence for (i.e., disconfirm) T. Similarly, the negative datum that *b* is not G can be positive evidence for T (if T predicts that fact) or it can be negative evidence for T (if T predicts the contrary).

What the Logical Problem contends is that, in the case of language-learning, there are very few *negative data* available: the child has access to very little explicit information to the effect that such and such string of words is not a sentence of the language he is learning. And what the generalized argument (introduced with the curry example in §9.3) maintains is that the failure of experience to supply negative data is universal. But what poses a problem for a learner whose hypothesis is overgeneral is not a lack of negative data per se; it is a lack of *negative evidence*—of the means to disconfirm that hypothesis. So what we need to find, assuming that we cannot rule out altogether the possibility that learners will project hypotheses that are too large, are sources of negative evidence *other than* those provided by explicitly negative data.

9.5.1 Non-occurrence as Negative Evidence

In discussions of the Logical Problem, it is often emphasized that the non-occurrence of a particular string in the linguistic data cannot function as a negative datum: from the mere fact that she has not heard s to date, the child cannot conclude that s is not a sentence of L. For most sentences of a natural language never have been and never will be spoken. Thus the child has no way of telling whether s's non-occurrence is due to its not being a sentence or whether it's simply due to the fact that no one has had occasion to utter it yet. This being so, the child cannot use non-occurrence as negative evidence.[17]

I want to suggest, however, that in many cases, the non-appearance of a string in the primary data can legitimately be taken as constituting negative evidence. The first, fairly obvious, way that a learner could use non-occurrence as a source of negative evidence is by making predictions on the basis of her current state of knowledge, and having them disconfirmed. Think of Edna, in the grip of the idea, widespread among preschool children, that all intransitive verbs can be used as causatives.[18] Her grammar will generate sentences like *I giggled her*, meaning 'I caused her to giggle,' in addition to the perfectly acceptable *I melted it*, meaning 'I caused it to melt.' Consider the scene witnessed by Edna: Father knocks over his coffee and utters the sentence *I caused the cup to fall from the table*. Edna's grammar, however, had generated *I falled the cup off the table* as appropriate to those circumstances. Her prediction was disconfirmed by her father's utterance. The non-occurrence, in that context, of the string predicted by Edna's grammar constitutes evidence that her grammar is inadequate.

Note that in this case, the *datum* is positive: Edna's datum is that *I caused the cup to fall from the table* is a sentence. But the *evidence* it supplies is negative: the occurrence of something other than what Edna's theory led her to expect constitutes evidence against her hypothesis. This evidence is not, to be sure, decisive. Other explanations for the failure of match are available. Perhaps Edna's father misspoke; perhaps she did not hear him aright; per-

---

17. Baker (1979:536); Lightfoot (1982:17); Pinker (1989:14).
18. See Pinker (1986:61ff.; 1994:275–76).

haps both *I falled it* and *I caused it to fall* are grammatical in that context; and so on. But, as I argued above (§9.4.1), the fact that a theory may always be saved in the face of recalcitrant experience is hardly news; and it's not news either that more than a single failure of prediction may be needed to overturn a cherished hypothesis. These general facts about the holistic and probabilistic nature of the relation between theories and their evidence should not lead us to ignore the fact that non-occurrence *can* constitute negative evidence against a theory: indecisive negative evidence, but negative evidence nonetheless.

There is a second, more interesting, way in which non-occurrence can serve as negative evidence: it can serve as evidence that whole classes of objects are not instances of the kind whose extension is being learned. Consider the following strings of English words, neither of which, I'll assume, have ever been uttered:

(1) Steve enjoyed the curry.
(2) Enjoyed curry Steve the.

I want to suggest that while the non-occurrence of (1) is *not* evidence that *that* string is not a sentence, the non-occurrence of (2) *is* in fact evidence that *that* string is not a sentence of English. The reason for the asymmetry is that in the case of (1), but not in the case of (2), we have independent evidence that strings of that kind *do* occur in English. First, distinguish a string *qua string* from a string *qua instance of a particular syntactic structure*, where by 'particular syntactic structure' I mean a phrase marker with the lexical items left out, or a tree of a certain shape with the terminal nodes left empty. Thus, (1a) and (2a) are rudimentary assignments of syntactic structures to strings (1) and (2), respectively:

(1a) $[_S[_{NP} \quad][_{VP}[_V \quad][_{NP}[det][_{NP} \quad]]]]$
(2a) $[_V \quad][_N \quad][_N \quad][det]$

The relation of syntactic structures to strings is one to many: for any given structure, there will be many strings that are instances of it and that can be obtained by substituting morphemes of an appropriate syntactic category into the vacancies left in the phrase marker. Intuitively, then, there are many strings that would serve as evidence that a particular structure is allowed by the language. The occurrence of any of the following strings, for example, would be evidence that the structure (1a) is a structure of English:

(3) Bruce loves a fight.
(4) Cats hate the rain.
(5) Curries are an art form.

Further, because these sentences are all evidence that (1a) is a structure of English, the occurrence of any one of them is evidence that all the other strings instantiating that structure are sentences of the language too, even if some of those other sentences never in fact appear in the primary linguistic data. So in cases where a given structure has been encountered before in the

data, the non-occurrence of a particular instance of that structure—like (1)—
is not evidence that that string is not a sentence. For we already have positive
evidence that structures of which (1) is an instance *do* occur in the language:
structures, so to say, trump strings. In cases where a particular structure has
never been instanced in the data, by contrast, further non-occurrences of
strings of that kind constitute further evidence that that structure is not
allowed in the language. Hence, the non-occurrence of a sentence like (2),
or indeed of any sentence having the structure (2a), provides evidence that
the structure (2a) is not allowed by the language. And this, in turn, is reason
to believe that (2), which exhibits that structure, is not a sentence of English.

In sum, the non-occurrence of a string like (2) constitutes negative evidence. But what makes it negative evidence is not merely its non-occurrence
qua string: what makes it negative evidence is its non-occurrence qua
instance of a particular syntactic structure. Again, not decisive evidence, but
evidence nonetheless. For similar reasons, non-occurrence can also be evidence against the existence of certain grammatical rules. The non-occurrence
of *On the table is tough to dance*, for example, is evidence that there is no
rule of 'Prepositional Phrase-Raising' in English; whereas the non-occurrence
of *The table is tough to dance on* is *not* evidence against the existence of a
rule for NP-Raising. For in the latter case, unlike the former, we have plenty
of positive evidence that NP-raising is permissible.

It's worth noting in passing that any even minimally concrete account of
language acquisition, nativist and nonnativist, will assume (as I have done
in the foregoing) that children are able to perform some kind of structural
analysis of incoming data. What is at issue here is not *whether* children
analyze the inputs to the language acquisition mechanism, but rather the
ends to which the analysis is put. It is also inessential to my argument in
this section what categories children turn out to use in analyzing incoming
strings and formulating their structural hypotheses. While I wrote in the
foregoing as if the various types of rules and structures hypothesized by the
child are stated in terms of familiar grammatical categories like NP and VP,
the argument works equally well on the perhaps more realistic assumption
that children analyze sentences differently at different stages of language
acquisition. So, for example, a child might reason that since there have been
plenty of sentences with the structure ACTOR–ACTION in the data, the non-
occurrence of a particular sentence (say, *Barney sucks*) is not evidence
against that string's being a sentence, given that there are independent
grounds for thinking that ACTOR–ACTION is an allowable structure in English; whereas the fact that there have been no sentences of the form ACTION–
ACTION–ACTOR–THING is evidence against that structure, and hence against
instances of it like *Hit kick Barney dinosaur*.

9.5.2 Positive Data as Negative Evidence

The Logical Problem asserts that the primary data can provide a learner
who overgeneralizes with no motive to 'shrink' her hypothesis. We have just

seen how, on the contrary, the non-appearance in those data of forms predicted by her grammar may supply the learner with the means to disconfirm
an overgeneral hypothesis. Pinker describes another method, which he calls
'constraint sampling,' whereby positive data too can lead the learner toward
a less inclusive grammar.[19] In constraint sampling, the learner uses her analyses of the *pld* as a basis for restricting the application of an overgeneral
rule. Given an input sentence, the learner randomly selects one feature of
that sentence and applies it as a constraint on the rule. Each possible constraint has a nonzero probability of being hypothesized at any given time,
and every constraint adopted is retained until a sentence violating it is encountered in the input, at which point it is dropped from the constraint set.
Eventually, the child attains the correct set of constraints on the rule, and
her grammar no longer overgenerates in that respect.[20]

A feel for how the procedure works can be got by considering how a
child might learn when to affix the suffix '-s' to the verb stem in a declarative
sentence.[21] In order to do this, the child must learn that '-s' encodes present
tense, imperfective aspect, and third-person-singular subject. Suppose she
heard the sentence *The boy wants a curry*. The most general rule she could
propose consistent with this input would be something like 'Always add
'-s' to the verb stem.' This rule, however, is overgeneral and would lead the
child to make errors like **I likes it*, **We wants them*, and the like. On
Pinker's theory, a child who projected such a rule would immediately start
hypothesizing constraints on it. Hearing, say, *Dad wants a beer*, she might
propose that the '-s' encodes for an animate subject. Hence, her rule would
be 'Add an '-s' only when the subject is animate.' This rule would generate
errors like **This pen write well* and would be straightforwardly falsified by
an input like *The curry tastes good*, at which point the learner would project
a different constraint—say, that the '-s' encodes for present tense. No inputs
violating this constraint would be encountered, so it would be retained and
further constraints added to the rule. Eventually, the learner will acquire the
correct set of constraints on the rule and never be forced by the input to
abandon them.

Pinker (1984) shows how the hypothesis that children employ constraint
sampling predicts quite specific facts to do with the kinds of errors they

19. See his (1986:67–70) for an overview; the theory is presented in detail in his
(1984).

20. I should note that although Pinker's constraint-sampling heuristic is quite general,
he is a nativist, holding that the space of possible constraints for a given rule type is
specified innately by UG. It seems to me, though, that if we allow (as all models of language-
learning in fact do) that a learner can use her current state of grammatical knowledge to
perform some preliminary syntactic analysis of the input, possible constraints might be
suggested by that analysis rather than (as in Pinker's model) being selected from an innately
specified set.

21. This example is mine, not Pinker's, and is intended only to provide a simple illus-
tration of the constraint-sampling procedure; it is not meant to be an account of the actual
process by which children learn the rule in question.

make and the overall course of acquisition. He points out that this approach involves "abandoning the assumption that the child is a completely rational hypothesis-tester, one who never abandons a hypothesis unless it is contradicted by some input datum" (1986:69). The constraint-sampling approach, that's to say, *builds in* the holistic and probabilistic view of confirmation that I urged in §9.4.1. It is perhaps for this reason that Pinker is able to see sources of negative evidence in the linguistic data that other theorists in the grip of the Logical Problem have missed.

Brent (1993) offers a mathematically more rigorous account of how positive data may be exploited by a statistical learner in order to acquire restrictive syntactic rules. His computer model, 'Lerner,' learns the syntactic properties of lexical items (such as verb subcategorization frames) from text. It attends to local cues provided by other lexical items (e.g., a word preceded by *the* is likely an N; *that the* typically indicates the beginning of a clause (1993:244)) and makes hypotheses about an item's syntactic features based on the distribution of that item relative to those cues. Since the cues can be misleading, however, (e.g., sometimes a V might occur after *the*), Lerner cannot consider a single occurrence of an item in conjunction with a particular cue as conclusive evidence as to its syntactic features. In order to control for such 'noise' in the data, Lerner estimates the probability that the item of interest will occur in a misleading context and then uses a standard hypothesis-testing method for binomial frequency data to calculate whether the item actually occurs in that context often enough that all those occurrences are unlikely to be errors—often enough, that is, that the putatively misleading context is not a misleading context at all. While Lerner uses cues (e.g., punctuation, capitalization) that are unavailable to children learning language, and hence cannot be taken as a model of how an actual child learns lexical syntax, Brent's model is of interest not just because it recognizes (as does Pinker's) that learning must proceed stochastically, but also because it specifies a method whereby error rates may be estimated, thus enabling the learner to extract a useful signal from noisy data.

9.5.3 Negative Data as Negative Evidence

The notion that there are virtually no negative data available to children— the notion that children have no access to information about what isn't a sentence of the language they are learning—forms the mainstay of the argument from the Logical Problem and is an outgrowth of research carried out by Roger Brown and his colleagues in the late 1960s and early 1970s.[22] One study in particular, Brown and Hanlon (1970), is invariably cited in support of the "no negative data" claim. Using their analysis of transcripts of conversations between three children and their mothers over a period of

---

22. E.g., Brown, Cazden, and Bellugi (1969); Brown and Hanlon (1970); Brown (1973).

years, Brown and Hanlon found, first, that parents were about as likely to comprehend a grammatical as an ungrammatical sentence uttered by their children, and second, that parents' explicit expressions of approval and disapproval did not correlate with the syntactic well-formedness of what their children said. From this, they concluded that children do not use negative feedback from adults in their acquisition of syntax.

Perhaps because overt failures of comprehension and explicit disapproval ("No, Hermie, that's not how you say it") are among the most obvious sources of negative data that might in principle be available to learners, Brown and Hanlon's findings were taken by learnability theorists and many within the linguistics community to demonstrate the non-existence and irrelevance of negative data *tout court*. Among developmental psychologists, however, the view that feedback and correction are not involved in the acquisition of syntax (or language more generally) has been much more controversial.[23] Noting that despite its influence among learnability theorists, "[t]he Brown & Hanlon (1970) result, unlike many other results in the language acquisition literature, has not been replicated or challenged" (1984: 82), Hirsh-Pasek, Treiman, and Schneidermann attempted to verify the earlier findings. Studying recorded conversations between forty mother–child pairs, they found, as did Brown and Hanlon, that explicit disapproval and approval are unrelated to well-formedness. However, they also found, as Brown and Hanlon did not, that nonetheless "the language learning environment does present subtle cues that distinguish between well-formed and ill-formed sentences" (1984:81). Mothers of two-year-olds, for example, repeated their children's ill-formed utterances significantly more often than they repeated well-formed sentences: 20.8% of flawed sentences were repeated, as opposed to 12.0% of well-formed sentences. Further, virtually all of the repetitions of flawed sentences corrected the children's error. While no similar patterns of differential response to the utterances of three-, four-, and five-year-olds were found—perhaps, the authors speculate, because children make fewer errors and hence need less correction as they get older (1984:86–87)—Hirsch-Pasek, Treiman, and Schneidermann conclude that the Brown and Hanlon (1970) finding "should not be taken so broadly to conclude that parents are INSENSITIVE to the forms of their children's utterances" (1984:87, emphasis in original) and suggest that "the environment might provide subtle cues that could help the child to narrow down his hypotheses about candidate grammars" (1984:87)

Expanding on this research, Demetras, Post, and Snow (1986) analyzed conversations between four mother–child pairs. They found that mothers' exact (i.e., verbatim) repetitions of their two-year-olds' utterances function like explicit approval (e.g., "Yes, that's right") in that they almost always follow the children's well-formed sentences. By contrast, mothers' contracted

---

23. E.g., Bohannon and Stanowicz (1988); Bohannon, MacWhinney, and Snow (1990); Demetras, Post and Snow (1986); Hirsch-Pasek, Trieman, and Schneiderman (1984); Moerk (1991); K.E. Nelson et al. (1984).

and expanded repetitions (which correct the child's error) and clarification questions ("What?"), all of which tend to break the "flow" of conversation, typically follow their children's ill-formed utterances. While acknowledging the limited size and diversity of their sample, Demetras, Post, and Snow conclude that "implicit . . . feedback does exist for these homogeneous dyads, and is produced differentially to [well-formed] and [ill-formed] utterances such that children could rely on it as a basis for adjusting or confirming their rules" (1986:286).

In an important and elegant study, Bohannon and Stanowicz (1988) broadened and systematized the search for negative data. They looked at the children's interactions not just with their mothers but with both parents and with other adults; they distinguished three types of child error (semantic, syntactic, and phonological); and they coded for ten different types of parental response: exact repetitions (verbatim repetitions of the child's utterance); contracted repetitions (repetitions of part of the child's utterance); recasts (utterances with the same meaning as the child's intended meaning, but in a different form); expanded repetitions (repetitions that add new information); clarification questions (like "What?"); exact, contracted, recast, and expanded repetitious questions (questions that repeat, with or without modification, part of the child's utterance); and nonrepetitious questions.

Their analysis confirmed Brown and Hanlon's finding that parents overtly correct almost all of their children's semantic errors (parents correct semantic errors 88 percent of the time; non-parents do only 6 percent of the time). However, their results (like those just discussed) cast considerable doubt upon Brown and Hanlon's findings vis-à-vis parents' ignoring of grammatical errors. Although they found that only 34 percent of syntactic errors and 35 percent of phonological errors receive obviously negative feedback (e.g., recasts, expansions, nonrepetitious clarification questions), Bohannon and Stanowicz argue that children may nonetheless extract reliable information as to the well-formedness of their utterances from such other, superficially neutral, types of feedback as do occur. For example, more than 90 percent of adults' exact repetitions follow children's well-formed utterances, whereas more than 70 percent of their recasts and expansions follow ill-formed utterances. A similar pattern was found for clarification questions. Moreover, Bohannon and Stanowicz point out (1988:687), not only do adults flag children's errors in these ways, they also provide corrected models for the children to review (parents provide this helpful service about twice as often as non-parents). In addition, all adults were twice as likely to correct utterances that contained a single error as they were to correct those that contained multiple errors (1988:687–88), thus facilitating the child's identification of her mistake. So although the different kinds of response distinguished by Bohannon and Stanowicz do not correlate anywhere near perfectly with the well-formedness of children's utterances, there is nonetheless a wealth of information about well-formedness to be gleaned from the regularities in others' reactions to a child's conversational efforts. Bohannon and Stanowicz conclude: "theories of language that use the no-negative-evidence issue as their raison d'être may be on shaky ground" (1988:688).

In another intriguing study, Moerk (1991) performed a reanalysis of some of Brown and Hanlon's original data, finding in the Brown "Eve" corpus (and displaying ruthlessly in his paper) numerous instances where Eve's mother corrects, challenges, requests clarification of, and outright repudiates the child's utterance. In the twenty-hour sample analyzed, Eve's misuse of noun labels is almost always challenged by her mother, who usually also supplies her with positive evidence as to the correct label, as in "No, not band-aids, rubber-bands" (Moerk 1991:225). Eve's failures correctly to use auxiliaries or to mark verb phrases for tense and modality are likewise frequent candidates for correction, as are her misuses of determiners and functors such as bound morphemes and prepositions. (Moerk remarks that almost all of Eve's mistakes in using prepositions were corrected, her mother at one time providing corrective feedback twenty times in one two-hour period.) Eve made few errors in word order, Moerk says, but those which occurred were almost always corrected by her mother, and many of her mother's conversational expansions of Eve's ill-formed utterances contained corrections of her syntax. While nonquantitative in approach, Moerk's paper is significant in that it demonstrates that even Brown's own transcripts reveal an abundance of corrective feedback in the primary linguistic data.

Brown and Hanlon (1970), it seems, is an outdated shibboleth in the learnability literature. Although it added an important nail to the coffin of behaviorism and constituted an essential incentive to the surge of empirical and theoretical investigations into the nature of the *pld* during the 1980s, this study can no longer be taken to be the last word on the existence or usefulness of negative data in the *pld*. The research discussed in this section confirms what any parent not personally involved in debates about learnability will tell you, namely, that it is simply false that parents do not correct their children's ungrammatical utterances. There are plenty of cues in the child's linguistic environment that a savvy learner (especially one who is sensitive to relative frequencies) could exploit in order to discover what *not* to say.[24]

9.5.4 Using Negative Evidence

As almost all the researchers in this area recognize, however, it is one thing to show that negative data exist and another to show that children can and do make use of them. Morgan and Travis (1989) argue that corrections occur with insufficient frequency and regularity to have any effect on language-learning, including children's ability to recover from overgeneralizations. Starting from Hirsch-Pasek, Treiman, and Schneidermann's observation that errors in older children tend to go uncorrected, Morgan and Travis argue that "if 3-, 4- and 5-year-olds make novel overgeneralizations

---

24. I am indebted to J. D. Trout for steering me toward the literature discussed in this section.

that are not corrected, then it must be concluded that sufficient negative evidence is NOT present in language input, even if corrections do appear briefly in the early stages of acquisition" (1989:537). For, they argue, negative evidence will be useful to the learner only if (1) "corrective responses [are] more likely to follow the ungrammatical than the grammatical form of the construction"; (2) "for each type of overgeneralization error the child makes, the child is systematically provided with some recognizable form of correction"; and (3) such "correction continues until the child succeeds in remedying that error" (1989:535).

Using Brown's transcripts of Adam, Eve and Sara, Morgan and Travis examined mothers' responses to three different kinds of overgeneralization error (viz., inflectional over-regularizations of past tenses, plurals, and possessives, as in *teached, mans* and *mine's*) and to the child's omission of inverted auxiliary verbs in Wh-questions (e.g., *What that?* as opposed to *What is that?*). Distinguishing between a variety of different types of parental response (none, expansion, imitation, clarification question, confirmation question, move on) and child utterance (grammatical, ungrammatical, lexical error, fragment, unintelligible), they ascertained that for two of the children, expansions and clarification questions occurred more often after ill-formed than well-formed utterances, and that for all children, expansions were more likely to follow ungrammatical utterances and imitations were more likely to follow grammatical utterances. However, although these results are broadly in accord with those of the studies discussed earlier, Morgan and Travis draw from them a quite different conclusion. Since (as they also observed) the likelihood of a child's receiving corrective feedback declines with age and tends to die out before the errors do, feedback could not, in their view, be contributing to the learning process. Moreover, they argue, because the frequency of correction is inversely proportional to the frequency of a given type of error, children do not get corrective feedback when they most need it, that is, when their errors have become entrenched. Hence, although "some parental responses may sometimes supply the perspicacious child with correction, we fail to see sufficient evidence to warrant the conclusion that language input generally incorporates negative information . . . we failed to find evidence supporting the possibility that children can recognize such [probabilistic] cues" (Morgan and Travis 1989:551).

Marcus argues likewise that feedback is irrelevant to language acquisition: maybe it exists, but children make no use of it. For, first, children in different families and/or cultures get different amounts and kinds of feedback (1993:69–77). Since all children are guaranteed to learn language despite the fact that not all children can be guaranteed the same sorts of feedback, "there is no evidence that noisy feedback is required for language learning" (1993:53). Marcus argues, second, that noisy feedback such as these studies describe could not be used in learning because it cannot provide decisive evidence for or against the grammaticality of a given construction unless extremely unrealistic assumptions are made about the learner's linguistic behavior and learning methods (1993:60–66). For example, he calculates that, given the kinds of feedback Bohannon and Stanowicz (1988) describe, a child would have to repeat a given string eighty-five times (and measure others' reactions to it) in order to reach a 99 percent degree of certainty in her judgments as to its grammaticality. Since children attain a state of reasonable certainty as to what the sentences of their language are *without* saying the same things over and over again like parrots, feedback must be playing no significant role.

But these sorts of conclusions are, I think, unwarranted. Morgan and Travis' requirement that all types of overgeneralization errors be systematically corrected until the errors disappear from the child's speech seems much too strong. That one type of error goes unremarked is surely no reason to think that feedback is not involved in the correction of other types of error. As Demetras, Post, and Snow (1986:287) argue,

> the failure of occurrence of negative feedback to some [ill-formed] utterances presents a serious problem to the child only if it is assumed that the child is working on acquiring the entire grammatical system at once and that every instance of positive feedback will confirm the rule the preceding child utterance instantiates. If the child is indeed working on different problems at different times, then some confirmation of [ill-formed] utterances [as occurs when a parent fails to react to an error] may not constitute a serious source of noise in the feedback system.

Nor does the fact that correction may not persist until the error disappears altogether show it to be inefficacious. As we have seen before (§9.4.2), confirmation—or in this case, disconfirmation—is holistic and probablistic. The fact (which seems to be entailed by all these kinds of results) that the information provided by feedback *alone* could not and does not suffice to falsify a rule, does not show that feedback plays no disconfirmatory role at all.

Similar remarks apply to Marcus' arguments. First, the fact that some children may be denied useful feedback does not indicate that those who are lucky enough to receive it do not exploit it in their acquisition of language. Nor does the fact that some children may use feedback in acquiring language show that a child who has no access to it is doomed to a life of muteness. For there is no reason to insist that all children must make use of the same sorts of evidence to the same extent. There are many different ways that children can exploit the linguistic environment for evidence bearing on their grammatical hypotheses. A child who lacks feedback will place greater reliance on other sources of negative evidence, while a child in a feedback-rich environment will presumably make free use of it. Feedback, in short, may be extremely useful to a language learner without being in any way 'required' for language-learning.[25]

---

25. MacWhinney likewise emphasizes that because there exist many sources of evidence about language in the child's environment, "the presence or absence of any particular support for language learning is not critical, since the other capacities can then move in to keep the system buffered and on track" (1989:99). K.E. Nelson et al. (1984) also point

Marcus' second argument is likewise flawed. First, while it is indeed implausible to think that a child will try out a given *string* eighty-five times to determine its grammaticality, it is not so implausible to think that she might repeatedly use a given *structure* or *rule,* and use feedback to judge the appropriateness of that structure or rule. Given that they can make some (not necessarily very sophisticated) analysis of their own and others' utterances, that is to say, children may achieve a high degree of certainty as to the appropriateness of a given string not by repeating the string itself, but by repeatedly invoking the rule that generates it or using the structure it instantiates. More important, while it may be the case that if noisy feedback were the *only* source of information a child had about her language, she would have to repeat a sentence eighty-five times to figure out whether it is grammatical, feedback about their own utterances is not the only source of information about language available to children. In judging that a sentence such as *I do not like green eggs and ham* is grammatical, for example, the child need not engineer eighty-five occasions on which to utter that sentence and wait for others' feedback. Instead, she can rely on the wealth of positive evidence as to that string's grammaticality that she has obtained through hearing it read to her fifty times every night for the past six months. Similarly, children can use myriad sources of information in addition to that provided by parental feedback in their judgments about ungrammaticality. The fact that no one else ever says *On the table is tough to dance* (or, indeed, any other string plausibly analyzed as an instance of prepositional phrase-raising), for instance, is evidence against that string's grammaticality that is quite independent of whatever evidence is supplied by others' failures to comprehend or corrections of the child's own utterance of it.[26]

In short, there is no reason to think that feedback cannot be used by children in learning language. On the contrary, there seems every reason to suppose that it could be, and there are inklings too in the empirical literature that it is. K.E. Nelson et al. (1984), for example, describe a number of ways that mothers' adjustments in their speech to their children's state of knowledge at various ages affect the children's linguistic development. Children (aged twenty-two to twenty-seven months) in their study whose mothers provided them with moderately recast versions of their own ungrammat-

to the likelihood that "there are *many* components of input for most children that are *not necessary* for their syntactic growth," while arguing that nonetheless "even limited quantities of certain important input elements may play sufficient or catalytic roles in acquisition, no matter how strong the evidence that they are not absolutely necessary elements" (1984:47).

26. Marcus' mistake in this argument is similar to that made by Gordon, who in defending the irrelevance of Bohannon and Stanowicz's findings to the issue of language acquisition argues that "the burden of proof is clearly on Bohannon and Stanowicz (1988) to demonstrate that natural languages are formally learnable without innate knowledge when partial and inconsistent feedback is available" (1990:219). But, as I've argued here, the task is to show actual learnability from actual data: that languages are not formally learnable from inconsistent feedback alone is neither surprising nor alarming.

ical utterances acquired language more quickly than those whose mothers did not supply them with corrected examples (1984:45–46). Farrer (1987) shows that children are more likely to repeat a morpheme from an adult recast than from a nonrepetitious adult utterance. Bohannon and Symons (1988) show that children are more likely to imitate adult recasts and expansions than they are exact adult repetitions (25.6 percent of recasts and expansions are imitated, while only 3.6 percent of exact repetitions are). So while Marcus, and Morgan and Travis may seek to minimize their importance, it seems to me that studies (such as those discussed in the previous section) demonstrating the existence of parental feedback are of critical importance to our understanding of language acquisition. They show that *negative data*—explicit information as to what sentences are not—*do exist* in the child's environment, albeit in a noisy form. As such, they do much to resolve, at least in principle, the Logical Problem of Language Acquisition. Of course it remains to be shown in more detail *how* children manage to make use of the negative data that feedback provides. But this question, while to be sure formidable enough, is nonetheless an empirical question, a question of detail. Rather than facing the mystery of how children could learn a restrictive grammar in the total absence of negative evidence, we now confront the problem of how they do in fact learn a restrictive grammar, given the kinds and amounts of negative evidence that are available to them.

In a recent survey of related developments in *Science,* Seidenberg (1997) argues that inquiry into the kinds of statistical or probabilistic learning models that could exploit these kinds of 'noisy' data promises to revolutionize our understanding of language acquisition. Studies like those just discussed show that negative data exist in the *pld*. Studies like those of Saffran, Aslin, and Newport (1996, discussed in §8.5.1) confirm that children possess an extraordinary sensitivity to, and facility for using, statistical information about their linguistic environment. Research into the formal aspects of probabilistic and statistical reasoning proceeds apace in a variety of fields, philosophy very much included. Computer science, especially with the advent of connectionism, promises us machines that can more naturally implement the 'softer' constraints of probabilistic reasoning processes.[27] The future of research into language acquisition is now, more than ever before, wide open and wildly exciting.

9.6 The Dialectical Role of the Logical Problem

What, then, of nativism? Seidenberg gleefully predicts the demise of nativist approaches to language-learning under the pressure of these new develop-

---

27. Though recall Brent's (1993) 'Lerner,' discussed in §9.5.2, as evidence that research on statistical learning is not exclusively the province of the connectionist.

ments: the new approach to modeling learning "retains the idea that innate capacities constrain language learning, but calls into question whether they include knowledge of grammatical structure" (1997:1599). I am not so sure as to nativism's long-term prospects. For, as we will see in chapter 11, there are other arguments that nativists may make in support of their contention that the mechanism for language acquisition is unique.

I am sure, though, that evidence for nativism will come, if it does, from sources other than the Logical Problem of Language Acquisition. My overall conclusion in this chapter has been that although the Logical Problem supports (DS), the claim that domain-specific information is necessary for language-learning, it does nothing to support (I), the claim that that information is innate. There are many domains in which learning unproblematically takes place in the apparent absence of negative data. So unless we are prepared to accept 'culinary faculties' for learning about curries, 'automotive faculties' for learning about cars, 'botanical faculties' for learning about trees and flowers, and so on, we should resist the inference to faculties in the linguistic case. In §§9.4–9.6, I attempted to show how the Logical Problem's apparent force derives from a conception of the learning task that is misleading in a number of ways, thus providing something more than mere intuition in support of my contention that an inference to nativism based on it is invalid. Among the problematic features of this conception are its failure to recognize the probabilistic and holistic nature of confirmation and its related conflation of negative evidence (which may have many sources) with explicitly negative data (which are claimed—erroneously, as it turns out—to be few and far between). Given these shortcomings, I conclude, the recent obsession in the literature on language-learning with the argument from the Logical Problem is just a mistake.

Or is it? Stephen Pinker has claimed in response to this kind of critique that the Logical Problem is not in fact *intended* by nativists to be an argument for their position (private communication). On his view, linguists' discussion of the Logical Problem is not meant to incline us toward any one type of learning theory over another: it is meant only to delineate the constraints that any acceptable such theory—of whatever stamp—must satisfy. But while I am prepared to believe that Pinker himself means to invoke the Logical Problem only to make vivid the difficulties involved in providing an acquisition theory, I do not think that his view of the Problem's overall dialectical role is entirely accurate. It seems to me that consideration of the Logical Problem, especially when supplemented with additional considerations like those adduced in §§9.2 and 9.3, *is* an argument for nativism over empiricism (though not, I have suggested, a particularly good one). And it seems to me, further, that when linguists *present* the Logical Problem of Language Acquisition, something very much like this argument is what they have in mind. Take Lightfoot, for instance. Immediately after presenting the Problem and discussing an example where children learn a rule in the absence of negative data, he writes—in what certainly appears to be an argumentative spirit:

> If the child's linguistic experience does not provide the basis for establish-
> ing some particular aspect of linguistic knowledge, some other source for
> that knowledge must exist. That aspect must be known a priori in the
> sense that it is available independently of linguistic experience. It may be
> available genetically or arise as a consequence of some other non-linguistic
> experience; I shall gloss over this distinction and speak only of genetic
> determination. (Lightfoot 1982:18)

Or consider Lasnik. Although he does not actually make the argument, Lasnik also seems to view the Problem as the basis of an argument for nativism,
beginning his (1989) paper on learnability with the following summation of
the status quo:

> Much of the recent discussion of language learnability has centered around
> the absence for the learner of negative evidence and the implications of
> that absence. The basic argument has been reiterated many times: If the
> child does not have access to negative evidence . . . then Universal Gram-
> mar presumably does not make available choices that can only be resolved
> by such evidence. (Lasnik 1989:89)

Even Pinker himself, in what may be a slip of the pen, seems at times to
invoke the Logical Problem in an argumentative vein. In his (1990), for
instance, he appears to be saying that the Problem provides us with reason
to abandon (a version of) empiricism and adopt (a version of) the nativist's
(DS):

> without negative evidence, if a child guesses too large a language, the
> world can never tell her she's wrong. This has several consequences. For
> one thing, the most general learning algorithm one might conceive of—
> one that is capable of hypothesizing any grammar . . . —is in trouble with-
> out negative evidence. Without negative evidence . . . there is no general-
> purpose, all-powerful learning machine; a machine must in some sense
> "know" something about the constraints in the domain in which it is
> learning. (1990:204)

In fact, the argument from the Logical Problem has now more or less
usurped other arguments for nativism in the introductory chapters and sections of books and papers on language acquisition. So while Pinker may be
right to maintain that the Logical Problem is not *always* intended to be an
argument motivating nativism, I think it must be conceded that the Problem's dialectical role is often highly ambiguous. If for no other reason than
to resolve this ambiguity, then, the argument deserves examination.

In the next chapter, we will continue our assessment of the APS and the
Logical Problem, and examine a second argument that nativists might
advance for (I), the claim that the task-specific information needed for
language-learning is innately known. This 'Iterated APS argument,' as I call
it, was outlined briefly in §9.1 and claims that since learning UG from the
pld is even harder than learning an individual grammar, one cannot sensibly
subscribe to (DS) without also accepting (I). I shall argue that, on the con-

trary, accepting (DS) and denying (I) is a perfectly reasonable thing to do in the light of the evidence and arguments so far considered. However, in chapter 11 we will examine a variety of other reasons for thinking that the constraints on language acquisition are not only domain specific, but possibly innate as well.

10

The Role of Universal Grammar in
Language-Learning

I argued in chapter 2 that one may be a nativist about a given domain in virtue of one's postulation of a task-specific acquisition mechanism to account for learning in that area. What makes a person an empiricist about that branch of knowledge, by contrast, is her contention that there is nothing particularly distinctive about the methods we use for mastering it. Chapters 8 and 9 dealt with arguments from the poverty of the stimulus, the preeminent means by which linguistic nativists have sought to motivate their conjectures about a dedicated language faculty. I argued that, contrary to received opinion, reflection on the poverty of the stimulus gives no support to nativism about language-learning. While the sheer number and variety of possible linguistic hypotheses indicate that learners' choices among competing views at particular times must be constrained by their prior knowledge about their language, there is no reason to think that the requisite constraints are known innately. Once young children's striking ability to extract information from their environment is appreciated, and the diversity and richness of the cues contained in the linguistic data are acknowledged, linguistic nativism loses its aura of invincible inevitability.

Running as a subtext to these arguments has been my contention that the explanatory resources of empiricism are more abundant than is generally recognized. In particular, I have argued, empiricists' postulation of a domain-neutral learning mechanism need not commit them to the implausible view that nothing but domain-neutral constraints on theory construction determine a learner's choice of linguistic hypotheses. An Enlightened empiricist can hold that the mechanism for language-learning is a general-purpose one, yet grant that at any given time (except $t=0$), learners' choices of theories will be conditioned by their prior linguistic knowledge, that is, by the knowledge about language *that they have previously gleaned from their experience*. Enlightened empiricism thus grants the nativist's insight that learning must be constrained by task-specific knowledge, while denying that those constraints are fixed, in advance, by features of the learning device. Although I certainly would not want to claim that the considerations adduced in the previous chapters "prove" empiricism about language, I do think they indicate that an empiricist approach to language-learning has far more potential than has recently been allowed. The notion that children could learn what they need to know about language without the help of a dedicated language faculty deserves a far more searching examination than it has been accorded over the last thirty-odd years.

10.1 The Argument from the Poverty of the Stimulus Reiterated

But, nativists will leap to object, the Enlightened empiricist's 'explanation' of language-learning is chimerical. In denying that the task-specific constraints on learners' linguistic theorizing are innately known, the empiricist leaves herself with no viable explanation of how those constraints are acquired. Her claim that the principles governing children's syntactic hypotheses are learned from experience is false, and quite demonstrably so. For in conceding the nativist's 'core' claim (DS), the Enlightened empiricist is apparently committing herself to the view that the Universal Grammar ('UG') is learned from experience, and learned from experience, moreover, prior to children's learning any particular grammar for their language. But how could this possibly be? If there is even a prima facie problem in explaining how a child learns the rules of a grammar from the primary linguistic data, there's a very much worse difficulty in explaining how she learns the more abstract and unintuitive principles of the UG from those data. No surveys of corpora or children's speech are needed to establish that a person who knows no languages at all is in no position to formulate, let alone test, universal hypotheses about languages qua languages. It's at best utterly unclear how a child could learn UG prior to learning her own natural language, and absent some explanation of how this feat is pulled off, the empiricist's explanatory pretensions are empty. Her 'answer' to the language acquisition problem is really only a deferral of it.

This 'iterated' argument from the poverty of the stimulus, as I'll call it, is perhaps the most rhetorically powerful item in the nativist's polemical toolbox. Even if co-opting the nativist's (DS) enables the empiricist to explain how children might learn that in English, one should not use *He thinks Steve should go* to mean that Steve thinks that he (himself) should go, it remains unexplained how they acquire the information—in this case, apparently, Principle C of Binding Theory—that enables them to do it. Whatever intuitive force is possessed by the argument from the poverty of the stimulus formulated (as in chapters 8 and 9) as concerning the learning of particular grammatical rules for particular languages, is possessed by it tenfold or a hundredfold when it is formulated as a puzzle about the acquisition of UG, the rules governing languages in general.

The iterated argument, however, depends on the assumption that in conceding the Weak nativist's (DS), the empiricist is thereby affirming the Chomskyan nativist's (U). It turns, that is to say, on the presumption that the domain-specific principles that the empiricist agrees are required for language-learning are those of the Universal Grammar. I argued in chapter 7 that this hypothesis needs defense. It seems on the face of it possible that the information that one needs for language-learning should turn out to be other than that supplied in the theory of UG. And if that were the case, then the ability of a child to acquire that information from experience remains at least an open question. To the extent that the Chomskyan case for (U) is plausible, then, Enlightened empiricism is implausible. But to the extent that it's not, empiricism still stands a chance. This chapter will be concerned to examine the evidence for (U), and thereby to evaluate further the empiricist's prospects.

10.2 Chomsky's (U): True by Stipulation?

Chomsky's conviction that Linguistic Theory is in some sense descriptive of the language faculty—and hence of relevance to understanding the sorts of information that constrain language learning—derives in part from his conception of the linguistic enterprise. On Chomsky's view, linguistics is a branch of psychology. As described in his (1988:3), it endeavors to answer four questions, each broadly psychological in focus:

1. What is the system of knowledge [that speakers of a language have developed]? What is in the mind/brain of the speaker of English or Spanish or Japanese?
2. How does this system of knowledge arise in the mind/brain?
3. How is this knowledge put to use in speech (or secondary systems such as writing)?
4. What are the physical mechanisms that serve as the material basis for this system of knowledge and for the use of this knowledge?

Linguistics as currently practiced, Chomsky admits, has nothing to say about question (4), which is "still on the horizon" (Chomsky 1988:6), and little to say about (3). The full explanation of how our knowledge of language is put to use, he argues, would involve finding answers to what he calls the 'perception problem' and the 'production problem.' And while linguistics can make a contribution to the explanation of how we interpret language (the perception problem), neither the linguist nor anyone else has much idea of how to deal with the production problem—with the problem of "what we say and why we say it" (Chomsky 1988:5). But, he maintains, linguistics does provide answers to questions (1) and (2). For the linguist's grammars *just are* descriptions of "[w]hat . . . we know when we are able to speak and understand a language" (Chomsky 1988:133). And Linguistic Theory *just is* a description of "the fixed and invariant principles that constitute the human language faculty" (Chomsky 1988:133)—that is, of the inborn cognitive substrate that, in interaction with our linguistic experience, enables us to learn the grammar of our native tongue.

To theorize about the grammar of a language, then, is the very same thing as to theorize about the competence of its speakers: a grammar is a theory about what speakers know about their language. And theorizing about UG (that is, doing Linguistic Theory) is theorizing about the initial state of the language acquisition device (or, as Chomsky sometimes calls it, LT(H,L))[1]:

> Proceeding in this way, the scientist can develop some rich and interesting hypotheses about UG, hence LT(H,L). . . . Linguistic theory is a theory of UG incorporated into LT(H,L). . . . Linguistic theory, the theory of UG . . . is an innate property of the human mind. (Chomsky 1975b:33–34)

> [W]e can proceed to spell out in specific detail a schematism that characterizes the initial state. Call this schematism "universal grammar." We may think of universal grammar as, in effect, the genetic program, the schematism that permits the range of possible realizations that are the possible human languages. (Chomsky 1978/1980:233–34)

So it simply makes no sense to ask whether a particular grammar is a true theory of speakers. And it makes no sense to ask whether a certain element of UG is implicated in language-learning. If it's part of the grammar, it's ipso facto part of speakers' competence. If it's part of UG, it's ipso facto incorporated into the initial structure of the acquisition device: "UG will specify what language learning must achieve, if it takes place successfully. Thus UG will be a significant component of LT(H,L)" (Chomsky 1975b:29).

Many linguists have followed Chomsky in taking their theories to be addressing such psychological questions and have accepted, seemingly, that (U)—the claim that describing UG and describing the constraints on learners' hypotheses are one and the same—can be made true by fiat.[2] Nonetheless, Chomsky's seconding of linguistics to psychology has received a certain amount of criticism. In the next section, I survey some pertinent complaints, with the aim of defending the contention of chapter 7 that, Chomsky's stip-

---

1. LT(H,L) is a function characterizing the Learning Theory (for Humans, in the domain of Language).

2. See, e.g., Koster, van Riemsdijk, and Vergaud (1980); Huybregts, Koster, and van Riemsdijk (1981:1); Lightfoot (1982:22); Sells (1985:3–6); van Riemsdijk and Williams (1986:3–5) for statements endorsing the Chomskyan position. Although it is difficult to overstate the extent to which this view dominates linguistics, there are some renegades. One breakaway group, led by Joan Bresnan, endorses Chomsky's idea that linguistics is psychological, but argues that if grammars are to be theories of speakers, they must take a form very different from that envisaged by the Chomskyan. See Bresnan (1978) and Bresnan and Kaplan (1982) for statements of the lexical functional grammarian's position. Another rebel coterie, inspired by Gerald Gazdar, denies the psychological interpretation for linguistics altogether. See Sells (1985:ch. 3) for an outline of Gazdar's generalized phrase-structure grammar. See Wasow (1985) for a survey of all three movements.

ulations notwithstanding, there *is* a real issue as to whether or not (U) is true.

10.3 What Is Linguistics About?

Chomsky dismisses questions, like mine, as to whether Linguistic Theory is true of the language faculty (or whether grammars are true of speakers' competence) as the manifestations of a misguided scrupulosity. Demanding to know "what is 'psychological reality' as distinct from 'truth, in a certain domain'?" (1980:107), he likens questioning grammars' 'psychological reality'—their truth in the domain of psychology—to questioning the reality of the entities and processes quantified over in chemistry:

> We may ask whether the linguist's constructions are correct or whether they should be modified or replaced. But there are few meaningful questions about the "reality" of these constructions—the "psychological reality," to use the common but highly misleading term—just as there are few meaningful questions about the "physical reality" of the chemist's constructions. (Chomsky 1988:6)

Asking whether a grammar is true of speakers' psychologies is just asking whether it is true, period. The notion that a grammar might possess theoretical virtues like truth or assertability or empirical adequacy (or whatever) and yet fail to be psychologically real is just nonsense.

But that there are substantive questions to be asked about the psychological reality of the linguist's constructs must, I think, be acknowledged. For while Chomsky is right that questioning the 'physical reality' of the entities and processes postulated in a true (assertable, empirically adequate, etc.) chemical theory would be silly, the case of linguistics is quite unlike that of chemistry. The interpretation of chemical theory is well understood and agreed to on all sides, and it is thus relatively clear what ontological commitments one makes in accepting chemistry as true (etc.).[3] By contrast, there is considerable controversy as to what the proper interpretation for theories in linguistics is, and it is correspondingly much less clear what commitments one makes in embracing a particular linguistic theory.

For as Chomsky freely acknowledges (1986:28–29), terms like 'grammar' (and related terms such as 'universal grammar' and 'linguistic theory') are used in modern generative linguistics with a three-way ambiguity. First, 'grammar' is used to refer to a *theory of a language*, where languages are considered in abstraction from the people who speak them, in much the same way as (say) political powers, like the power to veto an act of Congress, can be considered in abstraction from the individuals who exercise them. Chomsky calls languages in this sense 'E-languages' (1986:19), and though he asserts that "[this] concept appears to play no role in the theory

---

3. Pace the participants in the debate over scientific realism!

of language" (1986:26), and that "the concept of E-language has no clear status in the study of language and is best abandoned" (1991a:10), he himself has frequently used the term 'grammar' as if it were a theory of language in exactly this sense:

> [T]he syntactic component of a generative grammar [is] the rules that specify the well-formed strings of minimal syntactically functioning units . . . and assign structural information of various kinds both to these strings and to strings that deviate from well-formedness in certain respects. (Chomsky 1965:3)

> The grammar . . . simply characterizes the properties of sentences, much as the principles of arithmetic determine the properties of numbers. (Chomsky 1980:222)

Similarly, although he himself prefers not to speak this way, he acknowledges that there is a perfectly good sense in which UG can be said to be a theory that consists of "statements that are true of many or all human languages, perhaps a set of conditions satisfied by the E-languages that count as human languages" (1986:20).

> [W]e can define 'universal grammar' (UG) as the system of principles, conditions, and rules that are elements or properties of all human languages not merely by accident but by necessity—of course I mean biological, not logical, necessity. Thus UG can be taken as expressing 'the essence of human language.' (Chomsky 1975b:29)

Second, 'grammar' in Chomsky's writings is used to denote a *theory of competence*: grammars are theories of "exactly what one knows when one knows a language" (1986:24). "The person who has acquired knowledge of a language has internalized a system of rules that relate sound and meaning in a particular way. The linguist constructing a grammar of a language is in effect proposing a hypothesis concerning this internalized system" (1968/72: 26). Grammars in this sense are claimed to describe the "distinct system of the mind/brain" (1986:25) that constitutes a component of the larger psychological conglomerate that gives rise to speakers' linguistic performance, that is, to "the actual use of language in concrete situations" (1965:4). Chomsky still calls a grammar in this sense a 'theory of language,' only here, the language in question is the 'I-language,' that is, the "system of knowledge of language attained and internally represented in the mind/brain" (1986: 24). It is a "component of the mind/brain" (1991a:13) of the mature speaker. Correspondingly, UG, in this usage, is a theory of the initial state of the language faculty; it "is the study of one aspect of biological endowment, analogous to the study of the innate principles that determine that we will have a human rather than an insect visual system" (1986:40).

Third, 'grammar' has been used to denote not the *theory* of the I-language—not the *theory* of competence—but the I-language (competence) itself. Chomsky writes in his (1980:91), for instance, that he is "assuming grammatical competence to be a system of rules that generate and relate . . .

representations of form and meaning," and that "knowledge of the language of this [ideal] speech community is uniformly represented in the mind of each of its members. . . . Let us refer to this representation . . . as the grammar of the language." (1980:220). Similarly, 'Universal Grammar' and 'linguistic theory' are used to denote not merely the linguist's theory of the initial state of the language-learner, but also that state itself. So, for example, we read that "[l]inguistic theory, the theory of the Universal Grammar . . . is an innate property of the human mind" (Chomsky 1975b:34).

Chomsky appears unconcerned about the systematic ambiguity of 'grammar'—as denoting a theory of a language, a theory of a speaker's competence, or a speaker's competence itself—in his writings (see 1965:25; 1980: 220; 1986:29). But this three-way ambiguity is central to establishing the sensibleness and substantiality of questions about grammars' psychological reality. Corresponding to the different senses of the word 'grammar' are three different domains that might be thought to provide truth-makers for a grammatical theory: the language; the psychology of speakers; the contents of speakers' psychological states.[4] Hence, there are at least three different questions that could potentially arise about the truth of a grammar and three different ontologies that a grammar, if true, might commit one to. A given grammar could be true in one domain (that is, true under one interpretation) and yet false in another. A grammar could be true of language, for instance, but false of speakers' psychologies. Because there is more than one domain that linguistics might be concerned with, a theory's psychological reality need not follow from its truth *simpliciter*. We need in addition some reason to think that the proper domain of linguistics is, as Chomsky maintains, a psychological one.

10.3.1 Is Linguistics Psychological?

One might in general hesitate to tell a theorist that he doesn't know what he's theorizing about. Nonetheless, the Chomskyan belief that linguistics is psychological has come in for a good deal of criticism. Soames (1984a, 1985), Devitt and Sterelny (1989), and Katz (1981, 1985b) have argued that linguistics and psychology are, as Soames (1984a) puts it, "conceptually distinct" enterprises, and that generative linguists are simply wrong in thinking that they are developing psychological theories about speakers. They

---

4. The contrast drawn here between speakers' psychologies and the contents of speakers' psychological states is intended to reflect the difference between claiming that a grammar is *a theory of* speakers' competence and claiming that it *is* speakers' competence. I am assuming that the latter claim is true only if the contents of the grammar can be mapped very closely onto the contents of speakers' psychological states, whereas the former claim could be true if speakers' psychologies implemented the grammar in some looser sense.

base these claims on a consideration of the methodology of linguistics, as compared with that of psychology and cognitive science.

First, they argue, theories in each of these fields are on the face of it responsible for different domains of fact. Theories in linguistics seemingly seek to predict and explain facts about languages (e.g., that certain sentences are ungrammatical or ambiguous or necessary, or that languages may differ in their ordering of sentences' constituents). In contrast, theories in psychology are typically aimed at the prediction and explanation of facts about speakers of languages (e.g., that speakers judge certain sentences to be grammatical or ambiguous or necessary, or that they find certain rules easier to learn than others).

Soames (1984a) argues, second, that theories in the two domains are sensitive to different kinds of evidence. What is taken to confirm or disconfirm a grammatical theory are facts about the grammatical properties of sentences: the grammatical hypothesis that Spanish is a 'head initial' language, for instance, is confirmed by the fact that, in Spanish, the sentence *Juan habla inglés* is grammatical (Chomsky 1988:70). What confirms or disconfirms a psychological theory of language, by contrast, are facts about the linguistic behavior of speakers: the psychological hypothesis that most children know that Wh-trace blocks contraction is confirmed by the fact that most children never contract *want to* to *wanna* where a trace intervenes between *want* and *to*. (Crain 1991:604.)

And finally, as Soames (1984a:169–71), Devitt and Sterelny (1989:505), and Stabler (1984:167–69) note, the two fields appear to employ subtly different criteria in evaluating their theories. The linguist desires a grammar that characterizes languages through a maximally simple, general, and abstract system of rules. The psychologist wants a theory that accurately reflects the processes underpinning language acquisition and use. Since there's no guarantee that these desiderata will point in the same direction—since we lack a "justification of the idea that the linguist's idea of simplicity is tailored to relevant parameters of . . . human psychology" (Stabler 1984: 171)—there is no guarantee that theories that are optimal from the linguist's point of view will also prove to be optimal from the psychologist's. Thus, there is no guarantee that what turns out to be true of languages will be true of speakers too.

At the very least, these observations make problematic the Chomskyan insistence that theories in linguistics are correctly interpreted as being psychological in content. If linguistics really is a branch of psychology, why are linguists' methods so different from those of psychologists? On the view of Soames, and of Devitt and Sterelny, these methodological contrasts do more than problematize the Chomskyan interpretive stance: they falsify it. On their view, what these dissimilarities in method show is that theories in linguistics are—just as they seem to be—about different things from those in psychology. The former are theories about languages; the latter are theories about speakers of languages. Hence, they argue, to do linguistics is not to do psychology, and it is an empirical question, not one to be settled by stipulation, whether and to what extent theories in linguistics will turn out also to illuminate the psychology of speakers, however successful they might prove to be by linguists' lights.

10.3.2 Why This Issue Ought to Be Boring

The notion that it's one thing to theorize about languages and another to theorize about speakers of languages—let alone the further claim of Soames and company that linguistics is in fact about languages, not speakers—has generated enormous controversy. Where they have not been dismissed as pointless efforts to legislate what gets to be called 'linguistics' or 'psychology,'[5] arguments as to the distinctness of the two disciplines have been furiously rejected by Chomskyans as attempts, in the worst tradition of a priori philosophizing, to delimit the kinds of questions linguists can ask and to restrict the sorts of evidence they may appeal to in resolving them.[6] But the claim that linguistics is distinct from psychology is empirical, not stipulative, and should in my view be accepted as utterly uncontroversial.

As a matter of brute fact, which a glance at the relevant literatures will confirm, the subject matter and methods of linguistics *are* different from those of psychology. Linguistics and psychology are as different in their methods and concerns as are mathematics and psychology, or logic and psychology, or economics and psychology, or history and psychology. But so what? Nothing of any moment, so far as I can see, follows from this *except* the claim, which I made in chapter 7 and which (I hope) seemed so obvious there as hardly to bear stating, that it's an empirical psychological question whether grammars provide true theories of linguistic competence and an empirical psychological question too whether Linguistic Theory provides a good characterization of the mechanism of language-learning. To assert that linguistics and psychology are distinct is not to deny that each has the potential to achieve extraordinary growth and progress thanks to insights and ideas provided by the other. It is not to deny the possibility of symbiosis and mutual cross-fertilization. Cases where conceptually distinct theories have turned out to be, in Soames's phrase, 'empirically convergent,' are not unknown: chaos theory has proved useful in modeling global weather patterns, game theory has been used in explaining the emergence of altruism in species, and (although this is more controversial) formal logic has been argued to illuminate the psychology of reasoning. It is quite possible that linguistics and psychology might similarly converge. All that the proponent of conceptual distinctness contends is that this happy confluence, while doubtless to be desired, is something to be discovered, not simply declared.

5. See Fodor (1981c:206); Chomsky (1986:35).
6. See Fodor (1981c:198); Chomsky (1986:34–35); Antony (1991).

10.3.3 Why This Issue Seems So Interesting

Why, then, is the notion that linguistics is about languages so contentious? Chomskyans' vituperative rejections of such claims seem to derive from their view that if one rejects the psychological interpretation of theories in linguistics, one thereby commits oneself to some kind of Platonism about linguistic objects. But Platonism about languages, it is argued, is not only inherently implausible; it also makes a mockery of linguistics' pretensions to being an empirical, scientific discipline. Hence, Chomsky maintains, the idea that linguistics might be about languages considered in abstraction from speakers is "completely foreign to the empirical study of languages . . . [n]or has anyone ever indicated what sense it might have" (Chomsky 1993:19).

The bogeyman of Platonism is explicit in Fodor (1981c), where he defends what he calls Chomsky's 'Right View' about the domain of linguistics against a nonpsychological interpretation, or 'Wrong View,' which he equates with Platonism. "The only thing against Platonism," he contends, is that because it renders the study of language non-empirical, "deep down, nobody is remotely interested in it" (1981c:205). Similarly, Chomsky argues in a number of places that a nonpsychological interpretation of linguistics is untenable because it makes languages mysterious and ineffable entities, and linguistics nonscientific. In *Rules and Representations* (1980: 28–29), for example, he writes that it is important to distinguish his conception of UG (as constituting a description of the initial state, S_0, of the language faculty) from "a different one, which takes 'universal grammar' to be a characterization not of human language but of 'language as such.' " For whereas "[t]he study of the biologically necessary properties of language is a part of natural science. . . . the study of logically necessary properties of language is an inquiry into the concept 'language' . . . [and] is not an empirical investigation" In *Knowledge of Language* (1986), he pursues the same line of thought. Whereas internalized I-languages—"the steady state of knowledge attained and the initial state S_0" (1986:26)—are "real elements of particular mind/brains, aspects of the physical world" (1986:26), E-languages, languages considered in abstraction from speakers, are "artificial constructs" (1986:28): "languages in this sense are not real-world objects" (1986:27). Consequently, while "UG and theories of I-languages . . . are on a par with scientific theories in other domains; theories of E-languages, if sensible at all, have some different and more obscure status because there is no corresponding real-world object" (1986:27). Later in the same work, conceding that Platonists such as Katz (1981, 1985b; see also Katz and Postal 1991) would regard languages as very much a part of the 'real world,' given their opinion that they are abstract objects on a par with mathematical objects like numbers and sets, Chomsky, like Fodor, rejects the Platonist interpretation as both inherently uninteresting and untrue to the empirical character of modern-day linguistic theorizing: "Of course, one can construct abstract entities at will . . . and . . . define "linguistics" as the study of these abstract objects, and thus not part of the natural sciences, which are concerned with such entities as ɪ-language and S_0. . . . But there seems little point to such moves" (Chomsky 1986:33).

But although the idea that languages are abstract objects has been defended by one prominent critic of the Chomskyan interpretation of theories in linguistics, namely Jerrold Katz, the view that linguistics is about languages need not commit one to a Platonist conception of what languages are. Devitt and Sterelny (1989) suggest instead that languages are spatiotemporally located natural objects, analogous to the states, economies, governments, religions, and the like that are the subjects of other special sciences. On this view, which I am inclined to endorse, facts about languages supervene (albeit in a very complicated and poorly understood way) on facts about the beliefs, intentions, conventions, and histories of the people who use them, in much the same way that facts about economies, say, supervene (in a similarly ill-understood way) on facts about the people who operate within them. Languages so conceived are real-world objects of empirical study in the same way as are economies, political institutions, and other cultural objects. So while Chomsky is, I think, right to reject a Katz-style Platonism, it doesn't follow from this that linguistics must be about the psychology of speakers. ᴇ-languages, the objects of linguistic study, don't have to be viewed as alien objects lurking enigmatically in a transcendent Platonic heaven: they can and should be viewed instead as complex natural objects securely located in actual space and time. And linguistics doesn't have to be nonempirical if it's about languages rather than speakers. Since languages are natural objects, susceptible of empirical investigation, both grammars for individual languages and ᴜɢ are, as Chomsky wants them to be, empirical theories about real-world things.

So while the Chomskyan claim (ᴜ) that the task-specific knowledge required for language-learning is knowledge of ᴜɢ cannot be assumed to be true simply on the grounds that Linguistic Theory correctly describes linguistic universals, it remains an open possibility that the principles of ᴜɢ might nonetheless turn out to be just the constraining elements that are involved in language-learning. If so, then the iterated argument from the poverty of the stimulus (§10.1) has its major premise, and Chomskyan nativism looks unassailable. In the remainder of this chapter, we will examine the question of whether there is in fact any reason to think that knowledge of ᴜɢ is what drives language-learning.

10.4 Chomsky's (ᴜ): An Inference to the Best Explanation?

While Chomsky mostly takes the view that the truth of (ᴜ) is obvious, given what linguistics is about, he does occasionally offer an empirical argument to substantiate his claim that it is knowledge of ᴜɢ that constrains the learning mechanism. Taking Weak nativism for granted, he proposes that Linguistic Theory provides the most plausible account of what a child needs to know in order to learn a language. For, he argues, the hypothesis that speakers know UG explains and predicts novel facts about both languages and their speakers.

> A theory that attributes possession of certain linguistic universals to a language-acquisition system . . . implies that only certain kinds of symbolic systems can be acquired and used as languages by this device. . . . As a concrete example, consider the fact that, according to the theory of transformational grammar, . . . grammatical transformations are necessarily 'structure-dependent.' . . . One who proposes this theory would have to predict that although a language might form interrogatives, for example, by interchanging the order of certain categories (as in English), it could not form interrogatives by reflection, or interchange of odd and even words. . . . Many other such predictions, none of them at all obvious in an a priori sense, can be deduced from any sufficiently explicit theory of linguistic universals that is attributed to a language-acquisition device as an intrinsic property. (1965:54–55)

Since the hypothesis that the learning mechanism respects the principle of structure dependence enables us to explain and predict many different (and intuitively unobvious) linguistic phenomena, this hypothesis is to be preferred to any other speculations about the constraints on the language faculty. Thus, Chomsky argues, we should accept that it is our innate knowledge of UG's principle of structure dependence that is at work in language-learning, rather than suppose (as an empiricist might) that our choice of structure dependent rules has some other explanation. Generalizing the argument, Chomsky urges that we should accept his 'core' claim (U) for the same reason:

> There are, then, certain language universals that set limits to the variety of human language. The study of the universal conditions that prescribe the form of any human language is "grammaire générale." Such universal conditions are not learned; rather they provide the organizing principles that make language learning possible. . . . *By attributing such principles to the mind, as an innate property, it becomes possible to account for the quite obvious fact that the speaker of a language knows a great deal that he has not learned.* (1986:59–60, emphasis added)

I do not propose to criticize this inference to the best explanation on the grounds that Chomskyan nativism has not demonstrated its superiority to potential competitors such as Weak nativism and Enlightened empiricism. For (and this has been a recurrent complaint of mine in part III) the development of theories that might reasonably be expected to give Chomskyanism a run for its money has been stifled over the last three decades, and it is hardly fair to expect the Chomskyan to show that his theory is better than rivals that do not yet exist. Accordingly, I will accept that Chomskyan nativism is the best available theory of language acquisition—and argue that it provides no real explanation of language acquisition at all.

10.5 Hypothesis-Testing and Parameter-Setting

Chomskyan nativism purports to provide an explanation of—what? The question is not facetious: as we will see below (§10.9), there has been considerable discussion aimed at pinpointing the *explanandum* for which Chomskyanism is urged to be the *explanans*. As a first approximation, though, we may say that Chomskyan nativism explains how languages are learned. Since for Chomsky learning a language involves the speaker–hearer's coming to know or 'cognize' its grammar, the claim in the arguments above must be that Chomskyan nativism provides the best (or at least an) explanation of how speakers come to cognize grammars.

As we've seen before (§7.4), Chomsky's nativism has been elaborated in two ways, so there are two explanatory models to consider in evaluating this claim. In its early days, its assertion that language acquisition proceeds thanks to our innate knowledge of UG was cashed out in terms of a hypothesis-testing model of acquisition. Chomsky proposed that UG is innately known and facilitates language learning in the sense that (1) we have innate concepts of syntactic kinds as they are categorized in UG; (2) the hypothesis-generating part of the learning mechanism may only put forth grammars for languages that fall within the class of 'humanly possible' languages delimited by UG; and (3) in case more than one allowable hypothesis is compatible with the data, there is a determinate fact of the matter—fixed by UG's 'evaluation metric'—as to which one the learner should choose. Ideally, it was hoped, UG would so constrain the space of hypotheses and so finely distinguish competing hypotheses' rankings that at the end of the learning period, only one grammar—the grammar for the language being learned—would remain viable.

It proved hard, however, to articulate an evaluation metric for grammars that went beyond stipulating, in a decidedly empiricist vein, that learners should prefer grammars with fewer and simpler rules.[7] This difficulty, I suspect, was an important impetus to the advent of the 'Principles and Parameters' ("P&P") or 'Government-Binding' approach to syntax, introduced in Chomsky (1981). One advantage claimed for the P&P approach is that it so strongly constrains the class of possible grammars that only a very small number of hypotheses will be available to the learner. Thus the likelihood that the learner will be confronted with more than one empirically adequate grammar is greatly reduced, and so the need for an evaluation metric is apparently obviated.[8] With the P&P approach came changes in the Chomskyan conceptions of both UG and language acquisition. Rather than being conceived as a collection of generalizations about languages, UG came to be

---

7. See, e.g., Baker (1979), whose only suggestion (p. 538) about the evaluation metric is that it should value simpler grammars over more complex ones, where simplicity is conceived to be a function of the number of symbols used in stating grammatical rules.

8. See, e.g., Chomsky (1990); Friedin (1996).

envisioned more as a body of architectural constraints on tree structures. Talk of hypothesis-testing became unfashionable, and linguists began to speak instead of 'parameter-setting.'

Chomsky (1988:62–63) characterizes the parameter-setting orientation like this:

> The principles of universal grammar are exceptionless because they constitute the language faculty itself, a framework for any particular human language, the basis for the acquisition of language. But plainly languages differ . . . the principles of universal grammar have certain *parameters,* which can be fixed by experience in one or another way. We may think of the language faculty as a complex and intricate network of some sort, associated with a switch box consisting of an array of switches that can be in one of two positions. Unless the switches are set one way or another, the system does not function. When they are set in one of the permissible ways, then the system functions in accordance with its nature, but differently, depending on how the switches are set. . . . The data presented to the child learning the language must suffice to set the switches one way or another. When these switches are set, the child has command of a particular language and knows the facts of that language.

Lightfoot (1991) elaborates on the paradigm as follows:

> we have assumed that this unlearned information is genetically encoded in some fashion, and we have adopted (1) as our explanatory model:
>
> (1) a. trigger (genotype → phenotype)
>   b. primary linguistic data (Universal Grammar → grammar)
>
> The goal is to specify relevant aspects of a child's genotype such that a particular mature state will emerge when a child is exposed to a certain triggering experience, depending on whether the child is raised in, say, a Japanese or a Navaho linguistic environment. (1b) reflects the usual terminology: "Universal Grammar" contains those aspects of the genotype that are directly relevant for language growth, and a "grammar" is taken to be a phenotypic property, a part of a person's mental makeup that characterizes his or her mature linguistic capacity. The *primary* linguistic data are those data to which children are exposed and which actually determine or "trigger" some aspect of their grammars, having some long term effect. . . . Under current formulations of grammatical theory, the linguistic genotype, Universal Grammar, consists of principles and parameters that are set by some linguistic environment . . . the environment may be said to "select" particular values for the parameters of Universal Grammar. (1991:1–2)

Language acquisition is often described by parameter setters as a "selective" process rather than an "instructive" one. This reflects their view that experience is something of a tinkerer: its role is merely to fine-tune an inherently highly structured device or 'organ.' On an instructive view, by contrast, experience is a creator: its role is to "impart its character to the system that receives it, instructing what is essentially a plastic and modifiable nervous system" (Lightfoot 1991:2).[9]

Revealing though these sorts of characterizations are, the character of the parameter-setting approach is best grasped through an example. Accordingly, I will briefly recap Lightfoot's treatment of the 'bounding node parameter' (1991:24ff.) as a preliminary to our discussion.

Following up on Ross's (1967) discovery of the existence of 'island constraints' limiting the domain of application of transformational rules, Chomsky (1973) proposed that UG incorporates a 'Subjacency Condition,' a principle forbidding an element in a phrase marker to move 'too far' from its original position during the transformational phase of a derivation. He argued that an element moves too far if it crosses more than one 'bounding node' in a single transformational step, and that since the bounding nodes for English are s and NP, an English string will be ungrammatical if its derivation involves an element's moving (in a single hop) over more than one s or NP node.[10] Lightfoot (1991:24–25) recounts how in the early 1980s, Rizzi and Sportiche independently discovered that some languages (their exemplars were Italian and French, respectively) allow movement through two s nodes.[11] Rather than concluding from this that Subjacency was not after all a part of UG, Rizzi argued that it is a universal principle that is subject to *parametric variation*. If Italian and French selected $\bar{s}$ and NP (rather than s and NP, as English does) as bounding nodes, then sentences like those he and Sportiche discussed do not violate Subjacency; instead, they confirm it by demonstrating how it is upheld (albeit in a slightly different form) in other languages.[12]

For a parameter setter, findings such as these have implications for language-learning. Since the Subjacency Principle ("Don't cross more than one bounding node") remains invariant from language to language, we can assume that it is known innately, part of the initial, biologically determined state or 'genotype' of the language learner. The learner acquires a grammar that respects the above-described differences between English and the Romance languages French and Italian by setting the bounding node parameter one way (selecting s and NP) rather than another (selecting $\bar{s}$ and NP). These

---

9. Compare Piattelli-Palmarini (1986, 1989).

10. See Baker (1989/95: 297–300) for an explanation of Subjacency and related constraints on movement.

11. Sportiche's example was: *Voilà une list des gens à qui on n'a pas encore trouvé quoi envoyer* ('Here is a list of people to whom we've not yet found what to send'), analyzed as containing the phrase: [à qui$_i$] $_s$[on n'a pas encore trouvé $_s$'[[quoi$_j$] $_s$[envoyer e$_j$ e$_i$]]], in which *à qui* moves over two s nodes to its position at the front of the clause. Rizzi's was *Tuo fratello, a cui mi domando che storie abbiano raccontato, era molto preoccupato* ('Your brother, to whom I wonder which stories were told, was very troubled.'), which may be similarly analyzed to show movement over two s nodes (Lightfoot 1991:25).

12. $\bar{s}$ consists of an s and a complementizer (*that, whether, for*, etc.) with the structure $\bar{s}$[[COMP]$_s$[_____]]. Hence, for instance: $_s$[John believes $\bar{s}$[[that] $_s$[Mary loves Tom]]].

parametric choices are held to be triggered by the learner's linguistic experience, and most of the fun and challenge of the P&P approach to linguistics lies in figuring out what the parameters for language are and what their default settings must be in order that they could be set on the basis of the extremely limited (that is, largely positive) primary linguistic data held to be available. Thus Rizzi reasoned—and this is a ubiquitous argumentative pattern in the P&P literature—that S must be must be the default (or 'less marked') setting for the bounding node parameter. For if $\bar{s}$ were the default, then in order to effect the switch to S, English children would have to ascertain that certain kinds of movement are illegitimate in English. But these are negative data, and (allegedly) do not exist. By supposing that S is the default instead, though, one can explain how both Italian and English children learn what the bounding nodes in their languages are. English children will never be exposed to a triggering stimulus that violates the prohibition on moving over more than one S node, so their parameter will remain on the unmarked setting. By contrast, when a French or Italian child hears a sentence (like *Voilà une list des gens à qui on n'a pas encore trouvé quoi envoyer* or *Tuo fratello, a cui mi domando che storie abbiano raccontato, era molto preoccupato*) that violates Subjacency with the parameter so set, this causes the parameter to be set to the more marked setting, $\bar{s}$.

Lightfoot argues that these proposals are flawed because they assume that children have access to 'degree-two' data, that is, to sentences, like those just mentioned, containing two embedded clauses. On his view, the *pld* cannot be assumed to contain such complex constructions and the theorist must assume that "the trigger consists only of simple, unembedded material, and that everything can be learned from structures of 'degree-0 complexity.'" (1991:10; see also his 1989). He argues (1991:26) that on the assumption that they already know that NP is a bounding node for French, children could figure out that $\bar{s}$ is the correct setting for that language on the basis of a degree-0 datum such as *Combien as-tu vu de personnes?* ('How many people have you seen?'). In this sentence, *combien* moves over both an NP boundary and an S boundary, which would violate Subjacency if S were a bounding node in addition to NP.[13] So, given the child's knowledge that NP is a bounding node, hearing such a sentence would provide her with decisive reason to switch the parameter such that it takes the value $\bar{s}$. Similarly, he argues, although "comparable structures are not available to the Italian child" (1991:37), other fairly simple sentences are available that would suffice to set the parameter for Italian.[14]

Our task, then, in assessing the empirical adequacy of the nativist's explanatory schema, is to inquire whether either of these kinds of model—

13. Lightfoot analyzes the sentence as: Combien$_i$ $_s$[as-tu vu $_{NP}$[e$_i$ $_N$[de personnes]]] (1991:26).

14 Provided, however, one redefines what 'simple' means, understanding 'degree-0 complexity' now not in terms of no embedded clauses but of "unembedded binding Domains" (Lightfoot 1991:36–37).

parameter-setting or the earlier hypothesis-testing—provides a good account of how languages are learned. These issues will be dealt with in §§10.6 and 10.7. As a preliminary, I want briefly to address the question of how parameter-setting accounts are to be distinguished from hypothesis-testing models.

10.5.1 Hypothesis-Testing by Any Other Name?

We have just examined in some detail a parameter-setting account of how children come to cognize what the bounding nodes in their language are. Compare now the same story as it might be told by a hypothesis tester. He proposes that the hypothesis-generating mechanism in the child's language acquisition device is so tightly constrained by UG that the learner has available to her just two hypotheses about the Subjacency Condition, namely, SC_1 ("Don't move a constituent over more than one NP or S boundary") and SC_2 ("Don't move a constituent over more than one NP or $\bar{S}$ boundary"). On the reasonable supposition that the evaluation metric ranks SC_1 above SC_2, SC_1 will be the child's initial hypothesis as to the content of the Subjacency Condition. The child will abandon SC_1 and move onto the next-highly-ranked hypothesis, SC_2, only if she hears a sentence in the data that provides evidence falsifying SC_1. Whereas an English child will never hear a sentence falsifying SC_1 (hence SC_1 will be retained to form part of her mature grammar), a French or Italian child will abandon SC_1 for SC_2 when she hears a sentence—such as those discussed by Rizzi, Sportiche, and Lightfoot—that falsifies it. Since no data falsifying SC_2 will be encountered, she will retain SC_2 as part of her mature competence.

The terminological dissimilarities between this account and the parameter-setting theory are, of course, very striking. Rather than speaking of parameterized constraints, or the markedness of values, or the triggering of new settings by data violating the old ones, the hypothesis tester speaks of extremely strict restrictions on the space of possible grammatical hypotheses, of the way they are ranked by the evaluation metric, and of how they are falsified in the data and replaced. Still, it is not obvious to me that there are any real differences between the acquisition stories as told in these two different voices. While there are things that adherents of parameter-setting *might* say that *would* serve to demarcate their theory clearly from that of a hypothesis tester, there is no evidence that they are willing to make these kinds of commitments.

One obvious way, for instance, that a parameter-setting model might be distinguished from hypothesis-testing is if its talk of the 'triggering' of parameters reflected a commitment to the idea (familiar from part II) that the relation between the triggering stimulus and parameter values is 'brute-causal' in the sense of Fodor (1981b). Whereas the hypothesis-testing model sees the *pld* as providing evidence for and against the learner's grammatical hypotheses, the parameter-setting model, so elaborated, would view that relation as merely causal, fortuitous, and arbitrary, an 'intentionally opaque' (§4.5) by-product of natural selection's cavalier insistence on getting the job done by whatever means happen to be at hand. But, so far as I can see, parameter setters take no such view. On the contrary, they seem just as wedded as any hypothesis tester to the idea that there must be a strongly evidential relation between the selection of a parameter value and the experience that leads up to it. Thus Lightfoot (1991), for instance, is exercised not merely to find some simple stimulus that is reliably correlated with s̄ (rather than s) turning out to be a bounding node for a language—anything that was correlated with s̄ being a bounding node would, after all, do as a trigger for the parameter. Instead, he is concerned to find a simple sentence that *provides a reason* for changing the parameter from s to s̄. He, like virtually everyone else in the P&P game, takes it for granted that the inputs to language learning should not merely reliably cause certain parameter values to be selected, but also should justify or rationally compel the selections they produce. That being so, it is, as I said, hard to see what, aside from a change in terminology, the parameter-setting theory adds to our understanding of language acquisition.

This is not just a philosopher's nit-picking. How one conceives of the triggering stimulus has a direct bearing on the explanatory adequacy of parametric models. For example, Chomsky (1990:644–45) discusses a number of proposals as to how children learn whether or not their language allows the subject of a sentence to be omitted from the spoken string. (Remember, Italian and French do; English doesn't—§7.1.) According to Rizzi, the default value for the 'Null-subject parameter' is 'overt subject'—subjects must be expressed. On his account, when an Italian child hears a sentence like *Ho travato il libro* ('Found the book'), in which the subject is omitted, the parameter is reset to its 'subject optional' value and the child takes another step toward cognizance of Italian grammar. However, as Berman (1990) and Schlesinger (1991) argue, children in English-speaking families likely hear utterances in which the subject is omitted too, even though English is a 'nonprodrop' language in which subjects must ordinarily be expressed. Berman (1990:1137) gives the following examples:

I wonder why John's frowning like that. *Must be worried.*
We're going out for a pizza. *Want to come with?*

And other examples are easy to think of: *Couldn't give a damn, Wouldn't believe a word he said, Must have been the mailman*, etc. Why, then, given the existence in the *pld* of these sorts of data, does the English child's grammar stay set on 'subject overt'? Why, that's to say, does a type of input that apparently suffices to change the setting of the Null-subject parameter for an Italian child not change it for an English child too?[15]

---

15. Lightfoot (1991:14) notes the problem, but rather surprisingly offers no explanation of it.

There are explanations available, but only, it seems, to a hypothesis tester. Schlesinger, for example, proposes that English speakers' grammars remain on the default setting because subjectless sentences occur much less frequently in English than they do in Italian, suggesting that English children simply don't get enough evidence in favor of optional subjects to make the switch. Alternatively, a hypothesis tester may employ the approach of Weinberg (1991), who in addressing analogous problems, postulates an evidential 'threshold' that needs to be crossed before a parametric change occurs:

> [P]arameter values could be associated with initial probabilities. Unmarked settings . . . have greater initial probabilities. Probabilities can be incremented or decremented depending on the ability of the grammars they produce to provide an analysis of the strings in the child's linguistic environment. As one parameter value is incremented or decremented, the other . . . would be inversely affected until one parameter setting stabilized over some threshold and became the child's setting. (Weinberg 1991:637)

The proponent of hypothesis-testing may take such explanations on board because keeping track of relative frequencies, or incrementing and decrementing probabilities in response to the grammars' success in analyzing strings, *just is* gathering evidence pro and con grammatical hypotheses! But how does a parameter setter who clings to a brute-causal notion of triggering account for the fact that *Couldn't give a damn* doesn't trigger 'subject optional' in English children's grammars? How does she explain why a trigger that is causally sufficient in one case to reset a parameter is causally insufficient in another? Maybe there is an explanation to be had here—some kind of variation on Fodor's 'hierarchy of triggers,' for instance, might do the trick.[16] But it's certainly not obvious that the requisite story can be told.

So, if one tries to draw a substantive distinction between parameter-setting and hypothesis-testing by stressing their different conceptions of the stimulus to language-learning, parameter-setting models, so understood, are explanatorily worthless. When elaborated so as to succeed even prima facie in accounting for how language is acquired, though, parameter-setting models turn out to be mere variants on hypothesis-testing. Interesting variants, mind you: in talking of the setting of parameters rather than the testing of hypotheses, the parameter setter does make explicit just how dictatorial and repressive, on her view, the innate UG is. Her metaphor, that is to say, makes vivid the Chomskyan's conviction (post-1981) that the *pld* are so immensely impoverished that language acquisition cannot be explained unless learners have available to them only a small—a *very* small—finite number of possible grammars. But as to what more there is that might be distinctive about parameter-setting—or even whether parameter setters think that there is

---

16. See §§6.2.1 and 6.3.1. Note that it won't do to appeal to a breakdown of the mechanism in this context: a null-subject trigger must *reliably fail* to reset the parameter in English speakers at the same time as it must *reliably succeed* in resetting it for Italian speakers. Breakdowns are not this systematic.

something more that is exceptional about their approach—this, in my view, remains unclear.

10.6 Some Problems with Parameters

Setting aside now such conceptual worries, let's ask instead how well the parameter-setter's claim to explain language acquisition fares. This is a somewhat difficult issue to approach because there is no parameter-setting theory of language acquisition. Parameter-setting is less a theory of language acquisition than it is a theory-schema, or perhaps a collection of methodo-logical maxims. So what we have to evaluate is a dynamic mosaic of com-peting theory fragments, vying with each other for a position in the finished picture. I will suggest that, precisely because research into the principles and parameters of language is so energetic and vigorous, parameter-setting mod-els are not yet at a stage of development whereby their degree of explanatory success can accurately be judged. After discussing several different kinds of controversy that come up in the P&P literature, I will argue that although the existence of these debates does not reflect badly on parameter-setting as a research program, it does augur ill for any attempt a Chomskyan might make to ground an argument for (U) in the putative successes of that pro-gram to date.

10.6.1 Controversial Constraints

One piece of evidence in support of my contention that parameter-setting models are too underdeveloped at this time to be judged fairly in terms of their explanatory adequacy is to be found in the ongoing debate as to what, exactly, the linguistic parameters and their possible values are. Recall, for instance, Crain's (1991) discussion of *wanna* and *is* contraction (§8.6). He urged that children's respect for adult restrictions on contraction was a re-flection of their knowledge of Principle C of Binding Theory, and argued that since Principle C could not have been learned by two-year-olds from their experience, that constraint must be innately known. On Crain's picture of acquisition, then, Principle C is like the Subjacency Condition: it is one of the biologically-specified (and possibly parameterized) constraints that the child does not have to learn.[17]

Literally nothing in this little theory, however, is uncontroversial. Wasow (1991) starts at the top, objecting to Crain's analysis of children's linguistic behavior in terms of Principle C. Citing a 1982 paper of Pullum and Postal in which they give ten examples where contraction of *want to* to *wanna* is blocked, only two of which are explained by Principle C, he urges that

---

17. Lasnik in his *Essays on Anaphora* (1989) argues that there is interlinguistic vari-ation in the application of Principle C, which suggests that Principle C too is a candidate for parameterization.

Principle C has nothing to do with *wanna* contraction. He offers a competing analysis in which *wanna* is a verb, like *will*, that takes a bare, uninflected VP complement. On his account, *Who do you think they wanna help you?* is ungrammatical for same reason as *Who do you think they will help you?*, namely, that neither *wanna* nor *will* can take a complex VP like *help you* as a complement.[18] Slobin (1991) offers another explanation. Following Haiman (1985), he argues that contraction is blocked when there is a switch in reference: *Who do you wanna help you?* is ungrammatical because the verbs *help* and *want* have different subjects. By Wasow's and Slobin's lights, then, since Crain's data do not support the notion that Principle C is known, they certainly don't support the theory that Principle C is known innately, as one of the biologically mandated constraints on language competence. To the extent that "[e]ach of Crain's experiments is open to alternative explanations based on nonsyntactic factors . . . as well as different conceptions of syntax" (Slobin 1991:634), the acquisition theory based on those experiments is weakened. And the same is true across the board. So long as it's controversial how a given piece of linguistic behavior is to be analyzed, a parametric theory of how that behavior is learned is correspondingly dubious.

10.6.2 Fitting the Data

Even in cases in which there is broad agreement as to what kind of grammatical analysis a given phenomenon requires, further controversies erupt when P&P theorists attempt to explain how the relevant grammatical principles come to be known. Chomsky (1990:644–45) discusses one such debate, concerning the mechanism by which the Null-subject parameter is set. As we've already seen (§10.5), Rizzi proposes that the default setting for the parameter is 'overt subject' (subjects must be expressed), and that the 'subject optional' value is selected in children learning Null-subject languages by their exposure to a subjectless sentence like *Ho travato il libro*. One problem with this suggestion, as noted above, is that the data for a non-Null-subject language like English may sometimes include subjectless sentences (e.g., *Couldn't give a damn*). Another, noted by Hyams (1983), is that all children initially treat their language as if it were a Null-subject language (e.g., a two-year-old learning English will say *Want more juice* rather than *I want more juice*). Rizzi explains this away as evidence of performance errors in young children: although their grammar mandates subjects, they're as yet unable to produce them. To Hyams, by contrast, this fact about children's speech suggests that the default setting for the Null-subject parameter is 'subject optional,' not 'subject overt.' But if that is so, how do English-speaking children manage to learn that in English, subjects are obligatory? Assuming (as is standard in this literature) that they never get corrected or otherwise

---

18. Wasow also argues that *is* contracts to the left, not to the right (as Crain assumed), hence that trace theory is irrelevant to explaining the ungrammaticality of contracted forms involving *is*.

informed that their subjectless productions are ungrammatical, how do they figure out from positive data that in English, subjects must be (and not just may be) expressed? Hyams proposes that it is the presence of expletive subjects in the language (as in, e.g., *It is sunny*) that trigger the change. But as Berman (1990) argues, this solution presupposes that overt expletives and mandatory subjects co-occur. Yet this, she claims, is not strictly true. Hebrew is a Null-subject language, yet allows the expletive subject *ze (it, this, that)* in some contexts.[19] So if expletives are what trigger 'overt subject,' why do Hebrew speakers nonetheless stay fixed on 'subject optional'?

Puzzles and paradoxes such as these plague all even minimally explicit parametric theories. As more and more comes to be known about the variety of natural languages and how children use them, it becomes more and more difficult to fit parameter-setting models with the facts. Sokolov and Snow (1991) forcefully emphasize this point. Criticizing Crain's (1991) contention that Principle C is innately known on the grounds that one of his subjects consistently violated it, they argue that

> [t]heories that presume rapid and full-blown emergence of language structures on the basis of little evidence from the input will fail to connect with the large body of research concerning child development that documents numerous areas of developmental continuity between the prelinguistic and linguistic child, between the presyntactic one-word speaker and the grammar-user. Theories that focus only on universal processes in language development fail to connect with individual differences among children in the speed and ease of language learning. (1991:635)

'Fail to connect' here being a euphemism for 'are inconsistent with,' Sokolov and Snow's charge, like mine, is that the models of the parameter setter tend to be overly simplistic and hence vulnerable to challenge on the basis of empirical findings as to how languages are in fact acquired.[20]

10.6.3 Problems in Principle?

But it is always possible, as we saw in discussing the Null-subject parameter (§10.6.2), to tweak a parametric account so as to bring it in line with the facts. Perhaps, for instance, the subject who violated constraints on contraction in Crain's study was subject to nonsyntactic performance error (as Crain in fact argues). Or perhaps he was unaccountably suffering from some sort of developmental delay. (After all, as Chomsky is at pains to emphasize, "[c]apacities that are part of our common human endowment can flourish, or can be restricted and suppressed, depending on the conditions provided

---

19. E.g., **ze** *yafe kaxa lariv?* ('is it nice to fight like that?,' literally, 'it nice to so fight?'), *ze lo yafe* ('it's not nice,' literally 'it not nice'); *ma* **ze?** *nyar? lo, ze ha-kir* (what's **that?** paper? no, it's the wall') (Berman 1990:140–1). Roeper (1991: 630) likewise objects to Hyam's theory on the grounds that "there are prodrop languages that have expletives."

20. See Pierce (1991:629) for other cases in which children violate allegedly innate principles.

for their growth" (1990:634).) Or perhaps some other (as yet unstudied) parameter linked with Principle C had not yet reached threshold in the child, with the consequence that Principle C was not yet available in the child's grammar. Or maybe the kid was just a mutant.

Of course, the making of post hoc adjustments such as these to fit a theory with the facts is not objectionable in itself. However, there are, I think, structural features of the parameter-setting paradigm that indicate that its failure to fit (or 'connect') with the developmental data may prove both endemic and irremediable. For, as I will suggest in this section, there is reason to question some of the most fundamental commitments of the Principles and Parameters approach to language and language acquisition.

As we will see in §10.7, one of the embarrassments of the hypothesis-testing account is its inability to explain how language acquisition occurs within a developmentally credible time period. Although hypothesis testers can typically guarantee acquisition within a finite amount of time, finitely much time can be a very long time—more time, especially, than the average language learner has available to her. One of the advantages claimed for parameter-setting is that by so strongly limiting the hypotheses available to the child (or, if you prefer, by so strictly constraining the amount of possible parametric variation among languages), it has the capacity to minimize substantially the amount of data—and hence the amount of time—that children need for successful learning. Parameter-setting is claimed to be preferable to the older account because it can explain why language acquisition is so extraordinarily rapid.

In addition to strengthening the constraints on learners' hypotheses by employing ever more and more general and abstract formulations of UG, parameter setters make use of two further stratagems in cutting the learning task down to size. First, they help themselves to what is known as the 'Subset Principle.' Proposed and defended by Berwick (1985) as a way to ensure learnability from positive data, the Subset principle requires that parameter values be marked such that subsequent changes in the value of the parameter lead to ever more inclusive grammars. Thus, if one possible grammar is smaller than another (that is, if it generates fewer sentences than or is a 'subset' of another), then the smaller grammar must be triggered before the larger one. By constraining the learner such that she must always move from a smaller to a larger grammar—a change that can be effected, recall, on the basis of positive data (§9.2, figure 9.1)—the Subset principle is designed to prevent overgeneration and hence to reduce or eliminate any need the child might have for hard-to-find negative data that would slow the learning process.[21]

A second expedient by which parameter setters contrive to ensure quick and easy learnability is what I shall call the 'Cluster' principle. This principle derives from the P&P tenet that the properties of natural languages form

---

21. See also Roeper (1988:40–41).

clusters, such that if a language possesses one of the properties in the cluster, it will possess the others as well. So, for instance, the property of being a Null-subject language is thought to cluster with a number of other features in addition to that of allowing null subjects in simple clauses and deletion of coreferential pronouns in subordinate clauses. These other features include the use of expletive subjects, the use of subject–verb inversion (as in Italian) rather than subject–auxiliary inversion (as in English), and a high degree of morphological uniformity (Null-subject languages have either rich verb-agreement inflection or none at all).[22] Applied to language acquisition, the Cluster principle urges us to see the various modules of the grammar as being interlinked, so that setting a parameter in one module can catalyze a cascade of further effects throughout the rest of the grammar. Thus, it may be held, setting the Null-subject parameter also fixes a variety of other rules governing questions, morphology, and so on.[23] Here's how Pinker expresses his commitment to the Cluster principle. Speaking of children setting the Head parameter,[24] he writes:

> All they have to learn is whether their particular language has the parameter value head-first, as in English, or head-last, as in Japanese. . . . Huge chunks of grammar are then available to the child, all at once, as if the child were merely flipping a switch to one of two possible positions. If this theory of language learning is true, it would help solve the mystery of how children's grammar explodes into adultlike complexity in so short a time . . . they are just setting a few switches. (Pinker 1994:112)

Some, however, have questioned the parameter setter's deployment of the Cluster and Subset principles in pursuit of his goal to "provide a facilitating explanation for language acquisition" (Berman 1991:1136). By way of motivating suspicion, several writers have reflected that whereas the hypothesis-testing model seems to make language acquisition too slow, parameter-setting perhaps goes too far in the other direction. Lasnik (1991:624) describes how out of the drive to make the task of acquiring language as simple as possible, "a new, troubling question began to emerge: how is it that a child's acquisition of language is so slow?" MacWhinney urges that given the resources attributed to the child by a parametric theory, "the only really surprising thing about language acquisition is that it takes so long" (1989:90).

Suspicion of the Chomskyan's Subset and Cluster principles is approriate, in my opinion. It is common knowledge even among parameter setters that the Subset principle, at least in a strong form, is false. Children overgeneralize quite frequently during language-learning, so it simply couldn't be right to constrain them such that they *never* move from a more to a less

22. This list was taken from Berman (1990:1135).
23. See Roeper (1988:46–48) for further discussion motivating the Cluster principle.
24. The head parameter determines whether the head of a phrase precedes, follows, or has no fixed position with regard to its complement. See Pinker (1994:110–12).

inclusive grammar. What, though, of a weaker formulation, according to which one should construct one's parametric theories such that children *usually* don't move from a larger to a smaller theory? It may be that this is right. However, there is, so far as I can see, no reason to believe it. The Subset principle was motivated, recall, by the assumption that there is no negative evidence—evidence that would allow a child to disconfirm an over-general hypothesis—in the *pld*:

> One fact is now well-known, namely that triggering factors are all positive ones. The fact that correction is not a significant factor in acquisition means that the child is exposed only to positive evidence. . . . The fact that a child is exposed only to positive evidence leads to what has been called the *subset principle*. (Roeper 1988:40)

But this "fact," as we have seen at length in chapters 8 and 9, is no fact at all! Negative evidence (including negative data) is plentiful in the *pld* and children not only can but, apparently, do make use of it. That being so, it's not obvious a priori that approaches to language acquisition that abide by the Subset Principle are to be preferred to those that don't. One may therefore question the parameter setter's wisdom in basing her explanatory strategy on an empirical assumption (regarding the absence of negative evidence in the data) that is false.

As we saw in §10.6.3, Berman (1990) argues that what I've called the Cluster principle likewise derives from a badly mistaken conception, this time of the degree of uniformity to be found in the ways properties clump together in different languages. Pinker (1994), for example, exemplifies the parameter setter's tendency to exaggerate the degree to which the Cluster principle is true, "In English, the head of a phrase comes before its role-players. In many languages, it is the other way around—*but it is the other way around across the board, across all the kinds of phrases in the language*" (1994:111, emphasis added). By contrast, Berman argues that "these clusterings do not necessarily apply uniformly across or within languages" (1990:1136). For example, she points out that contrary to what Pinker here asserts, the head parameter does *not* always determine ordering in phrases 'across the board.' Both French and English are head initial languages, yet French adjectives sometimes precede the noun, and in English they always do.[25] As further exceptions to clustering generalizations, Berman points out that Hebrew, which is a Null-subject language (and hence should disallow expletive subjects) nonetheless allows them in some contexts, and that English subjects are sometimes dropped in conversational contexts, the Null-subject parameter's alleged setting to 'subject overt' notwithstanding.

In §11.1, we will look some more at the question of whether linguistic universals really are universal. For the present, it will suffice to see what

---

25. Nouns are the heads of NPs, hence in a head-initial language, a noun's adjectival modifiers should follow it (as in *la grammaire générale*) rather than precede it (as in *la jolie fille*).

conclusion Berman (1990) draws from her study of children learning Hebrew. Examining in particular their acquisition of the idiosyncratic rules governing subject expression in Hebrew, she found that although there are regularities in their acquisition of these rules, these regularities are not predicted by any version of parameter-setting theory currently on offer. She concludes from this that

> there is not necessarily one particular setting for . . . the null-subject [parameter] that is less marked for children across the board. There seems no need for such a strong version of the parameter-setting view of acquisition as formulated in [the various] attempts to solve the logical problem of language acquisition. (1990:1160)

10.6.4 Implications for Chomskyan Nativism

In this section, I have argued that the parameter-setting approach to language acquisition is problematic in a number of respects. We have seen, first, that it is unclear how parameter-setting differs substantively from hypothesis-testing; second, that particular models' claims to plausibility may be undermined by the controversial nature of their grammatical analyses and assumptions; third, that parametric models may be faulted for failing to accord with developmental and cross-linguistic data; fourth, that the parameter-setting orientation, as reflected in the Subset principle, is based on a badly skewed picture of the primary linguistic data; and fifth, that its assumption that there are significant regularities in the distributions of linguistic properties across languages may be much too strong. What conclusions should we draw from this? One moral that I would not urge at this stage is that the parameter-setting paradigm be abandoned. Parameter setters may claim, with some justice, that these sorts of controversies and unclarities merely reflect the facts that the parametric approach is still very young and that theories within it are now actively being developed, modified, and extended. Rather than showing parameter-setting to be in any way fundamentally flawed, the clamorous debates I've discussed bespeak a research program in its vigorous prime. That granted, however, one must, I think, beware of accepting any grandiose claims as to parameter-setting's explanatory capacities. I have argued that, as even some of its most enthusiastic exponents have acknowledged, "[t]o assume that parametric theory has already solved the acquisition problem is a grave misapprehension of current linguistics" (Roeper 1991:630). Parameter-setting may promise a spectacular future of explanatory triumph, but it remains very much to be seen whether and how such pledges will be redeemed.

What this means in the context of this chapter is that it is inappropriate for a Chomskyan to appeal to the success of the parametric approach as indicating the truth of his core claim (U). Chomsky argued, recall (§10.4), that one should accept his view that UG describes the domain-specific principles that a child needs to employ in language-learning because theories based on this core assumption provide good explanations of how languages are learned. I asked, in response to this, "What theories?" and "Do they?" In this section, we've looked at Chomsky's nativism as it has been implemented in the Principles and Parameters approach. I've argued that the explanatory successes of parameter-setting to date are hardly an appropriate basis for an abductive argument to (U). In the next section, we will examine those of the hypothesis-testing paradigm.

10.7 Hypothesis-Testing

I charged in the last section that parametric theories are both too sketchy and too controversial to ground Chomsky's inference to (U). Vagueness, however, is certainly not a criticism that can justifiably be made of the theories developed within the alternative, hypothesis-testing paradigm. On the contrary, hypothesis-testing theories of language acquisition have, from their inception, proved amenable to precise specification and searching formal investigation. As an added point in their favor, some hypothesis-testing theories provably guarantee language learnability. While parameter-setting theories are frequently claimed to be sensitive to learnability considerations, hypothesis testers have come up with the goods, producing demonstrable solutions to the Logical Problem of Language Acquisition (§9.1). Thus hypothesis-testing looks on the face of it like a much more stable and substantial ground on which to found an abduction to Chomskyan nativism. In this section, we will see how well this version of the Chomskyan argument fares.

Without a doubt, the most sophisticated, detailed, and careful exemplars of the hypothesis-testing model for language-learning are those developed with the tradition of formal learning theory (introduced in §8.5.2). At the instigation of Gold (1967), learnability theorists have sought to examine the power of various kinds of hypothesis-testing models of (especially) language acquisition. In so doing, they have had to develop precise accounts of what the inputs to learning are, of what its outputs are, of how hypotheses are generated and tested, and of how hypotheses are replaced.[26] Without a doubt also, the most sophisticated, detailed, and careful exemplar of the learning theoretic approach is that of Wexler, Culicover, and Hamburger.[27] In a truly monumental piece of work culminating in Wexler and Culicover's mammoth book *Formal Principles of Language Acquisition* (1980), these theorists took up the challenge, posed by Gold (1967), of demonstrating the learnability of natural languages from text, that is, from a sample of sentences such as children are exposed to.

26. Pinker (1979) explores a variety of such models.
27. See Hamburger and Wexler (1975); Wexler, Culicover, and Hamburger (1975); Wexler and Culicover (1980).

Gold, recall, had proved that if the space of grammatical hypotheses available to a learner is utterly unconstrained, classes of languages (including the class of natural languages) that include finite languages are unlearnable from data consisting solely of sample sentences in the language (§8.5.2). Wexler, Culicover, and Hamburger demonstrated that if two UG-like constraints, which they call the 'Binary Principle' and the 'Freezing Principle,' are imposed on the learner's possible hypotheses, then the transformational component of a grammar for a natural language is learnable from positive data. The Binary Principle, which is similar to UG's Subjacency Condition (§10.6.1), states that no transformation may have a structural description that refers to symbols in more than two adjacent levels in the deep structure. The Freezing Principle states that no transformation may apply to a configuration of symbols that could only have been created only by the previous application of another transformation. These principles serve to delimit the class of grammatical hypotheses the learner considers during learning: any grammar that does not satisfy them is simply not entertained. Wexler, Culicover, and Hamburger prove that given these constraints, natural languages are learnable from the primary linguistic data.

Now since since Wexler, Culicover, and Hamburger's constraints are so similar to those of UG, their work apparently provides support for the Chomskyan's identification (captured in his core claim (U)) of the principles of UG with whatever domain-specific information is implicated in learning. They themselves certainly take their work to be broadly confirmatory of the Chomskyan approach to acquisition, as do many others. Lightfoot, for example, writes that their work "specifies the boundary conditions for a theory of language-learning. . . . In fact it is likely that grammars are more restricted than they suppose, but at this stage it is useful to have a mathematical proof that at least some kind of transformation grammar is learnable under reasonable [i.e., Chomskyan] assumptions about the language learner" (1982: 35n.). I will argue, however, that it is in fact very unclear how much support results like these provide for the hypothesis that it is our innate knowledge of UG that is making language acquisition possible. What Wexler, Culicover, and Hamburger prove is that (the transformational part of) a language *could* be learned if learners knew UG innately. But this result does not by itself speak to the question of whether languages *are in fact learned* through learners' deployment of that knowledge. What needs to be shown in addition is that the Wexler model is in other respects a plausible model of children learning language. I shall argue that while Wexler, Culicover, and Hamburger's model is indeed constructed with an eye toward its psychological cogency, its primary aim is nonetheless to demonstrate learnability, and not to provide an accurate account of how real children learn languages. Since learnability, unfortunately, appears to be purchased at the expense of psychological plausibility, the successes of Wexler, Culicover, and Hamburger's model, brilliant though they are, provide no support for Chomsky's abduction to (U).

10.7.1 Learning and Learnability

One immediate locus of dubiety concerning work in mathematical linguistics generally is the concept of learnability itself. To prove a class of languages learnable is to prove that, given data from any one of the languages in that class, the learner will in some finite amount of time hit upon the correct grammar for that language and thereafter not be forced by the data to change her mind.[28] It is not, however, to prove the class learnable within some developmentally credible amount of time. Hence a standard learnability proof is at most a demonstration that it is *not impossible* that language could be learned from the available data, given certain assumptions about the class of natural languages (that is, given certain assumptions about the innate UG). But in general, proofs that some phenomenon is not impossible, given-so-and so assumptions, lend those assumptions little credence: as any child fed the cabbage-patch-and-storks account of baby-making instinctually recognizes, a 'how possibly' story is not always a 'how actually' account.

10.7.2 The Learning Algorithm

Another problem with viewing language-learning through the lens of formal learning theory derives from its idealizations of the learning strategy, the learner's method for formulating and testing hypotheses. Early models (e.g., Gold 1967) were criticized (e.g., Pinker 1979) because of their requirement that in order to test his new hypotheses, the learner must remember all the data to which he has hitherto been exposed. This is plainly an untenable requirement to impose on actual children. Furthermore, such models conceive of the learner as adopting and testing whole grammars rather than individual rules, and see him also as adopting whatever new hypothesis happens to be next in the enumeration rather than modifying his beliefs based on what he already knows. But there is no reason to think that this is how children actually proceed. A child whose grammar fails to generate some string in the data (say, *John left and Mary wept*) will surely not wipe the slate clean and adopt some wholly new (and likely unrelated) grammar for testing. Rather, he will simply add a rule for conjunction to the grammar he already possesses. The actual child, in contrast to the mathematical linguist's learner, approaches learning in a piecemeal and conservative manner (cf. §9.4).

Wexler, Culicover, and Hamburger (1975:225) claim that the learning function employed by their learner is much more plausible than the one just described, for their learner does not need to store all the data with which

---

28. Gold (1967). Wexler and Culicover (1980:40–41, 99) express the criterion of learnability in terms of there being some finite data set that enables the learner to select the correct grammar for her language. These formulations are equivalent for our purposes, for in these models the data are assumed to be presented sequentially, one datum per unit time. Hence finite data implies finite time, and vice versa.

he has been presented, instead making his theoretical decisions (that is, whether to retain or modify his hypothesis) on the basis of his present state of grammatical knowledge, together with the current input. Further, he does not project and test whole grammars, working instead at the level of the retention or rejection and/or replacement of individual rules. But while these are clearly advances over the earlier Gold-style learner, Wexler, Culicover, and Hamburger's creation remains a very poor model of the learning child. First, he modifies his hypothesis only when it is explicitly falsified in the data (that is, when it fails to generate an input sentence). Yet, as I argued in chapter 9, other kinds of evidence (such as evidence that certain forms do not appear in the linguistic data) can also bear on learners' hypotheses. Second, it is assumed that the learner can always tell when his grammar fails to generate a datum: his derivational powers are assumed to be unlimited. Yet it is far from clear that actual children may be assumed to be logically omniscient.[29] Third, when confronted with an unruly datum and deciding what action to take in response to it, Wexler, Culicover, and Hamburger's learner has unreasonably limited options: he may either add a single rule to his hypothesized grammar, so as to generate the datum in question; or he may delete one of the rules used in the unsuccessful derivation. But while restricting the learner's options in this way enables Wexler and company to avoid the charge that the learning function is implausibly holistic, the fact that children do seem at times to make major revisions in their state of linguistic knowledge suggests that the gradualness forced upon their learner perhaps errs too much in the other direction. Finally, and most importantly, the revisions Wexler, Culicover, and Hamburger's learner actually makes in the light of a disconfirming datum are unrealistically insensitive to the character of the evidence that provokes them. Wexler, Culicover, and Hamburger claim that when their learner decides whether to add or drop a rule (and if the latter, which rule to drop), "[t]his, of course, is done in a reasonable, not arbitrary, manner" (1975:225). As revealed in Wexler and Culicover's (1980:99ff.), however, 'reasonable' here means 'reasonable from the mathematical linguist's point of view,' not 'reasonable from the psychologist's.' For, on their model, all possible changes in response to a disconfirming datum are held to be equiprobable, the learner selecting one of them at random.[30] Yet as even Quine in his most holistic moods recognized, some revisions in the light of recalcitrant experience are always more likely than others.[31]

29. Thanks to Kim Sterelny for this point.

30. See Wexler and Culicover (1980:102 and n.30). E.g., suppose there were ten rules used in the unsuccessful derivation (hence ten rules any one of which could be dropped from the hypothesis set), and twenty new rules any one of which could be added to the set. Then, the learner has thirty options, each with a probability of 1/30 of actually occurring.

31. See Quine's (1953) insistence that despite the fact that any experience can be taken to bear on any hypothesis, some hypotheses are more "germane" to sense experience than others, hence more likely to be revised.

10.7.3 Inputs and Outputs

A third problem with Wexler, Culicover, and Hamburger's model concerns its assumptions about what gets learned during language acquisition and what it is learned from. In early versions of the theory (described in Wexler, Culicover, and Hamburger 1975:221–22), it was surmised that the learner learns only the Transformational component of a generative grammar, the Base being held to be innate. The latter assumption, however, is disputable. One difficulty, later acknowledged by the authors, is that since different languages order words and phrases differently, the base rules governing word order, at least, must be fixed by experience.[32] Another, unacknowledged difficulty is that in order to apply base rules correctly, the learner must know the subcategorization properties of lexical items. Yet it is implausible to hold that the lexicon too is known innately.

Later models attempted to mitigate the implausibility of the 'Universal Base Hypothesis' by supposing that, antecedently to the learning of transformations, the Base is learned from information concerning sentences' deep structures.[33] But the increase in acceptability gained with this move highlights a third kind of psychologically implausible hypothesis made by Wexler, Culicover, and Hamburger, this time concerning the inputs to learning. Learning the Base in the above model requires information about deep structures. But deep structures are not plausibly viewed as part of the primary linguistic data. They are theoretical entities postulated by syntacticians that, while perhaps playing a computational role in the production and/or comprehension of sentences, are surely not apparent to the casual ear of even competent speakers of a language. A fortiori, they are not apparent to the ear of the child who lacks even a grip on the most rudimentary phrase-structure—not to mention the transformational—rules of his language.[34] This problem, moreover, cannot be evaded by simply reinstating the Universal Base Hypothesis. For on all Wexler, Culicover, and Hamburger's models, learning transformations requires access to sentences' deep structures too: transformations are learned from inputs consisting of ordered pairs (b,s) of deep structures and surface strings. It is true, as Wexler, Culicover, and Hamburger (1975:222) point out, that their model gains in plausibility by using the more accessible surface *sentences*, not surface *structures*, as the second element, s, of the input pairs.[35] However the problem of ex-

32. See Wexler, Culicover, and Hamburger (1975:237).

33. See Wexler and Culicover (1974); Wexler, Culicover, and Hamburger (1975:237 ff.); Wexler and Culicover (1980:99f.).

34. E.g., even if one knew all the transformational rules (which this learner doesn't, since they haven't been learned yet), it is still no simple matter to extract a deep structure from a surface string.

35. It's nonetheless worth stressing here that the difficulty of extracting syntactic information, even something as mundane as a string of words, from the acoustic signal is one of the reasons nativists have argued that an empiricist-style general-purpose learner could not 'bootstrap' his way up from the data to grammatical competence.

plaining how the learner extracts the first deep structure element, *b*, remains. Wexler and Culicover (1974) and Wexler, Culicover, and Hamburger (1975: 237ff.) argue that deep structures may be extracted from data concerning sentences' meanings.[36] But the notion that meanings can be in any straightforward way 'read off' contextual clues is itself highly questionable. So, while one of the virtues of Wexler, Culicover, and Hamburger's learner is that he does not need negative data to learn a language, he nonetheless requires positive data of kinds that are, arguably, equally unavailable. For what actual children have access to during learning is streams of noise set against a bewildering background of people and things. Hence a model assuming their access to (*b,s*) pairs during learning is at most only potentially adequate.[37]

10.7.4 Implications for Chomskyan Nativism

I should emphasize that my object in this section has not been to denigrate the work of Wexler, Culicover, and Hamburger. Rather, my purpose has been to stress that achieving psychological verisimilitude is not the primary aim of formal learning theory. The Chomskyan nativist, recall, identifies the principles specified in (DS) as being needed for language-learning with the principles of the Universal Grammar. I argued that the identification of UG with the knowledge demanded by (DS) cannot be made a priori, and urged the need to supply empirical justification for this move. Here, I have argued that because its primary goal is not the provision of psychologically accurate models, work in formal learning theory offers no such validation. Since its intention is to expand our understanding of the computational demands of various types of learning task by showing how in principle learnability can be guaranteed, psychological plausibility frequently takes a backseat in the construction of the learning theorist's long and intricate proofs.[38] Precisely because "[m]any of the learning assumptions are motivated because of their simplicity or because of technical reasons involving proofs of learnability," as Wexler and Culicover (1980:100–1) put it, the appearance of a learner like Wexler, Culicover, and Hamburger's on the scene gives little support to

36. By assuming (1) that the ordering of elements in sentences' semantic representations is invariant across languages and (2) that the hierarchical relations in the semantic representations are retained in the deep structure (the 'Invariance Hypothesis'), they attempt to explain how learners extract deep structures from the linguistic input: once the rules governing the linear ordering of Base constituents have been figured out, deep structure representations may be read off sentence meanings, which in turn are extracted from contextual information.

37. Another potential source of controversy concerning the inputs to learning derives from Wexler, Culicover, and Hamburger's supposition that the primary linguistic data contain surface structures of degree-two complexity. As we've seen (§10.5), this is controversial.

38. Wexler and Culicover, e.g., are quite explicit about this. See their (1980:97–104).

the idea that UG is implicated in language acquisition. Although making this hypothesis does indeed enable us to envisage learners who may be sure eventually to discover the correct transformations without negative data, this certainty is bought only at the expense of making other undesirable assumptions about the learner and the context in which he learns.

Pinker has eloquently pressed the point that guaranteeing learnability is only a part of the task of explaining language acquisition. He articulates (1979:218) a number of conditions that a learning theory must satisfy in order to be a plausible psychological model. Weakest are the 'Learnability' and 'Equipotentiality' conditions, which jointly require that a model must entail the learnability of all natural languages. Stronger are the 'Time' and 'Input' conditions, which stipulate, respectively, that the model must allow for learning in a reasonable amount of time and under reasonable assumptions about the available evidence. And strongest are Pinker's 'Cognitive' and 'Developmental' conditions. These require that the model respect what is known about the general cognitive capacities of the learning child (by not assuming, for example, that she can remember every sentence she has heard), and that it reflect the actual course of language acquisition (by predicting, for instance, that children will erroneously regularize the past tenses of irregular verbs).

In his (1979), Pinker argued that "no current theory of language learning satisfies, or even addresses itself to, all six conditions" (1979:218). The situation is little better today as regards the provision of empirical validation for the notion that an antecedent knowledge of UG is what drives language-learning. As we saw in §10.6, parameter-setting models are too undeveloped to be appealed to in support for such a claim. In this section, we've seen that the hypothesis-testing model has been amply developed, but in the wrong sorts of ways. As a consequence, Chomsky's identification of the principles of UG with the information specified in (DS) remains unwarranted.

10.8 The 'Iterated' APS Defused

This chapter began with a consideration of the nativist's 'iterated' argument from the poverty of the stimulus. That argument urged that empiricism is barren as an explanatory approach to language acquisition. For the empiricist has no account of how learners could acquire from their experience the knowledge they need to constrain their theorizing about languages. What learners need to know (as Chomsky has established) is Universal Grammar, and it is near enough impossible that they could learn UG before (or even while) they learn the grammar of their native tongue.

In addressing this argument, I claimed that we need a reason for believing that knowledge of UG is indeed what drives language acquisition. I looked at two possible motives for accepting this claim. One derived from the Chomskyan conception of the linguistic task. If grammars and Linguistic Theory are empirical theories at all, this argument goes, then they must be theories of competence and the acquisition device respectively. I countered with the suggestion that theories in linguistics are (as indeed they seem to be) about natural languages, and proposed that Chomsky's opposition to this view rests upon the mistaken idea that realism about languages entails Platonism about languages. Following Devitt and Sterelny (1989), I claimed that languages are analogous, in point of their ontological status, to the economies, religions, governments, political powers, mechanisms of oppression, tyrannies, conspiracies, and the like that constitute the subject matter of other special sciences. They are real things in the world that can be (and, I maintain, are) studied empirically. The fact that such objects might supervene on the psychological states of individuals does not mean that the study of them constitutes a branch of psychology, nor does the fact that they supervene on such 'first order' facts in an as yet quite opaque way mean that they must be relegated to the realm of *abstracta*.

My purpose in making this argument was to defend the contention, made in §7.1 and reiterated in this chapter, that the Chomskyan nativist needs to adduce some psychological evidence in support of his claim (U), that Linguistic Theory describes the language faculty. In this connection, I then examined a second, abductive argument for (U) that has occasionally been made. Chomsky claims that the hypothesis that knowledge of UG undergirds language acquisition is justified by the fact that it provides the best explanation of how language is learned. To this I responded with two questions: What explanation does the nativist provide? and Is it a good one? In §10.6, I examined, and rejected as explanatorily unproven, parametric elaborations of Chomskyan nativism. §10.7 examined what is perhaps the most carefully articulated hypothesis-testing model in the Chomskyan tradition and urged that it, too, is inadequate as an explanation of language acquisition.

I concluded that there is in fact no reason to accept that UG describes the necessary constraints on the language acquisition mechanisms. Thus, there is no reason to progress from the Weak nativist's claim (DS) to the Chomskyan's stronger claim (U). Hence the fact (supposing it is one) that UG could not be learned from experience is utterly irrelevant to our prospects for developing an empiricist account of how languages are learned. The Chomskyan's 'iterated' argument from the poverty of the stimulus is unsound, for it rests upon an empirical premise, (U), that there is no reason to accept.

10.8.1 Three Caveats

Let me stress, first, that I am not arguing here that it is *impossible* that Chomskyan nativism might prove true. I do not rule it out that there may be UG-based models that would validate the claim that languages are learned in the manner Chomsky suggests. All I am urging is that before accepting Chomsky's nativism, we are entitled to see those models and assure ourselves of their empirical adequacy.

Let me say, second, that I do not regard it as in any way destructive of my position or arguments in this chapter that I do not have on hand any worked-out alternative to the Chomskyan picture of language acquisition. Chomskyans often write and speak as if their critics' lack of an alternative theory were in itself evidence for their view.[39] I disagree. In general, I think, the fact that we might lack alternatives to a given theory is reason to retain that theory only when there exist independent reasons to accept it. If there is no independent reason to believe a theory, though, then that theory's being the only game in town is no argument in its favor. What I have argued in part III is that *there are no* independent reasons to believe in Chomskyan nativism. Hence the fact that Chomskyan nativism lacks serious competitors is not in itself a motive for accepting it.

I hasten to add, third, that I do not regard Weak nativism in a similarly bleak light. As we will see in chapter 11, there are a good many reasons to think that the Weak nativist's faculties hypothesis may well be on the right track. As I have argued, though, reasons to believe Weak nativism do not automatically constitute reasons to believe the stronger Chomskyan position. Here again, I think, the widespread failure among theorists of language acquisition to distinguish between Weak and Chomskyan nativisms has done real damage. In encouraging us to ignore the fact that Chomsky's nativism adds to Weak nativism a substantive claim about the nature of the language faculty, the conflation of the Weak and Chomskyan positions has blinded us to the possibility that one may have good grounds for believing in a language faculty without thereby having grounds to believe in the language faculty as Chomsky conceives it.

10.9 Polemics and Concluding Truculence

Indeed, I think, the cognitive science community's largely uncritical acceptance of Chomskyan nativism may be even more unaccountable than I have hitherto implied. For not only does there prove on examination to be no positive incentive for accepting the Chomskyan's claim (U), it is arguable that there is independent reason to be skeptical of it. (U) states that the information we need to know to succeed in learning a language is contained in the Universal Grammar (and hence is described by Linguistic Theory). Linguistic Theory characterizes the essential properties of languages; it delimits the set of possible natural languages. But it is in general false that we need to know about the essential properties of a thing in order to learn about it. Biologists may worry about what makes cats cats, but a child's grip on cathood predates her excursions into zoology. Philosophers attempt to uncover the essential properties of persons, but it is not your knowledge of that essence that is helping you deal with your spouse. Mechanics, perhaps, theorize about the properties shared by all possible internal combus-

---

39. As one only moderately evangelical Chomskyan once asked me, in what he clearly took to be a decisive rhetorical victory: "Well, *how else* are languages acquired?"

tion engines, but no cognizance of those universals, thankfully, is necessary for our learning to drive. The point being that to the extent that it is *in general* false that theorizing about a thing's essential properties is the same enterprise as theorizing about what we must know in order successfully to learn about that thing, there is reason to doubt the Chomskyan's claim that UG describes not just the essence of languages but also the knowledge required for language acquisition to occur. Reflection on the nature of learning *tout court*, I'm suggesting, should have alerted us much earlier than this to the possibility that Chomskyan theories of language learning are on the wrong track.[40]

Now a Chomskyan could concede that one does not need a theory of the Universal Engine, or of Personhood Itself, or the Form of the Feline to learn to drive, or deal with one's spouse, or pick out Bruce-the-cat in a crowd. Yet he might maintain nevertheless that knowledge of essences *is* necessary to language-learning. Learning a language differs from these more trivial kinds of tasks in that it involves acquiring *cognizance* of grammar. And acquiring cognizance of a grammar, the nativist may urge, is a special kind of learning task, a task that one does need knowledge of UG to succeed in.

In order to sustain this line of argument, however, the Chomskyan must explain, first, what cognizance is such that a person's coming to stand in the cognizance relation to a grammar requires that she antecedently know the essential properties of languages; and he must explain, second, what cognizing a grammar (in that sense) has to do with knowing a language. Our primary *explanandum* here is how we come to speak and understand a language. The concept 'cognizance of grammar,' which was introduced by way of partial explanation of that ability, is of interest only insofar as it illuminates language mastery.

The project of explaining what cognizance is and what it has to do with language use and understanding, however, has a rather squalid history.

In the 1960s, Chomsky had had the temerity to use the word 'know' in characterizing speakers' relation to the grammar of their language, and philosophers, naturally enough, protested against this (mis)use of an epistemologically loaded term (e.g., Stich 1971). In response to their complaints, Chomsky grumbled a bit about terminological imperialism (1965:4ff.; 1976: 166; 1980:92ff.) but ultimately gave in, issuing in his (1980) a curt invitation to "replace 'know' wherever [he is] using it with the technical term 'cognize,' which has just the properties [he is] assigning to it" (1980:92). But what *are* the properties to be assigned to Chomskyan cognizance? Therein lay a research program, and the philosophy of linguistics during the last twenty years has been replete with attempts to elucidate a notion of cognizance that preserves and illuminates Chomsky's contention that cognizance of grammar is central to language use and understanding.

---

40. I would not want to claim that beliefs about the essences of Fs *never* play a role in learning about Fs. In some domains, e.g., mathematics, learning does seem to proceed at least partly through knowledge of essential properties.

Cognizance has been analyzed as tacit knowledge (Evans 1981/85:337–39; Davies 1987), as a 'subdoxastic state' (Stich 1978), and as neither, since what is cognized is not explicitly represented (Harman 1967, 1969).

It has been interpreted computationally, as reflecting our instantiation of "computational systems of rules that form and modify representations" (Chomsky 1986:5; see also Chomsky 1988:60ff., 93–101). Within the computationalist tradition, cognizance of grammar has been construed as indicating grammar's role as a 'level two' specification of an algorithm for language production or comprehension (Berwick and Weinberg 1983, 1984), as a 'level one' specification of the function that the language processor computes (Marr 1982), and as neither (Fodor, Bever, and Garrett 1974; Soames 1984a; Stabler 1984). Our cognizing of grammar has been claimed to reflect the fact that grammars specify the information that is 'drawn upon' during language processing, thus constituting theories at 'level 1.5' (Peacocke 1986a, 1986b), a suggestion that has been criticized in its turn (Schiffer 1986).

Cognizance has been claimed to be whatever relation obtains when there is *some* level of description at which grammars are true computational theories of speaker–hearers (Berwick and Weinberg 1984:39ff.). It's been held (by Devitt and Sterelny 1989) to have nothing to do with computational descriptions of language users at all and to be better understood in terms of rule-following. Most recently, cognizance has been argued, ironically, to denote speakers' complete ignorance of the grammar of their language (Devitt 1997).

The morass of empirical argument and counterargument and exegetical point and counterpoint that is exhibited in this literature reflects the fact that no one—including, I'd venture to say, Chomsky himself—has the least idea what cognizance of grammar might be, or of how it might be involved in the use and understanding of the languages that we speak. From a general philosophy of science point of view, this is nothing to worry about, of course. Technical terms are often implicitly defined by the theory that employs them, and as the causal role of the relation or process that a term is intended to denote is progressively better understood, so too the meaning of the term may shift. A theory (like Chomskyan nativism) that is in a state of flux should therefore not be expected to attach a stable meaning to its central theoretical terms; what one should expect instead is that a stable core of meaning will gradually emerge, as the theory is progressively elaborated and refined. That being granted, however, the semantic instability of 'cognizance' nonetheless constitutes a real problem for the nativist in the context of the argument we are presently considering. The nativist was defending Chomsky's (U) on the ground that 'cognizance' denotes a *special* relationship that speakers bear to grammars, a relationship that, intuitively, one could not even hope to enter into unless one had prior knowledge of UG. My point is that one cannot assess the cogency of this particular argument unless one knows what it is that 'cognizance' denotes! If it is unclear (as it manifestly is) what cognizance is, then the nativist is in no position to insist that we all accept his intuition that acquiring cognizance of grammar will require a Chomskyan explanation. A fortiori, he is in no position to insist that language learning is so distinctive among learning tasks that one must buy into the Chomskyan view that learning a language requires knowledge of UG even in the complete absence of any evidence to this effect.

Let me stress again that I am not denying the possibility that Chomskyan nativism could turn out to be true. I am quite willing to believe that there might be a relation, which we can call 'cognizance,' that plays a role in language mastery and is such that we can come to stand in that relation to a grammar only provided we antecedently know what constitutes a 'biologically possible language.' My point is just that, contrary to what seems to be assumed by both sides in this debate, the burden of proof here devolves upon the Chomskyan. Given the really rather striking paucity of evidence favoring his theory, it is the Chomskyan's responsibility to convince us that this account of language mastery and learning is correct. All that I have argued in chapters 7 to 10 is that, as of now, this responsibility has not been met.

11

Will the Evidence for Linguistic Nativism Please Stand Up?

In chapter 10, I argued that there is no reason to accept Chomsky's proposal, expressed in his core claim (U), about the nature of the language faculty. Hence, I argued, there is no 'back door' route to nativism opened up by consideration of whether the Chomskyan constraints on grammars are learnable from experience. In chapters 8 and 9, I argued that the poverty of the stimulus, that trusty innatist stalwart, likewise does nothing to brace the nativist position on language acquisition. The question nonetheless remains: Are there reasons to suppose that there is a special faculty for learning language, or should we abandon altogether the nativist paradigm and pursue a more empiricist path in investigating this domain? I want to end now on a more speculative and personal note, sketching in this concluding chapter some of the considerations that seem to me to bear on this issue. As will emerge below, I am inclined toward a Weakly nativist position as regards language acquisition: I think that there very probably is something very special about language, and that language-learning will likely turn out to have a basis in one or more distinct faculties of mind. I want to emphasize at the outset, though, that I regard none of the following arguments as in any way decisive. My view is that it has been and still is an (almost completely) open empirical question whether nativism about language acquisition is true. Nonetheless, it does seem to me that the evidence currently available tends on balance to support a faculties hypothesis. So if I absolutely had to bet, here, today, on how things will look when psychology is done—I'd put my money on the nativist.

11.1. Linguistic Universals

As Chomsky shows in *Cartesian Linguistics* (1966), the notion that there are properties shared by all human languages, and the hope that such universal properties may offer insight into how the mind is organized, date back at least to the early eighteenth century and the program of the Port-Royal grammarians:

> There are in the grammar observations that apply to all languages; these observations constitute what one calls general grammar.[1]
>
> Grammar, which has for its object the expression of thought by the help of speech, spoken or written, thus admits of two sorts of rules. One kind are immutably true and universally followed, they apply to the form of thought itself, they follow from the analysis of it and are only the consequence of it; the others are only contingently true. . . . The former constitute the general grammar, the others are the object of the various particular grammars.[2]

These early linguists regarded linguistic universals as illuminating the nature of our general intellective faculty. On their view, the theory of "general grammar" reveals "eternal truths" that are "the same as those which govern human reason in its intellectual operations."[3] Modern generative linguists, by contrast, take language universals to be revelatory not of Reason itself but, rather, of the odd and idiosyncratic, strange and unpredictable, eminently ungeneral-purpose structure of their hypothesized language faculty. As I've already made clear (§10.6.3), I do not accept the Chomskyan assumption that one can straightforwardly read off the characteristics of the language faculty from a consideration of what the linguistic universals are. The relation between how our language-learning mechanisms are structured and the properties languages display is sure to be much more complicated than this. Nonetheless, I believe that there is some plausibility to the claim, expressed by those within the Chomskyan tradition, that language universals are evidence of a distinct language faculty.

Chomsky argues that the idiosyncratic nature of grammatical rules and operations demands a faculties explanation (1988:41–48ff.). There seems to be no reason a priori why a natural language should not form a question by reversing the word order in a sentence or using a structure-independent rule like "Move the first *is* to the front" (cf. §8.1). Yet no human language

---

1. "Il y a dans la grammaire des observations qui conviennent à toutes les langues; ces observations forment ce qu'on apelle la grammaire générale." Du Maurais, *Véritables principes de la grammaire* (1729), quoted in Chomsky 1966:52.

2. "La grammaire, qui a pour objet l'énonciation de la pensée par le secours de la parole prononcée ou écrite, admet donc deux sortes de principes. Les uns sont d'une vérité immuable et d'un usage universel, ils tiennent à la nature de la pensée même, ils en suivent l'analyze, ils n'en sont que le résultat; les autres n'ont qu'une vérité hypothétique. . . . Les premières constituent la Grammaire générale, les autres sont l'objet des diverses Grammaires particulières." N. Bauzée, *Grammaire générale, ou exposition raisonnée des élémens nécessaire du langage* (1767), quoted in Chomsky (1966:52–53).

3. "La science grammaticale est antérieure à toutes les langues, parce que ses principes ne supposent que la possibilité des langues, qu'ils sont les mêmes que ceux qui dirigent la raison humaine dans ses opérations intellectuelles; en un mot, qu'ils sont d'une vérité éternelle." Beauzée, *Grammaire générale*, quoted in Chomsky (1966:53).

does so. The claim is not just that all languages are similar; it's that they are similar in ways that one wouldn't expect if language had been invented by us rather than by our genes:

> There is no logical reason why languages should use structure-dependent rather than linear rules. Languages can easily be constructed that use the computationally simpler linear rules. . . . This language would function perfectly well for the purposes of communication. . . . But it is not a human language. . . . Evidently the language faculty incorporates quite specific principles that lie well beyond any "general learning mechanisms." (Chomsky 1988:46–47)

Pinker too makes this case, in illuminating detail:

> All languages have a vocabulary in the thousands or tens of thousands, sorted into parts-of-speech categories including noun and verb. Words are organized into phrases according to the X-bar system. . . . The higher levels of phrase structure include auxiliaries (INFL), which signify tense, modality, aspect, and negation. . . . Phrases can be moved from their deep-structure positions . . . thereby forming questions, relative clauses, passives, and other widespread constructions. New word structures can be created and modified by derivational and inflectional rules. . . . Though many of these arrangements are in some sense useful, their details, found in language after language but not in any artificial system like FORTRAN or musical notation, give a strong impression that a Universal Grammar, not reducible to history or cognition, underlies the human language instinct. . . . The overall impression is that Universal Grammar is like an archetypal body plan found across vast numbers of animals in a phylum. (Pinker 1994:237–38)

Recognizing that this view predicts that "any basic property of one language should be found in all the others" (1994:239), Pinker argues (1994: 232–33, 239–40) that nativism is confirmed by the fact that even the apparent *dis*similarities between languages mask deeper underlying commonalities. English, for instance, is said to be an 'isolating' language. Its semantics is combinatorial in the sense that different meanings are expressed by recombining fixed semantic atoms in varying ways to form sentences (e.g., *The boy loves the girl* versus *The girl loves the boy*). In this regard, it is thought to differ from 'inflecting' languages (such as Latin) and 'agglutinating' languages (such as the Bantu language Kivunjo). In inflecting languages, different meanings are expressed by means of different affixes attached to the stem (*Puer puellam amat* versus *Puerum puella amat*). And in agglutinating languages, the words themselves are made on the fly by stringing many different elements together.[4] Pinker (1989:239) points out, however,

---

4. Pinker (1994:127–28) gives the example of the Kivunjo word *Näïkïm̀lyïïä*, which means 'He is eating it for her,' and is composed of the elements N- (indicating focus), -ä- (a subject-agreement marker that identifies the subject as falling into the first of sixteen gender classes), -ï- (indicating present tense), -kï- (an object-agreement marker, indicating that the object falls into gender class 7), -m̀- (a benefactive marker indicating that the action is taking place for the benefit of a member of gender class 3), -lyï- (the verb to eat),

that like inflecting languages, English too uses affixes to indicate subject agreement (*He walks* versus **he walk*) and marks the case of pronouns (*he, him, his*). Like agglutinating languages, it allows for the rule-governed generation of new words, as in *sensationalization* and *Darwinianisms*. The ostensible differences between the three types of language, then, are really just differences in the extents to which they make use of devices that may be found in every language.

The same is true, Pinker argues, for numerous apparent divergences between English and other languages. English's allegedly "fixed" word order is not really fixed, and the Aboriginal language Walpiri's "free" word order is not altogether free. English is a 'subject prominent' rather than a 'topic-prominent' language, yet like the topic prominent Japanese, allows topic constituents in some contexts (*Peaches I do like, pears I don't.*). English is an SVO language, but contains SOV archaisms like *Till death do us part*. English is a nonclassifier language (its nouns do not fall into gender classes), yet like classifier languages, it sometimes requires use of classifiers (*a piece of fruit*, not **a fruit*). So, Pinker argues, not only does a fixed core of language universals lie hidden, like a skeleton, under the surfaces of all languages; it's also the case that even those more superficial properties (such as being a fixed word-order or classifier or SVO language) that are commonly thought to distinguish languages one from another turn out to be mere variations on a universal theme.

Powerful as Pinker's reasoning here is, neither the existence of universals nor the inference from their existence to a specialized language faculty is uncontroversial. As we have already seen (§10.6) there are theorists, such as Berman (1990), who in questioning the Cluster Principle at least obliquely challenge the universality of some putatively general linguistic principles. Maratsos (1989) too expresses doubts as to how universal linguistic universals are. It is claimed, for instance, that all languages have devices for marking various syntactic properties such as case, tense, and number, and that this is evidence of our biologically based compulsion to construct languages of this particular form (see §11.4). Maratsos points out, however, that in tension with this universalizing tendency one finds wide variations in the medium of marking from one language to another: "linguistic systems exhibit nearly complete variety of marking the same meaning across different languages" (1989:111). For example, although all languages seem to have a mechanism by which to indicate the definiteness or indefiniteness of noun phrases (NPs), that distinction may be made in any of the following, quite disparate, ways. One may use (1) different words (as in English: *a, the*); or (2) different morphological markers placed on the stem (in Hebrew, the prefix *ha-* means *the*, and the suffixes *-echad* (m) and *-achat* (f) mean *a*); or

---

-ï- (indicating that in this instance the verb *to eat* has an additional role, namely someone who is benefited) and -à, a final vowel marking the mood as indicative (Pinker 1994:127–28). Kivunjo, Pinker says, echoing Bresnan, "[makes] English look like checkers compared to chess" (1994:127).

(3) the same morphological marker placed in different places on the stem (*en* in Finnish means *a* if it's at the end of a morpheme and *the* if it's at the beginning); or (4) variations in word order (in Hungarian, definite direct objects must precede the verb, whereas indefinite direct objects may come after it); or (5) variations in intonation patterns (as in some African tonal languages); or (6) variations in NPs' interactions with grammatical case to affect morphological marking (e.g., Turkish) or pronoun case and verb aspect marking (e.g., Tagalog).[5]

Maratsos argues that in addition to such divergences in how languages express widely made distinctions like definiteness and indefiniteness, languages differ too as regards the specific grammatical distinctions they make and the categories they employ. For example, he argues, there is considerable "cross linguistic variation in the basic underlying organization of formal syntactic categories, such as verb, adjective, subject and object" (1989:114). For these are functionally defined kinds. What makes something a verb in English is the role that it plays in the language as a whole: how it carries markings for past tense and negation, is used with infinitives, interacts with NPs to form the basic predicate–argument structure, and so on.[6] Since other grammars may have a very different functional organization—in Chinese and some American Indian languages, for instance, adjectives and verbs have almost identical syntactic roles—we cannot expect the functionally defined categories of English grammar to generalize. Hence the "four English major form class categories are certainly not universal" (Maratsos 1989:115). Indeed, Maratsos urges, "[a]cross languages, the only division guaranteed is that into noun and verb, or more neutrally, argument and predicate" (1989:115). And since the same is true also of grammatical relations such as subject and object, which although well-defined in English, are of dubious applicability to many other languages (1989:115–121), Maratsos concludes that "[s]urprisingly little, even of the most basic kind, is universal" (1989:122).

In addition to questioning the prevalence of general properties of language, Maratsos expresses skepticism about the inference from such universals as do exist to a dedicated language faculty. While granting that, for example, the split into argument and predicate, the deletion of redundant elements in certain contexts, and the tendency for important semantic distinctions to be echoed in the syntax may be global features of human languages, Maratsos urges that no special faculty need be postulated to account for their existence. Instead, the existence of universals like these can be traced either to language's communicative purpose or to general facts about the structure of human cognition:

5. All the examples here, except the Hebrew one (for which thanks to Diana Barkan), are taken from Maratsos (1989:111–12). As Barkan also pointed out to me, things can get even messier than this. In Romanian, a suffix *-ul* marks definiteness, and the indefinite gets its own word, *un*. Hence *omul*—the man, *un om*—a man.

6. See Devitt (1990:373–78) for a helpful discussion of the nature of syntactic properties.

All of these are accountable (at least in theory) in terms of more basic properties of the cognitive apparatus. The fact that certain major seman-tic–conceptual properties, such as definiteness, agency, actionhood, ob-jecthood and location, tend to recur could be traced to the functional and cognitive centrality of these notions in a reasonable analysis of cognition itself. (Maratsos 1989:122)[7]

Elman et al. (1996) argue further that even those aspects of language that might turn out not to have a teleological explanation in terms of commu-nicative pressures may be explicable in nonnativist terms. They argue that connectionist research reveals that very different kinds of 'intelligent' systems may come up with identical or very similar solutions to a given problem. It is common, for instance, for different networks modeling the visual system's extraction of a three-dimensional image from a two-dimensional array to develop units whose receptive fields mimic those of neurons in the mam-malian brain.[8] This shows, they suggest, that there may be "solutions which are contained in the structure of the problem space," solutions that "do not 'look like' the problem they solve but [that] are ubiquitous, if not universal" (1996:386). They propose that communicating thoughts over a one-dimensional channel (i.e., speech) may likewise be a problem so complex that it admits of but one kind of solution for organisms like us, namely, the one that we see in the languages spoken around us.[9]

Chomskyans claim that were a disinterested Martian scientist to come to Earth and examine its various linguistic sytems, she would be forced to conclude that everyone on this planet speaks the same language and that "knowledge of the language that is used is almost entirely inborn."[10] Mar-atsos or Elman and company, presumably, would envision her rather as marveling at the diversity of means that we Earthlings have invented to answer our pressing need to express what is within us. Who would be right? Strictly speaking, I don't see that there is any way at this point to choose confidently between these two competing pictures. Indeed, the existence of disputes like those described above makes me worry that to some extent, at

7. Note the echoes here of Putnam (1971). Unlike Putnam, who advocated an extreme empiricism about language acquisition (§8.2), Maratsos is concerned to advocate a "mixed" learning model, according to which a role is played in acquisition by both domain-specific and domain-neutral learning strategies. This seems very sensible to me.

8. The examples Elman et al. give are of units with center-surround and line-orientation receptive fields (1996:386).

9. See Sampson (1989:211). He argues, following Simon (1962), that "for statistical reasons, any complex structure that is built up gradually by trial and error from simple beginnings . . . can be expected to have certain hierarchical features . . . the 'hard core' linguistic universals identified by Chomsky turn out to match beautifully the properties which Simon's argument predicts will be found in any system built up by gradual evolu-tionary development."

10. Chomsky 1990:633. See also Pinker (1994:240, 232); Chomsky (1988:41ff.; 1991b:26–27).

least, language universals may be in the eye of the describer. Less strictly speaking, though, it must be admitted that it is very hard to read much of modern linguistic theory (especially that developed within the Principles and Parameters tradition) without coming away full of amazement at both the depth and the sheer weirdness of its generalizations about language. Language, if linguists are to be believed, is *very strange indeed*.[11] On the assumption that linguists' generalizations will prove to be robust, I am inclined to be somewhat skeptical of unsupported claims to the effect that the properties natural languages display simply reflect the lucky happenstance that our forebears chanced upon a workable solution to their interpersonal communication problems. Of course, it might be that the fact (say) that anaphors are bound and pronominals are free in their Domain is either the optimal solution to the language-design problem, or a consequence of some deep feature of human cognition, or else is (like driving on the right) merely an arbitrary rule that has through usage become conventionalized. But in the absence of any good evidence to this effect, or proposal specifying how, exactly, the human mind or its need to communicate is supposed to mandate this principle of Binding Theory, my view is that language universals like this, if they exist, constitute prima facie reason to think that there is a language faculty and that it constrains the shape of natural languages.

11.2 The Distinctiveness Of Language

Another intriguing kind of evidence that has been offered in support of the nativist's faculties hypothesis involves the claim that language is distinctive among human cognitive capacities. This distinctiveness is claimed to manifest itself in several different ways. First, it has been argued, a person's degree of linguistic sophistication does not reflect her overall level of intelligence or education. Second, there is evidence that language is localized in the brain, and that qua psychological process, it is significantly 'modular.' Finally, language has been claimed to be susceptible to genetic variability, and the existence of inherited language-specific disorders has been discussed. In each case, some connection is implied between language's independence from other cognitive systems and its being innate, that is, acquired via a special-purpose device. Let us examine these lines of argument in turn.

11.2.1 The Argument from Conververgence

Chomsky emphasizes that unlike other skills or domains of knowledge, which may display marked interpersonal variability and sensitivity to the particularities of experience and opportunity, language mastery is universally

---

11. As generative linguistics moves beyond its Government-Binding days and into the new 'Minimalist' era, the generalizations get deeper and weirder still. See Chomsky (1989/91, 1992/93, 1995).

attained. "Knowledge of language within a speech community is shared to remarkably fine detail, in every aspect of language from pronunciation to interpretation" (1990:635). He argues that the fact that all normal people in a linguistic community acquire essentially the same linguistic competence regardless of differences in either their experiences or their overall level of intelligence, education, or motivation, supports the view that language is subserved by a distinctive faculty of mind:

> To a very good first approximation, individuals are indistinguishable (apart from gross deficits and abnormalities) in their ability to acquire grammar. . . . Individuals of a given community each acquire a cognitive structure that is rich and comprehensive and essentially the same as the systems acquired by others. Knowledge of physics, on the other hand, is acquired selectively and often painfully, through generations of labor and careful experience, with the intervention of individual genius and generally through careful instruction. . . . Having discovered this much, s [an un-biased—perhaps Martian—scientist] should realize that humans are some-how specifically adapted to acquire grammar . . . as they are adapted to walk and not to fly. . . . s would [then] attempt to characterize this specific adaptation. (Chomsky 1975b:146–47)

Empiricists, such as Putnam (1971) and Sampson (1989), have responded that this line of argument is unsound since individuals do in fact differ in their levels of language mastery. Sampson goes further, constructing an ad hominem from Chomsky's acknowledgment of this fact: "In Piattelli-Palmarini (1980:175–6) Chomsky admits that . . . individuals who are more intelligent and/or educated than others have a greater degree of mastery of their common mother tongue. In view of this . . . it is not clear whether anything remains of the . . . argument from convergence" (Sampson 1989: 227).

But, first, there is no real inconsistency between Chomsky's 'admission,' on the one hand, that "two individuals in the same speech community may acquire grammars that differ somewhat in scale and subtlety" (1975b:38) and his frequent assertions, on the other, that "[t]wo individuals with the same genetic endowment and common experience will attain the same state, specifically, the same state of knowledge of language" (1980:46). For he is quite explicit that the claim of common knowledge or complete convergence is an idealization that is made for theoretical purposes: "Each individual has acquired a language in the course of complex social interactions with people who vary in the ways in which they speak and interpret what they hear and in the internal representations that underlie their use of language. . . . [W]e . . . abstract from these facts in [our] attempts at theory construction" Chomsky (1986:16).

In making this idealization, Chomsky is pursuing a strategy that is quite commonplace in cognitive science. Initially, one abstracts away from individual differences and attempts to develop a general account of the cognitive mechanisms at work; then, one shows how the general model predicts and explains such deviations from the norm as are in fact observed. So while the

Chomskyan idealization to complete convergence has had some unfortunate consequences for our (so to speak) *meta*theory of language acquisition (§9.4.3), it is, so far as I can see, completely innocuous in the context of developing an empirical psychology of language use and learning.

Second, and more to the point, it is irrelevant to the force of the argument from convergence that Chomsky appeals to the idealized, rather than the actual, facts of the matter in presenting it. For the nativist's case can be made just as well by an 'argument from almost complete convergence' that explicitly acknowledges some variability in language competence. "Look," the nativist could say, "there are things (such as walking and recognizing faces) that just about everyone is able to learn to do pretty easily; and there are other things (such as riding a bike or doing long division) that not every-one can learn to do easily, though almost everyone can learn to do them; and there are yet other things (like proving theorems in string theory or playing good chess) that only some people can learn to do, and that, usually, with considerable difficulty. Here is an empirical hypothesis: people find it easier to learn to do something if they are specially designed or adapted so as to be able to do that thing, or if doing that thing draws heavily upon other skills that they are specially designed to be able to do. Thus, learning to recognize faces is easier than learning to ride a bike because face-recognizing is something we're built to do; and learning to ride a bike is easier than learning string theory because it makes considerable use of other capacities (such as moving our legs up and down and keeping ourselves upright) that we are designed to be able to do. Now on this continuum, language is surely more like walking and recognizing faces than it is like riding a bike or doing long division—let alone doing string theory or playing chess! Just about everyone learns to do it, reasonably well and reasonably easily. Since we accepted a faculties hypothesis for faces and walking, therefore, we should accept the same hypothesis about language." The na-tivist's point, in other words, is *not* that nativism about language is plausible because everyone acquires the *exact same competence*. The point is, rather, that nativism is plausible because language looks to be one of those things, like walking and face recognition, that we are built to do, and *that* it is one of the things we are built to do is indicated by the simple fact that *we all learn how to do it*.

This conclusion is weak: it's that language is more like face recognition than it is like string theory in respect of its likely biological basis. But for that very reason, it doesn't matter that the premise from which it is derived is weak also. Of course the argument from convergence is not demonstrative. There are plenty of things we're not adapted to do that we all, nonetheless, do. (Using one's right foot to work the accelerator on a car, and having one's hair trimmed, and making funny faces are examples.) So it is certainly possible that language will turn out to be more like face-making than face-recognizing. But that it's possible doesn't mean that it's likely, and all the argument from convergence (as I understand it) aims to do is to offer a reason—not a decisive reason, just a reason—for thinking that language is probably innate. In this, I think, it succeeds quite well.

A second line of argument aiming to establish that language is distinctive emphasizes that it can be selectively damaged or obstructed, leaving other cognitive abilities intact. Here, the idea is that if there are "impairments that compromise language while sparing cognition and vice versa" (Pinker 1994: 46), then that is evidence of a distinct language faculty. Two broad kinds of linguistic dissociation, having different implications for language acquisition, will be distinguished and discussed in the next two sections.

11.2.2 Acquired Dissociations

First, there are a number of well-known syndromes in which a hitherto intact linguistic competence is damaged due to stroke or other brain trauma, leaving other mental functions more or less untouched. The characteristically 'telegraphic' speech that is symptomatic of agrammatic Broca's aphasia, for instance, reflects deficits not in cognition itself but, rather, in the processing of certain grammatical elements (e.g., inflections and function words) (Elman et al. 1996:379). Such dissociations between linguistic abilities and general cognitive abilities have been taken to show that aspects of language are encoded in very specific regions of the brain. Agrammatic Broca's aphasia is reliably associated (in right-handed individuals) with damage to particular areas of the left frontal cortex. This is taken to imply that the corresponding aspects of grammatical knowledge are represented at those loci in normally functioning brains.[12] And this fact, in turn, is sometimes taken to be evidence that language (or in this case, its grammar) is an "innate and domain-specific behavioral function" rather than a learned function, the latter being thought to be "distributed more broadly across neurological systems" (Elman et al. 1996:241). So Pinker, for instance, introduces a chapter titled "Language Organs and Grammar Genes" with a discussion of Broca's and Wernicke's aphasias (1994:297–314). Reasoning that "if there is a language instinct, it has to be embodied somewhere in the brain, and those brain circuits must have been prepared for their role by the genes that built them" (1994:299),

---

12. Müller (1996:622–23) offers an interesting insight into the complex argumentation that goes into establishing that a given language function is associated with a particular area of the brain. He contends, for example, that it's still controversial whether agrammatic aphasia is indeed a disorder of language (let alone syntax) rather than reflecting more general memory or processing difficulties. So even where it's known that lesions in a particular region are associated with certain clusters of symptoms involving (some aspect of) language, it is still no simple inference from this to the notion that *that aspect* of language is coded *in that region*. See also Ellman et al. (1996:380–81) for further evidence of the non-language-specificity of agrammatic Broca's aphasia. On their view, the deficits of such patients now are typically explained "with reference to processing deficits that are only indirectly related to grammar itself" (p.380).

Pinker apparently takes the specificity of these impairments, and the specificity of their locations in the brain, together to bear somehow on language's biological basis.

But, as Elman et al. (1996) argue, the fact that a capacity or function might be localized in the brain is compatible with its having virtually any developmental history, and similarly for those that are distributed over larger areas. They urge that regions of the brain may become specialized as a result of learning processes that are plausibly held to be neither domain-specific nor significantly under biological control—there is a region of the visual cortex, for example, that is specialized to recognize letter sequences that follow the spelling patterns of English words (Elman et al. 1996:242), and PET studies have shown that specific areas of chess masters' brains glow during specific parts of the endgame (Elman et al. 1996:378). Conversely, Elman et al. point out, specialized functions that may more plausibly be thought to be acquired via task-specific and genetically controlled processes may be distributed across large areas of cortex. Cortical stimulation studies indicate that there are many cortical areas where naming can be disrupted (Elman et al. 1996:243), and as Pinker himself recognizes (his earlier inference from neural specificity to innateness notwithstanding), "it would not be surprising if language subcenters are idiosyncratically tangled or scattered over the cortex . . . the brain does not need its functional parts to have nice cohesive shapes" (1994:315).

In other words, the developing cortex is a highly plastic organ. Functionally related tasks may be performed by noncontiguous areas of the brain, and functionally unrelated tasks may be carried out in physically very close locales. What task is done where is determined by a complex interaction of endogenous and exogenous factors; hence, although the neural specialization of (aspects of) language is consistent with language's being the product of a biologically driven and task-specific developmental process, it is also consistent with its being a product of human beings' remarkable ability to remake themselves in the light of their experiences. Consequently, no firm conclusions about how language is acquired can be drawn from evidence of its specific neural bases.[13]

Nor can such conclusions be drawn from data indicative of the (psychological) modularity of language processing (Elman et al. 1996:386–87). Double dissociations between syntactic and semantic processing, as are apparently found in cases of Broca's aphasia and fluent Wernicke's aphasia (in which patients' utterances are well-formed but nonsensical), seem to indicate that language has the so-to-speak 'vertical' or compartmentalized organi-

---

13. Elman et al. also argue (1996: 381) that the significance of localization studies is undercut by the finding (which Lenneberg (1964) was among the first to emphasize) that children who suffer even massive left-brain lesions are usually able to learn language to normal levels, so long as the damage occurs early enough. Other parts of the brain, presumably biologically hallmarked (if at all) for other tasks, are able to take over the language functions normally localized in the left brain.

zation that Fodor (1983) argues to be characteristic of modular psychological faculties.[14] Further, many aspects of language production and comprehension display other characteristics of Fodorean modules as well. Language comprehension, for example, takes place rapidly and involuntarily; its outcome is not easily influenced by the speaker–hearer's beliefs, desires, or preferences; and its underlying mechanism is not accessible to introspective investigation or conscious manipulation. The fact that language exhibits these marks of modularity suggests that it might also satisfy a further condition that Fodor argues to be characteristic of modules, namely, innateness. On Fodor's view, psychological modules are innately specified or 'hardwired,' so to the extent that it is modular, language may be thought also to be innate. But Elman et al. criticize this inference as well. They urge that many different sorts of skills for which it is *not* plausible to claim either biological control or emergence from a task-specific faculty can take on the hallmarks of modularity if they are practiced often enough. Shifting gears, playing a musical scale, and catching a fly ball can become, through learning, the outputs of processes just as rapid, unconscious, and inferentially-impermeable as are those involved in understanding or articulating a sentence of our language. So evidence of language's psychological modularity is again not good evidence of its being acquired through a task-specific learning mechanism.[15]

11.2.3 Developmental Dissociations

In the previous section, I argued that dissociation data deriving from cases in which normal language functioning is impaired as a result of brain injury are on the face of it irrelevant to the nativism issue. Whether taken as evidence of neural localization or of psychological modularity, acquired dissociations between language and cognition shed little light on the question we are concerned with, namely, "Is language acquired through a task-specific learning mechanism?" There is, however, another class of dissociations that is seemingly much more germane to this question. These are what might be called 'developmental dissociations,' to be found in cases where language development is selectively impeded or spared relative to other aspects of cognitive growth. Here the argument is that if one kind of knowledge or skill can be acquired where another cannot, then that is evidence that the two kinds of skill or knowledge are attained in different ways. In contrast to arguments from acquired dissociations, arguments to nativism

14. I set aside here the controversy among cognitive neuroscientists as to the conditions under which it is legitimate to infer the modularity of a psychological process from data concerning abnormal functioning and dissociations. But see, e.g., Shallice (1988, 1991) and Carramazza (1986).

15. Because functions or processes that it is not even remotely plausible to suppose are under biological control can apparently become modularized, Fodor's innateness criterion for psychological modularity should perhaps be dropped.

that are based on the existence of developmental dissociations are potentially much more convincing.

Recognizing the superior probative value of developmental as opposed to acquired dissociations, Lenneberg (1964, 1967) initiated the search for evidence that the ability to learn (or 'general intelligence') and the ability to learn language are poorly correlated. First, he claims, "[i]ntelligence is usually not affected" (1964:74) in individuals suffering from hereditary language disorders. Second, he maintains, "children acquire language at a time when their general power of reasoning is still poorly developed" (1964:78). Third, he argues, the ability to acquire language is independent of both brain size and IQ, two common measures of general intelligence. Nanocephalic dwarfs, whose mature brain weight is about 20 percent of normal (barely exceeding that of a newborn infant) are significantly retarded, yet nonetheless acquire the "rudiments of language" (1964:79), their proficiency approximately equaling that of a normal five-year-old. In children with Down syndrome, too, the growth of language is not dependent on—indeed, is anti-correlated with—IQ (1964; 1967:309–20).[16] Conversely, Lenneberg maintains, an absence of language does not imply reduced cognitive abilities, since congenitally deaf children who have had no exposure to language prior to attending preschool perform normally, once there, on nonverbal tests of intelligence (1964:80). From these data, Lenneberg concludes that language probably has a specific biological basis and is acquired as a result of distinctive developmental processes.

Lenneberg's arguments, assuming his data to be reliable, do seem to me to indicate that the capacity for language is in at least some respects distinct from general intelligence or IQ (whatever that is). More contemporary attempts to infer nativism about particular aspects of language competence from the existence of more specific sorts of developmental dissociations, however, are in my view less successful. Pinker (1994), for instance, searches for a dissociation, not simply between intelligence and language but between general smarts and the ability to learn grammar. He argues that a double dissociation between learning in general and acquiring cognizance of syntax is to be found in a comparison of children suffering from an apparently hereditary disorder known as developmental dysphasia or specific language impairment (SLI), and those suffering from another rare genetic disorder called Williams syndrome. Although SLI individuals tend to have normal nonverbal IQs, their language tends to be quite severely impaired, as Pinker's description indicates:

> They speak somewhat slowly and deliberately, carefully planning what they will say. . . . They report that ordinary conversation is strenuous mental work for them. . . . Their speech contains frequent grammatical errors,

---

16. Lenneberg's results suggest that as Down syndrome children's language proficiency steadily increases throughout the learning period, their measured IQ steadily decreases (1964:79–80). Lenneberg attributes this to the way the tests are scored.

such as misuse of pronouns and of suffixes like the plural and past tense. . . . In experimental tests they have difficulty with tasks that normal four-year-olds breeze through. . . . Apparently the defective gene . . . somehow affects the development of the rules that normal children use unconsciously. The adults do their best to compensate by consciously reasoning the rules out, with predictably clumsy results. (Pinker 1994:49–50)

In contrast to cases of SLI, where aspects of grammar (and especially morphology) are claimed to be degraded in the apparent absence of any other cognitive or linguistic (e.g., semantic or pragmatic) deficits, Pinker notes that "[f]luent grammatical language can in fact appear in many kinds of people with severe intellectual impairments" (1994:52), including people with autism, some schizophrenics, some hydrocephalics, and children with Williams syndrome (WS), a disorder associated with chromosomal defects. Pinker claims that while WS children tend to be "significantly retarded, with an IQ of about 50, and . . . incompetent at ordinary tasks like tying their shoes, finding their way, retrieving items from a cupboard, telling left from right, adding two numbers . . ." (1994:52), they are fluent conversationalists, observing all the grammatical niceties: "[l]aboratory tests confirm the impression of competence at grammar; the children understand complex sentences, and fix up ungrammatical sentences, at normal levels. And they have an especially charming quirk: they are fond of unusual words" (Pinker 1994: 53).[17]

Williams syndrome and SLI represent, Pinker argues, the two halves of a double dissociation that serves to "clinch the case" (1994:50) for the claims that "language is separate from intelligence" (1994:50) and that it develops—or, rather, that syntax develops—in its own proprietary way. Critics have argued, however, that attempts such as Pinker's to ground a specialized grammar faculty on the contrasts between SLI and WS ignore important empirical subtleties that, once recognized, cast doubt on any quick argument from the existence of these developmental disorders to linguistic nativism.

Elman et al. (1996:372ff.) discuss how both SLI and its putatively genetic basis sprang out from behind their qualifactory hedges to assume in the popular (and not-so-popular) imagination a stable and unassailable identity, quite at odds with their real empirical standing, as "well-known facts." They trace the birth of the 'grammar gene' and the emergence of SLI as an apparently unitary and uncontroversial disorder to a letter, written to *Nature* in 1990 by Myrna Gopnik (Gopnik 1990a). There, Gopnik reported the preliminary results of a study of a large family, the KE family, many members of which were diagnosed as suffering from SLI. She argued, first, that based

---

17. Compare the following description, given by an eighteen-year-old Williams subject of her life goals: "You are looking at a professional bookwriter. My books will be filled with drama, action and excitement. And everyone will want to read them. . . . I'm going to write books, page after page, stack after stack. I'm going to start on Monday" (Bellugi, Wang, and Jernigan 1994:27–28). The authors comment that this subject had an IQ of 49, the academic skills of a first-grader, and required a baby-sitter for supervision.

on the apparently Mendelian distribution of dysphasia throughout the family, the KE family members' language disabilities "may be due to one dominant gene" (1990a:715). She next argued that the KE's language impairments reflect very specific abnormalities in their knowledge of English grammar. On her view, the affected individuals are "feature blind" (1990a: 715): they have failed to grasp the rules of inflectional morphology and hence cannot determine how words and phrases should be marked for such critical syntactic features as number and tense.[18] Gopnik's first claim has since been confirmed: the KE's language deficits are due to a single, dominant gene, which was localized (and dubbed SPCH1) by Fisher et al. (1998). If she is right about her second claim—that SPCH1 codes for the rules of inflectional morphology—then her finding of a 'grammar gene' constitutes a stunning confirmation of Chomskyan nativism.

Gopnik's work has certainly been seen as a vindication of linguistic nativism, not only by Pinker, but by other academicians, journalists, and talking heads as well.[19] As Elman et al. (1996:374ff.) stress, however, Gopnik's speculations about the function of SPCH1 are highly controversial. While commending Pinker for his attempt (1994:297–9) to scuttle the notion that there is a single gene responsible for all of grammar, they condemn him and others writing about this issue for failing to take proper (indeed any) notice of the many critical discussions and controverting studies that appeared in the scientific literature subsequent to the Gopnik announcement.

It turns out, in fact, that almost nothing about SLI is uncontroversial. For although SLI is codified as a valid diagnostic category in the clinician's bible, the *Diagnostic and Statistical Manual* (DSM), and although most studies confirm that the disorder runs in families and seems to be partly inherited, opinions differ wildly as to exactly what the term "SLI" denotes. Bishop (1992) surveys the literature, teasing apart no fewer than six different theories as to the underlying causes of the linguistic deficits displayed by language impaired individuals. In addition to Gopnik's hypothesis (1) that the

18. See also Gopnik (1990c); Gopnik and Crago (1991:47).

19. Gopnik's findings generated enormous interest, both within and without the academy. In an article in *Science*, Pinker (1991) asserts that Gopnik's work "constitutes evidence that some aspects of use of grammar have a genetic basis." In a review article in *Nature*, Szathmary and Maynard Smith (1995) call Gopnik's study "[p]erhaps the most convincing evidence . . . for the belief that grammatical competence is to some degree independent of general learning ability" and claim that it "holds out the hope that we will in future be able to dissect language genetically, as we are today dissecting development." A story by AP science writer Paul Recer, filed on February 10, 1992, trumpeted that a "Gene Controls Learning of Grammar." Quoting Gopnik, Pinker, and other well-known experts, the article announced that evidence that "there is an inherited or genetic component to naturally learning grammar rules or in the ability to use individual words" had been presented at the recent meeting of the American Academy. In the *Los Angeles Times*, the headline read: "Language Defects Linked to the Grammar of Genes" (February 11, 1992, p. A24). In April that year, a long article in the *Guardian* promoted Pinker's and Gopnik's "doctrine of original syntax," stating that "there's one thing children don't have to learn: they're born with the gift of grammar," and asking "Is there a gene for it?"

symptoms of SLI sufferers derive from a defect in the language faculty itself, SLI has been traced to (2) impaired motor control, (3) an inability to 'translate' thoughts into a useable speech signal, (4) generalized deficits in conceptual development, (5) deficiencies in auditory processing skills which inhibit language learning, and (6) a global inability to cope with the kind of rapid information processing that language use demands. Evidence supportive of all these theories is available, as is evidence inconsistent with each. Thus although is comparatively easy to say whether a person is diagnosable with SLI, that diagnosis by itself gives little indication of what, exactly, is wrong with her.

Exactly this issue was raised in the next issue but one of *Nature*, where two letters appeared contesting Gopnik's claim that the deficits she observed in the KE family were deficits purely of grammar. Vargha-Khadem and Passingham (1990) claimed that their own study of the same family suggested that the deficits in the affected individuals were not limited to their abilities to apply the rules of morphosyntax, but included a variety of more general cognitive and motor deficits as well. Fletcher (1990:226) argued that the KE family is atypical, judging from Gopnik's description. He argues that "[SLI], outside the family studied, takes on more diverse forms than Gopnik envisages," listing "problems with verb complementation, temporal adverbials, and complex sentence formation" as being among the disorder's typical manifestations. He suggests, contra Gopnik, the SLI is more likely to derive from "phonological production problems," than from an impairment to the underlying grammar per se (1990:226).[20]

These suspicions were subsequently borne out by a number of further studies of both the KE family and other LI groups, indication that symbolic play, spatial imagery, aspects of nonverbal attention, and certain neurological soft signs were also impaired in LI individuals (Elman et al. 1996:369). Vargha-Khadem et al. (1995) confirm the claim of Vargha-Khadem and Passingham (1990) that the allegedly specific grammatical impairment found in the KE family in fact has "a broad phenotype which transcends impaired generation of syntactic rules and includes a striking articulatory impairment as well as defects in intellectual, linguistic and orofacial praxic functions generally" (1995:930). The 1995 study found that both the verbal and the non-verbal IQs of affected family members were on average twenty points below those of unaffected family members, and in addition hypothesized (in apparent confirmation of Fletcher's (1990) claim) that the reason why affected individuals were found to perform so badly on the kinds of morphological tests (making plurals, past tenses, etc.) administered by Gopnik was that they suffered from a congenital inability to control their facial muscles, a disability that especially affected deployment of crucial language articulators such as the lips and tongue.[21] In a study of a group of SLI children

20. Gopnik responds in her (1990b), which simply restates (though in rather stronger terms) the conclusions of her (1990a).

21. In apparent confirmation of Gopnik's postulation of an inherited grammatical def-

in San Diego, Tallal et al. (1991) also cast doubt on SLI's status as a specifically linguistic impairment. Although they confirmed the hereditary nature of SLI, finding that sufferers were significantly more likely than non-sufferers to have a first-degree relative with the disorder, they found that LI children with a positive family history were, in addition, more likely than nonsufferers or those without a family history of the disease to have other behavioral, emotional, perceptual, attention, and motor problems.[22] They too argue that inherited SLI is a result of more basic deficits—such as, perhaps, an inability to process rapid sequences of auditory stimuli[23]—and thus suggest that SLI is not a disorder primarily of language, its name notwithstanding.

Bishop (1994) argues that this confusion derives from the diagnostic criteria used for SLI. According to the DSM-IIIR, SLI is to be diagnosed if (1) language performance is significantly below age-level; (2) there is a substantial (twenty-point) discrepancy between children's verbal and nonverbal IQs; and (3) possible physical causes (e.g., hearing loss, acquired brain damage, abnormal structure of the articulators) or other causes (e.g., autism) of language delay are excluded (Bishop 1994:105). Bishop argues that these criteria are problematic. First, there are different ways to meet them, so a blanket diagnosis of SLI masks a number of distinct subtypes of the disorder, with symptoms ranging from phonological production defects, to productive grammatical problems, to receptive grammatical problems, to general comprehension or production difficulties, to cases where "children . . . speak fluently in complex sentences but . . . give tangential answers to questions" (Bishop 1994:106). In addition, the standard diagnostic criteria may be too strong. Many children who meet conditions (1) and (3) fail to meet condition

icit, however, Van der Lely and Stollwerck (1996) claim to have isolated a group of 'Grammatical SLI' children who display "a persistent and disproportionate impairment in the grammatical comprehension and expression of language" (1996:485) *without* presenting also with serious articulatory or phonological impairments. They found a significantly higher-than-chance incidence of SLI among first-degree relatives of affected individuals, and concluded from the distribution of SLI within families that grammatical SLI displays an autosomal dominant inheritance pattern. A problem with this study is that it scores for a positive family history if a relative is judged to have "a general or nonspecified SLI" (1996:491), where that judgment is made if the relative has or had a "speech, language, reading, or writing problem which required remedial help" (1996:491). But since the 'general or nonspecified' forms of SLI identified in relatives is (as the authors themselves note) a "heterogenous disorder" (1996:485) with a likely diverse aetiology, it is unclear what conclusions about the inheritance of *grammatical* SLI in particular can be drawn from these data. Müller (1996:618) argues that a similar problem pertains to the study of Tallal et al. (1991), see below.

22. Interestingly, though, they found (contrary to Gopnik's speculations about autosomal transmission) that males outnumbered females 3 to 1 among LI individuals with a positive family history, suggesting some kind of sex-linked inheritance.

23. Tallal (1988) found that training in which linguistic inputs are slowed down leads to a dramatic improvement in the language performance of LI children, leading Tallal et al. (1985) to argue that the problem derives from inability to process rapid visual and auditory stimuli. See also Curtiss and Tallal (1991).

(2), so by insisting on a twenty-point IQ discrepancy, one is "drawing an artificial distinction; many children with the same aetiology have equally severe language difficulties without a large IQ-language discrepancy" (1994: 108). Relaxing the discrepancy criterion so as to catch such cases, however, risks "an overinclusive definition that will select all children with borderline intelligence that has no known cause" (1994:108), for large variations among scores on verbal and nonverbal IQ tests are common in normal samples. Bishop ultimately defends SLI as a valid diagnostic category on the basis of twin studies showing a significantly higher incidence of co-occurrence of SLI among pairs of monozygotic twins than is found among dizygotic twins: her idea seems to be that since there is clearly something genetic going on here, we may as well keep using the diagnosis.[24] But while she concedes that researchers might want to keep the twenty-point verbal/ nonverbal IQ discrepancy criterion (condition (2) above) so as to minimize the risk of "selecting a heterogeneous mix of children with diverse aetiologies" (1994:108), she urges that in practical contexts (e.g., when deciding who should receive extra help at school) one should abandon condition (2) as arbitrary and misleading, and also drop the label 'specific language impairment,' which is justified solely on its basis.

In short, SLI seems to be an only marginally useful diagnostic category embracing a variety of language and other deficits with likely very heterogeneous etiologies. Cases of SLI, then, not only fail to support Pinker's claimed dissociation between grammar and general intelligence, but also give at best equivocal grounds for thinking that the capacity for language can be selectively impaired at all.

What, though, of Williams syndrome (WS), wherein language appears to flourish in the absence of most other higher cognitive capacities? Certainly, WS is on the face of it much more susceptible to confident diagnosis than SLI. It is a rare genetic disease associated with a rich cluster of physical and psychological abnormalities. Physically, afflicted individuals have characteristically 'elfin' facial features, irregular teeth, star-shaped irises, hypertension, low birth weight, vascular abnormalities, and hyperacuisis (an abnormal sensitivity to sound). WS brains display no obvious left/right asymmetries and are smaller than and differently proportioned from normal brains. Psychologically, WS subjects have low IQs (typically around 50–60) and display serious deficits on visuo-spatial, number, motor, problem-solving, and planning tasks. However, they also exhibit "suprisingly preserved linguistic and face processing capacities" (Karmiloff-Smith et al. 1995:200), being "almost at ceiling on certain tasks measuring understanding of syntactically complex structures" and scoring "as well as normal adults on the Benton, a face

24. The effect was seen whether strict or lax criteria were employed in determining who has SLI. If strict criteria are used, then 54 percent of monozygotic twins, as opposed to 30 percent of dizygotic twins had concordant diagnoses; if the 20 point verbal–nonverbal discrepancy requirement is dropped, then more than 70 percent of MZ and 41 percent of DZ twins receive the same diagnosis.

discrimination task" (Karmiloff-Smith et al. 1995:200). Behaviorally, WS children are anxious, have difficulty concentrating, and have poor social relationships with peers, although they tend to have good relationships with adults. They are also "empathetic and very sensitive to others' emotional displays" (Karmiloff-Smith et al. 1995:201). WS is definitely genetic in origin—it always occurs in both monozygotic twins—but most cases are thought to arise from new mutations. It has been speculated that WS results from disruption in brain growth due to aberrant calcium metabolism; more recently, it has been proposed that it derives from abnormalities on chromosome 7. (From Karmiloff-Smith et al. 1995:198–201; see also Bellugi, Wang, and Jernigan 1994, which compares the profiles of WS and Down Syndrome subjects.)

Some theorists have interpreted WS subjects' extraordinary facility with language as evidence for a specialized language module. Pinker (1991, 1994), as we've seen, interprets it as evidence for a grammar module, a suggestion echoed in Bellugi, Wang, and Jernigan (1994), who speculate that the "selective, non-deviant preservation of grammar in WS" supports the picture of grammar as "an independent, formal system" (1994:44). However, neither of these inferences is completely straightforward.

First, and contrary to the impression given by some of the literature in this area, it is untrue that the language of WS subjects is overall comparable with that of normal children. While "analyses of their language production indicates that lexical and grammatical abilities are remarkably spared in adolescent WS subjects, given the extent of their cognitive deficits" (Bellugi, Wang, and Jernigan 1994:28), there is evidence too that WS language is in many other respects quite abnormal. Vicari et al. (1996), for instance, conclude that the "language produced by WS children is really unusual" (Vicari et al. 1996:504) and survey recent research suggesting that although WS subjects appear to be good conversationalists, an appearance enhanced by the fluency of their language production, "the content of their speech is often odd or out of place in that social context" (Vicari et al. 1996:504). Bellugi, Wang, and Jernigan (1994) likewise stress the unusualness of WS subjects' vocabularies and semantic organization. In tasks requiring them to name as many animals as they can in a minute, WS subjects—in contrast to both Down subjects and normal controls—will include such items as *weasel, newt, salamander, chihuahua, ibex*, and *yak* (1994: 32). They also note pecularities in WS narratives. WS subjects tend to use affective prosody (marked by altered tone of voice, stress, and choice of words referring to emotion and affect) far more often than either Down Syndrome or normal children. Moreover, their use of such devices continues, even in their second and third retellings of the same story to the same audience, a persistence that, according to Bellugi, Wang, and Jernigan, "contrasts markedly with both normal child behavior and that of other disordered populations" (1994:35). These peculiarities reinforce the contention of Vicari et al. that it is a mistake to think of the WS child as developing normal language in the absence of normal cognitive development.

But the above-described peculiarities are, of course, consistent with claims, like Pinker's, that WS children "display a selective sparing of syntax" (1991:534), and hence with the argument that WS is revelatory of a distinct grammar faculty. However, there is also some evidence suggestive of serious and systematic impairments in WS subjects' grammatical performance too. Rubba (1991), for example, found that 19 percent of a WS subjects' uses of prepositions was deviant, and tentatively proposed that since the preposition use of normal children shows similar deviations from adult usage at certain stages of language acquisition, "we may have, in WS, a case of developmental arrest of linguistic retardation. expectable in subjects showing retardation in other cognitive domains" (Rubba 1991:4).[25] Vicari et al. also claim that in languages, like French or Italian, with more complex morphology than English, WS subjects display a number of other problems with grammatical gender, category fluency, naming, and comprehension of "complex morpho-syntactic sentences" (Vicari et al. 1996:504). In light of such findings, they conclude that the "language of WS children seems to be characterised by preserved phonological fluency but appears seriously impaired in grammer and semantic aspects" (1996:504). So while one certainly could not argue on the basis of such studies that claims as to the differential sparing of syntax in WS subjects are false, it is almost certain that as more and more is learned about the pockets of ability and disability displayed by WS subjects, blanket claims about "preserved syntax" and a "grammar module" will look oversimple.

Not only is there some unclarity as to how and where one should draw the spared versus not-spared line in WS subjects, there is controversy also as to how best to account for the strange cognitive profile that is emerging as characteristic of the syndrome. Pinker, as we have seen, wants to attribute the WS pattern to the selective sparing of a grammar module. Rubba (1991), however, urges that theorists consider the possibility that WS subjects "have greater impairment in their linguistic capabilites than was previously thought, and that the 'language faculty' has not been completely spared in this case" (1991:9). Neville, Mills, and Bellugi (1994) found that auditory processing of linguistic items in WS subjects was radically different from that of normals at any age, and argue that "the systems that mediate the preserved language in Williams are not the same as those that operate in normal control subjects" (1994:81). They speculate that "[t]he hypersensitivity of the auditory system in Williams subjects may in part underlie the sparing of and the precocious and hyperfluent nature of the Williams sub-

25. Examples of deviant uses by Rubba's subject "Crystal" include *He looked through his slippers, He was trying listen for sompin', He looked over [the log] and inside out it, So they stand to each other, This is your first experience of being on a [birthday] party* (Rubba 1991: Table 2, p. 11).

jects' language, and the fact that this development occurs following abnormal delays in the acquisition of auditory language." (1994:82)[26]

Another interesting theory sees WS as reflecting not the existence and sparing of a grammar module but, rather, that of a more general module for socially relevant cognition. We've already seen that WS children's speech displays heavy use of affective terminology. Their face-processing skills (in contrast to their visual–spatial abilities generally, which tend to be considerably impaired) are also unusually well-preserved. (Bellugi, Wang, and Jernigan 1994:37–41). In another study, Karmiloff-Smith et al. (1995) sought, and found, further evidence of the sparing of a cluster of 'socially relevant' skills in WS subjects. The WS subjects in their study displayed near-normal performance on a variety of 'theory of mind' tasks designed to evaluate the ability to understand and reason about the mental states of others. WS children were indistinguishable from normal controls and significantly better than an autistic group in inferring others' intentions and goals on the basis of the direction of their gaze, and 94 percent of the WS children (as opposed to 20 percent of autistic children) succeeded in simple 'false belief' tasks, which involve predicting another's behavior on the basis of his or her false beliefs, rather than the subject's own knowledge of the state of the world. In more complicated higher-order theory of mind tasks, which involve reasoning about what one agent A will do, given what he thinks about another agent B's thoughts, 88 percent of WS subjects succeeded in higher-order tasks involving knowledge attribution, a task that even high-functioning autistics cannot do, and that normal children succeed reliably in performing only at around nine to ten years of age. Finally, Karmiloff-Smith found that unlike autistic children, 80 percent of whom cannot understand metaphor and none of whom can recognize sarcasm, 50 percent of WS children dealt appropriately with both metaphor and sarcasm. These results suggest that at least some aspects of WS superior linguistic performance may be a consequence of a more general affinity for socially relevant tasks rather than being attributable to the preservation of a 'grammar module' per se.[27]

---

26. Müller likewise suggests that WS sufferers' linguistic facility may have a perceptual basis deriving from their "hypernormal auditory sensitivity" (1996:620). Alternatively, he speculates, the apparent language–cognition dissociation may derive from "nonlocalisableearly lesion effects" (1996:621). This hypothesis is supported by the fact that the WS profile (good language, severe visual–spatial deficits) is also seen in other cases of serious brain abnormality (e.g., hydrocephalus and spina bifida). If true, it would undercut inferences drawn from WS about normal neurological organization.

27. On the view defended by Karmiloff-Smith et al., (1995), spared social cognition could be only a *partial* explanation of WS children's overall linguistic success. They argue that the proposed 'social cognition module' likely contains subcomponents dedicated to the processing of stimuli relevant to language, face recognition, and theory of mind, since these abilities may be dissociated one from another. They hypothesize that although the social ur-module would likely include "all the communicative/pragmatic aspects of language," it would not include its syntactic and lexical components, hence that the superior ability of WS individuals in these domains must have in part a different explanation.

In sum although Williams Syndrome does much better than SLI at illustrating its half of Pinker's double developmental dissociation, even WS is not at this time well enough understood in its symptomatology or underlying causes to allow one to assert confidently on its basis that the development of syntax can be spared relative to other aspects of cognition. In 1964, Lenneberg asked "whether proof of language disturbance on a genetic basis is also evidence for the genetic basis of language *ability*" (1964:76). The arguments of this section indicate, I think, that we can do little better today than to echo Lenneberg's own answer to his question, which was, "Perhaps so, but more work will have to be done . . ." (1964:76).

11.3 Critical Period Effects on Language Acquisition

In addition to the dissociation data discussed above, Lenneberg (1964, 1967) cited two features of normal language acquisition in support of his faculty hypothesis. Language acquisition is remarkably robust (in the sense that it is very hard either to interfere with or to prevent), yet occurs only within a certain developmental window or 'critical period.' Lenneberg argues that the robustness and time-limited course of acquisition provide independent evidence of language's innateness.

All normal children in normal circumstances acquire language. So, as Lenneberg points out, do even severely handicapped children and those in highly abnormal conditions, such as congenitally blind children, those deaf from birth, children whose parents are mute, and children suffering from "gross and criminal parental neglect" (1964:67). Moreover, Lenneberg argues, the course of acquisition in typical and atypical cases alike is highly predictable. A learner's progression along the path to language competence is unaffected by the specific nature of her linguistic environment and is unaffected too by the particularities of her culture (1964:67; 1967:127–30, 136–139). Speech has a characteristic onset time (1967:127); children's first words are almost always words for classes, not individuals (1967:127); their first sentences tend to be two-word concatenations, often with subject/predicate form (1967:293); and their vocabulary expands at a rate that is highly correlated with identifiable stages in motor development (1967:129–30). Even in retarded individuals, the development of language follows this pattern, Lenneberg argues (1964:79ff.), noting that even among "feeble-minded" (Lenneberg 1964:79) children, including Down syndrome children, language develops normally (although more slowly) until puberty, when its growth ceases abruptly:

> the development of language . . . in all these patients, follows some general laws of evolvement which may be traced among all of these conditions [productive of mental retardation] and which, indeed, are not different in nature from the unfolding of language in healthy children. Among the retarded the entire developmental process is merely slowed down or stretched out during childhood and is regularly arrested during the early

teens. . . . the developmental arrest at puberty produces "frozen" primitive states which are inalterable at that age by further training. (Lenneberg 1967:309)

This brings us to a second respect in which the development of language, according to Lenneberg, is both robust and distinctive. He proposes that language is susceptible to what he termed 'critical period' effects. There is a 'window of opportunity,' open up to the age of about twelve years, during which language acquisition occurs unproblematically. Outside the critical period, however, language acquisition cannot occur normally, and if a child is not exposed to enough of the right kinds of stimulation during that period, her development of language will be permanently stunted, no matter what experiential reparations are subsequently made. Lenneberg cites a number of lines of evidence in support of his contention that there are maturational constraints on language acquisition, including the fact (mentioned above) that retarded children's language development ceases around puberty (1967: 154–55). Most revealing of a criticial period for language learning, he argues (1967:142–50), are differences in the abilities of children and adults to recover from acquired aphasias. In children younger than three years, severe brain trauma often causes a prolonged vegetative state. When the child regains consciousness, such language as had been acquired before the accident has usually disappeared altogether. Subsequently, however, the child relearns language in the same manner as normal children, passing (perhaps a little more quickly than usual) through the regular developmental stages. Adult aphasics, by contrast, typically do not regain the language they have 'lost.' Although some adult aphasics may recover some aspects of language function within three to five months after injury (as the body and nervous system make whatever repairs are possible), they do not pass through the same developmental stages as do children, and whatever deficits remain beyond this period are typically irreversible. In between these two extremes, the extent of language recovery is dependent on the age at which the trauma occurred. Children aged from four to ten who suffer lesions and exhibit aphasic symptoms very similar to those of adult aphasics typically recover language completely, and display no residual aphasic symptoms in later life. Older children, however, are more permanently impaired. Although they may make steady improvements over several years (unlike adults, who generally display improvement only in the first few months after the accident), the recovery of older aphasic children typically stops with puberty, after which time their prognosis is the same as adult patients'.

Lenneberg argues that aphasia in right-handed individuals is usually due to damage in the left hemisphere, and postulates that the different recovery profiles of aphasic patients of different ages correlates with and is likely a consequence of the extent to which the right hemisphere is able to take over the language functions of the damaged left side. Although considerable neural plasticity is possible up until puberty, hemispheric specialization is fully established at that time and the brain's capacity for major functional reorganizations declines (1967:152–54). Making an analogy with imprinting (which also displays marked critical period effects), Lenneburg tentatively suggests (1967:175–86) that the development of language has a specific biological basis and that "the capacity for language acquisition is intimately related to man's peculiar maturational history and the unique degree of lateralization of function" (1967:179–82).

While Lenneberg's proposals as to the neurological basis of the observed constraints on learning have not been supported in subsequent work (Newport 1990:13, n. 1), substantial evidence confirming the existence of the critical period itself was accumulated during the 1970s and 1980s. Curtiss (1977) recounts the story of Genie, a modern-day 'wild child' who had little or no exposure to language during a childhood spent alone in a room, tied to a potty chair. Despite intensive speech (and other) therapy in the years after her rescue at age eleven, Genie was unable to acquire more than the most rudimentary linguistic competence, and her case was taken by many as definitive proof of the critical period hypothesis.[28] Similarly confirmatory of the critical period hypothesis were a number of elegant studies of second language acquisition and deaf children's acquisition of ASL carried out in the 1980s by Newport and her colleagues. Newport (1984) found that the proficiency of adult speakers of ASL bears no relation to the overall length of time they had been exposed to the language, but does decrease linearly as the age of their first exposure to the language goes up. Johnson and Newport (1989) found that people's competence in a second language similarly declines with age of first exposure until puberty, at which point the curve levels off, with no measurable differences in competence being seen among those who began learning their second language after puberty.

That language acquisition occurs most easily, reliably, and 'naturally' prior to puberty cannot, I think, be doubted. Still, the extent to which these features support a faculties hypothesis is unclear. First, the inference from language's having a critical period to its being the product of a special faculty is sometimes based on a claimed analogy between language and other biologically controlled developmental processes. (This was Lenneberg's argument, as we saw above.) However, there seem to be disanalogies between the maturational constraints on language acquisition and those in those other cases that may weaken this line of reasoning. In particular, it may be urged, the ability to learn language does not cease altogether once the critical period passes: many adults learn a second language to a high degree of fluency, if not always to native-speaker standard (Sampson 1989:218). This contrasts with classic examples of maturationally bounded developmental processes, such as imprinting and the development of the visual system (Hubel and Wiesel 1963), in which the ability to acquire the competence in question ceases altogether at the end of the critical period.

28. Lane (1976) discusses another 'wild child' case. See also Curtiss (1988), an account of another language-deprived individual, Chelsea, who, deaf from birth, was isolated from language until age thirty-two.

Lenneberg (1967:176) anticipates this objection, arguing that the ability of adults to learn a second language may be explained by the fact that they had plenty of access to linguistic stimulation as they learned their first language. A better test case, the nativist might urge, is provided by someone like Genie, who was not exposed to much in the way of language at all during the critical period. Genie at first seems to support the nativist's analogy. Like Hubel and Wiesel's kittens, she was unable to acquire the competence in question once the developmental window had closed. Unfortunately, however, Genie's language deficits are not straightforwardly attributable to her lack of exposure to language as a child. Instead, they may be due, in whole or in part, to more general cognitive and emotional deficits produced by the extreme conditions of cruelty and deprivation in which she lived.[29] Interestingly, Lenneberg himself rejected so-called 'wild children' as evidence for the critical period for exactly this reason: "The only safe conclusions to be drawn from the multitude of reports [concerning such children's failures to acquire language] is that life in dark closets, wolves' dens, forests or sadistic parents' backyards is not conducive to good health and normal development" (1967:142).

I tend to concur. It seems to me that the similarities between language acquisition and imprinting or the development of the visual system are not well enough established at this time to support the inference to language's innateness. Since they're unlikely to be better supported any time soon (the requisite experiments being, thankfully, rare in nature and prohibited in the laboratory), I do not find this line of argument for nativism very convincing.

There is, however, another way to get from the unstoppable and time-bounded nature of language acquisition to its being the product of a special faculty. Rather than relying on dubious analogies with the development of peripheral processes like vision, or instinctual behaviors like imprinting, this argument takes the fact that language-learning occurs reliably and easily in early childhood to be simply another example of how language acquisition differs from most other kinds of learning. The fact that language acquisition is highly robust and in addition shows period effects, whereas the ability to learn other things (say math or physics) does not, is evidence that language is learned through a distinctive mechanism.

This argument for nativism has been challenged too, of course. Sampson (1989:219) raises the possibility that *all* learning (and not merely language-learning) is more difficult after puberty, and faults Lenneberg for failing adequately to address this possibility.[30] Elman et al. (1996:389) likewise

---

29. See Rymer (1992), which surveys some of the conflicting evidence on this point.

30. Lenneberg's only remark in this context is the—uncharacteristically vague and unsupported—assertion that there is "probably not" a general decline in the ability to learn post-puberty: "There are many skills and tasks that are much better learned during the late teens than in early childhood and a great deal of general learning has no age limitation whatsoever" (Lenneberg 1967:176).

suggest that age-related changes in the facility with which new knowledge is acquired are not specific to language, proposing that such changes in plasticity may be the result of learning itself. Connectionist modeling indicates that as ever more information is assimilated, neural structures may change in ways that make them unable to respond to new types of input. Thus, Elman et al. suggest, the maturational constraints on language-learning may simply be symptoms of the brain's increasing inflexibility. It is harder to learn a second language than it was to learn your first one because by puberty, your brain has, as it were, solidified around the sounds and structures of your native tongue. And it is hard, even impossible, to learn language if you have had no exposure to language during childhood for similar reasons: if things other than language are learned during the critical period, the ability of the brain to deal with linguistic information decays as a consequence.

Newport (1990) argues, against such suggestions, that language really is, as it appears to be, quite distinctive in the maturational constraints that it displays. Unlike learning "in most cognitive domains" (1990:22), which tend to support the "uncontroversial generalization" of developmental psychology that "big kids are better than little kids" (1990:12), language exhibits the opposite pattern, "with greatest success achieved by the *least* mature learners" (1990:22). However, Newport urges, one does not need a faculties hypothesis to account for this phenomenon. She proposes instead what she calls a "Less is More" hypothesis, according to which "language learning declines over maturation precisely because cognitive abilities increase" (1990:22). On her view, elaborated in Newport (1988, 1990), the fact that young children are not terribly proficient at learning in general is, almost paradoxically, what makes them so extraordinarily adept at learning language! Young children are unable to process complex stimuli, and hence must store and work with more abstract or "componential" (1990:24) representations of linguistic inputs. This limitation, Newport suggests, facilitates their representation of abstract syntactic facts, which, in turn, aids them in their extraction of linguistic rules and generalizations: "If children perceive and sort only component parts of the complex linguistic stimuli to which they are exposed . . . children may be in a better position to locate the components" (1990:24) and, hence, to formulate rules defined over them. Latecomers to the language learning game, by contrast, have developed the ability to "accurately remember and perceive complex stimuli" (1990:24). As a consequence, Newport argues (1990:23–26), they tend *not* to perform or store componential analyses of linguistic inputs, and hence fail in "consistently and uniquely analyzing the complex structures of language" (1990: 23). Since older learners are better than younger learners in perceiving and processing linguistic data in all their complex particularity, they have a correspondingly more difficult time than children in distilling linguistic generalizations from those data.

Newport's "Less is More" hypothesis certainly requires further investigation and elaboration. However, it does serve to demonstrate that the inference from observed maturational constraints on language acquisition to the existence of a language faculty is far from straightforward. Accordingly, I find this line of argument for nativism less than wholly persuasive.

11.4 Pidgins and Creolization

I shall end now with a brief look at another intriguing kind of evidence that has been cited in support of the nativist's language faculty. Discussed by Pinker (1994:32–39), this evidence concerns the process known as 'creolization,' wherein a 'pidgin' becomes a 'creole' as a result of being learned by children as their first language. A pidgin is a "makeshift jargon" (Pinker 1994:33), a "highly variably, extremely rudimentary language state" (Bickerton 1981:5) that is developed in societies where members of different language communities must live side by side and interact verbally in practical contexts. Often derived from the language of colonists or other powerful groups, pidgins are simple language systems "highly variable in word order and with little in the way of grammar" (Pinker 1994:33).

Now it is perhaps not suprising to think that a pidgin may become progressively more complex and sophisticated over time, eventually developing the marks of a mature natural language as originally disparate groups of speakers form more cohesive communities and have need to communicate more complex thoughts. However, it is suprising—or perhaps should be surprising to an empiricist—to think that the transformation from pidgin to creole could occur in one generation. Yet there is strong evidence that exactly this has happened—so strong, indeed, that Bickerton (1981) actually builds into his definition of a 'creole' the requirement that it "arose out of a prior pidgin which had not existed for more than a generation" (1981:4).

Bickerton (1981) compared the speech of two groups which emigrated to Hawaii at the end of the nineteenth century. Members of one group, who learned the Hawaiian pidgin (HPE, or 'Hawaiian Pidgin English') as adults, retained in their speech many of the characteristics (such as little regular structure, few syntactic markers, ambiguity, limited vocabulary) of the 'jargon' they learned on arriving in the islands. Members of the other group, by contrast, who had emigrated as children and had learned the pidgin as they were growing up, spoke quite differently. Their language—Hawaiian Creole English (HCE)—has a systematic grammar utilizing many of the syntactic elements that Hawaiian pidgin lacks, including articles (Bickerton 1981:22–26), auxiliaries (1981:26–30), sentential embeddings (1981:30–33) and relative pronouns (1981:34–42). Bickerton urged (1981:145ff.) that the latter group's language was evidence of how the innate language faculty, if left to its own devices, forces children to learn languages with a particular kind of structure, even when that structure is completely absent in the linguistic stimulus to which they are exposed. He supported this contention with the further observation that different creoles formed from unrelated languages bear "uncanny resemblances" (Pinker 1994:35) to each other as regards their use of movement rules, articles, complementizers, negation, Wh-words and phrases and the use of adjectives as verbs (Bickerton 1981: 43–70). These similarities, he argues, reflect the knowledge about language that we are born with.

As Pinker notes, Bickerton's argument is somewhat controversial, for it relies on his reconstruction of events (in particular, those surrounding his subjects' acquisition of language) that happened long ago. However, as Pinker then goes on to argue, the notion that children are compelled to invent a complex grammar even when none is present in the input language has recently been confirmed by studies of the sign languages of some of the world's deaf populations. Sign languages are known to be 'real' natural languages, marking most or all of the distinctions made in other languages. What is interesting is that signers too display the same patterns of acquisition as the Hawaiians whose language acquisition was reconstructed by Bickerton. For example in Nicaragua, as Pinker recounts (1994:37ff.), there were no offical sign languages until 1979, when the first schools for the deaf were created and LSN (Lenguaje de Signos Nicaragüense) was developed and came to be widely used in the deaf community. LSN as spoken by those who learned it in adulthood, according to Pinker, is "basically a pidgin. Everyone uses it differently, and the signers depend on suggestive, elaborate circumlocutions rather than on a consistent grammar" (1994:36). However, among those who learned sign language as children from speakers of the LSN 'pidgin,' an apparently very different language—called ISN (Idioma de Signos Nicaragüense)—has emerged. In ISN, unlike LSN, signs are standardized: everyone signs in the same way. The signs themselves are different: "[t]he signing is more fluid and compact, and the gestures are more stylized and less like a pantomine" (Pinker 1994:36). Further, ISN contains grammatical devices not present in LSN, such as the modification of signs to indicate subject–verb agreement and agent and patient roles (Pinker 1994: 36). On the basis of such characteristics, psycholinguists argue that ISN is a creole, "created" (like the Hawaiian creole) "in one leap when the younger children were exposed to the pidgin signing of the older children" (Pinker 1994:36–37).

Pinker also reports that a similar phenomenon—wherein the language a child learns to speak is more complex than the one he learns it from—has been observed in a deaf child, Simon, studied by Newport and Singleton. Simon learned ASL from his parents, who were also deaf and who had learned ASL as teenagers. Simon's parents' ASL skills were on the rudimentary side and "[i]n many ways . . . [they] . . . were like pidgin speakers" (Pinker 1994:38). For instance, they failed to learn the ASL rule for topicalization, and failed also to grasp its verb inflection system (Pinker 1994: 38). But

[a]stoundingly, though Simon saw no ASL but his parents' defective version, his own signing was far better ASL than theirs. He understood sen-

tences with moved topic phrases without difficulty and . . . he used the ASL verb inflections almost perfectly. . . . Simon must somehow have shut out his parents' ungrammatical "noise." He must have latched on to the inflections that his parents used inconsistently, and interpreted them as mandatory. . . . Simon's superiority to his parents is an example of creolization by a single living child. (Pinker 1994:39)

Nativism seems positively born to explain creolization. If language is learned by a mechanism that is constrained only to consider certain types of hypotheses, or that is designed to discard grammars that are regarded (by the inbuilt evaluation metric) as inelegant or unproductive or otherwise undesirable, then it is not surprising that if any language can be learned at all from degraded inputs such as pidgins, it would display features not contained in the input language. Empiricists, on the other hand, face a real challenge in explaining why children should add structure to the language that they hear spoken around them, for they must explain creolization by showing how the added elements could derive from more general constraints on cognition.

Potential empiricist explanations do exist. Perhaps, for instance, the additional structure is vital to the acquired system's being able to serve its communicative purpose. While the usefulness of particular grammatical features is controversial, some aspects of syntax have nonetheless been argued to facilitate communication. Pinker and Bloom's (1990) defense of the 'evolvability' of subcomponents of a grammar, for instance, depends on their making a case that those various components are functional. If aspects of grammar were at one time selectively advantageous because they enhanced our ancestors' ability to communicate, then perhaps they could be argued by an empiricist to improve the communicative capacities of individual children as well, and to be invented by them for that reason. Alternatively, it may be argued that people just aren't 100 percent accurate in learning languages. Sometimes they add structure (as in the cases we have looked at). But other times too they lose it, what is learned turning out to be less complex than what it is learned from. Lightfoot's (1991) discussion of historical language change makes clear that less complex languages (such as modern English) developed out of—and hence, presumably, can be learned from—more complex languages (such as Old English). Creolization might be an instance where learners err in the opposite direction.[31]

Still, and as I indicated at the outset of this chapter, I am not persuaded. Although there is much to be said for an empiricist approach to language acquisition, and although I have tried throughout part III of this book to say a lot more for it than has lately been consistent with a person's having any kind of future in cognitive science, I cannot shake the intuition that some form of nativism about language learning is overall more plausible

---

31. See also Deacon (1997:138–40).

than its rival. In this final chapter, I've tried to illustrate some of the grounds for this intuition. I've suggested that based on the preponderance of the evidence currently available, the nativist might be right after all about language acquisition.

11.5 Conclusory Moralizing

But lest I be suspected of closing this discussion of language acquisition, and of innate ideas in general, with a nice, definite 'Yea' or 'Nay' to linguistic nativism, let me stress that I regard all the pro-nativist arguments just discussed as highly provisional, in at least two respects.

First, it is important to stress that there is no reason to think that either nativism or empiricism will prove to be correct across the psychological board. It is likely, I think, that people will turn out to possess *both* general-purpose *and* task-specific abilities to learn, and hence that nativism is likely to be true in some domains and empiricism in others. As we have seen in this chapter, language displays certain marks that are suggestive of its having a nativist basis: the existence of language universals, the dissociation between children's acquisition of language and their acquisition of other skills of comparable complexity, phenomena like creolization. But there are other abilities that we have that do not display these sorts of characteristics and that seem more plausibly viewed as products of a powerful general capacity we humans have to learn from experience. Knowing what curries are; knowing one's multiplication tables and how to use them; recognizing a Mozart symphony or a David Bowie lyric; distinguishing an electron's track in a cloud chamber from that of an alpha particle; or picking the Chanel from among the Diors; writing a philosophy paper; or driving a car; or singing the National Anthem—these are abilities for which it seems, to say the least, far-fetched to postulate special faculties. The point being that *whatever* is the truth about language-learning, we are still going to need an empiricist-style general learning mechanism to account for some acquisition phenomena. Maybe it will turn out to be also the mechanism for language-learning, maybe not. But nativism is unlikely to be true in every domain. Hence it has been, in my view, a serious mistake to allow Chomsky-style arguments from the poverty of the stimulus to forestall—as they have forestalled throughout much of psychology and cognitive science—the development of nonnativist theories of learning.

And it is important to recognize, second, that the truth in a particular domain—whether it be language-learning or the acquisition of other competencies—must be discovered the hard way, that is, by finding the best overall account of the facts of acquisition and seeing the extent to which that account attributes inherent, task-specific structure to the learner. Although I have agreed in this final chapter that there are various indications that nativism about language-learning may well prove correct, I regard these arguments as highly defeasible in the absence of detailed, empirically adequate models of the actual processes by which languages are learned (§§10.5–10.7).

Let me end now by stressing that my intention here is not to pick on language-learning in particular, or to suggest that we are somehow more ignorant in the linguistic domain than we are elsewhere. My view is that learning *tout court* is *the* main unsolved mystery of modern cognitive science. It's unclear how we learn language—as I've argued. But it's unclear how we learn *anything!*

Take face-recognition, for instance. Like learning language, learning how to recognize the faces of people one knows is often cited as a strong candidate for a faculties explanation (e.g., Fodor 1983). As we've seen before (§6.4), people seem to have the concept of a human face innately, in the sense that minutes-old infants respond selectively to faces.[32] Two-day-old babies can discriminate their mother's face from that of a stranger; by six months, infants can discriminate old from young and male from female faces; and by seven months they can recognize as familiar faces that they have seen only briefly.[33] Their facility in performing these (extremely difficult) tasks of perceptual encoding and discrimination, in contrast with their otherwise largely undeveloped visual skills, suggests that learning how to encode and recognize familiar faces is specially facilitated. Furthermore, this ability has been argued to have a satisfying (and obvious) evolutionary explanation.[34]

Carey (1992:96–7) describes other studies carried out by herself and her colleagues that seem to provide further support for a nativist view of face recognition. First, children's ability to process faces improves more rapidly than does their ability to process inverted faces. Since faces and inverted faces are images of the same level of complexity, one would predict that they would place the same demands on a general-purpose pattern-recognizing mechanism. Children's differential success in dealing with the two kinds of images thus suggests that different mechanisms are at work. Likewise supportive of a faculties hypothesis is the fact that children's ability to encode and recall faces improves dramatically between the ages of six and ten years, whereas their ability to encode and recall stimuli consisting of randomly generated patterns of dots does not (Carey 1992:97). The phenomenon of prosopagnosia also is often taken to support a faculties hypothesis. Subsequent to brain damage, propsopagnosic patients lose not only the ability to recognize faces but also the ability to relearn how to do that

32. For example, infants less than ten minutes old showed a preference for following a moving schematic face over other images of comparable complexity (Ellis 1992:115).

33. Results surveyed in Carey (1992:96); see also Ellis and Young (1989:4–8).

34. Morton and Johnson (1991) argue that the 'specialness' of face recognition reflects the biological significance of faces to social species such as our own; Carey (1992:96) calls babies' early recognition of facehood a "running start" provided by evolution.

task. To the extent that these disabilities are specific to recognizing and learning about faces, the nativist hypothesis is supported.

On the other hand, though, there is evidence against a special 'face faculty' too. Ellis and Young (1989:13) quote Damasio's contention that prosopagnosia is not specific to human faces, and survey a number of studies indicating that many patients diagnosed with prosopagnosia also have difficulty distinguishing other classes of objects (such as foods and animals, cars, abstract symbols and birds) and kinds of stimulus (e.g. colors).[35] As regards the distinctiveness of the learning processes involved in facial perception, Carey (1992:96) discusses a number of experimental results in contravention of the faculties hypothesis. The steady improvement in face-processing that children display through about age ten undergoes a sudden and marked reversal during puberty. The fact that this disruption in performance is echoed in their processing of non-face stimuli as well suggests that there may after all be a significant common basis to the various processes of visual learning. Also confounding the interpretation of studies of face recognition is the fact that faces are extremely common stimuli in the human visual environment, which raises the possibility that children's superior processing of faces is due less to the operation of a dedicated face mechanism than it is to their having had so much experience with them. Another experiment of Carey's supports the latter explanation. Diamond and Carey (1986) reasoned that if familiarity and experience were (contra the faculties hypothesis) responsible for children's superior performance in dealing with faces as opposed to other, similarly complex stimuli (such as inverted faces), then similar dichotomies should be seen in other situations involving experts. They compared the abilities of both American Kennel Club show judges and dog-show novices to recognize previously encountered right-way-up and inverted dog faces. As predicted, the experts were better at recognizing the upright doggy faces than the inverted faces, whereas the novices were equally bad on both tasks. This Diamond and Carey took to indicate that experientially acquired expertise, rather than a special faculty for recognizing human faces, is responsible for our superior ability to process and remember those stimuli in comparison with others of equal complexity.[36]

There is, of course, much more to be said on the topic of face recognition and whether it is 'special' in ways that support a nativist learning theory in that domain. My point in discussing face recognition here is to underscore the fact that although face recognition is one of the best candidates for a faculties explanation that is presently to be had, the evidence for nativism

35. Ellis and Young find in their survey of the literature only one case in which prosopagnosia was apparently not accompanied by other agnosic symptoms (1989:14).

36. Ellis and Young (1989:9) question these results on the grounds that the experts proved no better than the novices in recognizing upright dog faces: they were better only at recognizing the inverted ones.

in that domain remains equivocal. Even more equivocal and difficult to interpret, I have suggested in part III, is the evidence in favor of nativism in the domain of language. Which suggests, I think, the following moral: If the jury is still out on face recognition—a process about which, after all, vastly more is known than about language use and understanding—how much more reluctant should we be to dogmatize about language acquisition!

So if—and this really is the end!—if I could urge *just one thing* as a 'take home' lesson to be drawn from the discussion of language learning in part III, it would be this: To understand a psychological phenomenon as complex and distinctive as language acquisition, we need to look everywhere we can for relevant insights, data, and techniques. We need to approach language with an open mind—a *tabula rasa* in the right sense!—and not with minds writ all over with a priori and ill-substantiated theoretical prejudices. Only when psychology is 'finished'—only when we have on hand a workable theory of how languages are learned—will we be in a position to say with any certainty whether or not nativism in this domain is correct.

Conclusion

In the last three decades, the perennial battle over innate ideas has once again been joined. This book has critically examined the contemporary resurgence of nativism about the mind in the context of both its historical development and modern advances in psychology and related fields.

Part I looked at the historical controversy about innateness, argued that standard interpretations of that debate are misguided, and developed a new account of what nativism is. According to the view I urged in chapter 1, it is incorrect to view nativism as a response to either of the two problems—namely, the justification of the a priori and the explanation of where our ideas come from—with which it has, historically, been associated. I suggested that what unites proponents of innate ideas is rather their denial of empiricism, a denial that manifests itself in nativists' tendency to defend two quite different (and prima facie incompatible) positions. On the one hand, as I showed in chapter 2, nativists assert a particular claim about the psychological processes responsible for our acquisition of ideas and beliefs. They hold that explaining how a mind gets furnished with its complement of mental states requires the postulation of dedicated, rather than general-purpose, learning faculties. On the other hand, however, as I showed in chapter 3, nativists are also driven at times by their more general views about the mind and its place in nature to express the nonnaturalistic suspicion that the project of explaining the genesis of our mental lives is in principle doomed to fail. By the lights of this neglected yet prominent component in nativist thinking, the interactions between mind and world that we ordinarily take to give rise to our cognitions are, and are overwhelmingly likely to remain, a mystery.

Parts II and III of this book examined the modern resurrection of innate ideas in light of this background.

Part II discussed Fodor's quondam nativism about concepts, surveyed his more recent repudiation of that position, and offered an alternative to his 'brute-causal' account of the concept-learning process. Chapter 4 sketched Fodor's arguments against empiricist accounts of conceptual development and introduced his radical concept nativism. I argued that Fodor's 'innateness hypothesis' should be understood as asserting that concept acquisition is nonpsychological, and I noted that in its denial that concept acquisition is susceptible of psychological explanation, Fodor's position bears a striking similarity to the non-naturalisms of earlier innatists. Chapter 5 then went on to discuss a problem with Fodor's earlier nativism, dubbed by Fodor (1998) the 'doorknob/DOORKNOB problem.' Contrary to what is predicted by Fodorean nativism, our concepts of F-ness are typically triggered by Fs. Whereas an empiricist may explain this regularity by noting that it is experiences of doorknobs that provide us with the materials to learn what DOORKNOB means, such intentional explications are unavailable to the Fodorean. Fodor offers two alternative explanations. His later, metaphysical explanation, I argued in chapter 5, fails to solve the problem: it is a serious mistake to think that the explanation of concept acquisition devolves upon the metaphysician. His earlier, 'brute-causal' account of concept acquisition likewise fails to explain how concepts are got from experience, as I argued in chapter 6. I urged that the acquisition of a concept in most cases requires our coming to possess some kind of recognitional capacity. While some of these recognitional capacities may well be innate, others depend on knowledge that is clearly learned through experience. Thus, I urged, in contradistinction to the pessimism evinced by the Fodorean nativist, psychology does have a role to play in explaining how our minds are furnished, for learning is frequently involved in concept acquisition, and what is learned needs to be intentionally described.

Whereas Fodor's nativism, I urged in part II, is of a kind with the second, mystery-mongering element in earlier nativisms, I argued in part III that Chomsky's nativism is continuous, rather, with the earlier nativists' postulation of special learning faculties.

Part III surveys the arguments and evidence bearing on language acquisition, rejects the Chomskyan account of the language acquisition mechanism, and ultimately defends a Weak (non-Chomskyan) version of nativism about language-learning. In Chapter 7, I articulated the five 'core' claims of Chomskyan nativism and argued that since these claims are largely independent of each other, there are a number of possible positions, of which Chomskyan nativism is only one, that could rationally be taken with regard to language-learning. I urged that failure to recognize these various possibilities has led to a situation wherein the evidence for linguistic nativism and against various forms of empiricism has mistakenly been taken to be much stronger than, in fact, it is. In chapters 8, 9, and 10, I argued that the celebrated 'argument from the poverty of the stimulus,' so often invoked by Chomskyans in support of their position, fails abysmally on both empirical and conceptual grounds to support nativism about language learning. Neither traditional poverty of the stimulus arguments, nor arguments from the alleged Logical Problem of Language Acquisition, nor the 'iterated' argument from the poverty of the stimulus discussed in chapter 10, offers the least reason to think that there is a special faculty for language acquisition. Nonetheless, I argue in chapter 11, we do have reason to think that there is a 'language faculty.' While the arguments that nativists have most insistently invoked in their own support are upon examination unable to establish their position, there are other lines of evidence, less cited but no less important, that suggest that the nativist's faculties hypothesis, rather than some form of empiricism, is the correct approach to take toward language acquisition.

Still, I argued, this conclusion is provisional at best. The current plausibility of nativism in the linguistic domain should not blind us to the need to develop empiricist (or general-purpose) accounts of learning in other areas. Nor, I urged, should it incline us to accept without question the rash of nativist theories about other aspects of human behavior that has developed in recent years. If the arguments of this book have any significance at all beyond the confines of academic philosophy, psychology, and cognitive science, that significance must lie in their demonstration that establishing a plausible account of the development of our cognitive (or other) capacities is no straightforward matter. Defending nativism—or its converse—requires that one show that that position provides the best overall account of how a given trait is acquired. So little is now known about the etiology of any trait that one must be wary of the kinds of glib and hand-waving conjectures as to the bases for a given trait that are currently fashionable. The truth or falsity of an innateness hypothesis, in whatever domain, must be discovered the hard way, that is, by developing an understanding of that trait's etiology, determining the extent to which it is susceptible of explanation at all, and if it is, whether that explanation requires the postulation of a dedicated learning faculty.

Bibliography

Adams, R. M. (1975). "Where Do Our Ideas Come From?" In Stich (1975) pp. 71–87.

Aitchison, J. (1987). *Words in the Mind: An Introduction to the Mental Lexicon.* Blackwell, Oxford.

Alper, J. S., and Beckwith, J. (1993). "Genetic Fatalism and Social Policy: The Implications of Behaviour Genetics Research." *Yale Journal of Biology and Medicine*, 66, pp. 511–24.

Antony, L. (1991). "Rabbit Pots and Supernovas." (Unpublished manuscript).

Ariew, A. (1996). "Innateness and Canalization." Paper delivered at the Philosophy of Science Association biennial meeting, Cleveland, OH, November 1.

Ayers, M. R., ed. (1975). *Berkeley: Philosophical Works, Including the Works on Vision.* 2nd ed. Everyman, London.

Baker, C. L. (1979). "Syntactic Theory and the Projection Problem." *Linguistic Inquiry*, 10, pp. 533–81.

Baker, C.L. (1995). *English Syntax.* 2nd Ed. MIT Press, Cambridge.

Bellugi, U., Marks, S., Bihrle, A. M., and Sabo, H. (1992). "Language, Cognition and Brain Organization in a Neurodevelopmental Disorder." In M. Gunnar and C. Nelson, eds., *Developmental Behavioral Neuroscience*, pp. 201–232. Lawrence Erlbaum, Hillsdale, NJ.

Bellugi, U., Wang, P., and Jernigan, T. L. (1994). "Williams Syndrome: An Unusual Neurophysiological Profile." In Broman and Graffman (1994), pp. 23–56.

Berlin, B., and Kay, P. (1969). *Basic Color Terms: Their Universality and Evolution.* University of California Press, Berkeley.

Berman, R.A. (1990). "On Acquiring an (S)VO Language: Subjectless Sentences in Children's Hebrew." *Linguistics*, 28, pp. 1135–66.

———. (1991). "In Defense of Development." *Behavioral and Brain Sciences*, 14, pp. 612–13.

Berwick, R. (1985). *The Acquistion of Syntactic Knowledge.* MIT Press, Cambridge.

Berwick, R. C. and Weinberg, A. S. (1983). "The Role of Grammars in Models of Language Use." *Cognition*, 13, pp. 1–61.

———. (1984). *The Grammatical Basis of Linguistic Performance: Language Acquisition and Use.* MIT Press, Cambridge.

———. (1985). *The Acquisition of Syntactic Knowledge.* MIT Press, Cambridge.

Bickerton, D. (1981). *Roots of Language.* Karoma, Ann Arbor, MI.

Billings, P.R., Beckwith J., and Alper, J.S. (1992). "The Genetic Analysis of Human Behavior: A New Era?" *Social Science and Medicine*, 35, pp. 227–38.

Bishop, D. V. M. (1992). "The Underlying Nature of Specific Language Impairment." *Journal of Child Psychology and Psychiatry*, 33, pp. 3–66.

Bishop, D.V.M. (1994). "Is Specific Language Impairment a Valid Diagnostic Category? Genetic and Psycholinguistic Evidence." *Philosophical Transactions of the Royal Society of London*, 346, pp. 105–11.

Block, N. (1986). "Advertisement for a Semantics for Psychology." In P. French, T. Uehling, and H. Wettstein, eds. *Studies in the Philosophy of Mind.* Midwest Studies in Philosophy, vol.10. University of Minnesota Press, Minneapolis.

———. (1995). "How Heritability Misleads About Race." *Cognition*, 56, pp. 99–128.

———. (1981). *Readings in the Philosophy of Psychology*, vol. 2. Harvard University Press, Cambridge.

Bohannon, J. N., MacWhinney, B., and Snow, C. (1990). "No Negative Evidence Revisited: Beyond Learnability or Who Has to Prove What to Whom." *Developmental Psychology*, 26, pp. 221–26.

Bohannon, J. and Symons, V. (1988). "Conversational conditions of children's imitation." Paper presented at the biennial Conferece on Human Development, Charleston, SC, April.

Bohannon, J. N. and Stanowicz, L. (1988). "The Issue of Negative Evidence: Adult Responses to Children's Language Errors." *Developmental Psychology*, 24, pp. 684–89.

Bostock, D. (1986). *Plato's Phaedo.* Clarendon Press, Oxford.

Braine, M. D. S. (1971). "On Two Types of Models of the Internalization of Grammars." D. I. Slobin ed., *The Ontogenesis of Grammar: A Theoretical Symposium.* Academic Press, New York.

———. (1976). "Children's First Word Combinations." *Monographs of the Society of Research in Child Development*, 41.

Brent, M. R. (1993). "From Grammar to Lexicon: Unsupervised Learning of Lexical Syntax." *Computational Linguistics*, 19, pp. 243–62.

Bresnan, J. (1978). "A Realistic Transformational Grammar." In M. Halle, J. Bresnan, and G. Miller, eds., *Linguistic Theory and Psychological Reality.* MIT Press, Cambridge.

Bresnan, J., and Kaplan, R. (1982). "Introduction: Grammars as Mental Representations of Language." In J. Bresnan, ed., *The Mental Representation of Grammatical Relations.* MIT Press, Cambridge.

Broman, S. H., and Graffman, J., eds. (1994). *Atypical Cognitive Deficits in Developmental Disorders: Implications for Brain Function.* Lawrence Erlbaum, Hillsdale, NJ.

Brooks, L. (1978). "Nonanalytic Concept Formation and Memory for Instances." In Rosch and Lloyd (1978) pp. 169–211.

Brown, R (1973). *A First Language: The Early Stages*. Harvard University Press, Cambridge.

Brown, R., Cazden, C., and Bellugi, U. (1969). "The Child's Grammar from I to III." In J. Hill, ed., *Minnesota Symposium on Child Psychology*, vol. 2. University of Minnesota Press, Minneapolis.

Brown, R., and Hanlon, C. (1970). "Derivational Complexity and Order of Acquisition in Child Speech." In J. R. Hayes, ed., *Cognition and the Development of Language*. John Wiley and Sons, New York.

Bruce, V., Burton, A. M. and Craw, I. (1992). "Modelling Face Recognition." *Philosophical Transactions of the Royal Society of London*, B335, pp. 121–28.

Bruner, H. G., Nelen, H., Breakefield, X. O., Ropers, H. H., and van Oost, A. (1993). "Abnormal Behavior Associated with a Point Mutation in the Structural Gene for Monoamine Oxidase A." *Science*, 262, pp. 578–80.

Carey, S. (1992). "Becoming a Face Expert." *Philosophical Transactions of the Royal Society of London*, B335, pp. 95–103.

Carramazza, A. (1986). "On Drawing Inferences About the Structure of Normal Cognitive Systems from Analysis of Patterns of Impaired Performance: The Case for Single-Patient Studies." *Brain and Cognition*, 5, pp. 41–66.

Carruthers, P. (1992). *Human Knowledge and Human Nature: A New Introduction to an Ancient Debate*. Oxford University Press, Oxford.

Chappell, V. (1986). "The Theory of Ideas." In A. O. Rorty, ed., *Essays on Descartes's Meditations*. University of California Press, Berkeley.

Chomsky, N. (1955). *The Logical Structure of Linguistic Theory*, Unpublished manuscript.

———. (1957). *Syntactic Structures*. Mouton, The Hague.

———. (1959). Review of Skinner's *Verbal Behavior*. *Language*, 35, pp. 26–58.

———. (1965). *Aspects of the Theory of Syntax*. MIT Press, Cambridge.

———. (1966). *Cartesian Linguistics: A Chapter in the History of Rationalist Thought*. Harper and Row, New York.

———. (1968). "Deep Structure, Surface Structure and Semantic Interpretation," M.I.T. mimeograph, Cambridge; published in N. Chomsky, *Studies on Semantics in Generative Grammar*. Mouton, The Hague, 1972.

———. (1968/72). *Language and Mind*. 2nd enl. ed., Harcourt Brace Jovanovich, New York, 1972. References are to the 1972 ed.

———. (1973). "Conditions on Transformations." In S. Anderson and P. Kiparsky, eds., *A Festschrift for Morris Halle*, pp. 232–86. Holt, Rinehart and Winston, New York.

———. (1975a). *The Logical Structure of Linguistic Theory*. Plenum, New York.

———. (1975b). *Reflections on Language*. Fontana, London.

———. (1978/80). "Language and Unconscious Knowledge." In J. H. Smith (ed.) *Psychoanalysis and Language, Psychiatry and the Humanities*, vol. 3. Yale University Press, New Haven, Conn. Repr. in Chomsky (1980), pp. 217–54, 287–90.

———. (1980). *Rules and Representations*. Columbia University Press, New York.

———. (1981). *Lectures on Government and Binding*. Foris, Dordrecht.

———. (1986). *Knowledge of Language: Its Nature, Origin and Use*. Praeger, New York.

———. (1988). *Language and Problems of Knowledge. The Managua Lectures.* MIT Press, Cambridge.

———. (1989/91). "Some Notes on Economy of Derivation and Representation." In I. Lakar and A. Mahajan, eds., *Functional Heads and Clause Structure.* MIT Working Papers in Linguistics, 10. Department of Linguistics and Philosophy, MIT, Cambridge; Repr. in 1991 in R. Friedin, ed., *Principles and Parameters in Comparative Grammar*, pp. 417–54. MIT Press, Cambridge.

———. (1990). "On the Nature, Acquisition and Use of Language." In W. G. Lycan, ed., *Mind and Cognition: A Reader*, pp. 627–45. Blackwell, Cambridge, MA, and London.

———. (1991a). "Linguistics, a Personal View." In Kasher (1991), pp. 3–25.

———. (1991b). "Linguistics and Cognitive Science: Problems and Mysteries." In Kasher (1991), pp. 26–53.

———. (1992/93). "A Minimalist Program for Linguistic Theory." *MIT Occasional Papers in Linguistics*, 1. Repr. in K. Hale and S. J. Kayser, eds., *The View from Building 20: Essays in Linguistics in Honor of Sylvain Bromberger*, pp. 1–52. MIT Press, Cambridge.

———. (1993). *Language and Thought*, Moyer Bell, Wakefield, RI, and London.

———. (1995). "Bare Phrase Structure." In Webelhuth (1995), pp. 383–439.

Chomsky, N., and Katz, J. (1974). "What the Linguist Is Talking About." *Journal of Philosophy*, 71, pp. 347–67.Repr. in Block (1981) pp. 223–37.

Churchland, P. M. (1981). "Eliminative Materialism and the Propositional Attitudes." *Journal of Philosophy*, 77, pp. 67–90.

Churchland, P. S. (1986). *Neurophilosophy: Toward a Unified Science of the Mind–Brain.* MIT Press/Bradford Books, Cambridge.

Clark, A. (1989). *Microcognition: Philosophy, Cognitive Science and Parallel Distributed Processing.* MIT Press, Cambridge.

Collins, A. M., and Quinlan, M. R. (1969). "Retrieval Time from Semantic Memory." *Journal of Verbal Learning and Verbal Behavior*, 8, pp. 240–48.

———. (1970). "Does Category Size Affect Categorization Time?" *Journal of Verbal Learning and Verbal Behavior*, 9, pp. 432–38.

Cornford, F. M. (1935). *Plato's Theory of Knowledge.* Oxford University Press, Oxford.

Cottingham, J., Stoothoff, R., and Murdoch, D., eds. and trans. (1984). *The Philosophical Writings of Descartes*, vol. 2. Cambridge University Press, Cambridge.

———. (1985). *The Philosophical Writings of Descartes*, vol. 1. Cambridge University Press, Cambridge.

Cowie, F. (1997). "The Logical Problem of Language Acquisition." *Synthèse*, 111, 17–51.

———. (1998). "Mad Dog Nativism" *British Journal for the Philosophy of Science.*

Crain, S. (1991). "Language Acquisition in the Absence of Experience." *Behavioral and Brain Sciences*, 14, pp. 597–615. (Peer commentary pp. 615–50).

Crain, S. and McKee, C. (1985). "Acquisition of structural restrictions on anaphora." Proceedings of NELS, 16, University of Massachusetts, Amherst.

Crain, S., and Nakayama, M. (1987). "Structure Dependence in Grammar Formation." *Language*, 63, pp. 522–43.

Crain, S. and Thornton, R. (1991). "Recharting the course of language acquisition: Studies in elicited production." In N. Krasnegor, D. Rumbaugh, R. Schiefelbusch and M. Studdert-Kennedy (eds.), *Biobehavioral Foundations of Language Development*. Erlbaum, NJ.

Culicover, P., and Wexler, K. (1977). "Some Syntactic Implications of a Theory of Language Learnability." In P. Culicover, T. Wasow, and A. Akmaijan eds., *Formal Syntax*. Academic Press, New York.

Cummins, R. (1989). *Meaning and Mental Representation*. MIT Press/Bradford Books, Cambridge.

Curtiss, S. (1977). *Genie: A Psycholinguisic Study of a Modern Day "Wild Child."* Academic Press, New York.

———. (1988). "Abnormal Language Acquisiton and the Modularity of Language," in F.J. Newmeyer (ed.) *Linguistics: The Cambridge Survey, Volume 2. Linguistic Theory: Extensions and Implications*. pp. 96–116.

Curtiss, S., and Tallal, P. (1991). "On the Nature of the Impairment in Language-Impaired Children." In J. Miller, ed., *Research on Child Language Disorders*, Pro-ed, Austin, Tx.

Danks, J.H. and Glucksberg, S. (1980). "Experimental Psycholinguistics." *Annual Review of Psychology*, 31, pp. 319–417.

Davies, M. (1987). "Tacit Knowledge and Semantic Theory: Can a Five Percent Difference Matter?" *Mind*, 96, pp. 441–62.

Demetras, M. J., Post, K. N., and Snow, C. E. (1986). "Feedback to First Language Learners: The Role of Repetitions and Clarification Questions." *Journal of Child Language*, 13, pp. 275–92.

Demopoulos, W. (1989). "On Applying Learnability Theory to the Rationalism–Empiricism Controversy." In R. J. Matthews and W. Demopoulos, eds., *Learnability and Linguistic Theory*, pp. 77–88. Kluwer Academic Publishers, Amsterdam.

Demopoulos, W., and Marras, A. (1986). *Language Learning and Concept Acquisition: Foundational Issues*. Ablex, Norwood, NJ.

Descartes, R. (1897–1913). *Oevres de Descartes*, Vols. I–XXII and Supplement, edited by C. Adam and P. Tannery. Leopold Cerf, Paris.

———. (1985). *The Philosophical Writings of Descartes*, vol.1, trans. J. Cottingham, R. Stoothoff, and D. Murdoch. Cambridge University Press, Cambridge.

———. (1988). *Descartes: Selected Philosophical Writings*, trans. J. Cottingham, R. Stoothoff, and D. Murdoch. Cambridge University Press, Cambridge.

Devitt, M. (1981). *Designation*. Columbia University Press, New York.

———. (1990). "A Narrow Representational Theory of the Mind." In Lycan (1990), pp. 371–98.

———. (1993a). "A Critique of the Case for Semantic Holism." In J. E. Tomblin, ed., *Philosophical Perspectives 7 & 8: Philosophy of Language and Logic*. Ridgeway, Atascadero, CA.

———. (1993b). "Localism and Analyticity." *Philosophy and Phenomenological Research*, 53, pp. 641–46.

———. (1996). *Coming to Our Senses: A Naturalistic Program for Semantic Localism*. Cambridge University Press, New York.

———. (1997). "Ignorance of Language." Paper presented at the Australasian Association of Philosophy Conference, Auckland, New Zealand, July.

Devitt, M., and Sterelny, K. (1987). *Language and Reality*. MIT Press/Bradford Books, Cambridge.

———. (1989). "Linguistics: What's Wrong with 'The Right View.' " In J.E. Tomblin, ed., *Philosophical Perspectives 3: Philosophy of Mind and Action Theory*, pp. 495–531. Ridgeway, Atascadero, CA.

Diamond, R. and Carey, S. (1986). "Why Faces Are Not Special: An Effect of Expertise." *Journal of Experimental Psychology: General*, 115, pp. 107–17.

Dodd, D., and Fogel, A. (1991). "Noninnatist Alternatives to the Negative Evidence Hypothesis." *Behavioral and Brain Sciences*, 14, pp. 617–18.

Dretske, F. (1981). *Knowledge and the Flow of Information*. MIT Press, Cambridge.

Ellis, A. W. (1992). "Cognitive Mechanisms of Face Processing." *Philosophical Transactions of the Royal Society of London*, B335, pp. 113–19.

Ellis, H. D. (1992a). "The Development of Face Processing Skills." *Philosophical Transactions of the Royal Society of London*, B335, pp. 47–54.

———. (1992b). "A Wise Child: Face Perception by Human Neonates." *Behavioral and Brain Sciences*, 15, pp. 514–15.

Ellis, H. D., and Young, A. W. (1989). "Are Faces Special?" In A. W. Young and H. D. Ellis, eds., *Handbook of Research on Face Processing*, pp. 1–35. Elsevier Science Publishers, Amsterdam.

Elman, J. L., Bates, E. A., Johnson, M. H., Karmiloff-Smith, A., Parisi, D., and Plunkett, K. (1996). *Rethinking Innateness: A Connectionist Perspective on Development*. BradfordBooks/MIT Press, Cambridge.

Estes, W. K. (1994). *Classification and Cognition*. Oxford University Press, Oxford.

Etcoff, N. L., Freeman, R., and Cave, K. R. (1991). "Can We Lose Memories of Faces? Content Specificity and Awareness in a Prosopagnosic." *Journal of Cognitive Neuroscience*, 3, pp. 25–41.

Evans, G. (1981/85). "Semantic Theory and Tacit Knowledge." In S. Holztman and C. Leich, eds., *Wittgenstein: To Follow a Rule*, Routledge and Kegan Paul, London. Rev. and Repr. in G. Evans, *Collected Papers*. Clarendon Press, Oxford, 1985. References are to the rev. version.

Evans, J. St. B. T., ed. (1983).*Thinking and Reasoning: Psychological Approaches*. Routledge and Kegan Paul, London.

Farrar, J. (1987). "Immediate effects of discourse on grammatical morpheme acquisition." Paper presented at the biennial meeting of the Society for Research in Child Development, Baltimore, April.

Feldman, J. (1972). "Some Decidability Results on Grammatical Inference and Complexity." *Information and Control*, 20, pp. 244–62.

Fisher, S., Vargha-Khadem, F., Watkins, K.E., Monaco, A.P., and Pembrey, M.E. (1998). "Localisation of a Gene Implicated in a Severe Speech and Language Disorder." *Nature Genetics*, 18, pp. 168–70.

Fletcher, P. (1990). "Speech and Language Defects." *Nature*, 346, p. 226. (Letter).

Flin, R., and Dziurawiec, S. (1989). "Developmental Factors in Face Processing." In A. W. Young and H. D. Ellis, eds., *Handbook of Research on Face Processing*, pp. 335–78. Elsevier Science Publishers, Amsterdam.

Fodor, J. A. (1975). *The Language of Thought*. Crowell, New York.

———. (1979). "On the Impossibility of Acquiring 'More Powerful' Structures." In Piattelli-Palmarini (1979), pp. 142–62.

———. (1980). "Methodological Solipsism Considered as a Research Strategy in Cognitive Psychology." *Behavioral and Brain Sciences*, 3. Repr. in Fodor (1981a), pp. 225–253.

———. (1981a). *RePresentations: Philosophical Essays on the Foundations of Cognitive Science*. MIT Press/Bradford Books, Cambridge.

———. (1981b). "The Present Status of the Innateness Controversy." In Fodor (1981a), pp. 257–316.

———. (1981c). "Introduction: Some Notes on What Linguistics Is About." In Block (1981), pp. 197–207.

———. (1983). *The Modularity of Mind*. MIT Press/Bradford Books, Cambridge.

———. (1984a). "Observation Reconsidered." *Philosophy of Science*, 51, pp. 23–43.

———. (1984b). "Semantics, Wisconsin Style." *Synthese*, 59, pp. 231–50.

———. (1987). *Psychosemantics: The Problem of Meaning in the Philosophy of Mind*. MIT Press/Bradford Books, Cambridge.

———. (1990a). *A Theory of Content and Other Essays*. MIT Press/Bradford Books, Cambridge.

———. (1990b). "Psychosemantics, or Where Do Truth Conditions Come From?" In Lycan (1990), pp. 312–37.

———. (1991a). "Replies." In Loewer and Rey (1991), pp. 255–312.

———. (1991b). "A Modal Argument for Narrow Content." *Journal of Philosophy*, 88, pp. 5–26.

———. (1994). *The Elm and the Expert: Mentalese and Its Semantics*. MIT Press/Bradford Books, Cambridge.

———. (1998). *Concepts: Where Cognitive Science Went Wrong*. Oxford University Press, Oxford.

Fodor, J. A., and Bever, T. (1965). "The Psychological Reality of Linguistic Segments." *Journal of Verbal Learning and Verbal Behavior*, 4, pp. 414–20.

Fodor, J.A., Bever, T. G., and Garrett, M. F. (1974). *The Psychology of Language: An Introduction to Psycholinguistics and Generative Grammar*. McGraw-Hill, New York.

Fodor, J.A., Garrett, M. F., Walker, E. C. T., and Parkes, C. H. (1980). "Against Definitions." *Cognition*, 8, pp. 263–367.

Fodor, J.A., and Lepore, E. (1991). *Meaning Holism: A Shopper's Guide*. MIT Press/Bradford Books, Cambridge.

Fodor, J.A., and Pylyshyn, Z. W. (1988). "Connectionism and Cognitive Architecture: A Critical Analysis." *Cognition*, 28, pp. 3–71.

Friederici, A. D., and Wessels, J. M. I. (1993). "Phonotactic Knowledge of Word Boundaries and Its Use in Infant Speech Perception." *Perception and Psychophysics*, 54, pp. 287–95.

Friedin, R. (1991). "Linguistic Theory and Language Acquisition: A Note on Structure-Dependence." *Behavioral and Brain Sciences*, 14, pp. 618–19.

Friedin, R. (1994). "The Principles and Parameters Framework of Generative Grammar." In R.E. Asher (ed.), *The Encyclopedia of Language and Linguistics*. Pergamon Press, Oxford.

Gazdar, G., Klein, E., Pullum, G., and Sag, I. (1985). *Generalized Phrase Structure Grammar*. Harvard University Press, Cambridge.

Garber, D. (1983). "Understanding Interaction: What Descartes Should Have Told Elizabeth." *Southern Journal of Philosophy*, Suppl. 21, pp. 15–32.

———. (1992). *Descartes's Metaphysical Physics*. University of Chicago Press, Chicago.

Glass, A. L., and Holyoak, K. J. (1975). "Alternative Conceptions of Semantic Memory." *Cognition*, 3, pp. 313–39.

Gleitman, L. R. (1986). "Biological Dispositions to Learn Language." In Demopoulos and Marras (1986), pp. 3–28.

Gleitman, L. R., and Wanner, E. (1982). "Language Acquisition: The State of the State of the Art." In Wanner and Gleitman (1982), pp. 2–48.

Godfrey-Smith, P. (1996). *Complexity and the Function of Mind in Nature*. Cambridge University Press, Cambridge.

Gold, E. M. (1967). "Language Identification in the Limit." *Information and Control*, 10, pp. 447–74.

Goodluck, H. (1991). "Language Development: Relatives to the Rescue!" *Behavioral and Brain Sciences*, 14, pp. 620–21.

Gopnik, M. (1990a). "Feature-Blind Grammar and Dysphasia." *Nature*, 344, p. 715.

———. (1990b). "Genetic Basis of Grammar Defect." *Nature*, 347, p. 26.

———. (1990c). "Feature Blindness: A Case Study." *Language Acquisition*, 1, pp. 139–64.

Gopnik, M., and Crago, M. B. (1991). "Familial Aggregation of a Developmental Language Disorder." *Cognition*, 39, pp. 1–50.

Gordon, P. (1990). "Learnability and Feedback." *Developmental Psychology*, 26, pp. 217–20.

Gould, S. J. (1981). *The Mismeasure of Man*. W. W. Norton, New York.

Greene, M. (1985). *Descartes*. University of Minnesota Press, Minneapolis.

Grube, G. M. A. (1981). *Plato: Five Dialogues*. Hackett, Indianapolis, IN.

Gulley, N. (1954). "Plato's Theory of Recollection." *Classical Quarterly*, n.s. 4, pp. 194–213.

Hackforth, R., trans. and comm. (1955). *Plato's* Phaedo. Cambridge University Press, Cambridge.

Hacking, I. (1975). *Why Does Language Matter to Philosophy?* Cambridge University Press, Cambridge.

Haiman, J. (1985). *Natural Syntax: Iconicity and Erosion*. Cambridge University Press, Cambridge.

Hamburger, H., and Wexler, K. (1975). "A Mathematical Theory of Learning Transformational Grammar." *Journal of Mathematical Psychology*, 12, pp. 137–77.

Hamer, D., and Copeland, P. (1994). *The Science of Desire: The Search for the Gay Gene and the Biology of Behavior*, Simon & Schuster, New York.

Hampton, J. A. (1981). "An Investigation of the Nature of Abstract Concepts." *Memory and Cognition*, 9, pp. 149–56.

———. (1982). "A Demonstration of Intransitivity in Natural Categories." *Cognition*, 12, pp. 151–64.

———. (1987). "Inheritance of Attributes in Natural Concept Conjunctions." *Memory and Cognition*, 15, pp. 55–71.

——. (1988). "Overextension of Conjunctive Concepts." *Journal of Experimental Psychology: Language, Memory and Cognition*, 14, pp. 12–32.

Hanson, S. J., and Burr, J. (1990). "What Connectionist Models Learn: Learning and Representation in Connectionist Networks." *Behavioral and Brain Sciences*, 13, pp. 471–518.

Harman, G. H. (1967). "Psychological Aspects of the Theory of Syntax." *Journal of Philosophy*, 64, pp. 75–87.

——. (1969). "Linguistic Competence and Empiricism." In Hook (1969) pp. 143–51.

——. (1979). "Meaning and Theory." *Southwestern Journal of Philosophy*, 9, pp. 9–20.

——. (1986). *Change in View: Principles of Reasoning*. MIT Press/Bradford Books, Cambridge.

Harnad, S. (1987). *Categorial Perception: The Groundwork of Cognition*. Cambridge University Press, Cambridge.

Harris, Z. S. (1951). *Structural Linguistics*. University of Chicago Press, Chicago.

Herrnstein, R.J. and Murray, C. (1994). *The Bell Curve: Intelligence and Class Structure in American Life*. Free Press, New York.

Hintzman, D. L. (1986). " 'Schema abstraction" in a Multiple-Trace Memory Model." *Psychological Review*, 93, pp. 411–28.

Hirsh-Pasek, K., Treiman, R., and Schneidermann, M. (1984). "Brown and Hanlon Revisited: Mothers' Sensitivity to Ungrammatical Forms." *Journal of Child Language*, 11, pp. 81–88.

Hook, S., ed. (1969). *Language and Philosophy: A Symposium*. NYU Press and University of London Press, New York and London.

Horning, J. (1969). *A Study of Grammatical Inference*. Technical Report CS139. Computer Science Dept., Stanford University.

Hornstein, N., and Lightfoot, D., eds. (1981). *Explanation in Linguistics: The Logical Problem of Language Acquisition*. Longman, London.

Hubel, D., and Wiesel, T. (1963). "Receptive Fields of Cells in Striate Cortex of Very Young Visually Inexperienced Kittens." *Journal of Neurophysiology*, 26, pp. 994–1002.

Hudson, R. A. (1994). "About 37% of Word-tokens Are Nouns." *Language*, 70, pp. 331–339.

Hume, D. (1977). *An Enquiry Concerning Human Understanding*, E. Steinberg, ed. Hackett, Indianapolis, IN.

——. (1978). *A Treatise of Human Nature*, L. A. Selby-Bigge and P. H. Nidditch, eds., 2nd ed. Clarendon Press, Oxford.

Huybregts, R., Koster, J., and van Riemsdijk, H. (1981). "Editorial Statement." *Linguistic Review*, 1, pp. 1–2.

Hyams, N. (1983). "The Pro-drop parameter in Child Grammars." In *Proceedings of the West Coast Conference in Formal Linguistics*, M. Barlow, D. P. Flickinger, M. T. Wescoat (eds.). Stanford Linguistics Association, Dept. of Linguistics, Stanford University, Stanford, Calif.

——. (1991). "Early Emergence of Linguistic Knowledge: How Early?" *Behavioral and Brain Sciences*, 14, pp. 623–24.

Jeffrey, C. R. (1994). "The Brain, the Law, and the Medicalization of Crime." In R.D. Masters and M.T. McGuire (eds.) *The Neurotransmitter Revolu-*

tion: Serotonin, Social Behavior, and the Law. Southern Illinois University Press, Carbondale, pp. 161–178.

Johnson, J. S., and Newport, E. L. (1989). "Critical Period Effects in Second Language Learning: The Effects of Maturational State on the Acquisition of English as a Second Language." *Cognitive Psychology,* 21, pp. 60–99.

Johnson, N. F. (1965). "The Psychological Reality of Phrase Structure Rules." *Journal of Verbal Learning and Verbal Behavior,* 4, pp. 469–75.

———. (1966). "On the Relationship Between Sentence Structure and the Latency in Generating the Sentence." *Journal of Verbal Learning and Verbal Behavior,* 5, pp. 375–80.

Johnson-Laird, P. N. (1983). *Mental Models: Toward a Cognitive Science of Language, Inference and Consciousness,* Harvard University Press, Cambridge.

Jolley, N. (1984). *Leibniz and Locke: A Study of the New Essays on Human Understanding.* Clarendon Press, Oxford.

———. (1988). "Leibniz and Malebranche on Innate Ideas." *Philosophical Review,* 97, pp. 71–91.

Jusczyk, P. (1997). *The Discovery of Spoken Language.* MIT Press, Cambridge.

Karmiloff-Smith, A., Klima, E., Bellugi, U., Grant, J., and Baron-Cohen, S. (1995). "Is There a Social Module? Language, Face Processing, and Theory of Mind in Individuals with Williams Syndrome." *Journal of Cognitive Neuroscience,* 7, pp. 196–208.

Kasher, A., ed. (1991). *The Chomskyan Turn.* Blackwell, Oxford.

Katz, J. J. (1981). *Language and Other Abstract Objects.* Rowman and Littlefield, Totowa, NJ.

———, ed. (1985a). *The Philosophy of Linguistics.* Oxford University Press, Oxford.

———. (1985b). "An Outline of a Platonist Grammar." In Katz (1985a), pp. 172–203.

Katz, J. J., and Fodor, J. A. (1963). "The Structure of Semantic Memory." *Language,* 39, pp. 170–210.

Katz, J. J., and Postal, P. (1991). "The Appearance of and Justification for Realism." *Linguistics and Philosophy.* 14.

Kenny, A. (1977): *Descartes: Philosophical Letters.* University of Minnesota Press, Minneapolis.

Kevles, D. J. (1985). *In the Name of Eugenics.* Alfred A. Knopf, New York.

Koster, J., van Riemsdijk, H. and Vergaud, J. R. (1980). "Glow Manifesto: Concerning the Object of Inquiry." *Glow Newsletter.* Foris, Dordrecht, Holland, 5, pp. 40–44.

Kripke, S. (1980). *Naming and Necessity.* Harvard University Press, Cambridge.

———. (1982). *Wittgenstein on Rules and Private Language: An Elementary Exposition.* Harvard University Press, Cambridge.

Krushke, J. K. (1992). "ALCOVE: An Exemplar-Based Connectionist Model of Category Learning." *Psychological Review,* 99, pp. 22–44.

Lagefoged, P., and Broadbent, D. E. (1960). "Perception of Sequence in Auditory Events." *Quarterly Journal of Experimental Psychology,* 13, pp. 162–70.

Lane, H. L. (1976). *The Wild Boy of Aveyron.* Harvard University Press, Cambridge.

Lasnik, H. (1986). "On Certain Substitutes for Negative Data." In Demopoulos and Marras (1989), pp. 89–105.

Lasnik H. (1989). *Essays on Anaphora*. Kluwer Academic Publishers, Dordrecht.

Lasnik H. (1991). "Language Acquistion and Two Types of Constraints." *Behavioral and Brain Sciences*, 14, pp. 624–5.

Leibniz, G. W. (1981). *New Essays on Human Understanding*, P. Remnant and J. Bennett trans. Cambridge University Press, Cambridge.

———. (1989). *Philosophical Essays*, R. Ariew and D. Garber trans., Hackett, Indianapolis, IN.

Lenneberg, E. (1964). "A Biological Perspective of Language." In E. H. Lenneberg, ed., *New Directions in the Study of Language*, pp. 65–88. MIT Press, Cambridge.

———. (1967). *Biological Foundations of Language*. Wiley, New York.

LeVay, S. (1993). *The Sexual Brain*. Bradford Books/MIT Press, Cambridge.

Levelt, W. J. M. (1970). "A Scaling Approach to the Study of Syntactic Relations." In G. B. Flores d'Arcais and W. J. M. Levelt, eds., *Advances in Psycholinguistics*. American Elsevier, New York.

Lewontin, R. C., Rose, S., and Kamin, L. (1984). *Not in Our Genes: Biology, Ideology and Human Nature*. Pantheon, New York.

Lightfoot, D. (1982). *The Language Lottery: Toward a Biology of Grammars*. MIT Press, Cambridge.

———. (1989). "The Child's Trigger-Experience: Degree-0 Learnability." *Behavioral and Brain Sciences*, 12, pp. 321–34.

———. (1991). *How to Set Parameters: Arguments from Language Change*. Bradford Books/MIT Press, Cambridge.

Loar, B. (1981). *Mind and Meaning*. Cambridge University Press, Cambridge.

———. (1982). "Conceptual Role and Truth-Conditions." *Notre Dame Journal of Formal Logic*, 21, pp. 272–83.

———. (1991). "Can We Explain Intentionality?" In Loewer and Rey (1991), pp. 119–35.

Locke, J. (1975). *An Essay Concerning Human Understanding*, P. H. Nidditch, ed. Oxford University Press, Oxford.

Loewer, B., and Rey, G., eds. (1991). *Meaning and Mind: Fodor and His Critics*. Blackwell, Oxford.

Lycan, W. G., ed. (1990). *Mind and Cognition: A Reader*. Blackwell, Oxford.

McClelland, J. L. (1981). "Retrieving General and Specific Information from Stored Knowledge of Specifics." *Proceedings of the Third Annual Meeting of the Cognitive Science Society*, pp. 170–72. Berkeley, Ca. August 19–21.

McClelland, J. L., Rumelhart, D. E. and the PDP Research Group. (1986). *Parallel Distributed Processing: Explorations in the Microstructure of Cognition*, 2 vols. MIT Press/Bradford Books, Cambridge.

MacWhinney, B. (1989). "Competition and Teachability." In M. L. Rice and R. L. Schiefelbusch, eds., *The Teachability of Language*, pp. 63–104. Paul H. Brookes, Baltimore.

Marantz, A. (1995). "The Minimalist Program." In Webelhuth (1995), pp. 349–82.

Maratsos, M. P. (1982). "The Child's Construction of Grammatical Categories." In Wanner and Gleitman (1982) pp. 240–66.

——— (1989). "Innateness and Plasticity in Language Acquisition." In M. L. Rice and R. L. Schiefelbusch, eds., *The Teachability of Language*, pp. 105–125. Paul H. Brookes, Baltimore.

Marcus, G. (1993). "Negative Evidence in Language Acquisition." *Cognition*, 46, pp. 53–85.

Marr, D. (1979). "Representing and Computing Visual Information." In P. H. Winston and R. H. Brown, eds., *Artificial Intelligence: An MIT Perspective*, vol. 2. MIT Press, Cambridge.

———. (1982). *Vision: A Computational Investigation into the Human Representation and Processing of Visual Information*. W. H. Freeman, New York.

Matthews, R. J. (1984). "The Plausibility of Rationalism." *Journal of Philosophy*, 81, pp. 492–515.

Mazurkewich, I., and White, L. (1984). "The Acquisition of Dative Alternation: Unlearning Overgeneralizations." *Cognition*, 16, pp. 261–83.

McGinn, C. (1982). "The Structure of Content." In A. Woodfield (ed.) *Thought and Object*. Clarendon Press, Oxford, pp. 207–58.

Medin, D. L., and Shaffer, M. M. (1978). "Context Theory of Classification Learning." *Psychological Review*, 85, pp. 207–38.

Medin, D. L., and Smith, E. E. (1984). "Concepts and Concept-Formation." *Annual Review of Psychology*, 35, pp. 113–38.

Mervis, C. B., Catlin, J., and Rosch, E. (1976). "Relationships Among Goodness-of-Example, Category Norms and Word Frequency." *Bulletin of the Psychonomic Society*, 7, pp. 283–4.

Miller, G. A. (1962). "Some Psychological Studies of Grammar." *American Psychologist*, 17, pp. 748–62.

Millikan, R. G. (1984). *Language, Thought and Other Biological Categories*. MIT Press/Bradford Books, Cambridge.

———. (1991). "Speaking Up for Darwin." In Loewer and Rey (1991). pp. 151–64.

Moerk, E. (1991). "Positive Evidence for Negative Evidence." *First Language*, 11, pp. 219–51.

Moravcsik, J. (1971). "Learning as Recollection." In G. Vlastos ed., *Plato: A Collection of Critical Essays*, vol. 1, *Metaphysics and Epistemology*, pp. 53–69. Anchor/Doubleday, Garden City, NY.

More, H. (1653). *An Antidote Against Atheism*. Roger Daniel, London. Repr. in Patrides (1970). pp. 213–87.

Morgan, J. L., and Travis, L. L. (1989). "Limits on Negative Information in Language Input." *Journal of Child Language*, 16, pp. 531–52.

Morton, J., and Johnson, M. H. (1991). "CONSPECT and CONLERN: A Two-Process Theory of Infant Face Recognition." *Psychological Review*, 98, pp. 164–81.

Müller, R. A. (1996). "Innateness, Autonomy, Universality? Neurobiological Approaches to Language." *Behavioral and Brain Sciences*, 19, pp. 611–75. (Includes peer commentaries.)

Murphy, G. L. and Medin, D. L. (1985). "The Role of Theories in Conceptual Coherence." *Psychological Review*, 92, pp. 289–316.

Nehamas, A. (1985). "Meno's Paradox and Socrates as Teacher." *Oxford Studies in Ancient Philosophy*, 3, pp. 1–30.

Nelson, J. O. (1967). "Innate Ideas." In P. Edwards ed., *Encyclopedia of Philosophy*, vol. 2 pp. 166–8. Macmillan.

Nelson, K. E., Denninger, M. S., Bonvillian, J. D., Kaplan, B. J., and Baker, N. D. (1984). "Maternal Input Adjustments and Non-adjustments as Related to Children's Linguistic Advances and to Language Acquisition Theories."

In A. D. Pellegrini and T. D. Yawkey, eds., *The Development of Oral and Written Language in Social Contexts*, pp. 31–56. Ablex, Norwood, NJ. 1984.

Nesse, R. M. (1994). "An Evolutionary Perspective on Substance Abuse." *Ethology and Sociobiology*, 15 pp. 339–48.

Neville, H. J., Mills, D. L., and Bellugi, U. (1994). "Effects of Altered Auditory Sensitivity and Age of Language Acquisition on the Development of Language-Relevant Neural Systems: Preliminary Studies of Williams Syndrome." In Broman and Graffman (1994), pp. 67–83.

Newport, E. (1977). "Motherese: The Speech of Mothers to Young Children." in N. Castellano and D. Pisoni, eds., *Cognitive Theory*, vol. 2. Lawrence Erlbaum, Hillsdale, NJ.

———. (1984). "Constraints on Learning: Studies in the Acquisition of American Sign Language." *Papers and Reports on Child Language Development*, 23, pp. 1–22.

———. (1988). "Constraints on Learning and Their Role in Language Acquisition: Studies of the Acquisition of American Sign Language." *Language Sciences*, 10, pp. 147–72.

———. (1990). "Maturational Constraints on Language Leaning." *Cognitive Science*, 14, pp. 11–28.

Newport, E., Gleitman, H., and Gleitman, L. (1977). "Mother, Please, I'd Rather Do It Myself: Some Effects and Non-Effects of Maternal Speech Style." In Snow and Ferguson (1977), pp. 109–50.

Nisbett, R., and Ross, L. (1980). *Human Inference: Strategies and Shortcomings of Social Judgment*, Prentice-Hall, Englewood Cliffs, NJ.

Noble, E. P., Blum, K., Ritchie, T., Montgomery, A., and Sheridan, P. J. (1991). "Allelic Association of the D2 Dopamine Receptor Gene with Receptor-Binding Characteristics in Alcoholism." *Archives of General Psychiatry*, 48, pp. 648–54.

Nosofsky, R. M. (1988). "Exemplar-Based Accounts of Relations Between Classification, Recognition and Typicality." *Journal of Experimental Psychology: Learning, Memory and Cognition*, 14, pp. 700–8.

———. (1991). "Tests of an Exemplar Model for Relating Perceptual Classification and Recognition Memory." *Journal of Experimental Psychology: Learning, Memory and Cognition*, 17, pp. 3–27.

O'Neill, E. (1987). "Mind–Body Interaction and Metaphysical Consistency: A Defense of Descartes." *Journal of the History of Philosophy*, 25, pp. 227–45.

Osherson, D. N., and Smith, E. E. (1981). "On the Adequacy of Prototype Theory as a Theory of Concepts." *Cognition*, 9, pp. 35–58.

———. (1982). "Gradedness and Conceptual Conjunction." *Cognition*, 12, pp. 299–318.

Oyama, S. (1985). *The Ontogeny of Information: Devlopmental Systems and Evolution*. Cambridge University Press, Cambridge.

Patrides, C. A., ed. (1970). *The Cambridge Platonists*. Harvard University Press, Cambridge.

Peacocke, C. (1986a). "Explanation in Computational Psychology: Language, Perception and Level 1.5." *Mind and Language*, 1, pp. 101–23.

———. (1986b). "Replies to Commentators." *Mind and Language*, 1, pp. 388–402.

Peters, S., and Ritchie, R. (1973). "On the Generative Power of Transformational Grammars." *Information Science*, 6, pp. 49–83.

Piattelli-Palmarini, M. (1986). "The Rise of Selective Theories: A Case Study and Some Lessons from Immunology." In Demopoulos and Marras (1986), pp.

———. (1989). "Evolution, Selection and Cognition: From 'Learning' to Parameter Setting in Biology and in the Study of Language." *Cognition*, 31, pp. 1–44.

———, ed. (1979). *Language and Learning: The Debate Between Jean Piaget and Noam Chomsky*. Routledge and Kegan Paul, London.

Pierce, A. E. (1991). "Acquisition Errors in the Absence of Experience." *Behavioral and Brain Sciences*, 14, pp. 628–29.

Pinker, S. (1979). "Formal Models of Language Learning." *Cognition*, 7, pp. 217–282.

———. (1984). *Language Learnability and Language Development*, Harvard University Press, Cambridge.

———. (1986). "Productivity and Conservatism in Language Acquisition." In Demopoulos and Marras (1986), pp. 54–79.

———. (1989). *Learnability and Cognition: The Acquisition of Argument Structure*. Bradford Books/MIT Press, Cambridge.

———. (1990). "Rules of Language." *Science*, 253, pp. 530–35.

———. (1994). *The Language Instinct: How the Mind Creates Language*. HarperCollins, New York.

Pinker, S., and Bloom, P. (1990). "Natural Language and Natural Selection." *Behavioral and Brain Sciences*, 13, pp. 707–84.

Pinker, S., and Prince, A. (1988). "On Language and Connectionism: Analysis of a Parallel Distributed Processing Model of Language Acquisition." *Cognition*, 28, pp. 73–194.

Posner, M. I., and Keele, S. W. (1968). "On the Genesis of Abstract Ideas." *Journal of Experimental Psychology*, 77, pp. 353–63.

———. (1970). "Retention of Abstract Ideas." *Journal of Experimental Psychology*, 83, pp. 304–8.

Powers, D. M. W. (1991). "Language Acquisition in the Absence of Proof of Absence of Experience." *Behavioral and Brain Sciences*, 14, pp. 629–30.

Pullum, G.K. (1996). "Learnability, Hyperlearning, and the Poverty of the Stimulus." In *Proceedings of the 22nd Annual Meeting: General Session and Parasession on the Role of Learnability in Grammatical Theory*, J. Johnson, M. L. Juge, and J. L. Moxley (eds.), pp. 498–513. Berkeley Linguistics Society, Berkeley.

Putnam, H. (1971). "The 'Innateness Hypothesis' and Explanatory Models in Linguistics." In J. Searle, ed., *The Philosophy of Language*. Oxford University Press, London, pp. 130–39. Repr. in Block (1981), pp. 292–99.

———. (1975). "The Meaning of 'Meaning.' " In *Mind, Language and Reality: Philosophical Papers*, vol. 2, pp. 33–69. Cambridge University Press, Cambridge.

Quine, W. V. O. (1960); *Word and Object*. MIT Press, Cambridge.

———. (1953). "Two Dogmas of Empiricism." In *From a Logical Point of View*, 2nd ed. Harvard University Press, Cambridge.

———. (1969). "Linguistics and Philosophy." In Hook (1969) pp. 95–98.

Read, C., and Schreiber, P. (1982). "Why Short Subjects Are Harder to Find." In Wanner and Gleitman (1982), pp. 78–101.

Reed, S. K. (1972). "Pattern Recognition and Categorization." *Cognitive Psychology*, 3, pp. 382–407.

Remnant, P. (1979). "Descartes: Body and Soul." *Canadian Journal of Philosophy*, IX, pp. 377–388.

Riemsdijk, H. van, and Williams, E. (1986). *Introduction to the Theory of Grammar*. MIT Press, Cambridge.

Rips, L. J., Shoben, E. J., and Smith, E. E. (1973). "Semantic Distance and the Verification of Semantic Relations." *Journal of Verbal Learning and Verbal Behavior*, 12, pp. 1–20.

Roeper, T. (1988). "Grammatical Principles of First Language Acquisition." In F. J. Newmeyer, ed., *Linguistics: The Cambridge Survey*, vol. 2, Linguistic Theory: Extensions and Implications, pp. 35–52. Cambridge University Press, Cambridge.

———. (1991). "We Need a Team of Gene-Mappers, Not Principle-Provers." *Behavioral and Brain Sciences*, 14, pp. 630–31.

Roeper, T., and Williams, E. (1987). *Parameter-Setting*. Reidel, Dordrecht, Netherlands.

Rosch, E. (1973). "Natural Categories." *Cognitive Psychology*, 4, pp. 328–50.

———. (1975). "The Nature of Mental Codes for Color Categories." *Journal of Experimental Psychology: General*, 104, pp. 192–233.

———. (1978). "Principles of Categorization." In Rosch and Lloyd (1978), pp. 28–72.

Rosch, E., and Lloyd, B. B., eds. (1978). *Cognition and Categorization*. Lawrence Erlbaum, Hillsdale, NJ.

Rosch, E., and Mervis, C. B. (1975). "Family Resemblances: Studies in the Internal Structure of Categories." *Cognitive Psychology*, 7, pp. 573–605.

Ross, J. (1967). "Constraints on Variables in Syntax." Ph.D. dissertation, MIT.

Rubba, J. (1991). "Preposition Use in a Speaker with Williams Syndrome: Some Cognitive Grammar Proposals." CRL Newsletter (University of California, San Diego), 5, pp. 1–11.

Rumelhart, D. E., Hinton, G. E., and Williams, R. J. (1986). "Learning Representations by Back-propagating Errors." *Nature*, 323, pp. 533–36.

Rumelhart D. E. and McClelland, J. L. (1986). "On Learning the Past Tenses of English Verbs." In McClelland, Rumelhart and the PDP Research Group (1986), vol. 2, pp. 216–71.

Rymer, R. (1992). "A Silent Childhood." *The New Yorker*, April 13 and April 20.

Saffran, J. R., Aslin, R. N., and Newport, E. L. (1996). "Statistical Learning by 8-Month-Old Infants." *Science*, 274, pp. 1926–28.

Samal, A., and Iyengar, P. A. (1992). "Automatic Recognition and Analysis of Human Faces and Facial Expressions: A Survey." *Pattern Recognition*, 25, pp. 65–77.

Samet, J., and Tager-Flusberg, H. (1991). "Maturation, Emergence and Performance." *Behavioral and Brain Sciences*, 14, pp. 631–2.

Sampson, G. (1980). *Making Sense*. Oxford University Press, Oxford.

———. (1989). "Language Acquisition: Growth or Learning?" *Philosophical Papers*, 18, pp. 203–40.

Savile, A. (1972). "Leibniz's Contribution to the Theory of Innate Ideas." *Philosophy*, 47, pp. 113–24.

Schiffer, S. (1986). "Peacocke on Explanation in Psychology." *Mind and Language*, 1, pp. 362–371.

Schlesinger, I. M. (1991). "Innate Universals Do Not Solve the Negative Feedback Problem." *Behavioral and Brain Sciences*, 14, p. 633.

Schmaltz, T. M. (1992). "Sensation, Occasionalism and Descartes's Causal Principles." In P. D. Cummins and G. Zoeller, eds., *Minds, Ideas and Objects: Essays on the Theory of Representation in Modern Philosophy*. North American Kant Society Studies in Philosophy, vol. 2. Ridgeview, Atascadero, CA.

———. (1998). "Descartes on Innate Ideas, Sensation, and Scholasticism: The Response to Regius." In *Studies in Seventeenth Century Philosophy*. Oxford Studies in the History of Philosophy, vol. 2. Oxford University Press, Oxford.

Scott, D. (1987). "Platonic Anamnesis Revisited." *Classical Quarterly*, 37, pp. 346–66.

———. (1988). "Innatism and the Stoa." *Proceedings of the Cambridge Philological Society*, 214, pp. 121–53.

Seidenberg, M. S. (1997). "Language Acquisition and Use: Learning and Applying Probablistic Constraints." *Science*, 275, pp. 1599–1603.

Sells, P. ed. (1985). *Lectures on Contemporary Syntactic Theories: An Introduction to Government-Binding Theory, Generalized Phrase Structure Grammar and Lexical-Functional Grammar*. Center for the Study of Language and Information, Stanford University Press, Stanford, CA.

Sergent, J. (1989): "Structural Processing of Faces." In A. W. Young and H. D. Ellis (eds.) *Handbook of Research on Face Processing*. North-Holland, Amsterdam, pp. 57–91.

Shallice, T. (1988). *From Neuropsychology to Mental Structure*. Cambridge University Press, Cambridge.

———. (1991). "Précis of *From Neuropsychology to Mental Structure*." *Behavioral and Brain Sciences*, 14, pp. 429–69.

Slobin, D. I. (1966). "Grammatical Transformations and Sentence Comprehension in Childhood and Adulthood." *Journal of Verbal Learning and Verbal Behavior*, 5, pp. 219–27.

———. (1991). "Can Crain Constrain the Constraints?" *Behavioral and Brain Sciences*, 14, pp. 633–4.

Smith, E. E. (1980). "Concepts and Thought." In R. J. Sternberg and E. E. Smith, eds., *The Psychology of Human Thought*. Cambridge University Press, Cambridge.

———. (1988). "Compositionality and Typicality." In S. Schiffer and S. Steele, eds., *Cognition and Representation*, pp. 37–52. Westview, Boulder, CO.

Smith, E. E., and Medin, D. L. (1981). *Categories and Concepts*. Harvard University Press, Cambridge.

Smith, E. E., and Osherson, D. N. (1984). "Conceptual Combinations with Prototype Concepts." *Cognitive Science*, 8, pp. 337–61.

Smith, E. E., Osherson, D. N., Rips, L. J., and Keane, M. (1988). "Combining Prototypes: A Modification Model." *Cognitive Science*, 12, pp. 485–527.

Smith, E. E., Shoben, E. J., and Rips, L. J. (1974). "Structure and Process in

Semantic Memory: A Featural Model for Semantic Decisions." *Psychological Review*, 81, pp. 214–41.

Smolensky, P. (1988). "On the Proper Treatment of Connectionism." *Behavioral and Brain Sciences*, 11, pp. 1–74.

Snow, C., and Ferguson, C., eds. (1977). *Talking to Children: Language Input and Acquisition*. Cambridge University Press, New York.

Soames, S. (1984a). "Linguistics and Psychology." *Linguistics and Philosophy*, 7, pp. 155–79.

———. (1984b). "What Is a Theory of Truth?" *Journal of Philosophy*, 81, pp. 411–429.

———. (1985). "Semantics and Psychology." In Katz (1985a), pp. 204–26.

———. (1989). Review of G. Gazdar, E. Klein, G. Pullum, and I. Sag, *Generalized Phrase Structure Grammar*. *Philosophical Review*, 98, pp. 556–66.

Sober, E., ed. (1984). *Conceptual Issues in Evolutionary Biology: An Anthology*. Bradford Books/MIT Press, Cambridge.

Sokolov, J. L., and Snow, C. E. (1991). "The Premature Retreat to Nativism." *Behavioral and Brain Sciences*, 14, pp. 635–36.

Stabler, E. P. (1984). "Berwick and Weinberg on Linguistics and Computational Psychology." *Cognition*, 17, pp. 155–79.

Sterelny, K. (1983). "Natural Kind Terms." *Pacific Philosophical Quarterly*, 64, pp. 110–25.

———. (1989). "Fodor's Nativism." *Philosophical Studies*, 55, pp. 119–114.

Stich, S. P. (1971). "What Every Speaker Knows." *Philosophical Review*, 80, pp. 476–96.

———. (1972). "Grammar, Psychology and Indeterminacy." *Journal of Philosophy*, 69, pp. 799–818; repr. in Block (1981), pp. 208–22. References are to Block.

———. (1978). "Beliefs and Subdoxastic States." *Philosophy of Science*, 45, pp. 499–518.

———. (1983). *From Folk Psychology to Cognitive Science: The Case Against Belief*. MIT Press, Cambridge.

———, ed. (1975). *Innate Ideas*. University of California Press, Berkeley.

Sutherland, S. (1993). "Evolution Between the Ears." *New York Times Book Review*, p 16, March 7.

Szathmary, E., and Smith, E. M. (1995). "The Major Evolutionary Transitions." *Nature*, 374, pp. 227–32.

Tallal, P. (1988). "Developmental Language Disorders." In J. F. Kavanagh and T. J. Truss, eds., *Learning Disabilities: Proceedings of the National Conference*, pp. 181–272. York Press, Parktown, MD.

Tallal, P., Stark, R., and Mellits, D. (1985). "Identification of Language Impaired Children on the Basis of Rapid Perception and Production Skills." *Brain and Language*, 25, pp. 314–22.

Tallal, P., Townsend, J., Curtiss, S., and Wulfeck, B. (1991). "Phenotypic Profiles of Language-Impaired Children Based on Genetic/Family History." *Brain and Language*, 41, pp. 81–95.

Thornhill, R., and Thornhill, N. W. (1992). "The Evolutionary Psychology of Men's Coercive Sexuality." *Behavioral and Brain Sciences*, 15, pp. 363–75.

van der Lely, H. K., and Stollwerck, L. (1996). "A Grammatical Specific Language Impairment in Children: An Autosomal Dominant Inheritance?" *Brain and Language*, 52, pp. 484–504.

Vargha-Khadem, F., and Passingham, R. E. (1990). "Speech and Language Defects." *Nature*, 346, p. 226. (Letter).

Vargha-Khadem, F., Watkins, K., Alcock, K., Fletcher, P., and Passingham, R. (1995). "Praxic and Nonverbal Cognitive Deficits in a Large Family with a Genetically Transmitted Speech and Language disorder," *Proceedings of the National Academy of the Sciences, USA*, 92, pp. 930–33.

Vicari, S., Brizzolara, D., Carlesim, G. A., Pezzini, G., and Volterra, V. (1996). "Memory Abilities in Children with Williams Syndrome." *Cortex*, 32, pp. 503–14.

Vlastos, G. (1965). "Anamnesis in the *Meno*." *Dialogue*, 4, pp. 143–167.

Wanner, E., and Gleitman, L. R. (1982). *Language Acquisition: The State of the Art*. Cambridge University Press, Cambridge.

Wasow, T. (1985). "Postscript." In Sells (1985) pp. 193–206.

———. (1991). "Debatable Constraints." *Behavioral and Brain Sciences*, 14, pp. 636–37.

Webelhuth, G., ed. (1995). *Government and Binding Theory and the Minimalist Program*. Blackwell, Oxford and Cambridge, MA.

Weinberg, A. (1991). "Parameter Setting and Early Emergence." *Behavioral and Brain Sciences*, 14, pp. 637–38.

Wexler, K. (1982). "A Principle Theory for Language Acquisition." In E. Wanner and L. R. Gelitman (eds.) *Language Acquisition: the State of the Art*. Cambridge University Press, Cambridge, pp. 288–315.

Wexler, K. and Culicover, P. (1974). "The Invariance Principle and Universals of Grammar." *Social Sciences Working Papers*, 55, University of California, Irvine.

Wexler, K. and Culicover, P.W. (1980). *Formal Principles of Language Acquisition*. MIT Press, Cambridge.

Wexler, K., Culicover, P., and Hamburger, K. (1975). "Learning-Theoretic Foundations of Linguistic Universals." *Theoretical Linguistics*, 2, pp. 215–53.

White, S. (1982). "Partial Character and the Language of Thought." *Pacific Philosophical Quarterly*, 63, pp. 365–74.

Williams, G. C., and Nesse, R. M. (1991). "The Dawn of Darwinian Medicine." *Quarterly Review of Biology*, 66, pp. 1–22.

Wilson, E. O. (1975). *Sociobiology*. Harvard University Press, Cambridge.

Wilson, M. D. (1978). *Descartes*. Routledge and Kegan Paul, London.

———. (1991). "Descartes on the Origin of Sensation." *Philosophical Topics*, 19, pp. 293–323.

Wright, R. (1994). *The Moral Animal: Evolutionary Psychology and Everyday Life*. Pantheon Books, New York.

———. (1995). "The Biology of Violence." *The New Yorker*, March 13, pp. 68–77.

Yolton, J. W. (1956). *John Locke and the Way of Ideas*. Oxford University Press, Oxford.

Zadrozny, W. (1994). "From Compositional Semantics to Systematic Semantics." *Linguistics and Philosophy*, 17, pp. 329–42.

Index